Unfinished Man
and the Imagination

Unfinished Man and the Imagination

Toward an Ontology
and a Rhetoric of Revelation

Ray L. Hart

Herder and Herder

1968
HERDER AND HERDER NEW YORK
232 Madison Avenue, New York 10016

Contents

... Would it have been worth while,
To have bitten off the matter with a smile,
To have squeezed the universe into a ball
To roll it towards some overwhelming question . . .

T. S. Eliot, "The Love Song of J. Alfred Prufrock"

... In any investigation in this field, where "the thing itself is
deeply veiled," one must take pains not to overestimate the results.
For in such an inquiry one is constantly compelled to face the possibility of disclosing an even more primordial and more universal
horizon from which we may draw the answer to the question,
"What is 'Being'?" We can discuss such possibilities seriously and
with positive results only if the question of Being has been re-
awakened and we have arrived at a field where we can come to
terms with it in a way that can be controlled . . .

Martin Heidegger, *Being and Time*

... Imagination . . . is an art hidden in the depths of the human
soul, whose true processes we shall hardly ever extract from nature
and bring unveiled to view . . .

Immanuel Kant, *Critique of Pure Reason*

... Because in Him the Flesh is united to the
      Word without magical transformation,
Imagination is redeemed from promiscuous
      fornication with her own images. . . .
Because in Him the Word is united to the
      flesh without loss of perfection,
Reason is redeemed from incestuous fixation
      on her own Logic . . .

W. H. Auden, "For the Time Being"

For Fern

Foreword

What It's All About in a few words in advance of the many is out of the question—is, that is, if language is not to be denied its indissoluble link with apprehension. Whether we speak in order to become *aware of* and not merely to communicate, as Merleau-Ponty maintains, or in order to take our revenge on those thoughts that drive us wild in their ghostly pre-linguistic state, as Nietzsche thought, is doubtless a question of some importance. However that may be the issue is the same: what it's all about emerges in the language itself and is understood only retrospectively. So much is true if a fundamental thesis of this study is also true, that we live out of the future but understand out of the past. The point may be scored in Merleau-Ponty's characteristically precise terms: "The reason why the thematization of the signified does not precede speech is that it is the result of it . . . The consequences of speech, like those of perception (and particularly the perception of others), always exceed its premises."

It is not alone the relation between language and apprehension that qualifies the value of summarizing and mapping the terrain from Here to There. Of less but considerable importance is the fact that when the author gets to his Foreword he is, by reason of his condition, under suspicion of something less than calm judgment. At the far end of labor and delivery he bears a relation to his book not unlike that of mother to newborn. As regards the birth of ideas Nietzsche advanced some apt observations: (i) "One can be pregnant only with one's own child." (ii) "Whoever has to give birth is sick . . ." (iii) "Whoever has just given birth is unclean." In a state of postpartum psychosis there is in the author ". . . an order of rank in psychic conditions which approximates to the order of rank in the problems

11

to be solved." In mounting schizophrenia he is likely hell-bent for either of two fallacies, the "intentional" (my darling is what I mean him to be) or the "affective" (take the thing out of my sight, let him be as he strikes you).

Artists, never to be confused with professors, are wiser parents of their progeny—linguistic, graphic, or plastic. They experience even more acutely the terrors of incubation and parturition, of stabs and rending, where pain and surcease are all but indistinguishable. But for them the act of delivery is also the act of clean discovery; the afterbirth is quickly sloughed; and the work of art lives its own flesh, gurgles its own joys and weeps its own sorrows. Discursive writers cannot, at least do not, follow this model; and that in no small part because they do not produce art objects. Yet in a book that makes pretensions to examine the relations between aesthetics and theology at several points in the cognitive spectrum—the ecology of theological knowledge, as it were—it would be ridiculous not to honor the thing up for explication from the outset. That thing, of course, is the genesis of meaning through imaginative disclosure and articulation.

So in this place we may evade the temptation to take the All into our confidence; and instead set the reader in propinquity with some of the problems hereafter to be hovered over, give the bark a shove toward the current. In a different metaphor we may heed Nietzsche once again: ". . . it is best to do with profound problems as with a cold bath—quickly in, quickly out!" The long warm soaker can be saved for the body of the book itself.

From its origins Christian theology has experienced difficulties with either or both of its extremities (not to mention the broad middle) in the full spectrum of knowledge: to the left the language of avowal, circumspection, and mytho-poetic disclosure; to the right the language of reflexivity, explication, and rational conceptuality. Christianity-and-the-modern-mind or "relevance" theology has tended to assume it is the segment to the right that is blurred; that a fundamental constancy of apprehension is there and needs only to be focussed by the optics of contemporary rationality. This movement, whose courage and fortitude ought not for an instant to be sniggered at, has thus recognized

12

and come to terms with the historicality of reason but not that of imagination. Because of this recognition by halves many a modern has exclaimed with Hamaan, "When I wandered into the forecourts of knowledge I lost the vocation I had thought I had for Divinity!"

In theology today, indeed in human culture itself, the problems at *both* ends are nothing less than a thunder-clap in our ears. That rationality in which theology can and must take an interest is one appropriate to the contemporary imaginative circumspections through which its ownmost "given" broaches its claims and engages human complicity. But the circumspections that reach us by inheritance are recondite by reason of the accretions of historical imagination; in them the fundamental human decisions have already been taken, so that we are in bondage to a fated imagination. The boiling question, the father's secret revealed now in the son (Nietzsche), was put in "East Coker" by T. S. Eliot:

> *Had they deceived us*
> *Or deceived themselves, the quiet-voiced elders,*
> *Bequeathing us merely a receipt for deceit?*

To this inevitable question "demythologization" arose inevitably in theology. But the demythologizers conducted us not to a more primordial imaginative language but rather to a more recondite language. What is required is Augustine's "taming of the tongue," that shrew which screams (in Stanley R. Hopper's telling phrase) ". . . the literalistic reminiscences of the unbroken conceptual mirror" tricked out in figural dress; and a loosening of the tongue so that it may speak, and so apprehend, in an authentically contemporary imaginative idiom that gospel that is both "good" and "news." That is to say something understood hardly if at all in departments of homiletics and systematic theology in divinity schools today: that preaching cannot be a piece of "mind-milliner's work" (Horace Bushnell) on faded systematic flowers, and that systematic theology cannot be a piece of *haute couture* cut on yesterday's religio-mythic mannequins.

The full spectrum, from left to right extremity, comprises

13

"revelation" in its ontological/rhetorical complexity—although there is no concealing the fact that I judge the left to house the crucial problematic for theology (and politics!) today.

Among the neo-orthodox giants of the recent past revelation was a central category. The break with the older liberalism was a break consummated in the neo-orthodox understanding of revelation, a break aided and abetted by poignant remembrance of Kierkegaard and others who, not being understood in their own time, had the chance of saying something important. Neo-orthodox theology certainly—and probably its mistress, existentialistic theology—is now in a state of terminal illness. The reasons are many; a fair share are extratheological. Which is the case: that we cannot theologize any longer out of a neo-orthodox frame because its enervating doctrine of revelation no longer strikes us as viable, or that its doctrine of revelation cannot secure our fealty precisely because we see the dead end to which it leads in its comporting theological structures?

Doubtless it is treacherous to think against the backdrop of the immediate past alone. But against that backdrop, coupled with the fact that neo-orthodox theology never got its tap root down in the New World, we in America today are in the position of being able to think through the scope of theology without being tyrannized by a Great Vogue in doctrine of revelation. We therefore can think through the scope of theology and the character of revelation *together;* and this is a kind of *kairos* for us.

We are called now to the labors of "fundamental theology," if that venerable term can be rescued from some of its older Roman Catholic nuances; and if it cannot, then to "theology of culture." Such reflexive theology will be neither *natural theology* (either that of the older liberalism or that of the new: establish the scope of theology, then determine what revelation can mean within it), nor *dogmatic theology* (either that of neo-orthodoxy or that of its contemporary mannerists: establish the contours of revelation, and take them as the contours of theology *überhaupt*). Fundamental theology is *like* neo-orthodox theology in that it has no essentially apologetic interest: it wishes to conceive itself without giving too many hostages to cultural ecology. It is *like* the older and newer liberalism in that

14

it wishes to conceive itself precisely in its contact with what is fundamentally human. Fundamental theology is *unlike* the older liberalism because it is determined not to turn its formal analysis into a material resource. That is, it means to conceive itself in such a way as to gain access to the material tradition as a life-giving source. It is *unlike* neo-orthodox theology in that it will not freeze the content of the material tradition by means of its formal packaging.

Talk of revelation in fundamental theology will be talk that is carried forward, in so far as it touches ontological matters, in the language of fundamental ontology. It will be talk that gains its intelligibility from the recognition that the situation to be described is one which man already inhabits. This situation is not one to which man has to be brought but rather is one which has, by phenomenological means, to be brought under re-cognition. Those means include the technique of "bracketing" or *epoché:* that shock of the active imagination which decomposes the patina of recondite reality-sense. *The problematic in revelation is the problematic of man in his ontologically emergent manhood.* In the end this problematic is of such depth that we can only make approximations of it, set ourselves in contiguity with it from soundings taken from various historical vantages. As with viewing a rich work of art—one perspective requiring that another be struck immediately—each approximation, just to the degree of its success, forces us to another until the visual and auditory space has been filled.

* * *

During the ten years or so in which this blood has been turned into ink I have had ample occasion to sense the wisdom in the warning of Jonathan Swift: "Going too long is a cause of abortion as effectual though not so frequent as going too short, and holds true especially in the labours of the brain." If abortion has been averted in this long stretch, that owes to many mid-wifing hands. Even if the longish list of teachers, mentors at large, and graduate students be omitted, the remainder to be mentioned are only a sign.

First, there are those Foundations and universities that have

15

given me money and had the good sense to let me alone: The American Academy in Rome, The Society for Religion in Higher Education, The American Association of Theological Schools, Drew University, and Vanderbilt University (especially the Vanderbilt Research Council).

Second, there are those colleagues who have taken such interest in the scope of these pages as to give themselves unstintingly to its nurture at various stages: in the halcyon days at Drew, Professors John and Jane Dillenberger, John Godsey, Will Herberg, Stanley Hopper, Carl Michalson, David Miller, and Nelle Morton; at Vanderbilt, Professors Walter Harrelson, Peter Hodgson, Charles Scott, and my graduate assistant, Mr. Lewis Myers.

Third, among colleagues the *primus inter pares* so far as the emergence of these pages is concerned has been Professor Robert W. Funk, whose *Language, Hermeneutic, and Word of God* represents his end of the conversations over the years from which this book has come at my end. Together we have sought incipiently to overcome the no less silly than anachronistic partitions of the conventional theological enterprise. Language is indeed a shaking reed for expressing what I owe him for evoking, cajoling, shaming, and otherwise extracting more lines in this volume than I should care to count.

Fourth and finally, it is to my family to whom I am supremely indebted: to my parents, Albert and Ruby Hart; to my own Xanthippe, Fern, to whom these pages are dedicated, who I am glad to say did not type a single line (in compassion for the copy-editor) but rather brought her philosophical training and knowledge of contemporary *belles lettres* to bear at decisive points; and to my sons, Morgan and Bracken, who burst into the study often enough with fly-rods amenacing to remind me of what only a pedant could forget, that the only thing more important than theology in this world is fishing.

Polebridge
North Fork of the Flathead
Montana
July, 1968

16

Unfinished Man
and the Imagination

PART ONE

Contemporary Foci
of the Problem of Revelation

I. The Underside of Theology as Hermeneutic

Outline

I. INTRODUCTION

The contemporary theological essay typically begins with an anatomy of frustration. There may be here and there a whiff of nostalgia for those grandiloquent salutations with which Paul could open his letters:

Grace and peace to you from God our Father and the Lord Jesus Christ. I am always thanking God for you. . . . You possess full knowledge and you can give full expression to it, because in you the evidence for the truth has found confirmation.[1]

In the main, however, contemporary theology finds its state of health (*salus*) more reliably diagnosed in the salutation thrown

[1] I Cor. 1:3–7 (New English Bible).

21

out by Peter, in Christopher Fry's *A Sleep of Prisoners,* as he turns toward the nave:

Dearly beloved brothers
In a general muck-up, towzers included . . .[2]

The general muck-up which contemporary theology participates may once have had its surrogate in the private terror of an occasional isolated God-seeker; today, thanks to media both "hot" and "cool," it extends well beyond the individual and the groves of academe to the public at large.

While it is no part of the intention of this essay to advance yet another piece of theological muck-raking, it may be useful initially to offer a quickly recognizable example of the way in which the theological problematic has shifted in relation to the American political experience. It is a commonplace that the establishment and character of colonial governments and even of the government of the federal republic owed much to religious imagery that had been revivified and reconfigured by a transatlantic crossing. Of the several strands comprising this imagery one in particular may be noticed. That strand of Reformed Theology running through the Low Country religious dissidents, the English Puritans, and the American Great Awakening was a strand dominated by governmental, "federal," economy-of-order-and-rule images. On crossing the Atlantic this imagery underwent a subtle change, a change not unmixed with the political aspirations of its bearers. The imagery remains fundamentally governmental; but God as the "Sovereign Lord" is displaced by the image of God as the "supreme Magistrate."[3] Thus eternal reprobation, modeled on the whim of a sovereign

[2] Christopher Fry, *A Sleep of Prisoners,* in *The Modern Theatre,* ed. Robert W. Corrigan, (New York: Macmillan and Co., 1964), p. 1047.
[3] Samuel Davies, influential theologian and early president of the College of New Jersey, said that he knew "hardly anything of so much importance to give us just sentiments of the proceedings of God with his creatures, as that we should conceive of him as moral Ruler, or the supreme Magistrate of the world." *Sermons on Important Subjects by the Reverend Samuel Davies, A.M., President of the College of New Jersey, with an Essay on the Life and Times of the Author, by Albert Barnes,* ed. Albert Barnes, (New York: Robert Carter and Brothers, 1849), Vol. I, p. 335.

22

King, is replaced by conditional election according to the fulfillment of law. In the obedience of rightly established law, judged by duly constituted magistrates, man is to find his temporal good; and from the cosmic frame on which the temporal is modeled, his eternal good as well.

That man was being given the chance to establish salvific law in the New World was itself accounted an act of God, an act that would prove the giving of the Decalogue pale by comparison. "Great was the rescue on the banks of the Red Sea," wrote Samuel E. McCorkle, one of the founders of the University of North Carolina, "but to this I can contrast ours on the banks of the Delaware."[4] "God has done more for United America, and thereby for all mankind," McCorkle continued, "than he ever did before for Israel, or for any other nation."[5] Moreover, Christianity in alliance with civil government was specifically charged to subdue the New World and, indeed, every savage spot on the earth. While the decadent civilization of tyrannical monarchies was to be left on European shores, Christianity was to take up civil-izing anew. If Christianity could not survive in a civilization gone to seed, neither could it ". . . flourish in the savage, wandering, hunting-state." The first obligation laid on New World Christianity if it would civilize anew, then, was the introduction of ". . . the settled, wealthy, respectable state of agriculture." Thereby "honor and wealth" would be brought upon the new nation; just *this* righteousness would exalt United America among the nations of the earth.[6] Salvific law would, in the end, heap coals of fire upon the

4 Samuel E. McCorkle, *A Sermon on the Comparative Happiness and Duty of the United States, Contrasted with Other Nations, Particularly the Israelites; Delivered in Salisbury, on Wednesday, February 18; and at Thyatira, on Thursday, February 19, 1795; Being the Day of General Thanksgiving and Prayer Appointed by the President of the United States,* (Halifax, North Carolina: Abraham Hodges, 1795), pp. 10–11.

5 *Ibid.,* p. 15.

6 Samuel E. McCorkle, *A Charity Sermon, First Delivered in Salisbury, July 28; and Afterwards in Other Places in Rowan and Counties Adjoining; Particularly at Sugar's Creek, in Mecklenburg County at the Opening of the Synod of the Carolinas, October 2; and Last at the Meeting of the Hon., the General Assembly of North Carolina in Fayetteville, December, 1793,* (Halifax, North Carolina: Abraham Hodge, 1795), p. 8.

decadent nations of the earth, burning up the dross of atrophied political systems and illuminating penumbral pockets as yet unreached by perdurable order.

It is unnecessary to dwell on the vast difference between the perceptions of the average educated American today and the mind-set of this colonial and early federalist era and its permutations in our history. Even so this mind-set, albeit often subconsciously, is a specter that haunts our apprehensions as a people and our rhetoric vis-à-vis the world community. That is the case whether it be affirmed in a nostalgic and dogmatic way, or whether it be denied as irretrievable. If we may simplify greatly and resist entering upon the guessing game with respect to the proportions of the populace to be assigned to each, two segments of contemporary American opinion may be identified.

In the first, the intuitions of a former era are brought forward in the form of dogmas. These dogmas embrace all those concepts that go with the view of the United States as a nation "having the soul of a church" (in Professor Sidney Mead's phrase); and come to a head in one form or another of the dogma of "manifest destiny." From such a consortium of dogmas the "commitment" of the United States in Vietnam today is typically "justified." What counts against the force of such dogmas, or indeed any dogma, has been pointed out by Professor Perry Miller in his monumental study of early New England America. When dogma is severed from its root in religious imagination it becomes merely a counter "in an intricate intellectual chess game" or a piece of outright ideology (i.e., a rational explanation of a position taken on non-rational grounds).[7]

In a second segment of American opinion, neither the images of an earlier era nor their appropriate dogmatic deductions are regarded as affording the framework out of which we are to comport ourselves today and bring ourselves to speech. With that, to be sure, lines with the past are not cut absolutely. Rather, whatever of value came to expression formerly by image and concept must now come to expression anew in images and concepts indigenous to altered time and circumstances. Since these circumstances signal at least in part the fundamental

[7] Perry Miller, *The New England Mind*, Vol. I: *The Seventeenth Century*, (Boston: Beacon Press, 1939), p. 6.

24

theological problematic to which subsequent pages will be devoted, it may be useful to single some of them out.

(1) In the first place, what has come out of America-the-melting-pot is a stew in which no single religious ingredient can claim, for the whole hungry populace, to be the meat. Religious pluralism is a fact, where religion counts at all, and is a fact nowhere so much as where it counts as "common denominator" religion. (2) Where Christianity has retained identifying characteristics, it has lost its formative influence upon society; and the prospects of regaining such an influence in an institutional way are all but hopeless. (3) Because of astonishing developments in the sciences on the one hand and the socio-political reconfiguration of the world by wars and revolutions on the other, a mind-boggling gap has emerged between the generations. A thousand years of pre-twentieth century time would be required to account for the difference between the lived perceptions of today's college student and those of his living grandfather (if not those of his father). (4) Because of this generation gap and everything that has worked to widen it, the rites of passage from present to past and from past to present have, like most other rites, deteriorated to the point of demise. With its penchant for "frontier," now transmuted to technology, outer space, and "protecting the free world," the United States has never had much more than a negative sense of the past. As Santayana shrewdly observed, the United States is the land of the dominance of foreground. But that dominance could hold the public only so long as the background-past was sufficiently secure to require no taking notice of. This time is no more; and now that we need them, the ways of passage are clogged. (5) Finally (to make an end of a list that could go on), the inherited religious symbols no longer function symbolically. They survive, of course, as objects of study and analysis. But by and large they exert no immediate pressure upon the will, as they fail to configure experience and knowledge of man and nature. That they lack immediacy means that they do not mediate their putative intentionality with instantaneous impact.

Theology with any purchase on viability today proceeds with an ecological ear cocked to these circumstances. That hardly means that the subject matter of theology is without remainder

25

one more variable in the interdependent product-mix of society. Theology means to say its own piece and no other, but can do so only with an ear to "acoustics." Hearing goes with *what* is said, not just *how* it is said. Theology therefore has to find in itself forms of apprehension and levels of discourse that are commensurate with kinds of disclosure reflected in such circumstances as those described above, precisely in order to say what it and it alone can say.

At least, that task of theology will be honored here. It is important to note, however, that the example above was just that: an example of the way in which the theological problematic has shifted. Happily, the theological enterprise in the United States today is pluralized and diverse: each circumstance named above has some form of theological work leaning into it. If the work of these pages is not directed specifically to all or even one of the circumstances named, that owes to the fact that we have not yet sketched a sufficiently inclusive horizon for the problem we are to worry. In gaining the high places by a circuitous route, from which to take a reading on that inclusive horizon, we do well to heed the injunction of Professor Stanley R. Hopper. He warns on the one hand against putting into figural dress ". . . the literalistic reminiscences of the unbroken conceptual mirror," and on the other hand against fashioning literalistic concepts of unbroken images.[8]

Theology conceived as "translation" or "hermeneutic" is a kind of theology that has sought to heed these timely warnings. Let us begin to mount the problem by considering the task of translation and its difficulties.

II. THE TASK OF TRANSLATION AND ITS DIFFICULTIES

We have to find a meaning in the development of language, and conceive of language as a moving equilibrium. For example, certain forms of expression having become decadent by the sole fact that they have lost their "expressiveness," we shall show how the

---

[8] *Interpretation: The Poetry of Meaning,* ed. Stanley Romaine Hopper and David L. Miller, (New York: Harcourt, Brace, and World, Inc., 1967), p. x.

26

gaps or zones of weakness thus created elicit from speaking subjects who want to communicate a recovery and a utilization, in terms of a new principle, of linguistic debris left by the system in process of regression. It is in this way that a new means of expression is conceived of in a language, and a persistent logic runs through the effects of wear and tear upon the language and its volubility itself.[9]

Every word must be watched, and every sentence pass through the process of double reflection.[10]

If the subject matter of theology has receded, a conservative voice will be heard to say, that is so because theologians have forsaken the tried-and-true language of tradition through which that subject matter has impinged upon humanity in the past. Instead of hewing to the great old words (the rebuke goes on), contemporary theologians pander the language of philosophy, psychology, sociology, or whatever seems à la mode.

There is a point here if we do not stumble over it. If academic theology holds an integral subject matter in view, it will do so (like every other discipline) through a language having distinguishable contours. We do not first get hold of a subject, then shop around for just the right language in which to package it. Language and apprehension (at least, that apprehension susceptible of articulation) arise together in the mind's act. Language, to be sure, has a way of freeing itself from the first-order context of apprehension. Only by courtesy of such "distancing" are many people able to use a common language without stuttering over every word. But in the individual, apprehension may outrace language in common currency; and while that apprehension must float to the surface by clinging to "linguistic debris" (Merleau-Ponty's phrase), since language cannot be created *de novo,* it does so in a new configuration of language. Thereby one surprises a fresh first-order context of apprehension, which serves to order language's own debris into a new house of "meaning."

[9] Maurice Merleau-Ponty, *Signs,* trans. Richard C. McCleary, (Evanston: Northwestern University Press, 1964), p. 87.
[10] Søren Kierkegaard, *Concluding Unscientific Postscript,* trans. David F. Swenson and Walter Lowrie, (Princeton: Princeton University Press, 1944), p. 223.

First-order language preserves that body-heat intimacy which obtains between apprehension and the reconfiguration of linguistic debris which expresses it; as such, first-order language is eventful.[11] Second-order language withdraws from the language-event in order to place it in a larger frame, to connect it with apprehensions embedded in the language of common currency, and so to enhance its communicability in and to the public domain. When second-order language runs aground (i.e., completely outdistances the language-events from which it withdraws), it furnishes the debris from which first-order language is built up. *A crucial question for theology, since its language is of the second-order, is whether its own linguistic debris can be used in raising a new house of first-order language; i.e., can be used to bring the subject matter of theology to language-event.*

Theology's technical term for its own linguistic debris is "tradition." A huge and exotic tradition it is; no other discipline carries a larger inventory. While the words of tradition are not his only inventory-item, the theologian has a penchant for keeping a supply of them in excess of demand. And if the demand is slight, he shifts the inventory from shelf to shelf so as to create the impression of doing business. (This enterprise is called "systematic theology" in seminary curricula.) No, the theologian is not speechless: his problem is less poverty than wealth of words. But it is often the wealth of currency robbed of gold reserves, money deprived of purchasing power by rampant linguistic inflation. Are the words "cashable," will they be accepted as tender: can anything be gotten for them or through them? Does anything "real" impinge through them? These questions (perhaps not so crudely put) arise no less in the minds of cultured lovers than in cultured despisers of Christianity when they hear such terms as God, Jesus Christ, Holy Spirit, Trinity, supralapsarianism, dispensationalism, sin, grace, redemption, faith, atonement, resurrection, eschatology, etc.

[11] For a perceptive study of "language-event" in Heidegger, Bultmann, Fuchs, and Ebeling, see Robert W. Funk, *Language, Hermeneutic, and Word of God,* (New York: Harper & Row, 1966), pp. 20–71.

28

In the conviction that these words once intended the subject matter now gone out of perspicuous focus, that through them man reckoned with both the proximate and ultimate meaning of his existence, Christian theology asks the question: how can that which once came to expression through them come to expression anew, so that it is the proximate and ultimate meaning of *our* existence that is engaged? Especially, how are the words of tradition to serve a maieutic (mid-wifing) role in the delivery of such a new configuration? In pursuit of these questions the systematic theologian is pressed into hard historical work, as Gerhard Ebeling has both urged and demonstrated.[12] The morphology of theological language over the centuries is itself instructive for the systematic task. Already in scripture and at decisive turning points in the church's history one discerns language growing tired and weak, then bursting out in a new birth of volubility.

The project for getting the intention of traditional theological language into contemporary linguistic equivalents has been called "translation." Simplifying greatly, we may look at two ways of prosecuting this project since the rise of modern theology. The first is essentially negative and is practiced by the theological undertaker; the second is or aims to be positive and is practiced by the theological miracle-worker. Most modern theologians have had a little of both in them.

The theological undertaker decides which of the traditional words simply will not translate (say: heaven, earth, and Gehenna: the three-storey universe of biblical cosmology): what they intend cannot be understood, much less accepted, in the language into which translation is to be made. Flaunting the feathers of his modernity, the theological undertaker shoves these feeble if not expiring words into the grave. Dead theology does not bury its dead; and many a contemporary theologian thinks that "Let me first go and bury my father" is *not* a delaying tactic but rather precisely the spadework he must do *in order* to "spread the good news of the Kingdom of God."

---

[12] See especially *Word and Faith*, trans. James W. Leitch, (Philadelphia: Fortress Press, 1963), and "Theologie," *Die Religion in Geschichte und Gegenwart*, 3rd. ed. (Tübingen: J. C. B. Mohr [Paul Siebeck], 1962), pp. 754–770.

(Assuming, of course, the "Kingdom of God" is not numbered among the interred.)

Some theological words are in fact dead; the vital sap for evoking and invoking some claiming dimension of reality has trickled out past nursing back. The common linguistic landscape is cluttered enough without corpses, and the theological undertaker does yeoman's service by burying those under his care. Still, if he knows the sick-list of history in some depth, he has some cause for nervousness as he presides over the obituary column. In the past some theological concepts have *appeared* dead when they were really merely dormant; the *form* of antiquated words has often been a poor clue to their *intention*. In the midst of his spadework the theological undertaker must surely wonder whether these bones will rise again, and whether just such resuscitation is not his proper vocation.

So he changes hats; or, more likely in an age in which even theology has been revolutionized by specialization, he calls in the miracle-worker. Now if there is a more hazardous enterprise than burying a theological word it is surely the attempt to revive one. Still, throughout its history, Christian theology has found it necessary to go back in order to go forward. In the past forty years or so Continental and (some) American theologians in the Protestant tradition have been piping tunes to Reformation bones; English Protestants and Roman Catholic theologians have been ripping up the graves of the Fathers; and in the Reformation itself Luther and Calvin found it necessary to unseal the lips of Augustine and Paul. But this is to mention only some of the major pieces of miracle-working that have managed to pass muster. Not a few were badly botched. Graveyards are widely known to be the favorite haunt of ghosts. When the theologian turns graverobber he may well tangle with a ghost that can live only on blood sucked from his veins. Thus some of the liveliest heresies in Christian history have been ghosts parading as revivified theological concepts fresh from the grave.[13]

[13] Dare we risk a contemporary example? One thinks of the revivification of "Christology" in recent Neo-Reformation theology which, in H. Richard Niebuhr's phrase, verges on "Christomonism." (The phrase shows up as well in Althaus' critique of Karl Barth. Paul Althaus, *Die*

The project of "translating" the tradition presents temptations and difficulties beyond those already mentioned. An acute temptation is the sophistic one: to warm up the leftovers of theological tradition according to the tastes of the contemporary palate. The question overriding hermeneutical interrogation of the past then becomes, "What will Jones swallow?" William Temple dealt with this way of putting the matter with sound theological instinct. Twitted by Ronald Knox for being ostensibly preoccupied with "what Jones will swallow," the Archbishop replied, in effect, "You have it wrong. In the first place, *I* am Jones. In the second place, the question is not 'What will Jones swallow?' but rather 'Is there anything to eat?' "[14] The gravity of the latter question exposes the shabbiness of what might well be called "consumer research theology." What modern man can *understand* is indeed a crucial question; what modern man will *buy,* in the storehouse of what he understands, is hardly theology's first preoccupation.[15]

A second temptation is to busy oneself with showing that the translation has already occurred, albeit in a covert way. One can recognize at least three idealized forms of this project, sometimes touted as "theology of culture." The opening gambit of the first is, "Let me tell you about your presuppositions." The boat of western civilization is rowed back to its Judeo-Christian headwaters; from that vantage point one can then see how western civilization branches out downstream, how it diversifies the primal spiritual substance. A second form is similar to the first, although subtler. According to its lights, the *intentionality* of outmoded theological language survives covertly but viably only in the cultural side-effects of the long Christian tradition. Theology therefore is to employ the underside of culture to retrieve its own proper task. In a third form, theology attempts to win the "contours" of the intentionality of outmoded theological language from its own linguistic morphology. Theology

---

Christliche Wahrheit, 2d. rev. ed., [2 vols.; Gütersloh: C. Bertelsmann, 1949], Vol. I, pp. 67–73.)

[14] See Ronald Knox, *Some Loose Stones;* cited by O. Fielding Clarke, *For Christ's Sake,* (New York: Morehouse-Barlow Co., 1963), p. 51.

[15] Shabbier still is the emulation of the Madison Avenue subliminal trick: make the customer buy *before* he understands—that he doesn't need it!

then makes these "contours" serve to identify those areas of culture upon which it will draw in order to flesh out its intentionality. The difficulty with all these idealized forms, however, is that for none of them is translation so covert as it is made to appear. For each of them, what is alleged to be covert translation can be seen to be covert only as overt acts of translation are executed. At all events, we shall seek to recommend another view of "theology of culture." When theology shall have found within its own rhetoric levels of discourse commensurate to culture in *its* modes of disclosure, the formal ground for a theology of culture will be found, and not before.

There is a major difficulty with the "translation" of tradition as the central means whereby theology's subject matter is gotten into view. In ordinary usage the "translator" is one who has a reasonably thorough grasp of the languages involved. The American New Testament scholar will know, at the very least, Koine Greek and English; the patrologist will know (say) fourth-century Latin and Greek, and English. Now a phrase like the following shows up in the controversy at Nicea: the Son is said to be *homoousion to patri*. How should this phrase be translated? "The Son is of the same essence as the Father." But does the carrying over of sense from one language to another involve merely finding equivalents in one language for words in another? Do we understand the *intentionality* of the *English* phrase, an "accurate" translation? Before answering too readily, it would be well to remember that many of the parties to the Nicene dispute did not understand the *Greek* phrase, even though Greek was the mother tongue of some. How to account for that? Because the Greek phrase *was itself a translation,* an attempt to turn a real intentionality into the horizon of their own linguistic resources. What each party held in view, no doubt influenced by the language tradition he knew, was (to put it as blandly as possible) the sort of reality Jesus was. Disputes between the *Homoousians* and the *Homoiousians* were then disputes about the translation of *this* intention. Translation achieves its purpose if it brings the intentionality of the words into view, and gains *common* consent if a common intentionality is linguistically focussed.

The problem of the contemporary hermeneutical translator

32

is thereby made vivid: in order to translate he must presuppose the results of translation. That is, the intended subject matter of the language he proposes to translate must be in view. But if in view, it is in view through language; there is no apprehension without language. What the hermeneutical translator yearns for is, so to speak, intention in the nude: the first-blush datum before it came on the stage in linguistic dress. But the second-order language of tradition obeys obscenity laws to the letter: whatever it carries forward is done so through words.

Well, then, the hermeneutical translator—somehow and in some mode—has a glimpse of the subject matter, and he has it through language. But through *what* language? (i) If entirely through the language being translated, the project is bootless; in that case the language did not need translation. Tired language is language that requires thinking about.[16] Strong language is never self-conscious: it lets us think the subject matter, not itself. So if language lets the subject matter within the range of vision it is already strong. (ii) But suppose the language being translated is weary and heavy-laden, and that the subject matter heaves into view through the language into which one is translating. In that case the project is not so much bootless as it is lacking in intrinsic connection with the language being translated. If the subject matter comes into focus through *this* language, what is its connection with the subject matter of *that* language? After all, was it not the subject matter of *that* language that was under scrutiny? If the intention focalizes itself through *this* language, why have recourse to *that*?[17]

[16] Of tired language Iris Murdoch has written: "We are like people who for a long time looked out of a window without noticing the glass—and then one day began to notice this too." *Sartre: Romantic Rationalist,* (New Haven: Yale University Press, 1953), p. 26.

[17] More than any other on the contemporary scene, it is Rudolf Bultmann who has brought these problems to the fore and who illustrates the second horn of the dilemma. For him the horizon of theology's subject matter is established by the contemporary language of self-understanding, a language framed by Heidegger's "existentials." This ontological grasp of theology's subject matter serves to *identify* the non-mythological intention of primitive kerygmatic language. When shorn of its literalization, kerygmatic language is seen to be about man's self-understanding too. Contemporary language of a certain sort and antique language of a certain sort are seen to have a common intention. But if this be "translation," wherein lies the *increment* of understanding?

33

There appears to be an impasse (to call it that temporarily) between (i) and (ii). Not an impasse, someone will say, but the sign of a difference between two enterprises. There is a road that starts back there and comes to here; "historical theology" starts here and goes back there on that road. There is a road that starts here and goes forward into the future; "systematic theology" loads up with whatever is available here and sets out for the sunrise. One road ends and somewhere

---

There is none: the identification of a similar or identical subject matter for antique language in no way adds to the ontological (generalizable) self-understanding available through contemporary language. (See "The Historicity of Man and Faith," in *Existence and Faith*, trans. Schubert M. Ogden, [New York: Meridian Books, Inc., 1960], pp. 92–110.) Presumably one turns to primitive language, through the process of demythologizing translation, to rob it of weirdness. Having seen that such language also holds human self-understanding in view, one may then be open to its use in the sermon. Proclamation, the sermon, intends to bring the Word of God to event: to radicalize one's general self-understanding by calling one to concrete decision concerning that understanding. But proclamation and decision are *ontic* affairs (their reality is of an individual and incommunicable sort) and therefore cannot afford an increment of *theological* understanding. It would appear then that, on principle at least, Bultmann depends altogether upon contemporary language to focus theology's subject matter in ontological contour; and further that he leaves a lacuna if not an aporia between the subject matter of theology and that of preaching.

I may fairly draw the charge of stylizing Bultmann and of foreshortening the options [above, (i) and (ii)] in order to make a point. No doubt one may hold an intention focalized in one language up to an intention focalized in another language for the double purpose of correcting and enlarging the first, and correcting and enlarging the second. The juxtaposition of the two provides *distance* for each in the opposite direction. Unquestionably, Bultmann intends the achievement of such distance through his prosecution of "the hermeneutical circle" in the translation of a text. The point I wish to score is that the distance appropriate to theological thinking requires attention to the rhetoric of the movement from the ontic to the ontological and from the ontological to the ontic, for want of which attention Bultmann tends to deliver theology from captivity to the logic of one kind of language (the archaic mythological) to captivity to the logic of another kind of language (that of Heidegger's existentials). This is to miss theology's authentic increment of meaning, and is indeed to evade theology's fundamental linguistic predicament. Theology must bring its ontic circumspections to speech in *whatever* language is at hand, and can do so only by bursting the seams of that logic (since that logic repeats the ontologically unspoken). These matters are treated explicitly under the rubric of the hermeneutical spiral in Chapter II, and in Chapters IV–VI, *passim*.

34

else the other begins; there can be no interchange between roads that are parallel at no point. Thus the historical theologian asks what the word meant then and there; and the systematic theologian puts together words out of present stock which he defends as true, meaningful, or useful.

This description of the difference between the two enterprises rests on the assumption, now under broad-scale attack, that historical theology is under the dominion of positivistic historiography and that systematic theology brings its subject matter into view without recourse to scripture or tradition. The difference may be stated again with this assumption in mind. The positivistic historian turns to the language of a past era "on its own terms." If all foreign matter and anachronisms (such as the question: what is the intention of these antique words in contemporary language?) are kept out of the inquiry, if the full context of the era is considered, etc., etc., the intention of language by its users in that era can be made plain. This project is one not of "translation" but rather of straightforward "historical recovery": the words meant thus and so then and there. The systematic theologian yawns and says: "That no doubt is interesting to those who are interested by that sort of thing. But does one have to see the world through the eyes of a second-century African eremite in order to be a Christian today?" His answer is a no, thank you: systematic theology will get its subject matter in hand by means of contemporary linguistic resources, or at least against a contemporary linguistic canon.

Since hermeneutical theology has headed the phalanx in assaulting any radical distinction between historical and systematic theology, it has every reason for distress should the impasse referred to above prove to be unbreachable or insurmountable. Indeed, the impasse must be breached, not celebrated; the rite could only be a pagan one. But the breach can hardly be worked with supplies so far packed along for the translation project. What this means straight out is that translation cannot be considered an irreducible theological problem. Theology of whatever school is indebted to the "new hermeneuticians" for having exposed this fact, as well as some clues as to what the more fundamental problems are. But it is now clear that hermeneutic itself can be carried forward only by attending to certain problems on the underside of "translation." We may turn now to these problems as they constitute the broad horizon of problematic in which the special problem of this book will be set, the problem that is the fundamental problem for theological hermeneutic, viz., how revelation enters into the expansion of human being and rhetoric.

III. THE PERENNIAL FOCI
OF THEOLOGICAL PROBLEMATIC

Stated *paucis verbis* and so in high abstraction, three perennial problems may be summarized in advance of detailed development. A. There is the problem of theology's foundation, of what is *given* to be intended and attended to by theology; and the problem of how to allow that given to bear upon the execution of the theological task so as to keep theology faithful to the given's ownmost cognitivity. B. There is the problem of the complication of the *given* when set in frames other than that of its "mere givenness," and the consequent proliferation and diversification of its cognitivity when set in those frames. This problem is that of the scale of mental acts in correlation with the scale of revelatory presence (and/or evasion). C. The third problem is the convergence of the other two upon one of the modes of historical time, viz., the past. It is therefore the problem of the power of tradition to re-present (give) what once was presented (given) in the present, and that knowingly. This third problem thus opens out upon the problem of the co-inherence of the modes of historical time, and the rhetoric of fully historical speech.

Since these problems are intertwined, a rather fuller treatment of the first will permit a more compressed examination of the second and third. It should be noted too, for reasons that will appear in the following chapter, that problematic can be approached fruitfully only circumambiently. The following then should be taken as initial readings, as a first scent of the quarry to be tracked to various lairs.

36

A. The Given

To raise the question of theology's given in the first breath is already to say some things about the theological enterprise. Theology is founded on or in the face of something more primitive (primordial) than itself; it is therefore a derivative, responsive, second-order enterprise. Moreover, theology is not just the "Aha!" which such a given might evoke; it is the response of *mind,* the response of *cognition,* or understanding.[18] Even these laconic sentences serve to expose the problem of the connection between knowing and being for theology, the relationship between theology's response and what it responds to. This problem might be divided into (i) the problem of *sterility* in the foundation, and (ii) the problem of *infertility* in the response; yet the two go so closely together as not to permit separation in examination.

Perhaps it will be useful to see why "God" as the *obvious* answer to the question of theology's primordial given has been diminished in immediate force for some theologians and laymen in growing numbers. Most concrete religions (one can hardly say *all* in view of the phenomena, say, of Buddhism) take their origin from hierophanies, the divine manifestation, or the manifestation of the divine. Not that alone, but also the manifestation of the divine in contest with the gods of the world—with tellurian principalities and powers mythologized as gods. (Did not Yahweh put the pagan gods to shame and Jesus exorcize the demons?) The divine manifestation may be indirect, but in that case something in the world succeeds in getting itself taken as a clue to the divine or the divine action in conquest of all but countervailing powers. Simplifying greatly, one can go two ways with such a clue to the *given.* One can prescind from the tellurian contest between divinity and the demi-divine to divinity

---

[18] On this note the decently brought up reader may fall out of his chair: can the cognitivity of this or that be established by announcement? The statement above is not meant to establish the cognitivity of this or that proposition, but rather to stipulate that the response of *theology* is cognitive (negatively, that what is non-cognitive in any sense of the term cannot be *theological* response). It remains to be explored what senses "cognition" bears in the scale of theological response.

a se (as Christian theology often has in its doctrine of the Trinity), or one can prescind from that contest to what it is within the world against which the divine contends.

The former way, that of working from and toward God as the sole given, appears on etymological account to be the way of *theo-logy*. Since God himself would be its given, such theology could take no primary interest in the psychology or sociology of divine manifestation: from whatever "something in the world," it abstracts to God in himself. Such abstraction would be only the first step in a course which seeks to make the discourse of theology coincident with the divine discourse, which takes the human mind to the point at which God speaks himself: to the interiority of the divine *monologium*.[19] But if such theology succeeds in holding such an object steadily in view, it does so at the price of dissolving itself as an enterprise of human discourse, since for that is substituted the beatific audition of the divine *monologium*. Just this dissolution is theological pantheism, the homing instinct of the "religious" temperament. Such theology, both in principle and in performance, is a dehumanizing and a detemporalizing enterprise. Its derogation of humanity is achieved precisely by means of preoccupation with *God*. In fact, it *illustrates* "original sin" through its preoccupation with God in the way that only God can be preoccupied with himself. (Original sin: the arrogation by man of a relation to God that only God can have to himself.) This dissolution of human discourse, and ultimately of human being *coram Deo, in exaltatio humanae naturae in consortium divinae naturae,* comes of ignoring that *given* means (among other things) given *to,* and especially given to and in the world.

The other way is to prescind from the contest and the divine combatant to that in the world which is actually or possibly in contention. On this reading theology takes careful notice of psychology, sociology, philosophy—whatever serves to adumbrate vying forces in the human Colosseum. In recent decades it has been "existentialism" (an exceptionally complex and by

[19] As Professor Julian N. Hartt once put it, "where *natura naturans* nods to *natura naturata* . . ." "Some Metaphysical Gleanings from Prayer," *The Journal of Religion,* Vol. XXXI, No. 4 (October, 1951), pp. 254–263.

no means uniform phenomenon, extending well beyond philosophy in cultural impact) that has re-identified the old and ever new "principalities and powers" which contend for human fealty. This re-identification, moreover, has been accomplished without resort to explicit mythology (i.e., without referring vying mundane forces to transcendent agencies). A contest remains, to be sure; but since the mundane parties (e.g., guilt, meaninglessness, death) have not the status of demidivinities no superior divinity is required to slay them. In this phenomenon, which truly is the "appearance" of the modern mind, is to be seen the intelligibility of "God is dead" and "post-Christian" theologies. That is, God need no longer be counted upon to solve problems in the world; the problems—at the level at which divine intervention would avail—have been dissolved. Here too is the logical end of a certain kind of "demythologization:" if the world is demythologized, the demythologization of God cannot be far behind.[20] At all events if theology attends first, foremost, and exclusively to what the given is given *to,* it winds up with nothing *given* to. More especially it does not allow the given to identify the world and its decisive strifes, to interrogate the world and the world's self-analysis, and to establish that world in which man is to be housed in fulfillment.

These two ways then are ways of diverting theology's *given,* or of taking a part of it and fabricating the rest. To be sure such a judgment in the end requires a standpoint placed by some discernment of *what* the given is. Yet even a formal analysis of the words "given to" discloses deficiencies in theologies which neglect either the *given* or the *to.* Theology, let it be reiterated, is recurrently responsive (and indeed the conditions of human response are a part of the "to" of the *given to*). When theology fabricates its given it may be some sort of enterprise (among other things, an enterprise that does not understand the word "given"), but not a theological enterprise.[21]

20 It would make a substantive difference in theological program if one *began* with the demythologization of God. This, I think, is what Bonhoeffer did in his later work. Such a point of departure seems to be the *prius* of his "world come of age," rather than vice versa.

21 Need it be said that theology is scarcely distinguished from other

Theology may not ask, without ceasing to be theology, *whether* there is a given with which it has to do: its given is its formal *a priori*. Theology will ask incessantly what the contours of this given are and how it impinges. Thus, to drill near some nineteenth- and twentieth-century nerves, theology will not roll out the available nets of cognition (or those of "ordinary language use") and cast them upon the waters, thence to peer among the catch—mayhap to find something that can sustain theological life. The tentativity of theology is owing not to the various mesh sizes available, to the nets through which other enterprises let data come to it. *Tentativity* in theology is owing rather to the givenness of its given in concert with the course of historical reality. Thus two things are to be avoided if the problem of the given in theology is not to be short-circuited: delivering the given into the power of the human *subject,* and establishing it in the status of the self-same *object* which is steadily "there" on the horizon of conception.

That the given evades (seems not to give itself in speech with power) and/or that response is infertile, so that theology is apparently without issue—without a son to bear the name, except perhaps yet another bastard, which she wearies of bearing—this is the most profound problem before theology today. Any claim to take the problem on, even to expand the problematic, requires the stance of a theological position as a whole. Yet three zones may be marked off which theology cannot circumvent but only think its way through if it is to have issue.

(1) Theology must come to terms with the *mediation* of its given. The catch-word for the mediacy of theology's given is

---

enterprises, formally, by being responsive to what is given to it in such a way as to be faithful to that given? So are physics, philosophy, literary criticism: what is excepted?

It should be noted that the category of the given, not to mention its misleading surrogate the "pure datum," has had a long career in an enormous philosophical repertory, a career that cannot be brought into critical review here. (For such a review, see Dorothy Emmet, *The Nature of Metaphysical Thinking,* [London: Macmillan and Co., 1949], pp. 19–95, *passim.*) Let us initially understand the *given* to mean: that which is logically antecedent to response and thus that which is neither a mode of response nor something generated in response. This definition will require expansion later (Chs. V–VI) when we consider the model of the art object and that of the work of art.

"tradition." Tradition must be dismantled to see what it mediates, what it handed around and hands on. Mediating only in dissolution, tradition furnishes debris for building up the structure to house what it could not hold against the flood of time. What tradition of the previous epoch could not hold except in fragment was the given in new contour. The given in new contour could only cling to fragments of the old expression, could only appear in confusion of its newness by coming to expression in the language at hand. To dismantle the tradition means to see how it worked and works in the constitution of historical reality, and how the fortunes of concrete history carved and carve the linguistic artifacts of tradition. The opposite of dismantling the tradition is a type of cohobation whereby from a single temporal substance diverse distillates are derived, which then ossify as the quaint world-views of discontinuous epochs. The archenemy of tradition as a mediator of theology's given is *historicism* which, ironically, really views history as a series of epochal eternities held together occasionalistically by some *deus ex machina;* and which often claims however paradoxically (in a scale extending from fundamentalist Christianity to Marxism) that at least *one* of these eternities is so transparent to the immediate given as to lay its mediate language upon succeeding eternities.

The formal reference of tradition as used here is theology's linguistic heritage. That heritage is shaped first and foremost by scripture and the church's historic confessions, but the hermeneutical language by which scripture and confession reach theology is and always has been the language at hand, which is to say: language reflecting alliances between scripture-creed and other sub-traditions of culture at large. In taking up the mediacy of its given, therefore, theology takes up obliquely the phenomenon of language itself and especially the relation between language and being.[22] Yet this is no merely general task, but

---

[22] Consider in this light the ever-stunning prologue to the Gospel according to John: "When all things began, the Word already was. The Word dwelt with God, and what God was, the Word was. The Word then, was with God at the beginning, and through him all things came to be; no single thing was created without him. All that came to be was alive with his life, and that life was the light of men. . . . So the Word became flesh . . .", John 1:1–14.

41

one oriented to theology's own concrete language. That orientation cannot blink the fact that such language is held together by cultural alliances which cannot be undone.

Enough has been said to indicate that tradition is only potentially authoritative. Here two propositions, one from Schleiermacher and the other from Ebeling, may be set side by side in restraint of each other. "The Christian Church . . . is not in a position ever and anon to begin the development of its doctrine over again from the start . . ."[23] "A purely traditional relation to God is only a special form of godlessness."[24] To confer actual plenary authority upon tradition and thus to make it co-extensive with revelation of the given is to accept the mediacy of antiquated language as the sole mode of the given's presence. This yields in the end an authority whose authoritativeness can be experienced, like that of the state, only under the wielding of extrinsic power.

(2) Theology must come to terms with the *immediacy* of its given and the modulation of that immediacy. If there is no immediate apprehension of the given, what serves to identify *that* a body of language mediates the given and check *what* it mediates? On the other hand, what if anything serves to identify *that* apprehension is immediate and that *what* is so apprehended is *theology's* given (and not, say, a gastric disturbance)? Here, in restricted compass, is the problem of the relation between prayer, sacrament, and sermon on the one hand and theology on the other. For worship is the "zone" of immediacy, as theology is the "zone" of mediacy. Great distance between these zones and the sparseness of each are signs of imminent receivership for the church. In every renewal of the church the two zones have been concentric, two planes of one circle. No

---

This prologue is a good example of what later will be called "the interlacing of regions" (Ch. III), as it is also an example of the increase of language. Thought originally to have been an early Christian hymn and thus a piece of first-order language, the prologue in its Johannine form still reflects the immediacy of the given in new contour while deflecting that immediacy to a more inclusive universe of discourse.

[23] Friedrich Schleiermacher, *The Christian Faith*, trans. H. R. Mackintosh and J. S. Stewart, (Edinburgh: T. & T. Clarke, 1948), Prop. 16, Postscript, p. 82.

[24] Ebeling, *Word and Faith*, p. 339.

42

renascence of theology lives without a new birth of worship, and vice versa.

But lament and hortatory comment are scarcely the way out. From history we learn the perils of denying to "immediacy" the force of its meaning. Thus an instinct to discriminate "scripture" from "tradition," scripture serving as the immediate presentiment of the given, against which to check tradition. But how to check scripture—already a doubt of scripture's immediacy? By the Spirit? But what takes the measure of Spirit (what is the check against Montanism)? Well, scripture—dictated by or through the Spirit. How then did the dubiety of scripture's immediacy arise in the first place?

Even these hoary controversies bore a point not to be lost sight of. The tradition (which however includes scripture) does not check itself: it sleeps, conceals, forgets. Tradition left to itself is, in Heidegger's phrase, "the forgetfulness of being." It belongs to tradition to forget and then to forget the forgetting. Having his being in large measure out of tradition, man cannot remember because he cannot remember forgetting.[25] The processes of memory have then to come into view if the mediacy-immediacy question is to be addressed. Memory, like tradition of which it is the personal bearer, is a vast field of potency which requires "seeding" in order to deliver fruit. That is, it provides ground and nutrience but not the plant. What seeds memory, takes it out of lying fallow, are *events:* which are nothing considered in themselves but the immediacy of some given.[26]

Theology has been all too ready to rest after associating the immediacy of its given with *event.* Going together with this association is the claim frequently made that "events" and "timeless truths" (or "propositions") are to be contrasted and that theology is founded upon the former. This has the look

[25] This formulation owes much to Funk, *op. cit.,* Ch. I.

[26] There is at hand in the American South today a publicly visible instance of these processes. Recent events at Selma and other events like them have served for some people to crack the forgetfulness of the Southern tradition and to provide life for the all too spindly plant of equal justice. For others, alas, the same events serve to petrify forgetfulness, to bind the future through the form of the past.

of an elementary category confusion, a contrast of apple and orange. That confusion can be removed only by bringing into view the cognoscibility of events and the eventfulness of truth; and with the removal of category confusion the claim of contrast between "events" and "timeless truths" may prove to have been misdirected.

To say, as I think must be said, that theology's given in immediacy is "the Word of God as the event of God's Word in human audition" is to say nothing not in need of extensive comment. For one thing, it is a piece of unspeakable arrogance for any particular theologian to turn theology into the horizon of his own eventful existence, much less to assume that the Word of God eventuates itself with such continuity in his own existence as to give theology a steady intention. Theology, instead of that, looks to events (hereafter called "paradigmatic" events) which left the stamp of their immediacy upon language: which brought something new to be through language. Only in this way does theology work not only *from* event but also *toward* event; *from* language all but tapered out from "initiating" event *to* language glowing with the near-immediacy of present occasion. But this is to say that theology, *qua* theology, never has its given in *sheer* immediacy; it works from the linguistic effects of immediacy toward the new vocation of the Word, and thence over again.[27] Theology lives out of the future, understands out of the past.

(3) The impingement of reality in the present. Theology moves *from* event by attending to the ways in which its given impinged upon and constituted historical reality in the past, and *toward* event by its openness to the impingement of its given upon and through historical reality as that reality is experienced in the present. It goes without saying then that theology must maintain the greatest possible openness to the experience of reality in the present. As Gerhard Ebeling has said, ". . . what does not stand in any demonstrable and intelligible connection with the experience of reality that can be

[27] The interposition of systematic theology ("systematic symbolics") between the mediacy and the immediacy of the given, between the language of tradition and the rhetoric of first-order speech and act, is developed in Chapter VI below.

44

expected of me, cannot be responsibly appropriated by me at all."[28]

Like that of any other discipline, theology's language cannot avoid abstractions. Abstractions, as in some forms of mathematics, may serve as counters for amusement; but they have finally to touch home base in the world (which of course may be that important world that comes to expression in the comic). Theology's language forms no amusement game; everything is thrown over if its language has no real reference. Theology loses its nerve when it does not listen to the tolling of reality in multifarious contemporary scale; and when it does not chime with its own "head tones." This means nothing less than that theology enters the ontological lists and disputes reality. And that precisely does not mean that it advances a systematic ontology of its own as the heteronomous condition for experiencing its own given.

The distinction between "reality" and "being" is one which Christian theology (with teeth) cannot let go, as it cannot let go either of the two things discriminated.[29] Christianity is of course a concrete historical religion: it confesses to real impingement of a certain sort upon persons in the past, and casts that impingement in personal language. Not only that, Christianity confesses *paradigms* of real impingement which emerged in history and have been perpetuated by historical process. Christianity is perpetually tempted to remain yet another con-

---

[28] *Word and Faith,* p. 339.

[29] This distinction is elaborated below in Chapter IV, pp. 116–119. It may be noted here, however, that the distinction lies at the heart of the Christian doctrine of creation. In the biblical account(s) of creation there is, to be sure, an ambiguity which classical theology has been able to reckon with only by striking a bargain between "creation" and "redemption." This ambiguity may be sketched as follows. On the one hand the creation story borrows freely from available mythological stock: thus there is a note of the earth's reality as the adumbration or mirror-image of the being of God or the gods. On the other hand the "heavens" of "the heavens and the earth" are mentioned only to be dropped (Gen. 1:1). Thereafter man and earth are pictured as so constituted in their reality as to be ordinated toward a "condition of being" (for want of a better phrase) that is neither already a possession by virtue of creation nor yet something laid up in the heavens to be emulated. This "condition of being" is to emerge historically and eschatologically, between man's "subduing and having dominion" and the covenantal relation *coram Deo.*

crete religion in history by confessing its own patterns of impingement. But it is perhaps no exaggeration to say that Christianity was spared the fate of eclipse that lay in wait for other ancient Near Eastern religions (with the exception of Judaism which in this respect shows parallels to Christianity) by the emergence of *theology*. Theology takes for one of its tasks to show that its own paradigms of historical *reality* are the manifestation of the "maturation" of historical *being*. (To show that, to come to the heart of the matter, in Jesus Christ we reckon with the very historical being of manhood.) Early on, Christianity was saved from the status of yet another religion by its alliance with ontological philosophy. And if it be shrieked "But that was Greek ontology!," one can only ask why, if *Greek* ontology was the decisive ingredient, Greek *religion* fell upon a failure of nerve. The point is that in Greek ontological reflection Christian theology found categories through which to argue that its confessed impingements of reality disclose what *is* and *is to be,* or at the very least, through which to interrogate the common presentiments of mere "reality." From this one is to conclude not to a specific archaic (or contemporary) ontology as the singular substratum of Christian theology, but only to the use of ontological categories at hand which are appropriate for framing faith's own ontic apprehensions. Thus Christian theology can forsake neither its own concrete tradition nor the alliance of that tradition with the maieutic force of ontological philosophy without becoming on the one side just another religion in the sweep of history or on the other just another system of ontological philosophy. The problem for theology, *in nuce,* is how to keep both "reality" and "being" in view.

B. Theology and the Scale of Mental Acts

It was remarked at the beginning of this section that the three perennial problems are intertwined, that any one of them appears on the palimpsest text of the other two. In trying to run down the problem of theology's given in its "mere giveness" have we not already come upon the problem of its complication? And touched at many points different senses of knowledge? We

46

have, and need not repeat. What must now come into focus is the problem of the scale of mental acts activated by theology's given.

It may be useful to collect and tidy up by means of catch-words. For the mode of its given's presence theology uses the term "grace." *Faith* is response to the given present by grace; it is the response of the self, identified and interrogated by the given, to the given. *Theology* is at once a movement of mind from grace to faith, and a transposition of faith to understanding (*fides quarens intellectum*). Now, is the given in grace, faith, and theology altogether self-same and identical, and thus singular in modality? If the analysis under *A.* above possesses merit, the answer must be negative. Anyone contending for a "primal thinking" that embraces grace, faith, and theology has laid upon him the task of showing that the given is singular in modality. But to contend for the complication of the given, and thus for a complex of cognitive frameworks, entails no lesser responsibility; for thereby one courts the danger of transmuting the given rather than tuning to the various wave lengths of its modalities, and beyond that lies the danger of introducing such discontinuity between the frames of cognition as to fracture the unity of the subject matter as a whole (and thus make it impossible, for example, for preaching and theology to inform each other). To take such responsibilities on as a fundamental part of theological work is to assert that "how" questions are inseparably bound up with "what" questions. The "how" of faith is not finally the differentia of faith's content, but it does afford the base for phenomenological reflection whereby faith's content is brought to understanding in its connection with human existence at large.

Does theology have access to what can count for *grace?* A cognitive circuit from the generating apparatus in "event" to the bulb of illumination in understanding? If not, in any sense, it appears that the project of raising faith to understanding is doomed, at least "shorted," from the outset. For if there is *no* connection between the grace-faith event and the mechanics of understanding, then, at best, faith becomes immediacy without content (faith mysticism, or fideism) and theology becomes wholeness without presence (inventive rationalism). It

47

is more than passing strange that so much recent theology should have emphasized "faith raised to understanding" as the heart of the theological task, all the while ignoring what that emphasis rests upon if it be possible of realization, viz., the circuit of cognition from event to understanding.

To take the most difficult case straightaway: to what does theology have access in scripture? To the creation event, the exodus event, the crucifixion event, the resurrection event?[30] The obvious answer, that theology has access to none of these "events," is so obvious as to arouse suspicions. If event is something *entirely behind* language, some X without residue, *no* past event is accessible. What theology has access to in scripture is language and that in various literary types. In some of these types theology finds language in an ordered conceptual frame; and this language is clearly accessible to theology— because such language is a piece of theology. There the event is already interpreted, and contemporary theology can re-interpret the antique interpretation (of what?). That, however, is not to breach the impasse, but to celebrate it. Nor will it do to posit the *that* of the Word of God as event "behind" the primitive kerygmatic sentences, since a *that* without a *what* is nothing, at least nothing that can be brought to speech.

If theology has access to what counts for grace and has direct access only to language, the event of grace can only lay its potency upon the future by giving rise to language which actualizes that potency. Such a statement opens the Pandora's Box which houses the question of the complex intercausality of language and event. This question must be addressed, complexity and all, if theology is to raise not another piece of theology to understanding, but faith itself. It will mean that what theology turns to first in scripture is that language which is nearest (in a logical, not a temporal sense) the event—that language which "inverbalizes" the event. Event-inverbalizing language is incorrigibly imaginative language.[31] That of course

---

[30] As if these were "events" in the same sense!

[31] Theology turns as well to other sorts of language, to that of didactics, creedal confession, etc. To get the meaning of such language in view, however, theology must recover its plurisignative intentionality; and that means to track its imaginative origins. Here Husserl's dictum is pertinent: *Sinn* is a function of *Sinngenesis*.

48

raises the problem of how events give rise to images and images to events, and thus no less the role of imagination in the constitution of historical being than its function in the scale of mental acts. It is the aim of this book to address just these questions as a first step toward getting in tandem with the three fundamental problems laid out in this chapter.

To examine these things is to attempt a phenomenological description of the cognitive stations in the movement from grace through faith to theology, and thus to expose the hermeneutic of revelation. Not that alone; it is to reckon with the episodic character of unfolding personal-historical human being and the shape of man's linguisticality. That a study of imagination is made central to the prosecution of these tasks is scarcely to be justified in a way that theology has surely outgrown: by isolating a function of mind, in which to house revelation, that is secure against embarrassing epistemological questions. Not only is that impossible; it moves against the current of faith's own movement toward understanding. The imagination is settled upon for inquiry because (i) historical being is built up and perpetuated, whether enhancingly or destructively, through imaginative activity (a claim that has to be specified in meaning) and (ii) because event-inverbalizing language is imaginative language.

C. The Re-presentative
and Cognitive Potency of Tradition

On the one hand, profitable theological inquiry evades the interdicts which are trapped in the ceaseless sedimentation of theological language, and thus suppresses all proprietary and "curator" instincts. On the other hand, theology can speak only with its own tongue; and that is a tongue laden with language which cannot simply be cursed but rather must be broken and made to yield its intentionality to language aborning. No more than any other discipline can theology shed its linguistic skin in the twinkling of an eye and take up speaking wholly in neologisms.

If theology cannot have done with its past, that owes, for

one thing, to the fact that man himself cannot excise himself from his past and the fund of potency established by him and for him in the past. It owes as well to the claim that revelation always involves a temporal prius or, to put the matter more broadly, that revelation is constituted in concert with the course of historical reality. This raises acutely the question of the modalities of historical time (past, present, future) and their lived co-inherence; and especially visible is the problem of gaining access to the past in its establishment of plural potency (i.e., breaking the bonds of historicistic fate). Obviously these matters want less laconic naming, not to mention fuller elaboration.[32]

IV. PROLEPSIS

Since we can proceed only one step at a time, *solvitur ambulando,* it will be salutary now to take the long view lest we trip over our own feet. It is our intention to descry the formal contours of the genesis of meaning, the formal lineaments of the maturation of human be-coming in historical time, and the formal rubrics of the rhetoric of articulation: all as occasioned by revelation, and as descriptive of its character. Revelation, as faith meets its fundamental trajectory and as it passes *qua* category among theologians, cannot be approached with conceptual directness. In the present chapter, certain perennial theological problems have been brought forward in the form occasioned by an especially promising but by no means trouble-free fresh start on the category of revelation, viz., that of hermeneutical theology. But it is impossible to line Kewpie "problems" (without making strawmen of them) neatly in row, and then just as neatly to pepper them off with "answers." This impossibility needs, however, to be spelled out through a consideration of *problematic* itself within the context of a view of what will be termed the "hermeneutical spiral"; this project will be the task of Chapter II. In Chapter III we shall listen in on the resonance of the word "revelation," follow the word into its use as a theological category, and seek its force as the fundament of

[32] See below, Chapters III, IV, and VI.

50

man's career *coram Deo*. There the threefold perennial problematic of Chapter I will be tightened to embrace a threefold problematic of revelation.

Chapters IV–VI, by far the bulkiest, amplify the signals telegraphed ahead in the problematic of Chapters I-III, while at the same time renewing the problematic in pertinence to work that lies well beyond the end of the volume. Thus Chapter IV takes up an ontology of revelation, Chapter V a rhetoric of theological discourse that intends fidelity to revelatory disclosure, and Chapter VI a description of systematic symbolics in relation to a phenomenology of tradition.[33] The whole should be viewed as a piece of meta-theology: a recommendation as to what at least one kind of theology should be about today, and how it should go about what it is about.

[33] The fundamental argument of the book is carried by Chapters II-VI in a systematic-abstract frame. Appendix IV shows how the argument is rooted in an assessment of the tradition; it develops the argument in a systematic-historical frame from soundings taken along the chronological line. Appendices I-III comprise studies in the history of the category: imagination.

II. Problematic and the Hermeneutical Spiral

Outline

I. Introduction
II. Problematic and the Horizon of Subject Matter
   A. The Breach of Surface Unity, the "Loosening" of the Subject Matter through Problematic
   B. Problematic and Determinate Lines of Reference
   C. Problematic in Relation to Presuppositions and their Re-alignment
   D. Problematic and "Horizon-Fusion": Subject Matter and Subject
III. The Hermeneutical Spiral
   A. Circle and Spiral
   B. Hermeneutical Spiral: The Relation between Being and Knowing
   C. Contemplation and Dialectic (Reflection and Reflexion)

I. INTRODUCTION

Inquiry is more loquacious than discovery. Demanding takes longer than obtaining; and the hand that knocks is more active than the hand that receives.[1]

> We dance round in a ring and suppose,
> But the secret sits in the middle and knows.[2]

[1] Augustine, *Confessions*, XII, I, 1; in *Augustine: Confessions and Enchiridion*, trans. Albert C. Outler, (Philadelphia: Westminster Press, n.d.), p. 270. (Cited hereafter as Outler.)
[2] Robert Frost, "The Secret Sits," in *Complete Poems of Robert Frost*, (New York: Henry Holt and Company, 1949), p. 495.

52

In the theological game of "May I?" we have so far sneaked a few steps forward, duck waddles though they may have been. The Leader was not all that unaware; he commands us to take five giant steps backward. If we step back with alacrity, it is due neither to abject obedience nor yet to make a strategic retreat, but rather in order to see how strides may be taken in theology. Strides that may be taken and kept are those that revolve on question and answer. But before we take up striding again, and as a measure of protection against mere gamboling, we may fall back for a look at the rationale or legitimation for this way of proceding.

In fine, we need to see why there is no such thing as a pure problematic, why there is no blank screen of questions upon which to project answers. That understood, it will be apparent why it is impossible to post a debit column of problems and then a credit column of fulsomely correlated answers. Analytic is shot through with constructivity; construction continues analysis. Although constructivity may be muted while analytic is amplified, the process must subsequently be reversed or rather, as we shall see, spiraled. Thus Chapters I–III will lavish care upon the problematic of revelation, but without suppressing signals of comporting constructive statement. Chapters IV–VI will amplify those signals, but without suppressing the ensuing reprogramming of theological problematic. Viewed internally, this is the way theology grows (or, at least, changes).

The rationale of these notions may now be sought under two rubrics, that of *problematic* itself, and that of "the hermeneutical spiral."

II. PROBLEMATIC
AND THE HORIZON
OF A SUBJECT MATTER

The capacity to put the pertinent question and the capacity to know are capacities that cannot be separated. They are distinguishable but inseparable, as Plato has it, because each has something of the other in itself. Plato prosecuted knowledge, at least in the "Socratic" dialogues, through the question and

53

through the interrogation of the question. This is possible because within each question, which *qua* question is a "not-knowing," there is some kind of "knowing"; otherwise the question could not be grasped as pertinent. But within each answer, which *qua* answer is a "knowing," there is some kind of "not-knowing," because the answer without ceasing to be answer leads into an expanded problematic. It is no less true of *understanding* than of being: *ex nihilo nihil fit.*[3] Knowledge cannot arise from sheer ignorance, as ignorance is unintelligible apart from some modality of knowledge. We shall return to this set of considerations momentarily under the heading of the "hermeneutical spiral."

By the "problematic" of a subject matter is meant that set of basic (i.e., vis-à-vis *this* subject matter, irreducible) questions through which the subject matter is apprehended, understood, and related to other subject matters. So stated it is clear, together with the foregoing polarity of question and answer, that the problematic of a subject matter establishes the *horizon* within which inquiry concerning that subject matter is meaningful.[4] The basic questions preside over meaning in this sense: they point the direction in which explicit answers will have to move. That only can be recognized as answer which moves in such-and-such direction. It could not be otherwise, as answer is present in the question in some dumb modality.

Four ways in which the problematic of a subject matter establishes its horizon may be specified.

A. The Breach of Surface Unity, the "Loosening" of a Subject Matter through Problematic

In the first place, it belongs to the interrogative character of problematic to deprive a subject matter of that surface unity

[3] See Ebeling, "Der hermeneutische Ort der Gotteslehre bei Petrus Lombardus und Thomas von Aquin," *Zeitschrift für Theologie und Kirche,* Bd. 61, Heft 3 (November, 1964), pp. 284-326, esp. p. 307.

[4] It is of course a major philosophical problem whether there is a problematic, in this sense, that embraces *all* subject matters, and so establishes a common horizon for all meaning.

54

which it has only by courtesy of convention and the laziness of mind with which it is commonly approached. (One thinks for example of that shattering of Euclidean space which comprised in part the problematic issuing in Einstein's theory of relativity.) The question, set in motion by a fresh but dumb apprehension of some other configuration of the selfsame subject matter, disfigures the interrogated reality. To "open" is the function of the question. The *loosening* power of an authentically problematical question is felt precisely when the old answers *lose* their meaning, i.e., their power to answer. In its pure problematic (which no doubt is a pure abstraction), a subject matter is utterly bereft of closure and therefore of unity. This is a pure abstraction because in any subject matter under inquiry question and answer are in tension, no matter how great the preponderance of the one over the other. To say the same thing another way, a subject matter utterly bereft of closure and therefore of unity is no longer subject matter: it simply falls out of the mind's consideration.

B. Problematic and Determinate Lines of Reference

Genuine problematic opens the subject matter in a determinate way and therefore establishes definite lines of reference. Hermeneutical interrogation of a subject matter does not loosen or open that subject matter to the point of chaos. (Of course, this would not disallow the dissolution of any particular subject matter in conventional form, either to be absorbed into a more encompassing subject matter or to be proliferated into more integral units of other subject matters. The cultural history of the West abounds with instances of such dissolution, absorption, and proliferation.) If it were necessary to say above that problematic robs a subject matter of its conventional unity, here it is necessary to say that problematic likewise thwarts the tendency of subject matter to disintegrate into chaos when loosened from the bonds of custom. When the subject matter under inquiry is "revelation," this point bears underscoring. For many, the notion of revelation has indeed been opened, loosened, shaken; its conventional meaning has fallen away. For many

55

also, this falling away has led (with strict reference to the subject matter of revelation) into chaos, into sheer dubiety. What may well have begun as a movement of real problematic ceased at some point so to be. We have already recognized that a subject matter may simply fall out of the mind's entertainment. When that occurs the most to be hoped for is the emergence of genuine problematic. What that might mean in any specific case, with respect to revelation, is difficult (and probably unprofitable) to predict. It might well mean that sheer dubiety would be coaxed into doubt of something; that the reconfigured remnants of the subject matter of revelation, proliferated and absorbed in other subject matters, would provoke some hermeneutical interrogation. At all events, only so long as the mind be intrigued by the subject matter of revelation in some form can revelation be problematical for the mind. Sheer dubiety can be no nearer the problematic of revelation than naïve credulity (oh hard truth for today's theologian, who doubts with the best of them), for sheer dubiety is, like Plato's "many without a one," nothing that can be brought to speech. And that is because sheer dubiety is shaped by no prevailing question, and hence abuts no subject matter.

Perhaps the point can be made this way: the horizon established by problematic can be entered either by that loosening and opening of the subject matter that occurs with the naïvely credulous when their knowing becomes not-knowing, or by that arranging and disposing of the subject matter that occurs with the prodigally dubious when their not-knowing becomes wanting-to-know or even, in a veiled way, a knowing.

The horizon of a subject matter as its problematic refers to that fundamental interrogation which brings to pregnancy the possibilities within the subject matter. One is tempted to say that this interrogation brings the new shape of possibility to birth. But that would milk out of interrogation its problematical character, would turn its not-knowing into a kind of knowing that it does not know. It belongs to the new shape of possibility, as it emerges from an authentic problematic, that it forms the backdrop for all projective inquiry, and yet comes to light as genuinely possible only through the projection. The "backdrop" afforded becomes visible through what is projected upon it.

56

C. Problematic in Relation to Presuppositions and their Re-alignment

In the problematic of a subject matter presuppositions with respect to that subject matter wield their force near the surface. One hears of "buried presuppositions." But does it not belong to the way in which a presupposition works that it is buried? It is not a datum among the data that it shapes, *per impossible*. At that deep level at which presuppositions work upon act and thought (as distinguished from the way in which thought may work upon presuppositions!), little distinction is drawn between presuppositions according to family-types and origins: those of a civilization, a culture, nation, racial stock, region, family, individual. So it goes when the major subject matters of one's existence maintain a steady course. Not so when one or more becomes really problematical. When a subject matter so crucial for the Christian as revelation becomes problematical, the "families" of presuppositions come into conflict (to take the trite example, the conflict between the presuppositions of a particular Christian communion and those of physical-and-life-sciences mentality). There is, of course, as our age knows only too well, the problematic of culture itself. When the central subject matters of a culture become problematical for large numbers of people (and such subject matters can be *identified* as central only as they become problematical), "family" presuppositions conflict with each other on such a massive scale and in such visibility as to be the subject of empirical study.

But our business is not cultural criticism; and the tempting question, whether presuppositions in *open* conflict function any longer as presuppositions, can be touched only by innuendo. The question of "presuppositions and thought about subject matter" is an enormous one and is entered upon the lists here because the brief discussion of problematical interrogation gives some hints as to how presuppositions function and how they are realigned. Presupposing, like hermeneutical questioning, is a kind of not-knowing; what is presupposed is not known as what is known by its means. "All questioning and wanting-to-know," writes Gadamer, "presuppose a knowing of not-knowing." But, he continues, "it is a determinate not-knowing which leads to a determinate question."[5] This "knowing of not-knowing" characterizes presuppositions as they function in inquiry attending a subject matter. "Philosophy will never seek to deny its 'presuppositions,' but neither may it simply admit them."[6] That means, in the terms used here, that in problematic the "not-knowing" in a presupposition is raised to prominence; it is loosened from correlation with the old "knowing"; it becomes a newly determinate not-knowing and so open to a new knowing. In short, the presuppositions of a selfsame subject matter come under reform and alteration only in the state of problematic.

D. Problematic and "Horizon-Fusion": Subject Matter and Subject

We have so far seen that problematic establishes the horizon of a subject matter by disfiguring its customary unity and by laying out the lines of new configuration or possibility; and that one of the ways problematic achieves both of these is by exposing presuppositions in conflict. The fourth way in which problematic establishes horizon is really an expansion of the third. It may be called the process of "horizon-fusion."[7]

There is one sort of horizon-fusion to which *all* subject matters are potentially subject in problematic, a sort to which we have already alluded. That is, when a subject matter becomes problematical and thus loses its customary moorings, it is opened to the possible fusion of its horizon with the horizon of other subject matters. To repeat, such horizon-fusion is a matter of record in western intellectual history; and the fusion has always occurred in the wake of intellectual problematic of revolutionary

[5] Hans-Georg Gadamer, *Wahrheit und Methode,* (Tübingen: J. C. B. Mohr [Paul Siebeck], 1960), p. 348.

[6] Martin Heidegger, *Being and Time,* trans. John Macquarrie and Edward Robinson, (London: SCM Press, 1962), p. 358.

[7] The term is Gadamer's (*Horizontverschmelzung*), although I scarcely use it in his richly elaborated sense. See *Wahrheit und Methode,* pp. 289ff., pp. 356ff. The same applies to my use of the term "prejudice" (Gadamer's *Vorurteil;* see pp. 255ff.)

proportions. The question remains outstanding, prosecuted from Plato through Hegel to Teilhard de Chardin, whether an absolute horizon-fusion of all subject matters can be actualized. Theology, after a heady experiment with queening, experienced an acute horizon-*diff*usion during several centuries following the high Middle Ages. Yet recent decades have seen the rise in America of new sorts of limited theological horizon-fusion; thus "theology of art," "theology of politics," "theology of sex," etc.

There is another sort of horizon-fusion which characterizes *some* subject matters when they become problematical. Just which these are need not detain us, as theology is clearly included. Horizon-fusion of this sort refers not to the overlaying of one subject matter with another, but to the radical juxtaposition of the horizon of the subject matter and the horizon of the person for whom the subject matter has become problematical. Just as problematic disturbs and realigns the presuppositions at work in a subject matter, so it interrogates the prejudices (or to use the nice word, pre-understandings) of the person. The disturbance of conventional unity in the subject matter has its backlash in the everyday selfhood of the person. What is at stake in the crumbling horizon of the subject matter therefore is the crumbling horizon of one's own personal existence. Where horizon-fusion of this sort obtains, the problematic of a subject matter is the problematic of the subject as well. The racial problematic in the United States today is perhaps the most visible public instance of specific horizon-fusion in this sense.

Theology offers perhaps the paradigm-case of horizon-fusion of this second sort. None of its categories comes under problematical status without engaging the full horizon of the person for whom they are problematical. That means, minimally, that whoever has promised to love, honor, and obey his prejudices should steer clear of theology. The alternative to that, and the one commonly opted (outside the groves of academe, of course), is to systematize prejudice and call it theology. Only by that route is one secure against theological problematic.

In genuine theological problematic the exposure and the realignment of presuppositions at work in theological subject

59

matter are indissolubly connected with the exposure and interrogation of personal prejudice. Out of authentic problematic, theological reformulation brings personal involvement in tow. To be sure, this does not mean that theology causes "conversion." So to put the matter is entirely to miss the point. Problematic in a subject matter does not "cause" a reaction in the subject, or vice versa. "Horizon-fusion" in theology means that the problematic of subject matter and that of subject are coincident. Just in that coincidence lies the immediate "relevance" of theological problematic. Only in concrete "horizon-fusion" will theological problematic have significance for us.

III. THE "HERMENEUTICAL SPIRAL"

At the beginning of the consideration of problematic I referred to the "hermeneutical spiral." Since the hermeneutical spiral refers above all to the relation between knowing and not-knowing with respect to an item up for interpretation, and since this relation has been our major concern now for some pages, it is appropriate that direct attention should be settled upon it. To reiterate, this concern can only be prosecuted at once in a formal fashion and by anticipation of the projective effort hereafter.

A. Circle and Spiral

I use the phrase "hermeneutical spiral" rather than the more common phrase "hermeneutical circle" for two reasons. (1) The "hermeneutical circle" has come to characterize the special difficulty one experiences in interpreting a *written text*. Dilthey so named this difficulty, and described it as follows. "Herein lies the central complexity of all hermeneutic. The whole of a work must be understood from its individual words and their relations, and yet the full understanding of individual words already draws upon the understanding of the whole."[8] Now the part-whole scheme in which this complexity of interpretation is stated may well be the most appropriate one in which to cast the difficulty of textual interpretation. But the item up for interpretation may not be a written text; it may be anything at all: a potsherd from an archaeological dig, a sharp pain in the chest, a crucifix, or "the subject matter of revelation." If there is to be a consideration of problematic which can embrace such diverse things, such a consideration must extend to whatever can put itself forward to the mind as comprising some significant union of knowing and not-knowing. To undertake such a consideration, of course, is to assume that "meaning" is not *there* as a self-standing something, but rather has to be won from what brings itself forward.[9]

(2) Beyond the part-whole connotations which the phrase "hermeneutical circle" has taken on within a school of hermeneutical theory, there are needlessly troublesome connotations which attach to the metaphor "circle." Thus the "hermeneutical circle" arouses suspicions of a "vicious circle." Moreover and more seriously, the metaphor "circle" is inadequate to the relation between being and knowing. This point can best be made by moving directly to the "hermeneutical spiral."

B. Hermeneutical Spiral:
The Relation between Being and Knowing

Thinking is protected against sterility of the given and infertility of response only as it honors the relation between being and knowing as a relation which can be envisaged as that of a *helical spiral*.[10] There *is* a circularity of motion (as the wire of

[8] Wilhelm Dilthey, *Gesammelte Schriften*, (Göttingen: Vandenhoeck & Ruprecht, 1958), Vol. V, p. 330.

[9] *"Le sens n'est pas un fait donné, il est plutôt une tâche, une vision à conquérir."* C. A. van Peursen, "Phénoménologie et ontologie," *Rencontre/Encounter/Begegnung:* Contributions à une psychologie humaine dédiées au Professeur F. J. J. Buytendijk, (Utrecht: Uitgeverij Het Spectrum, 1957), p. 317.

[10] For rusty geometricians: a helical spiral is the curve assumed by a straight line drawn on a plane when that plane is wrapped around

a helical coil goes around but does not come back to the same point). The relation is circular because knowing presupposes being (minimally, that of the knower and that of the known) and being presupposes knowing (at some level of apprehension of some dimension of being's givenness). Yet this is not a true circle, and therefore not a cognitively vicious circle. The circuit "beginning" (who can say where the circuit begins?) with the point marked "something being given" does not return to the same point on the same circumference, but to a point "above" it; and likewise with the point marked "knowing." Every spiral involves an enriched cognition of the field of the something-given, and every expansion of field furnishes impetus for another cognitive circuit: thus an expansion of the knowing mind and of the given itself. Without some such model as that of the helical spiral to adumbrate their nature, being and knowing stand over against each other as blocks of stuff never to have intercourse, as though the givenness of being were never enhanced through knowledge (or constricted through ignorance) and as though what knowledge responds to is an incarceration of itself.

From this it will be clear that there is no such thing as a simply-being-given (or a being-simply-given), or rather that any something-being-given is not immediately intelligible: such a thing would be immediately intelligible only to a being for whom the distinction between being and knowing could not be drawn. The *ontically* given thing does not give itself in a simple way. That is, the very givenness of a thing is modalized by the various cognitive kinds of mental reception. Moreover, insofar as the thing is truly "other," i.e., is neither recondite nor derivative, it gives itself from its own internal principle of order or concentration and in concert with whatever else goes to make up the event in which it is manifest. *What* is given to *focalized sensual intuition* is the delineated thing, not its internal principle of order. Herein is the mystery of every ontic given for the hermeneutical mind: it gives and withholds simultaneously. This giving and this withholding ground epistemological

---

a cylindrical surface, especially a right circular cylinder (e.g., the curve of a screw thread, or the wire of a spring).

and ontological discourse respectively, and account for the spiral between knowing and being.

C. The Inverse Relation
between Extension and Intension

Hermeneutics (the theory of interpretation) cannot avoid epistemological discourse because any interpretable datum will have *extension* beyond its immediate presence, nor ontological discourse because the datum will have *intension* beyond the power of the mind to know (in a straight empirical sense.)[11] *It is the inverse relation between extension and intension that makes the spiral move.* What this means is that the more we have of a datum's immediate presence (its internal unity) the less we have of its character ("whatness") in relation to the field in which it is presented (its external range), while the more we have of its character in relation to the field in which it is presented the less we have of its immediate presence. Knowledge, wrote Paul Weiss in an early article, "always involves a synthetic unification of externals, referring to an internal unity not had."[12] (I should want to qualify this to say: "knowledge *by rational extrication* or abstraction always involves . . .") The knowing mind sets out from a datum to explore the extent of the datum's range, sets out on a circuit to unify this datum with the field in which it appears; and knowing reaches the farthest arc of the spiral when the datum cannot follow (i.e., removes its pres-

[11] One cannot choose between the alternatives posed by Plato's Euthydemus: "What I know, is" or "What is, I know." To accept either is to fail to understand the helical relation between knowing and being. In the later dialogues Plato himself came close to this point of view without, however, writing a treatise in explication of it. (This thesis is enlarged in my article, "The Imagination in Plato," *International Philosophical Quarterly,* Vol. V, No. 3 [September, 1965], pp. 436–461.) The understanding of the "hermeneutical spiral" presented here owes much to the later Plato and the early Paul Weiss. In addition to Weiss's article cited in the following footnote, see his book, *Reality,* (Princeton: Princeton University Press, 1938).

[12] Paul Weiss, "Metaphysics, the Domain of Ignorance," *Philosophical Review,* XLII, No. 256 (July, 1934), p. 404.

ence), when it becomes doubtful that knowing yet refers to the datum from which it set out.

One can hardly lay out all at once a full phenomenological description of the cognitive circuit as such; that would amount to a phenomenological equivalent of Kant's *Critique of Pure Reason* (as Husserl saw!). It is enough to note that, with respect to its own representations of the initiating datum, reason proceeds cataleptically. The cognitive circuit is made episodic by various kinds of cataleptic pauses; indeed whether the procedure (vis-à-vis the initiating datum) is to be viewed as a spiraling circuit or as a nonreversible straight line depends upon the kind and number of cataleptic pauses. Two examples may be noted. (1) One such pause occurs at that point at which reason becomes dubious of its reference to the initiating datum, at which the sense of the datum's presence becomes weak. Only by courtesy of such a pause does the problem of *verification* arise. Confronted with this problem reason may bend back, by means of other sorts of pauses, to the datum. But it may not, too. It may proceed away from the datum, verifying/falsifying solely with reference to principles of reason (as in the "coherence" view of truth). (2) A second pause is one in which the sense of the initiating datum's presence is utterly lacking, in which reason functions without reference to its delineated presence. The physicist is not thinking about nothing when he thinks about "light"; but he is not bound to his light bulb either. He is thinking the concept light, light in full extension. (These two sorts of catalepsis are mentioned here for purposes of exemplification. No one will suppose that they exhaust the stations along the way of cognition.[13])

That only can be a datum for *hermeneutical* interrogation about which we *know* ourselves to be *ignorant* (to state it in the curious way one must).[14] In a way that the mind cannot

[13] The epistemological matters broached here are treated in Chapter V below.

[14] Knowledge can never be accounted for if it be assumed that the state prior to knowledge is absolute ignorance. No one ever found himself in such a state. One kind of cognitive discourse can only be incited or excited by another kind of cognitive discourse. I am incited to thought only by something being given in my field of percipience or conception

leave alone, such a datum both "gives" and "withholds" itself. It is given in that it diverts the mind's attention from other claims to its own; it provokes or beckons the mind to search out along its own lines, a search that activates the apprehensive, synthetic, and projective machinery of metal powers. Such a datum withholds by its power to draw the mind back, to be sure to a novel but connected constellation, when abstract concepts have lost all sense of its concrete presence. This is not to deny that there may well be data which do not serve as the subject matter of hermeneutical investigation. Physicists may someday attain such an understanding of light that they will no longer be bothered by any delineated instance of it. In that case the light of a flashlight will be some sort of datum, but not an hermeneutical one. Likewise with the data of theological tradition: we shall take no notice of them unless they both give and withhold, unless they provoke in us a dumb knowledge of being ignorant about something important harbored in them. Only so do they become data for hermeneutical interrogation.

D. Contemplation and Dialectic
(Reflection and Reflexion)

This elaboration of the hermeneutical spiral makes connection with some hoary motifs in classical philosophy and with those thinkers on the contemporary scene (Farrer, Marcel, Jaspers, Heidegger, et al.) who, in speaking of "the mystery of being," recall Aristotle's dictum that "Philosophy begins in wonder." The nerve of ontological reflection is astonishment that something should be and wonder at our ignorance of that order at the source of its givenness. Paul Weiss means to characterize such reflection in the most favorable sense when he says that it is trained upon ". . . the domain of ignorance, profound and inexhaustible."[15]

---

in such a way that it puts itself upon me as something about which I *know* I am ignorant. Such a way of speaking presupposes there are different modes of cognition, and to that subject we shall have to turn hereafter.

[15] Paul Weiss, *art. cit.*, p. 402.

To the "wonder" of reflection and *contemplation* must be added however the "wander" of *dialectic* and reflexion. The process of thinking is under way when, in the face of the ontically given, an almost passive wonder combines with an active quest for knowledge of its outreach and inreach. Consequently the supporting poles to which the hermeneutical *Anlage* gives rise are contemplation and dialectic; and in the notable "systems" of thought, as in a structural arch, the tensions of man's engagement with being are so deflected into these poles that they must bear the weight of any superstructure of doctrine. If in the thinker's thought one pole loses its restraining, deflecting, and supporting relation to the other, he becomes either a mere mystic or a mere logician. The separation in modern western thought has usually taken a logical direction, although there are signs in more recent European philosophy of a renaissance of the mystical motif.[16] Logicism and misologism, mysticism and the rationalism of the imperialistic concept: any and all, we have implied, are breaches of the hermeneutical spiral.

It may be useful, finally, to offer an example of the hermeneutical spiral, one which takes leave of the highly abstract and formal setting in which it has been necessary to broach this notion. In the *Psalms* and wisdom sayings of the Old Testament there is to be found language at once as concrete and abstract as scripture can afford. In these literary genres the concrete ever bends into the abstract, while the abstract makes its point by curving back for a fresh load of the concrete—and thence over

[16] Merleau-Ponty writes, "It [philosophy] will double back upon itself indefinitely, then, and will be, as Husserl said, an infinite dialogue or meditation. To the extent that it remains faithful to its own intention, it will never know where it is going. The incompletion of phenomenology and the allure of its inchoative state are not signs of its failure. They are inevitable because phenomenology has for its task the revelation of the mystery of the world and the mystery of reason." And again: "The world and reason are no problem; let us say rather they are mysterious. But mystery defines them: there is no question of dissipating the mystery by some solution, for they are prior to solutions." *Phénoménologie de la Perception,* (Paris: Gallimard, 1945), Avant-Propos, p. xvi. (A somewhat different translation than the above will be found in Merleau-Ponty, *Phenomenology of Perception,* trans. Colin Smith, [London: Routledge & Kegan Paul, 1966], pp. xx–xxi).

66

again. One may satisfy himself on this score almost at random, say, in the *Psalms* and *Job*. The stunning thing is that the "same" phenomena are ever in view, yet they are never *just* the same by reason of the hermeneutically spiraling circuits through which they are being taken by the religio-lyrical spirit.

Consider Psalms 8 and 104, and Job 28. Psalm 8 is pallidly characterized in the textbooks as "a meditation of man's place in creation." It is that; but it is above all a piece of the Psalmist's reflex figuration in the face of the phenomena of the heavens, of the awesomeness of moon and stars. What these phenomena excite and incite in him is a reflex awareness of the astonishing fact that he should be able to have these phenomena appear to him without having the ground melt beneath his feet. For that awareness the only appropriate response is

> *What is man that thou shouldst think of him,*
> *And the son of man that thou shouldst care for him?*

This response is then bent into the phenomena of earth: the question is "answered" by a display of "the beasts of the field" over which man is to take dominion.

But that answer is not a final one. In Psalm 104 the Psalmist turns to the "same" phenomena, those of the heavens and the earth. Here, however, praise has refunded these phenomena: what now appears is not something to induce reflexive awareness in man of his own domination, but rather awareness of a limit in the phenomena upon his domineering. Clouds are the chariot of the Lord, the wings of the wind his messengers, flames of fire his ministers: with his license to dominion, man is up against something wondrously good and holy.

Yet again, the phenomena present another visage in Job 28. Man may set an end to darkness by removing from its depths the precious things of the earth. He may put forth his hand to the rocks, turn the mountains upside down, and cleave rivers in the bedrock. From stone will issue copper, gold from the secret seams, and out of the underground bubbles water for a thirsty land. But where can wisdom be found? It is none of these, and is rarer than they. If wisdom is not to be had by

67

infinite extension from the phenomena of heaven and earth, to put the matter discursively, that owes to the fact that wisdom has no absolute locus of intensive presence. So man can only harken to those phenomena which renew *this* giving and withholding Presence, and adopt the policy: "the fear of the Lord, that is wisdom."

III. Revelation: Word, Fundament, Category

Outline

I. INTRODUCTION

To this point we have been preoccupied with grasping the contemporary form of theology's perennial problematic; and with seeing why the very notion of problematic is essential to the vitality, even the possibility, of theological reflection. The problem of revelation has been spied only at great distance—like having seen mountains for the first time from afar, known to be *mountains* only from the map (otherwise they might have been a dark cloud-bank, a pinking-sheared ribbon of shadow upended against the sky). On the one hand we must not be tyrannized by the map: "Oh yes, that must be the Sangre de Cristo range." That is, we must not allow the theological textbooks to identify "the problem of revelation" without remainder. But if we give ourselves to the lived phenomenon and its landscape, we must prepare to steel ourselves against what Emerson called the compulsion "to utter twenty-four sentences simultaneously." What cannot be seen all at once cannot be spoken all at once. Perhaps it is more accurate to say that our language at hand, with its immanent predispositions, will not let us see everything there is to see all at once. This will become apparent as we worry the word "revelation" itself.

As the ablest of contemporary cinematographers have taught us (and occasionally have been able to achieve[1]), the perspective to strike is that from which the thing to be seen itself perspectivizes the world and thus establishes the horizon of the world's reality. No less a task lies ahead, made more difficult by its discursive character: viz., to project against the general backdrop already lowered the central problem under study, and that in such a way that backdrop and problem contribute to mutual specification.

As a way of broaching the matter, the word "revelation" may now be sounded for its bearings. Those bearings will then "locate" a discussion of the familiar distinction between revelation as content and as process. At best, these considerations can only conduct us to the antechamber of the phenomenon, to the point at which a fresh purchase on the fundamental problematic of revelation may be essayed. That will require a discrimination of revelation as *fundament* and revelation as theological category.

[1] One thinks especially of *Blow-up, L'Ecclisse, The Pawnbroker, The Seventh Seal.*

70

II. THE WORD "REVELATION"

A. The Hermeneutical Complexity of the Word

One need not look past the word "revelation" for an illustration of hermeneutical complexity in theological language. Of all theological concepts that lurch out of the shadows of the past none is more likely to send a spasm through the trigger finger of "the contemporary mind." For some the word has lost all powers of connotation; it has become denotative, and that with a graveyard-bell ring of supernaturalism. For others the word retains connotative tone, but without limit, and thus is freighted with multifarious and all but unaccountable associations. In many circles the mere use of the word "revelation" will serve to have its user classified with those who yet believe the earth is flat, who traffic in recipes for divining brews, and who have such morsels of belief and information served up fully prepared in their cerebral synapses by direct electrical action of deity. That revelation can any longer be identified with or serve as a surrogate for such beliefs is only slightly less bizarre than the content of the beliefs themselves.

Such is the fate-laden character of language, however, that a term cannot be made through instant determination to slough everything save its putative essential intention. The speaking and hearing of words comprise, for one thing, the intersection of personal histories. Built up at that intersection, the signification of a word develops head-on and thus through body contact. Altered usage arises from wreckage at the point of impact, from the debris of shattered speaking and hearing. It would be odd then if a word like "revelation," with such a rich history, were not on a collision course. Just in that lies its possibility for a revivified purchase on its own intention.

If the word "revelation" is *utterly* sedimented, there is nothing to do but put it behind glass in the Theological Museum of Antiquities. Whether the word is so hardened can only be determined by its careful use in the situation of speaking and hearing.[2] The word that will not bend in favor of its intention,

[2] Words are to be used with a sensitive ear cocked to the acoustical situation: as noted earlier, hearing is the thither end of speaking. When

that will not assist in the formation of other words for its own intent, is beyond usefulness. If the word "revelation" has come upon such days, theology must bring its intention to speech through other categories, just as the word "revelation" itself was brought forward when other words failed to intercept personal histories and the world's horizon of self-interpretation.[3]

B. The Immanent Coign of Vantage

In the terms developed in Chapter II, unless the word "revelation" puts itself upon us as comprising some important "not-knowing," as in some way inciting and exciting the hermeneutical spiral, something to collide with, it will be ignored and dropped from our personal vocabulary. (Or it will be used in a Pickwickian sense, as some eighteenth-century poets used its surrogate, "inspiration," play-acting with their Muses when the ink refused to flow.) At this point theology's face goes red as its breath grows short. There is no denying that much of yesterday's "revelation" is today's falsehood. Among sophisticated hearers, that surely is one of the pieces of debris the word "revelation" has brought into the common linguistic pool. Theology that means to rehabilitate the word "revelation" will therefore take great care to discriminate that *not-knowing* which goes with revelation *qua* fundament of human being and which incites hermeneutical knowing, from that not-knowing which turns out to be simply *false knowing*. If theology has learned anything from its history, it will not attempt to make this discrimination entirely from its own resources. One can scarcely exaggerate, for example, the positive role the sciences have performed in bringing theology to the consciousness that its proper not-knowing is not to be confused with that false knowledge of the world

---

Zarathustra failed to make his language score, he fell silent with the exclamation to himself: "I am not the mouth for these ears." Friedrich Nietzsche, *Thus Spoke Zarathustra,* I, 5; trans. Marianne Cowan, (New York: Henry Regnery Co., 1957), p. 9.

[3] It will be the burden of Appendix IV to see how the intentionality of the word "revelation" came into theological language before the word came into use.

which it is the business of science (to state that business negatively) to dispel.[4]

Fundamental theology, to put the matter positively, is preoccupied with its own not-knowing and knowing, although it prosecutes that preoccupation in the broadest humanistic framework. Bustled into mental act by the not-knowing that heralds its own given, it brings that not-knowing to various modalities of knowledge through the hermeneutical spiral.

The theological problematic of revelation will be developed, consequently, without recourse to a standpoint outside itself, i.e., in terms of its own immanent development. Only so can formal and material considerations in theology remain connected from the outset, however much the formal be brought to the fore. But the intentionality of the word "revelation" historically has been confined to no single categorial alembic; and therefore an entirely immanent coign of vantage, like a position taken in a river constantly shifting its current, is something to be aimed at rather than steadily achieved. So what it means to establish oneself in "the immanent coign of vantage" needs tarrying over.

(1) The immanent point of vantage may be described initially, in Bergson's phrase, as the point where an act of "intellectual auscultation" is exercised, the point where one listens to what the tradition has brought to speech in the word "revelation" and its hermeneutical equivalents. This may not be done in such a way as to overtop the problem. Listening from an immanent vantage would require listening not to language on holiday with its engine idling (Wittgenstein), but to language on the job at high throttle. To strike the immanent vantage,

[4] Here is the reason a certain kind of apologetic enterprise should be abandoned forever, that in which theology sets out to identify certain types of not-knowing within a culture, thence to bring their patrons up the garden path to revelation's knowing. The record of this enterprise is inauspicious: time and again not-knowing (say, the "gaps" in science) has been traded for revelation as false knowledge. The integrity of any type of not-knowing must be left to excite its own appropriate interpretive mechanisms: that is the "culture" with which theology has properly to do. If the analysis of the hermeneutical spiral in Chapter II possesses merit, there will be formal similarities in all acts of interpretation. But the physicist's reckoning with the not-knowing that provokes his interest in *light* cannot, without abutting false knowing, be made the veil of some profound theological not-knowing.

73

we shall find it necessary to advance heuristic categories; categories which formally open access to revelation *qua* fundament, and thus to the broad range of what came to expression in historically conditioned language.

(2) To aspire to the immanent coign of vantage, in reckoning the fundamental problematic of revelation, is therefore precisely to evade the standpoint from which the *possibility* of revelation is made the first question. From the immanent vantage it is not the possibility but rather the actuality of revelation *qua* fundament, as that actuality has distributed itself in history and language, that is the overriding question. As noted before, theology may not ask, without ceasing to be theology, *whether* it has a given.

(3) Finally, the *immanent* coign of vantage bespeaks a human, not a divine, point of view. From the divine point of view, we may suppose, there is scarcely any "problematic of revelation."

The last point can only be urged strenuously against those who mean effectively to subvert the immanent coign of vantage, and thus content themselves with explicating revelation through the metaphor of a "leap." It is of course true that, if theology is not to have recourse to a standpoint outside its own problematic, theological reflection "begins" in some sense on the hither side of revelation itself (i.e., it assumes the profferment of grace). But that hardly binds us to a *silentium altissimum* (whose protagonists are, ironically, exceptionally talkative): to saying, the chasm was just there, we leapt, and did not look back in philosophical anger. It is true that ". . . we have to respect the mystery of the given-ness of this fact . . ."[5] But we have already seen that respect for mystery is only a part of the hermeneutical tale. It is by no means clear that the effort to follow and execute the hermeneutical spiral, the effort to understand the "how" of the givenness of faith's mystery, is any more rash or subversive of that mystery than is some vaunted *silentium*

[5] Karl Barth writes: "We have to respect the mystery of the givenness of this fact . . . without making any rash or subversive attempt to understand its How." *Church Dogmatics,* trans. G. T. Thompson and Harold Knight, Vol. I/2, (Edinburgh: T. & T. Clark, 1956), p. 233. Also: ". . . Faith only needs to confess that it has happened. It has happened for us, but it has happened without us . . ." *Ibid.,* Vol. IV/1, p. 249.

altissimum, especially if it is the whole intention of revelation to bring the Word to understandable speech.

C. Verbal and Substantive Resonances in the Word

In the word "revelation" there is a tension of resonance to be noted from the outset. While not strictly a verbal noun (that would require "revealing"), the word "revelation" is a noun derived from a verb. One hears in the word an internal tension between its verbal and its substantive resonance. A noun denominates, names something; a verb asserts or shows an activity or state. As distributed between these resonances, the word appears to emit its force to two hearings.

(1) On one hearing, the note struck is primarily verbal; and the voice of verbal resonance is predominantly *active.* (That is the minimal meaning of the claim that in revelation man is placed under "summons.") Even when its verbal voice verges on state, revelation is not *static* (to put the matter in the curious way English requires). The active voice sounds in the noun revelation even when revelation denominates a state, thing, or condition. It could be said, consequently, that revelation is indeed deed (a legacy bequeathing something) only in deed (in *act*).

(2) On a second hearing, revelation is primarily and above all a noun denominating something. That "something" possesses the stability requisite for denomination. Revelation signifies *this* something and no other. If there is a note of verbality in the noun, that can only mean the active disclosure of *what is there* in substantive state and named by the noun. "Reveal" can only mean the disclosure of "revelation," or the manifestation of the "revealed."

D. "Revelation": Content and Process

The verbal-substantive tension, just now signaled, may now be amplified by tracing it into the much discussed question of revelation as "process" and revelation as "content." Process

75

refers to the act or "how" of revealing, the *fides qua creditur* or the *modus praedicandi;* content to what is revealed, the *fides quae creditur* or the *res praedicata.*

It is first necessary to see why the issue of process and content in revelation (and their interrelation) is an important one. As far back as the community of faith reaches, revelation involves a temporal prius ("God at sundry times and divers places . . .").[6] Revelation *now* involves remembrance, recollection, recommencement.[7] What is recovered, so that now there can be an uncovering? What has been circulated, handed around and on, that is essential to the fertilization of faith's flower? Some *content,* some body of truths, insights, wisdom, or attitudes —a content that is to shape the vision and interpretation of my present reality? Some *process,* which it is necessary to undergo in order to bring presently experienced reality into meaningful focus? Does the necessity of remembrance and circulation mean that *something* once for all delivered must be believed, or that some *way* of believing once for all established must be followed? In short, just in what respect is revelation normative or prescriptive? Moreover, is the prescriptivity of revelation attached altogether to its quality as a temporal prius?

Now it will be useful to see how questions of these sorts are replied to in each of the two positions recently discriminated. The one construes revelation as primarily content, the other as primarily process. Each position will be stylized for purposes of contrast (I do not intend that either should be attributed to a particular school or theologian). Through the exposure of weakness in each by running commentary, we shall see how neither position, nor a simple combination of them, affords an irreducible statement of revelation's fundamental problematic.

(1) In the first position (which for efficiency's sake will be referred to hereafter as the first view), revelation attaches first and foremost to content, a body of truth. The body may take the form of scripture, confessional formulae closely related to scripture, church dogma, or some combination of these. At all events, revelation encapsulates an *original given* in such fashion as to be communicable intact. Bearers of the body of truth are

---

[6] See below, III., A., 4.
[7] See below, III., A., 5.

themselves so "inspired" as to keep it pure, i.e., so as to keep it in harmony with its original deliverance. While such a body is intrinsically true, *per se notum,* it functions "truthfully" only under the condition of acknowledgment or assent.[8] Assent means two things minimally, that the bearer (e.g., scripture or ecclesiastical hierarchy) is credited with authority (purity of transmission), and that the body of content is believed as binding. The *form* of this body of content may admit of some diversification, to be sure under the watchful eye of an inspired bearer. The simplest form, the one least susceptible of pollution, is that of the straightforward *proposition.* On this way of construing revelation, for example, "God created the world" is an item of revealed truth; with other cognate items it is handed on and around, mayhap to find some persons who will acknowledge or assent to it.

On this first view, there can be no question about the character of revelation's *continuity.* That continuity is nothing other than the pure transmission of an original body of truth; perhaps one should say, revelation is an original discontinuity that is handed around and on continuously in unitary form. What counts as revelation *now* must perforce be in unity with that originality. The conditions of assent in no way qualify the originality and unity of what comes by the route of an inspired course. Whatever the shape of one's experience hitherto, experience now is to be conformed to the hegemony of a set of interpretive propositions secured against meddling.

(2) The second position (hereafter referred to as the second view) begins, logically, with some such affirmation as this: ". . . every generation has the same original relation to revelation."[9] This point of departure indicates a quite different way of discriminating content and process in revelation; content is itself a function of process. The content of revelation is like manna given the Israelites, proportioned to immediate vital need and incapable of surviving the exigencies of the day. Revelation cannot be preserved through the pressure cookery of

[8] Etienne Gilson writes, ". . . the problem of revelation requires that there is some divinely made statement to which we must bow." *Reason and Revelation in the Middle Ages,* (New York: Scribner's, 1938), p. 97

[9] Bultmann, *Existence and Faith,* p. 89.

77

ecclesiastical confession, dried for quick energy on the endurance hike through the wilderness of existence, or packaged as "general principles" in the deep-freeze of metaphysics. The *real* process of revelation is the result of no prior processing; revelation neither opens jars nor thaws for a Birdseye view. Revelation has no horizon but that of the *immediate now* and the felt exigencies of the individual *qua* subject. Thus the "subject" of revelation takes total priority over the "subject matter" of revelation, or rather makes subject matter the function of the subject. Taken to extremity, this view shunts aside the *what* of revelation in favor of a certain *how,* so that revelation concerns not a specially shaped subject matter but rather a special way of viewing (or "deciding") all subject matter.

What then survives the moment? In what does the continuity of revelation consist? Certainly not content, if that means a fixed subject matter viewed in anything like a fixed way. The answer can only be that nothing survives the moment since the immediate moment of revelation is an event; and an event (on this view) is not perdurable and so not communicable. Faith is not thereby necessarily claimed to be without content, however occasionalistic such content would have to be. Faith's content could only be the whole subject matter of one's existence in the present moment. This content is not however a communicable content, or at least is not communicable in its revelatory aspect.[10]

The second view comes down heavily on the side of revelation as a radically contingent affair with respect to both its content and its process. As such the position intends to specify the meaning of revelation as *grace* and to restrict the content of revelation to what emerges through grace alone. Yet such an account scarcely makes any advance upon a classical problem in Evangelical theology, viz., what it remains for *theology* to do in the face of revelation so conceived. All modes of discourse are effectively reduced to proclamatory modes (notably, preach-

[10] "What 'revelation' means in general cannot be any more exactly and completely specified by the man of faith than by any man of unfaith. . . . The only new thing that faith and faith alone is able to say about revelation is that it has become an event and becomes an event." *Ibid.,* p. 100.

78

ing), to the invocation of the occasion for decision. It is, however, a notorious problem how occasionalism can sustain itself as a viable possibility. To his great credit Malebranche saw that an occasionalistic view must make appeal finally to God as the principle of continuity between finite occasions. Yet he did not see—and in this he has been joined by many a theological occasionalist—that this was to reinstate what he (and many a theologian) set out to discredit, viz., a *deus ex machina.* One of the acute ironies in this theologically "existentialistic" view is that, unless it be willing to give up the continuity of revelation absolutely, it abuts what is surely self-contradictory: a mechanical Spiritomonism.

This train of reflection allows a problem to come into view. Are revelation under the aspect of content and revelation under the aspect of process *contingent* in the same way? Here is a tricky problem indeed. The first view holds that the content of revelation is in no way contingent; only the process whereby it functions *qua* revelation (viz., assent) is contingent. On the second view it is precisely the contingency of the subject which shapes the content ("subject matter") of revelation, as also the process of revelation.

What is at stake here? Two things: an understanding of the church and an understanding of theology. If the content of revelation is entirely noncontingent, the church (or scripture, or whatever) as its bearer is co-ordinately non-contingent; the church is a quasi-eternal ship sailing the historical waters of contingency, casting lines hither and yon, now and then getting a strike of assent. Theology for its part presides over the fixed supply of tackle and bait. If on the other hand the content of revelation is *absolutely* contingent, there can be no continuous instrument of the Kingdom in history: what would it have to say? Theology for its part could ruminate on contingency *überhaupt,* develop a handbook on angling, and tie its own flies. If *de rigeur* it is held that the content of revelation is absolutely contingent *and* that the church is the continuous instrument of the Kingdom in history, then God can only be a *deus ex machina,* i.e., called in to solve the contradiction. What we are to conclude from this is that the church which invokes faith and the faith that is called for (or the content of revelation

79

handed around and on and the process whereby that content illumines present existence), while both contingent, cannot be contingent in the same way. That is, they cannot be contingent in the same way without giving up absolutely the continuity of revelation, or without establishing such a continuity upon a ground absolutely to be counted upon. Another way of putting the same matter is that the contingency of the *mediacy* of revelation cannot be identified in kind with the contingency of the *immediacy* of revelation. As for theology, its special problem is the contingency of mediate revelation: which however would not be *mediate* if it were absolutely contingent. These statements obviously will bear further elucidation subsequently.

If to this point the second view has drawn considerable fire, that is scarcely to suggest that the first view is less vulnerable. It is in fact caught in a veritable *enfilade*. Excepting all fundamentalistic Protestant and some (how much?) Roman Catholic theology, contemporary theology is convinced in the main that, whatever else it may mean, the *process* of revelation cannot refer to some special way of communicating a body of truth already won and therefore already shaped; and, as the terminus of process, to *assent* to such a body. No proposition would gain wider acceptance than the following one: "the *content* of revelation is not a body of propositions to be accepted as the condition of faith."

Is there nothing to pause over that what revelation is *not* can be stated propositionally, while what it *is* cannot? If there is such a positive hold upon revelation as to permit the statement of what is *not* revelation (and without that "hold" should the negation be credited?), what prevents the "hold" from issuing in propositions concerning what revelation *is?* Does not everything turn on the transit from "positive hold" to proposition? If that transit were gotten in view, however, could we allow it to propositions of negation but not to propositions of affirmation? These questions are hardly broached as a start on rehabilitating "revealed truths." That notion is sick past resuscitation, primarily because of what "revealed" and "truth" mean in it. But if truth is not first and foremost a matter of propositions and their agreement, if propositions are rather an invocation to truth—a beacon to guide the hermeneutical retracing of the transit back to the "hold" which gave rise to them—the affirmative proposition has as much to say for itself as (indeed more than) the negative proposition. Thereby, to be sure, a nice piece of work is cut out: the elaboration of the "transitory spiral" from positive hold to proposition and back again.

On the first view, to come back to that, confessional formulae and scripture (propositions) are the material cause of revelation and assent is the efficient cause of revelation. While there is no going back to such a view, there is no denying that it had purchase of several extraordinary advantages when it carried conviction. For one thing, there could be no doubt of the framework in which theology has its "given." The given, in the form through which theology had to reckon with it, was steadily there in the body of transmitted propositions. For another thing, as one can see in the art of those periods in the West when this view has prevailed, revelation could function as some sort of a material cause in culture even when there was no absolutely uniform cultural assent. Culture could display some formal relation to the material content of revelation without being grounded in revelation as such (i.e., revelation as the unity of content and process). That was made possible by a community of discourse in which the language of revelation's content and the language of cultural intercourse could co-exist peacefully. When that peaceful co-existence broke out into conflict, the content of revelation could survive only as a linguistic heteronomy. And that is to point to the Achilles heel in this view of the content of revelation, viz., to its *fixity*. Such fixity presupposes a host of cognate theological presuppositions; and that this view has come on hard times means that just those presuppositions have come under re-alignment and alteration. The view can only presuppose that historical reality marches a straight course, or at least that the vagaries of historical reality have to be adjusted to eternal light. More radically questionable, it assumes that God's relation to the world is an unaltering one and that historical time, apart from a single original divagation (viz., in Jesus Christ and in him to disclose eternity), in no way qualifies the divine profferment of grace. The fixity of the content of revelation would then have no greater validity than these cognate concepts.

81

If the first view of revelation's content is thereby dissolved, that is not to point us to an account of revelation exhaustively and without remainder on the basis of revelation's process. That is so because "process," whether with respect to being or knowledge, is always connected with something irreducible to process. What the process of revelation is connected with is, in a sense that has to be brought into view, *given*. What is so given is not alone the distillate of preceding theological reflection, the residue of the past in the form of systematic axioms. Such axioms may indeed serve to order reflection upon what is given as the content of revelation by another route. Or they may not: that is the terrible decision the thinking man of faith must make afresh in each generation. He must discriminate among such axioms according to the normative and the merely traditional-historical; and that task is hardly made easier by the fact that the content of revelation (under its aspect of mediacy) reaches us by an historical route.

In Chapter I the analysis of theology as a project of translation disclosed an underside of threefold problematic. Our analysis of the word "revelation" yields a not dissimilar result. The double resonance of the word "revelation," verbal and substantive, was traced into two kinds of theology. Where primordiality is accorded to process in the one and to content in the other, a conflict breaks out that threatens to dirempt revelation of its integrity. (Thus those who take up the cudgels for revelation as content are charged with "objectivism," while those who enter the lists for revelation as process are tarred with "subjectivism.") The sheer longevity of this conflict offers as little reason for perpetuating as for celebrating it.[11] The conflict, as just now pressed, directs us to the proper horizon of the problem, even though the conflict in itself leads into a dead-end street.

In what follows immediately we shall not hold out of mind

[11] Barth treats of this conflict Christologically. ". . . The event of the incarnation of the Word, of the *unio hypostatica,* has to be understood as a *completed* event, but also as a completed *event.*" As a *completed* event Christology has a static-ontological reference. But as a completed *event,* Christology has a dynamic-noetic reference. Barth further notes that the Lutheran and Reformed traditions have made these emphases, respectively, without however unifying them. *Op. cit.,* Vol. I/2, pp. 165ff.

those issues which dramatize the question of process and content in revelation. We will essay, however, a more basic discrimination, that between revelation as fundament of theology (and, of course, as fundament of the meaning of our own being) and revelation as a theological category. Withal we attempt, formally, to establish ourselves in the "aura" of the meaning that is sought.

III. REVELATION AS FUNDAMENT
AND AS CATEGORY OF THEOLOGY

A. Revelation as Fundament

In order to see how "revelation as fundament" sublates the previously noted nuances of the word "revelation," while setting them in a more primordial frame, it will be necessary to bring up the klieg lights on the phrase "revelation as fundament." Revelation refers, we shall maintain, now to the intentional fundament of faith, now to the category under which that fundament is considered theologically. The first of these references needs first and most attention.

The intentional fundament of faith (what brings faith into being and nourishes it) is often enough honored in contemporary theology, however honorifically from the standpoint of reflexion. There is talk of the "that" of faith, the "event" in and through which faith attains its incipient reality, the *terminus a quo* which scarcely makes any claims for an *ad quem*. There is also talk of the "moment of revelation," a moment that is qualitatively different from succeeding patterns of interpretation. In that moment wholistic powers of percipience are said to be vastly intensified as fragmentary and ambiguous meanings are subjected to the litmus of ". . . a summons to be acted upon and acted out." While this summons ". . . takes on an intentional life and power of its own . . ." within the moment, it neither founds nor induces activity when the moment is over.[12]

---

[12] Cf. Hartt, *Being Known and Being Revealed* (1957 Tully Cleon Lectures), (Stockton, California: Pacific Philosophy Institute, 1957), pp. 50-57, *passim*. "One decides to become a Christian in the sense of

Fundamental revelation is consequently restricted to "the moment of revelation."

Talk that ends at these points is talk that will not allow revelation as fundament to be interrogated; and what cannot be interrogated cannot be understood. The question of revelation as fundament is at bottom the question of the radicalization of the foundation of faith. Where the question of faith's foundation is radicalized, whether under the category of revelation or some other, the question of revelation as fundament is present and voting. That the question of faith's foundation has been radicalized is a fact spread in profusion across the contemporary landscape. If this fact is not to take its revenge upon what remains of faith's superstructure, ways must be found into the problem of revelation as fundament.

Toward this end, I shall proceed with some propositions concerning revelation as fundament. No one will be fooled by the indicative form of these propositions; the questions caged in them will shriek out in their own voice. Perhaps it is well, however, to leave little to chance; and so at the end, the major questions lurking in the interstices of indicative statement will be brought into view, and that in such a way as to advance and specify the threefold problematic of Chapter I in pertinence to the basic problem under inquiry.

In advance of propositioning our subject, it may be profitable to linger over the word "fundament." Perhaps, in the word "fundament," the sensitive ear will register overtones of Husserl's *Fundierung*. Certainly the *problem* Husserl had in mind when he used the word *Fundierung* is here in view when the words "founding" and "constituting" are used. As richly prosecuted in phenomenological literature, that problem is too complex to enter upon here.[13] The barest indication must suffice. From no standpoint taken in recognizable experience can the constitutive function refer to a radically (i.e., *de novo*) productive or creational activity on the part of an ego secured against interference. Ego, other egos, and the world: all are already

identifying oneself with the christian community as a repository of interpretative schematisms, in a way fundamentally different from the way in which he grasps in 'Christ' the meaning of his existence" (p. 51).

[13] See my "Heidegger's *Being and Time* and Phenomenology," *Encounter*, XXVI, No. 3 (Summer, 1965), pp. 309-329, esp. pp. 312ff.

there, and are already there in commerce. Yet the constitutive function comes into play in just these discriminations, and indeed wherever meaning lays a claim upon consciousness. For nothing is just "there" in its *meaning.* Conceptual meaning is reflexively retrieved as we understand how phenomena are built up for our own situated consciousness. (*Sinn,* Husserl was fond of saying, is the function of *Sinngenesis.*) Constitutive consciousness is therefore consciousness that understands by way of participating the founding of its own multi-dimensional noemata.[14]

(1) Fundament: triadic constitutive process. Revelation as fundament refers first and foremost to that constitutive process whereby the *what* or substantive bearing of revelation is built up as the intentionality of human being in historical time. *This constitutive process comprises an inseparably triadic movement; fundament refers to the already founded, to founding afresh, and to the yet to be founded.* Revelation as fundament therefore founds human being on and in the co-inherence of the modes of historical time.

From the characterization of fundamental process as triadic it will be seen that the process cannot be understood to coincide with an "object," if object be taken in its predicative or naturalistic sense. In the natural or post-predicative attitude an object coincides only with "the already founded"; it is, so to speak, ascribed as a mature monad with its own driver's license. If the exhaustive coincidence of fundament with the already founded (and thus with an "object") is forestalled, that owes to reflexion which seeks to become equal to reflection; i.e., equal to the lived world as reflected in pre-predicative circumspection. Such lived experienced is marked by a triadically spiraling process. In illustration of this point we need not have recourse to abstruse examples. Let us take note of two.

[14] The noema is the intention or referent of the noetic act. Noema is not a simple surrogate for "object," if object is understood in an ordinary or naturalistic sense. A particular tree, for example, is taken by the mind under various noemata, as the referent of various noetic acts (perception, conception, imagination). It is of course one of the oldest of philosophical problems, how the noemata, with respect to a singular object, have both identical and varying aspects when intended by different noetic acts.

Phenomenologists characteristically turn to lived *perception:* how do perceived things have meaning? The tree I perceive through yon window, surely enough, is already there and could not be perceived without being already founded in the world. But does that foundedness alone ground my singular perception and account for its backworld of complexity? My body is the organon of perception; it too is "already founded" in the world. But neither or both of these "foundeds" (the tree, my body) exhaustively constitutes the noemata, the noetic reference which shapes the meaning of the backyard Hackberry for me. For one thing, these noemata are (in part) in process of afounding, of being constituted. That I inhabit a world means, among other things, that my corporeity is founded on intercorporeity and interspirituality. The meaning of this tree is something afounding before my eyes; its meaning is something building up as it is inserted in perceptions by my family, as my wife spreads a picnic beneath it and as my sons climb it. For another thing, the noemata of full perception are charged with proleptivity. Already the tree is taken under the future: the plans for a treehouse with a secret trap-door and a rope ladder. Now comes the news that our family friend must be uprooted to allow passage of a water main, forcing the question of the meaning of the whole phenomenon upon us acutely. The "to be founded" is bent back upon the "founded."[15]

[15] The example above is restricted to perceptional noesis. The "same" tree is of course subject to conceptual and imaginative noeses. The meaning of the tree "in the round" would require us to consider the constitution of the noemata intended by all these noetic acts. (See note 14 above.)

On the movement of the process of founding, cf. Merleau-Ponty: ". . . The forces of the constitutive field do not move in one direction only; they turn back upon themselves . . . the spring of constitution can no more be found in its beginning than in its terminus. . . . Since constitution is neither just the development of a future which is implied in its beginning, nor just the effect which an external ordering has in us, it escapes the alternative of continuous or discontinuous. It is discontinuous, since each layer is made from forgetting the preceding one. It is continuous from one end to the other because this forgetting is not simply absence (as if the beginning had not existed) but a forgetting what the beginning literally was to the profit of what it has subsequently become . . . From its position, each layer takes up the preceding ones again and encroaches upon those that follow; each is prior and posterior to the others, and thus to itself." *Signs,* pp. 173-176.

The triadic constitutive process may also be seen at work in a linguistic frame. In expressing an apprehension I can, initially, only resort to words at hand; and that means to words whose meaning is already founded. These words enable me to reconnoiter what is heaving into view; their use is a first tactical move in "a raid on the inarticulate" (T. S. Eliot). But the founded meaning of these words, which is what makes them initially useful, becomes burdensome on the march. If I sight the apprehension through them alone, I express not the novel apprehension but the meanings already founded and therefore sedimented in them. They must then be slowly jettisoned just as they concatenate other words, words which invest *this* apprehension with expressibility in my own and the public domain. Every expressive sentence is a movement from "founded" to "founding" linguisticality. And not only that. Since it never coincides strictly isomorphically with reality, language strains against its own logic to bring the noematic overplus of apprehension within its acoustical range. When "founding" language unfounds founded words, there yet remains the "to be founded" which presses linguistic logistics into another circumambient foray.

From these elaborations of the triadic constitutive process it will be clear, *mutatis mutandis,* that theology's dator noemata (and thus its *given*) may not be restricted to the "already founded." Theology is thereby deprived of an all but congenital proclivity, viz., to be pathologically preoccupied with an archaeology of its own primitive foundation. The same is to be said, however, of the other two phases of the triadic movement, whether of present or proleptic founding. Revelation as fundament refers to that triadic movement in which no phase can gain exclusive ascendancy without arresting the movement as such. In classical theological terms, this movement is the intention of the interlacing of the doctrines of creation, redemption, and eschatology.

In sum to this point, revelation as fundament is that from which, against which, and toward which theology thinks. That

This theme, developed in a different literary mode, is to be found running through William Faulkner's novels. It is directly stated in *Intruder in the Dust*: ". . . Yesterday won't be over until tomorrow, and tomorrow began ten thousand years ago." (New York: Random House, 1948), p. 125.

on which hermeneutic is trained, it is the thing to be thought or interpreted. Yet it is not a "thing," not even a datum, if by datum is meant a self-standing quantity that is altogether externally related to its field of presence. What is founded in fundament suggests the given, and therefore "datum." But datum only partially expresses fundament, since revelation qua fundament exceeds the founded. The founding or giving (*dare*) of revelation is also active and present; it is the "giving" which establishes theology's direction now, and which puts all deviations from that directionality into question. Thus *datum* yields to, or latches onto, *dandum*.[16] This giving carries with it, however, a future that is not yet ours; a future into which we are called and out of which we are summoned to live. So it will be seen how theology thinks from, against, and toward its fundaments. If theology were only "data processing," it would be at best a luxury of intellectual excess, not a necessity for the realization of full-orbed revelation.[17]

(2) Fundament: multi-dimensional noemata and the interlacing of regions. *Revelation as fundament refers to plural and multi-dimensional noemata. These noemata are the mode under which particular interlacings of regions are presented in and to human selfhood as man's authentic place to dwell.*

In these propositions, two things obviously call for elaboration. The first is "plural and multi-dimensional noemata," and the second (which extends the first) is "particular interlacings of regions."

(a) We have already said that revelation as fundament does

---

[16] The analogy of human giving is weak. What sort of gift could a friend give that could, together with our response to it, confer or clarify the meaning of our existence? Yet there is some analogy, itself as rare as the genuine giving and receiving of gifts between friends. Admen speak of the "gift that keeps on giving"; and it is indeed such a gift that it is blessed both to give and to receive. Such a gift refuses to stay on the mantel, and intercepts every stylized response. Selected on the basis of intimate acquaintance with the one to whom given, the gift interdicts his forgetfulness of the giver. Whether by beauty, utility, or humor, it qualifies every situation in which it is perceived. Having the first mark of being, the power to present itself, the genuine gift is not by accident also called a "present."

[17] See below, Appendix IV: All the ancient Mediterranean and Near Eastern religions trafficked in revelation, but only the Judeo-Christian heritage construed theology to be essential to full-orbed revelation.

not afford an entitative foundation among others on the single base of which a theological edifice is to be built. Still less does it disclose an additional reality that now has to be integrated with other real things, like a wart noted on one's body for the first time. Thus in revelation as fundament there is no sudden animadversion of God's reality which is then bolted into contest with the reality of other things. This much was understood about revelation as fundament long before the category of "revelation" took such prominence as it has today, and that in one of the longest-lived traditions in western Christendom. I refer to the explication of revelatory fundament heading up in Augustine, the doctrine of "illumination." For Augustine (drawing on Plato, who construed the Good under the metaphor of the sun), revelation is the fundament of theology in the way that light is the foundation of seeing. Light establishes the range of vision and so makes it possible to see what falls within that range. One would not look into the light as one more real thing to take account of (unless he would risk blindness for his trouble).

In the history of theology the doctrine of illumination, however, has not been an unmixed blessing. The early illuminists (especially Augustine) managed to depose "an additional reality" from revelation's purview, and thus to save theology from becoming riveted to a single monolithic noema. But this deposition was worked in the later illuminist tradition at the price of construing revelation as fundament exhaustively and without remainder from the side of noesis, i.e., at the price of removing noemata from the syndrome of revelation altogether. How this came about may be sketched in broad strokes. For the illuminist, light in man proceeds from the knowing eye. From differing accounts of the presence of this light in man, differing possibilities for construing revelation as fundament emerge. In one stream of the illuminist tradition light was secured by the presence in the mind of eternal exemplars, themselves the residue of Eternal Light. Revelation was therefore in principle already founded in the mind. The residual presence of Eternal Light ultimately trivialized the things seen: one attended finally to the exemplar, not the *exemplatum* (hence *ontologism*). In other streams of the illuminist tradition, where there is no transcendent enlightenment to account for knowing light in man, either of two possibilities emerge with respect to revelatory noesis: skepticism or fideism. The history of illuminism from the side of noesis alone, whether in medieval Augustinian or in modern Kantian traditions, has been the history of three temptations: ontologism, skepticism, fideism. It was Thomas Aquinas (and to a lesser extent, Bonaventura) who laid out a program for contruing revelation as fundament at once from the side of noesis and from the side of noemata.[18] That program, but neither its conceptual apparatus nor its results, must be taken up afresh if the full problematic of revelation as fundament is to come into view. There is "light" in events and "light" in the mind. In anticipation of subsequent chapters we may say that mind is possessed of a light whose rays chip a larger aperture in events: sometimes, as in poetry and scripture, to be met with a light more intense than itself. Such a light, in search of enlightenment, is active imagination.

(b) The point has been reached at which the consideration of "plural and multi-dimensional noemata" becomes blended with the elaboration of the phrase "particular interlacing of regions." The conjunction of mind and event in mutual illumination, just now referred to, is an example of the interlacing of regions. "Mind" and "event" are, to be sure, very broad regions indeed. Not only that: mind for example is only one region of personhood, as event is the concentration of a host of subsidiary regions. To understand the particular interlacings of regions which afford theology its noemata, it will be necessary therefore to enter subsequently upon a formal account of the regions of personhood and those of historical event (Ch. IV).

When we speak of an interlacing of regions apart from a particular reticulation, nothing is said that pertains to theology alone. The regions inhabited by historical humanity are legion in number and elastic in boundary. Their identification and constitution, not to mention their interspersement, are among the hoariest of philosophical problems. Classical metaphysics was out to find the minimal number of regions (e.g., existence, essence, substance, form) and the point of their maximal interspersement, in order to locate the habitat of any being whatsoever. Classical philosophical theology could then take this

[18] See below, Appendix I, "Imagination and Conformation."

minimal number of regions and their maximal interspersement and, by various analogical maneuvers, read them as cartographical characterizations of a unitary region, that of Being-itself or God.

Proceeding according to its own *métier* Christian theology does not reckon with regions and their reticulation in this way, although it has profited from and even participated in this way. Theology orients itself to particular conjunctions of regions, to conjunctions made and dyed in historical time. From these particular conjunctions, theology thinks toward regions not so immediately conjoined or reticulated but which nonetheless are ingredient in human existence and meaning. To take the obvious example: theology thinks that language which reflects the events of Jesus' career as apostolically participated. From these interlacings of regions, the Apologists could extrapolate Incarnate Logos in a movement of thought toward discarnate logos.

It would however belie the triadically constitutive character of revelation's fundamental noemata if they were restricted without remainder to some interlacing of regions in the past, and so constricted to an interlacing already founded for all time. This point was covered, in high abstraction, in the discussion of "horizon-fusion" in Chapter II. Nothing counts as fundament which does not intercalate present selfhood and its destiny in the horizon of regional interspersement. The particularity of "particular interlacing" is in part the particularity of my own selfhood and its historical regionality. So much is put in evidence by the very language I use to bring the fundamental noemata under recognition. To every particular conjunction of regions I bring an understanding of regions that is manifest in the first slip of the lip. My initial "fix" is managed through collective representations housed in speech at hand (representations of "God," "man," "thing," etc.). While these representations make communication possible at an abstract level, they suffer from lack of check and warrant by primordial dator noemata, from the particular interlacing of regions in which reference is constituted. That is, these representations do not re-present. (Thus revelation as the fundament of human being is also the refunding of language.) In this restricted sense, the interrogation of pre-understanding in theology is like that in so-

91

called regional ontology. Regional ontology, prosecuted with language as the fund of collective representations in view, is the attempt to wrest presentations of essence (of whatever region) from the ontic as primordially constituted.

Concerning theology's fundamental noemata we have said so far that (i) they are built up in a triadically constitutive process, (ii) they are plural and multidimensional, (iii) they are concatenated by an historically particular interlacing of regions, and (iv) they are intercepted and encroached upon by language. If theology cares to attain a formal understanding of these matters in depth, it can only engage for its own account in regional ontology and in a phenomenology of linguisticality. With that, however, substantive Christian theology (what in Chapter VI will be called "systematic symbolics") will scarcely have begun; only a formal, circumscriptive, reflexive awareness will have been attained. Revelatory dator noemata of theology are not terminal (except as *a quo*) and conclusive but rather are, for the appropriate noeses of reflective-historical consciousness, inceptive and provocative; they incite the Word to speech. Theological noemata possess immanently a transcendent thrust: they are continua to be extended by and in the human self, by and in the mind's act, by and in the will's political involvement. "Mind's act" refers to no discarnate cerebration but rather finally to incarnate celebration of the Word tented in the world just by that act.[19] If substantive theology has as its major goal

[19] A case in point is the sacramental act, say the sacrament of the Lord's Supper. All liturgy intends the concrete instancing of transcendence. That is the meaning of talk about "the real presence of Christ" in the Eucharist: the noemata take a name and a habitation in my flesh. And this incarnation of transcendence is something which by no means reaches its *terminus ad quem* in the back eddies of my own liturgical experience. Fritz Buri has scored the point well: "This enactment within represents only a threshold of their [the sacraments'] redeeming activity; for from the inner experience they demand to become operative again in the outwardly visible existence, in the behavior of the individual and the formation of the community. Only in this formative power for human life and corporate life do they find their fulfilment—so far as one can speak of fulfilment in history as such. The means of salvation are by nature not content with a mythological incarnation in symbolic speech and action, but wish—from the perspective of the self-understanding occasioned by them and by means of the self-actualization of existence produced by them—to transform the individual and corporate life of man in accord with their meaning."

the development of transcendence nestled and restless in its fundamental noemata, that is not to say that it strikes out for atemporal perfection. The "perfection" theology sets upon is that inceptively present in what is noematically presented, and which requires extending in the only frame of reality man knows, viz., historical *time:* the "perfection" of transcendence is an historical perfection. The fundamental noemata, tested again and again against their primordial bonds, have to be followed (in Merleau-Ponty's phrase) "into their final prolongations."[20] "Final" here means temporal finality, the perfection appropriate to the unity of the modes of historical time.

(3) Fundament: logical prius and the modes of noetic schematization. The analysis of revelation as fundament so far has touched the question of *noesis* or cognition only obliquely. Points of contact may be noted briefly. For one thing, revelation as fundament is intentional: when faith comes to consciousness and so into language, something is "in mind." There is consciousness of something and speech about something; and theology purports to hold consciousness and speech to the forms which this something requires. For a second thing, fundamental noemata are plural and multi-dimensional and so require noeses that are plurisignative. That means, for a third thing, that theology cannot be reduced to a single modality of noesis since it encounters no singular noema. From these oblique connections we may turn to the heart of the matter.

In the mode of knowledge peculiarly appropriate to it, viz., faith, revelation as fundament is circumspective, nonreflexive, pre-theoretical, and pre-thetic. Faith's unique noesis is therefore pre-theological, pre-homiletical, and pre-ethical.

In ramification of this claim several points require notice.

(a) Negatively, the propositions above mean that revelation as fundament is irreducible to a categorial schematism or to a scale of noeses within theological aspiration. The irrefragable dator force of revelation as fundament consists in its power to refund and reconfigure categorial schematization.

(b) While faith's knowing is a circumspective participation

Theology of Existence, trans. Harold H. Oliver and Gerhard Onder, (Greenwood, S.C.: Attic Press, 1965), p. 99.
[20] Cf. Merleau-Ponty, *Signs,* p. 175.

93

of the triadic genesis of authentic human being, faith never attains a concretely perduring unity of mind with constitutive genesis. Authentic constitutive genesis is listened in upon and consciously participated only for the shortest segments (e.g., the high moments of love between two persons). Faith turns to theology, in part, in order to transpose a fleeting coincidence with authenticity into a more perdurable noetic mode, from which it may hope to win its way to fresh presentiment.

(c) As already noted, theology does not plant its scale of noetic schematizations in the theologian's own circumspections (save as horizon-fusion makes that unavoidable). That scale anchors wherever the first-order language of authentic human genesis is spoken, but above all in scripture.

(d) "Why a theological schematization of revelation as fundament at all?" The answer to this question is that nothing can be got into our heads and on our tongues, and thus in the venue of publicity, without schematization (Kant). For revelation as fundament to come under schematization is for it to be granted a change of venue; in theology as in the courts a change in venue is granted in order to gain a public hearing on what transpired in the event (the pre-schematical noesis). Everyone knows absolute justice could be meted out only in the venue in which the event occurred, participated by witnesses totally unclouded by prejudice. But, alas, the venue of faith's circumspections has no county seat (save in wholly non-discursive noesis).

(e) While the hermeneutical spiral moves from circumspective presentiment through interpretive schematization to circumspective presentiment afresh, there is a danger in the counsel: back to the primordial. Our time is marked, like every time that does not know how to go forward, by an enormous passion for going *back:* to the archaic, the nocturnal, the oneirotic, the primordial, the infantile, the instinctual, to the very birthplace of apprehension and language. (Think of Cassirer, Husserl, Heidegger, Nietzsche, Gaugin, Lévy-Bruhl, Durkheim, Rousseau, Thoreau, Freud, Jung—yes, even Neo-Reformation theologians!)

In emphasizing the circumspective noesis that goes with revelation as fundament, we have to get it absolutely straight that

94

there is a certain kind of "going back" which cannot be under-taken without all sorts of silly self-deception. There is simply no recovery of an absolutely pre-critical attitude toward hi-erophany, or anthrophany either for that matter.[21] The problem of fundament and starting place in theology is entirely miscon-ceived if it be assumed that we have to leap backwards over some barrier in order to set out.[22] If the proposition above is correct, that revelation as fundament is circumspectively appre-hended, theology *is* marked in its logical origins by a certain naïveté. But this *theological* naïveté is "second" or post-critical naïveté; it registers in the "aura" of the meanings to be ex-plicated, moving in a firmament of images in order to surprise their meaning for post-critical man. The firmament of images is the primal noncategorial schematization of revelation as fundament. This "firmament" is, however, a galaxy in motion and in process of formation and decay. That process and its implications for the task of systematic symbolics can be laid aside for subsequent inquiry. The point to emphasize now is that, just in the face of revelation's fundamental circumspective-ness, theology registers a second immediacy and proliferates that immediacy in a plurality of schematical modes. Its hermeneutic of images aims to be, as Paul Ricoeur has said, "the postcritical equivalent of the precritical hierophany."[23]

(4) Fundament: temporal prius. *Revelation as fundament refers not only to a logical but also and especially to a temporal prius.* (One thinks of those churches in Rome—say, San Clemente—whose foundations settle in the debris of centuries, bottoming in Mithraic temples whose own foundations blend

[21] This point is brilliantly developed along essentially compatible lines but out of quite different philosophical, theological, and literary tradi-tions by Paul Ricoeur and Owen Barfield. Cf. Paul Ricoeur, "The Hermeneutics of Symbols and Philosophical Reflection," *International Philosophical Quarterly*, Vol. II, No. 2 (May, 1962), pp. 191–218. This article appeared originally in *Il problema di demittazione* (Archivio di Filosophia di Roma), (Padova, 1961); extracts from it appeared as "Le symbole donne à penser," *Esprit,* Nouvelle Serie, Nos. 7–8, (Juillet-Août, 1959), pp. 60–76; translated as "The Symbol: Food for Thought," *Philosophy Today,* Vol. IV, No. 3/4 (Fall, 1960), pp. 196–207. Cf. also Owen Barfield, *Saving the Appearances: A Study in Idolatry,* (London: Faber and Faber, 1957), esp. Chapters IV, VI, and XX.

[22] This theme is taken up again in Chapter VI below.

[23] Ricoeur, *art. cit.,* pp. 202–203.

imperceptibly with bedrock and whose baptistries are underground streams.)

The triadic constitutive process itself signals the necessary and proper temporal dimensions of revelation as fundament. Revelation as fundament is past *illic et tunc,* present *hic et nunc,* and future *illic et tunc.* As the fundament of the church's confession of faith, revelation came to expression in times and places long and far removed from my here and now. The circulation of that confession through the continuum of centuries and over a variegated terrain has always and everywhere been thought, within the mainstream of Christian life and reflexion, to be essential to the emergence of faith here and now. When revelation as fundament is viewed without recourse to a standpoint outside itself, the single intentionality of faith is exercised by the spiraling of a triple maieutic: (a) the potentially cognitive residue of a past time and another place, handed on and around by the church's confession, is actualized for me (b) only in this time and place; yet simultaneously that mere potentiality is worked up into genuine compossibility by the quality of my being now in this place (c) as I stand under and into the future.

This triple maieutic is held in mind when it is said that revelation as fundament is *historical.* Revelation as fundament is historical not only because it has an inexpugnably *eventful* character (interlacing of regions) but also because any present revelatory event occurs by and is interpreted through the residue of past revelatory events, those which lie at the foundation of the church's confession. Moreover, without the present event under the sign of the future (as opened to receive it), the residue of the past functions as fate; functions, that is, not as the *traditio* and *traditum* of revelatory fundament, but rather as an excrescence of the church's traditionalism.

(5) Fundament and theology's recommencement. It follows from what has been said and implied to this point that, with revelation as its fundament, theology does not start anything independently as it does not stay with anything stationary. When the sirens chant otherwise, theology like Ulysses ties itself to the mast and puts wax in the sailors' ears. What theology may not do and hold its fundamental intentionality in view is to say

96

with Gertrude Stein, "There is no there there." *Theology does not so much begin as continue; not so much endure as recommence.*[24] With revelation as its fundament, theology is free for reflexion only because and if it has access to reflect-ion, to a precomprehension already resident in language, ". . . a latent reason to transform into a patent reason."[25]

The point may be put another way. *To say that theology continues, with revelation as its fundament, is to say that it never stops beginning because it never really begins to end.* The beginning in theology can never be anything other than the reflex of its end; an authentic start on truth is the reflex of final truth. The "final truth" with which theology has to do, however, vests in the co-inherence of the modes of historical time; and so an authentic start on this truth entails a spiraling of the modes of time. Indeed, to say that theology never stops beginning because it never begins to end is just to say that it coincides with the hermeneutical spiral through which revelation as fundament registers in meaning.

B. Revelation as Category

We have now to speak of revelation as a theological category. So far we have tried to get at the intention of revelation (i.e., to revelation as fundament) formally by resorting to "helping" categories. These categories have been largely of a philosophical sort (noema, noesis, interlacing of regions, etc.). They are heuristic ("helping") categories in the sense that the word

[24] Cf. Ricoeur on the hermeneutic of symbols: ". . . A meditation on symbols starts from the fullness of language and of meaning already there; it begins from within language which has already taken place and in which everything has already been said; it wants to be thought, not presuppositionless, but in and with all its presuppositions. Its first problem is not how to get started, but, from the midst of speech, to recollect itself. . . . It is therefore no yearning for a sunken Atlantis that urges us on, but the hope of a re-creation of language. . . . First the giving, then the positing . . . all has already been said in enigma and yet . . . it is necessary ever to begin and re-begin everything in the dimension of thought." *Ibid.,* pp. 192–193.

[25] Pierre Thévenaz, *What is Phenomenology?,* ed. James M. Edie, (Chicago: Quadrangle Books, 1962), p. 109. In reaching the formulations above I have been greatly aided by this book.

97

"revelation" gives way and gives rise to them as we give ourselves *formally* to the intent of the category of revelation. The intent of the category of revelation in its formal aspect can come to speech, into expressibility, only in this way.

Let us be clear on what is meant by the intention of revelation in its formal aspect. I do *not* mean that there is a universal act of mind, revelation, which is to be deduced transcendentally in a Kantian manner so as to gain access to its formality of operation. From the beginning, especially in the account of the hermeneutical spiral and also in the insistence that the *theological* problematic of revelation is sighted from an immanent coign of vantage, a radical separation of the formal and material dimensions of revelation has been disallowed.[26] Both pure formality and pure materiality are unknown to Christian theology. There is, for example, no purely formal way of stating the content of revelation as fundament.[27] What is fundamental is what is revealed; revelation as the *concrete* fundament of my being is material. Sheer material concrescence, sheer eventfulness, cannot however come directly into language. Rather, material concrescence comes into language under a plurality of cognitive modes, all of which are necessary to its being understood. If we are to grasp the way in which this concrescence is taken into a scale of cognitive modes, there is no choice but to attend to revelation in its formal aspect. Nor are we to suppose that this is exclusively a philosophical project, avoidable by material or substantive theology. Theology schematizes revelatory concrescence whenever it uses such "material" categories as grace, creation, and salvation. The study of revelation in its formal aspect is the study of revelation as fundament taken under formal schematization (whether of an imaginative, perceptual, or conceptual sort).

Revelation as a total phenomenon is complex: that much so far is clear. If this total phenomenon is embraced by a single category or name, "revelation," that is so because the mind can

26 When such a separation is allowed, one has a different sort of problematic (e.g., philosophical, sociological, psychological, etc.)

27 This is the answer to the reader who has been wondering what the foregoing analysis of revelation as fundament has to do with Jesus Christ, salvation, the Church, and other "material principles" of revelation.

only take phenomena however complex under singular significations. In addition to what has been said already about linguistic expansion at the intersection of personal histories, language grows, a singular word expands in signification, by hewing to the complexity of the phenomenon. A category grows beyond its fixity of signification by having bent back into itself the significatory increment of those additional categories spawned by it as its own intention comes more clearly into view. This increment of signification is hermeneutical "translation" of the central category. Were this category perfectly adequated to its intent, it would need no translation precisely because it would already be perfect translation.[28] If the category cannot introduce us to its own intent and thus spark additional categories, or if it cannot receive back into itself an increment of signification, it ossifies and falls into "dead language."[29] Of that, enough has been said under the hermeneutical spiral in Chapter II.

There is then no choice but to use the category of revelation until we see, by its studied use, whether it is translatable. This makes for an ambiguity in the use of the word which doubtless has become apparent already, an ambiguity I have tried to reduce by referring to revelation *as fundament,* or revelation *as this or that.* Ideally every additional category, spawned by the central category of revelation, exceeds that central category and works reflexively to compound its ambiguity while expanding its significatory power. Thus "revelation" is a category or concept, yet *qua* fundament revelation is not categorial or conceptual. So too, "revelation" embraces (a) that which incites the hermeneutical spiral and also (b) this "that which" taken into human understanding, the movement of the hermeneutical spiral itself. We are of course obliged to reduce ambiguity, but only in commensuration with increased significatory power.

[28] Christian theology knows no such translation in the mode of perfection save in the Word translated as flesh (penultimately in the Israelite community, ultimately in Jesus Christ), and that is to be counted among theology's logical and temporal "primitives."

[29] Those who claim that the fundament of Christian theology can be translated only by means of the category of revelation have the burden of Christian history against them, unless they resort to hermeneutical categorial equivalents of the category of revelation. In that case they have recourse to the very translation which is denied. See Appendix IV below.

Language "means" when a balance is struck between ambiguity and signification; perhaps we can say, when ambiguous words signify. Let us repeat: if the category of revelation has become altogether sedimented in its significance or if it is rendered totally ambiguous by ostensibly incremental categories, it can only be consumed (in Augustine's phrase) in "the daily furnace . . . [of] the human tongue."[30]

C. Three Areas of Problematic with regard to Revelation

We have finally to make good on the promise to highlight those major problems which doubtless arise in connection with the propositions advanced concerning revelation as fundament. The most useful course to follow will be one which draws attention to three large areas of problematic, areas in which we have been working and which comprise the subsidiary questions expressed and implied in this chapter. It will be the task of Chapters IV, V, and VI to correlate with these three areas of problematic, respectively.

(1) A primary problem so far partially exposed is that of an ontology of revelation as fundament, an ontology of the fundamental trajectory of events in and by which human being is authentically constituted. This problem concerns itself above all with the "what" and the "there" of revelation, the intention of revelation. What revelation intends, and its being there to be intended, are questions compressed already in talk of the triadic movement of "founding" or "constituting." We see how richly and yet perplexingly complex the what of revelation is when we speak of it as an interlacing of regions that is food for thought by virtue of multidimensional noemata. Add to that the claim that the "there" of revelation's intent is qualified by a "then," indeed by full-scale temporality, and one brings certain questions in an ontology of revelation to an acute stage.

There is obviously the question of *contingency*, the perdurability and steadiness of revelation's intention. We have denied a universal revelatory noesis, at least as a foundation for bringing

[30] *Confessions*, X, 37, 60; Outler, p. 237.

the formality of revelation into view. Shall we take the next step and deny universal revelatory noemata, and if so how shall we speak of the perdurability, extension, and publicity of revelation's intentionality (have we not already spoken of *particular* interlacings of regions?)? That is, how shall we speak *ontologically* of the revelatory event? If we do not take that step, i.e., if we do affirm universal revelatory noemata, how shall we speak in any other way *but* ontologically, so that theology would wind up as philosophy after all?

There is contingency's twin, the question of *continuity*. Traditionally this question has had both a vertical and an horizontal plane. In the vertical plane, the ancient and medieval question was often one of giving the subject into the dominion of revelation's subject matter (e.g., the mystical union of the self with God); whereas the modern question is often one of giving the subject matter to the hegemony of the subject. In the horizontal plane, there is the question of the identity of the subject in his inescapable affair with the world, with situated subject matters; and the question of his "extending" revelatory noemata to embrace and so redeem these subject matters as they shape the horizon of his and his neighbors' world.

Of course, an ontology of revelatory event must not be confused with "revealed ontology." An ontology of revelation is an account of the orders involved in the revelatory event, the regions of being and becoming reticulated as the intent of a revelatory noetic act. An ontology of revelation is prosecuted in the same way as, for example, an ontology of a work of art.

(2) A second large area of problematic is that of revelation and its cognitive (noetic) scale. Equally appropriate is the designation of this problem as that of revelation and the hermeneutical scale. Within the horizon of this problem the prior question is not "Is revelation cognitive?" but rather "What cognitive form or forms does revelation assume?" So far the latter question has been pocketed in such phrases as "dator noemata and their appropriate noeses."

The heart of this problem is the scale or transit between revelation as pre-thetic circumspection and revelation construed in a conceptual frame.[31] (In analogy: We circumspect the bodily

[31] By "pre-thetic circumspection" I mean prehension in advance of

101

touch of someone we love. We also conduct experiments of a psychological and physiological sort on tactile responses. But we are able to do so only by keeping in touch with touch, while gaining conceptual distance on it.) On such a scale turns the relation between faith and theology. If faith remains entirely bound to its own circumspections, it is delivered to the furies, not to mention the duration, of honeymoon love. (It is no accident that revelatory circumspective language, in most religions, is shot through with sexual metaphor.) In that state revelation takes the form of one oracle against another, the state of one primitive religion against another, the quandary of lovers in their first honeymoon quarrel. Unless revelation households in a conceptual frame (to mention only *that* segment of the cognitive scale), even if only as a temporary tenant in a temporary housing development, there is no way to discriminate and judge between competing "revelations"—between Delphic oracles and primitive Christian numinal words, between the circumspections of Father Divine and Paul Tillich. Let it be remembered that heresy could only arise with theology. At the level of primordial circumspection there can be only *difference* between competitive visions, not heresy. Heresy is a matter of infidelity to circumspection, a failure to keep the noetic scale tethered to its own circumspective ground.

The last comment on heresy helps us correct the emphasis of the preceding paragraph and so to see the particular import of this whole area of problematic in its contemporary force. "Christianity-and-the-modern-mind theology" has indeed pressed the movement from circumspection to conception. But it is the inverse movement which constitutes the problem in its most acute form, the form which today carries the most forceful cultural impact. I refer to the difficulty of bringing revelation under circumspection through the route of theological concepts (as it were, the difficulty of moving from the top to the bottom of the scale). Theological concepts which putatively schematize revelation must be judged heretical if they block the circumspectibility of revelation as fundament. To have lumbered on this point is the striking insight of contemporary "God is

_____
theses being laid down or upon the prehended reality, the primitive grasp prior to conscious positing or predication.

102

dead" theologians (whether or not they are right that it is the concept of God which blocks circumspectibility), a point all the more underscored by cries of Heresy! directed against them. These cries proceed from a view of heresy as the contest of concepts. Thus the concept of God can be accepted by the nominal Christian (ergo Orthodoxy) and then be traced into whatever substrate of circumspective religiosity, or circumspective socio-economic self-interest, for that matter; or rejected by the honest pagan who cannot trace the concept into any circumspection that does not admit of other schematizations. In neither case does the concept serve a genuine hermeneutical function; it does not interpret a circumspection of revelation as fundament, a logical and temporal prius with its own claims. With that, however, we trench on another major area of problematic.

(3) The third principal area of problematic is that of revelation in relation to tradition and scripture. We have just spoken of concepts that lose their hermeneutical connection with revelation as fundament. Such concepts may of course simply be laid aside, in which case revelation dissolves its problematical character and becomes a matter of indifference. But if the problematic remains intact (though the concepts deliver no "message," as "messengers" they still haunt[32]) and if revelation as fundament involves a temporal prius, there is nothing to do but work hermeneutically with the very thing blocking hermeneutic, viz., the tradition which putatively embodies revelation's schematization. In its most acute form the problem is just this: the present foreshortens the past, the past tyrannizes the present, and the net result is that the future is blind. The present has no machinery but what the past has washed ashore; we can turn to the past materially only with its own residue. The present, however, is not the past; the residue is the background of our present being, but we stamp it with our present grasp of reality.

To break out of this paralytic situation, we are called upon to reform the *theological* equivalent of an act of historical re-

[32] Among the ancient meanings of *hermeneia* was the message delivered by the divine herald or messenger. A splendid history of this term and its cognates is furnished by James M. Robinson, "Hermeneutic Since Barth," *The New Hermeneutic,* ed. James M. Robinson and John B. Cobb, Jr., (New York: Harper & Row, 1964), pp. 7–77, esp, pp. 1–19.

covery, or in a botanical analogy, to retrace decaying substance into its life source and thence out again to fruit ripe for the plucking. The botanical analogy is faulted by the suggestion of an automatic process, so let us stay with the analogy of historical recovery. Traditional theological concepts are like the historian's artifacts. From potsherds, pieces of agricultural implements, bits of weapons of war, fragments of documents, from civilization ravaged in tatters, the historian has imaginatively to enter households, battles, and salons of culture: to envisage what was whole and vital from what is partial and mordant. He sets out from artifacts (and to be sure, takes note of what previous historians have gleaned from them), but he brings his imaginative circumspections to speech in a way that evades them, i.e., he takes them through a new revolution of the hermeneutical spiral. What artifacts provoke, the historian evokes.

I have said tradition *and scripture.* Scripture is itself tradition, but a decisive piece of tradition. It is decisive for a number of reasons. (i) Like all tradition, it refers to revelation as temporal prius. (ii) But scripture above all refers to particular interlacings of regions, i.e., particular events, which are held to be paradigmatic of authentic human being. (iii) This decisive piece of tradition survives in language (to be sure, of various literary types) which intends to be event-inverbalizing language.[33] (iv) That means, scripture stands as the primal schematization of revelation as fundament, and therefore as the indispensable heuristic for bringing revelation under circumspection anew.[34] (v) Therefore it is with scripture that theology perpetually recommences.

Tradition and scripture are *there,* but revelation as fundament, while there in them, is not *there* in them in the way that they are there: that is the core of this area of problematic. They are there in language, but from them revelation as the fundament of my being will have to find its own tongue. Theology is

[33] We have already recognized that scripture is replete as well with other sorts of language: discursive, narrative, theological, etc.

[34] Cf. Augustine: "My heart is deeply stirred, O Lord, when in this poor life of mine the words of thy Holy Scripture strike upon it." *Confessions,* XII, I, 1; Outler, p. 270.

the legatee of language conveyed in such a way that it can become *currency* and be spent only if the will (testament) is broken. Otherwise the linguistic legacy of theology is used in support of what Nietzsche called "monumental history."[35] Theology's linguistic legacy is its venture capital, the stake off which it lives while panning for the nugget of circumspection. Such a bequest affords only a head start on time, not a retirement home.

[35] Cf. *The Use and Abuse of History* (*Vom Nutzen und Nachteil der Historie für Leben*), trans. Adrian Collins and ed. Julius Kraft, (New York: The Liberal Arts Press, 1949), pp. 20–25.

PART TWO

Unfinished Man, Imagination, and Revelation

IV. Unfinished Manhood: Toward an Ontology of Revelation

Outline

I. "Toward an Ontology of Revelation"
   A. Ontology
      1. The "Ontological Difference"
      2. The Reflexive Character of Ontological Thinking
   B. Revelation
      1. The Modest Scope of an Ontology of Revelation as Undertaken Here
      2. Summational and Proleptic Propositions Concerning Revelation, as Bearing on an Ontology of Revelation
      3. The Convergence of Themes from Ontology and Revelation
II. The Agent-Self
   A. The Self vis-à-vis Itself and the World
   B. The Will as Clue to the Ordering Power or Principle of Selfhood
   C. The Self and "Continuous Ingredience"
      1. Background
      2. Foreground
      3. Concentration
   D. The Self and "Discontinuous Ingression"
      1. The "Other"
      2. "Event"
   E. Manhood Finished and Unfinished, and the Classical Ontological Categories
      1. "Form"
      2. "Essence"
      3. "Essential Form"

F. The Self *qua* Finished and *Potentia Obedientalis*

G. The Structure of Revelation: The Historio-Personal Existential

I. "TOWARD AN ONTOLOGY OF REVELATION"

The task of this chapter may be broached by examining the subtitle, "toward an ontology of revelation." We shall pause over the constituent terms themselves with a view to making sense of their combination.

A. Ontology

Ontology is the study of Being in disclosure and realization, and all that pertains to the disclosure and realization of Being. Ontology cannot admit a perspicuous focussing of Being as such, an intuition of the plentitude of Being; for that would amount to a quashing of ontological thinking in principle—would amount, in the classical term, to *ontologism*.

(1) The matter may be put positively, with Heidegger, by saying that " the ontological difference" characterizes every datum for ontological thinking. Between Being and beings there is a root difference that accounts for the impetus to ontological thinking. Being is disclosed and realized in beings (things, persons, etc.); beings are the locus, the "there" of Being. But beings are at the same time the locus of Being's non-coincidence with itself, the dwelling of Being's concealment and evasion. One cannot start from Being without beings for that would be to start from nowhere, from no "appearance" or presentation of Being. Nor can one start from beings without Being, for it is just that beings *are* and how they are (not to mention that they are not fully null and how they are not fully null) that is the nerve of ontological wonder.[1] For these reasons, one cannot point unambiguously to a *something* as the exhaus-

[1] This circularity is discussed in my article, "Heidegger's *Being and Time* and Phenomenology," *loc. cit.,* pp. 317f.

tive referent of ontological thinking, especially since in the natural (customary) attitude toward that something the question of its Being is suppressed or repressed.

Ontological philosophy as prosecuted by recent phenomenologists has sought to score these points by reproaching the western metaphysical tradition, while at the same time seeking to bring the intention of that tradition forward. Even if one cannot accept Heidegger's charge against the metaphysical tradition, as an historical judgment, that it has confused or identified the question of Being with that of beings, one can scarcely blink the tendency of main-line metaphysics to absolutize being in a certain "locale" or "region."[2] Realistic-scholastic metaphysics ramified Being as the Absolute Transcendent, modeled on the "object" of the natural attitude, the mundane "in-itself" that is a terminal reality. Modern idealistic metaphysics construed Being as the Absolute Transcendental, modeled on the "subject" of world-constituting consciousness, the source of the "for us" of the world. With each of these metaphysical types Being comes to rest in an absolute locale, so that all kinds of beings must be seen to be flora and fauna of that region. And thought becomes bound to the logic deposited in language by metaphysical "conclusions."

(2) Ontological thinking protects itself against dialectical catalepsis, and so against an absolute *ex machina,* only insofar as it is a thoroughgoingly *reflexive* enterprise. This reflexive enterprise is identical with that of the hermeneutical spiral. In unremitting alternation, reflexive thinking comprises the centripetal and centrifugal acts of mind vis-à-vis the phenomena of man and world; it is the alternating ascesis and dilation of consciousness which aspires to think the coincidence and noncoincidence of man, world, and Being.

These remarks on the reflexive character of ontological thinking require development. They are of a piece with the discussion of the hermeneutical spiral in Chapter II, but that in itself needs to be made clear. More important, the material thought on

[2] Cf. *Was ist Metaphysik?,* 5th ed., (Frankfurt: Klostermann Verlag, 1949), p. 8. Cf. also, on St. Thomas as an exception to Heidegger's judgment, Johann B. Lotz, S.J., "Denken und Sein nach den jüngsten Veroffentlichungen von M. Heidegger," *Scholastik,* Bd. XXXIII, (1958), p. 83.

which we are embarked in this chapter will be aided by an expansion of its logic. It will be necessary to use some language from the classical tradition in prosecuting that thought; there is no serious alternative to using the language of that which we are out to overcome.[3] The intrinsic relation between language and thinking, indeed our very historicity, will see to that. Only a vigilant reflexivity will permit us to refrain from thinking *merely* what is deposited in the language at hand. Ontological thinking aspires to a "radical beginning" within its historical context which, if successful, will contribute to the refunding of language and a fresh apprehension of the modulations of being. Let us see now what is involved in reflexive thinking of this sort.

(a) In ordinary usage a reflexive movement is a refluent, ebbing movement. Thus a reflexive thought or action is one that is turned, bent, or directed back upon the thinker or agent. (In the English reflexive pronoun this sense is captured directly: "He shot himself.") Ontological thinking is originally and inescapably reflexive in this sense. The ontological question invariably recoils, boomerangs on its asker. The question of Being cannot be pressed without inserting the question of the being of the questioner, of man himself. It is not alone wonder that things are, or that they are not nothing, that excites ontological thinking, but also the fact that man numbers himself among such things and sees himself at stake in the modulation of Being.

Reflexive *ontological* thinking is by no means the same thing as ontic circumspection. Ontic circumspection concerns *my* pre-reflexive establishment in the world, the prehension of my disposition concretely in Being. Ontological thinking is the reflex in the mind of ontic circumspection, the conceptual ebbing of my lived onticity. As distinguished from my ontic intuitions, shot through with personal history as they are, ontological thinking (*qua* anthropological) thinks the modulated Being as such of man, or the Being of man as such. It does so by spiraling through lived experience, and not by linear abstraction from

[3] Cf. Ludwig Wittgenstein: "In giving explanations I already have to use language full-blown. . . ." *Philosophical Investigations*, trans. G. E. M. Anscombe (Oxford; Basil Blackwell, 1958), pp. 48e–49e, (#120).

112

experience. It aims at bifocal vision: to keep both the pre-reflexive and the reflexive self in the picture, so that the reflexive self (man himself) is the *extension* of the pre-reflexive self (I myself) and the pre-reflexive self is the *intension* of the reflexive self.

(b) The reflexive character of ontological thinking would be seriously misunderstood if it were taken to mean that, without remainder, the question of Being is bent back upon the self. Reflexivity also means that the self is turned into the horizon of its establishment, the world. With that, thinking only cuts reality at its circumspected joints: environment is a world for human beings; being human is being in a world. Ontological thinking is therefore doubly reflexive; more strictly, it is unceasingly reflexive. The reflux of the ebb-tide (i) is the flow-tide (ii). The tide in the affairs of Being has to be taken both at the ebb and at the flood.

As Hegel saw with magnificent amplitude, there is no dialectical step that can be an *absolute* beginning for ontological thinking. Such a beginning would itself constitute the Absolute; we would have to inhabit the Absolute in order to take the absolutely first step. But then there would be "no place to go," and hence no need for reflexivity. In short, Being simply would not be experienced in its modulation. Ontological thinking is already under way, if it occurs at all (i.e., if the ossifications of the customary attitude are evaded and "quick absolutes" are avoided), by virtue of submission to the revolutions of "the ontological difference." So the origin of ontological thinking can be located not in the "subject," the "object," or the Absolute, but rather only in the recoiling of the ontological difference upon itself in connection with anything which presents itself. For many, no doubt for most, ontological thinking is already under way only covertly, only in dumb surrogate, only in non-discursive awareness of their own enhancement and attrition on the shores of Being.

Under (a) we have noted the ebbing, afferent motion of ontological thinking; under (b) the flowing, efferent action of ontological thinking; and we have emphasized that, as waves both ebb and flow, reflexive ontological thinking ceaselessly alternates between afferent and efferent motions. Pursuing the

113

analogy further (and going along with the old myth), we now ask after the "moon," the question as to what tilts the earth on its axis so that ebb-tide becomes flood-tide and vice versa. In a stricter metaphoric sense, since reflexive thinking goes on in human selves, we come to the "heart"—the biblical metaphor for the *will*—where afferent action becomes efferent, efferent action afferent; in short, where "circulation" occurs.

(c) But let us back up and see how this question necessarily arises. We said that ontological thinking roots in the recoiling of "the ontological difference" upon itself, and that reflexivity in thought is just the hermeneutical equivalent of that recoiling. Unqualified, this assertion assumes (i) that the recoiling of the ontological difference is "there" positivistically as a fact, and (ii) that, confronted by this fact, the mind automatically thinks reflexively. Both assumptions are transparently erroneous.

(i) On the table before me there is an apple. But "the ontological difference" is not there in the way that the apple is there for standard perception. How the ontological difference is there is an exceptionally complex matter, and need not detain us here. (It is there in the question of the redness of the apple, for example. But it is also there, to take an even more complex example, in the apple Eve ate: in that case, in the mythological frame, not even the apple is an *ens*.) It is enough for present purposes to note that the ontological difference is not there as an entity, although occasioned by entities, and is a datum only for hermeneutical consciousness.[4]

(ii) In the customary attitude, I do not automatically think about the apple reflexively. In that attitude I am unlikely to think it seriously at all (unless desparate for an example, and it catches my eye!). Catches the eye: there is the nub. Thinking is governed by the kind of access perception gives to its object; and perception is figurated. More strictly speaking, the seat of connection between perception and thinking is imagination; and the imagination is never an empty transcendental power, but rather is stocked by the course of historical accretion and

---

[4] That is, the ontological difference is a datum only as we seek to interpret an entity within its field of being. Such an interpretation need not by any means be limited to technical ontological philosophy. It may be largely nondiscursive interpretation, as in the arts.

114

attrition.[5] So I "spontaneously" perceive the apple as a red, juicy thing, good to eat. Since my imagination has not been programmed in mythological figure, I do not spontaneously perceive it as a focal incarceration of cosmic temptation, as the Devil's Fruit. If the latter is to be a thoughtful possibility, or if the apple is to be thought otherwise than as an object of appetite, a realignment of imagination is necessary. The reality-sense has so to be jarred as to permit the perception of the object in an other than standard way.[6]

Our question was, What tilts the tides of reflexive ontological thinking? It is not the ontological difference as an object "out there," since access to the ontological difference as instantiated in or in connection with an object is itself a function of hermeneutical reflexivity. Nor is it some *a priori* sequence of mental acts that guarantees just such an access. Setting these negative conclusions with a claim made above, we will be in a position to suggest an answer to our question and at the same time offer a preliminary rationale for the ontological thinking that follows.

(d) We claimed: ontological thinking aspires to a "radical beginning" within its historical context which, if successful, will contribute to the refunding of language and a fresh apprehension of the modulations of being (p. 112 above). A radical beginning will be one, obviously, that begins with the radix, the root. The radix in all radicalism, as Pierre Thévenaz, has said, is the *will*.[7]

(i) The will is the seat of the reality-sense in man (a point we shall return to later), but in a way that engages if not fuses

[5] These claims are developed at length in the following chapter.

[6] Of course, an unsettled reality-sense is not a sure sign of impending ontogical thinking. (It may be a sign of incipient mental illness!) That an unsettled reality-sense in a healthy mind does not issue in explicit ontological thinking may be due either to a want of sophistication, the *lack* of an ontological language tradition, or to a surfeit of sophistication, the *failure* of an ontological language tradition.

[7] Cf. Thévenaz: "All philosophical radicalism implies by that very fact the will and the responsibility of man at the heart of the absolute principle that he poses and of the apodictic evidence that he is looking for. From the start it goes beyond epistemology, the level of critical judgment, and aims at fusing together the moral will and the grasping of evidence, the ethical and the metaphysical. It is the will which wills the beginning and which untiringly brings reflexion back to it." *What is Phenomenology?*, p. 96.

115

both ethics and ontology. That is "physically" real which sets a "physical" limit on my will (yon wall which I cannot walk through); but that also is real which sets a limit on my will by virtue of my valuation of it (my wife and children). Consequently, the will is invariably involved in the grasping and forming of what counts for 'evidence' (i.e., what appears or presents itself).[8]

It is necessary to will a radical beginning. But a radical beginning (let it be said again) is not an absolute beginning; it is the point at which thought already in motion is "circulated," turned toward new presentiment, and thus the point from which evidence is grasped and formed. Reflexive thinking requires willing, yet the will so to think is exercised by and upon the will itself. This requires a discrimination of modalities of the will's act. The will upon which willing to think reflexively is exercised, is the habituated will. The will—through imagination, its mental mode—establishes the range of perception and so delimits what can count as "real" evidence for thought.[9] That thought, however, could never be reflexive which is oriented to such evidence, since it could only advance in a unilinear way to the evidence and find its terminus therein. Thought is made reflexive by a jarred reality-sense, by the turn of the will upon its own domestications, and so by the turn of imagination in active upon passive mode.

(ii) The point we are making will be made clearer by bringing out a distinction on which it depends. That is the distinction between "reality" and "Being." Elemental sanity requires this distinction, for many sorts of things possess reality (e.g., nightmares) for which "Being" claims would be made not at all or only with severe qualifications. Reality invariably has will-

---

[8] This is a point of the greatest importance for both philosophy and theology. Cf. Alfred North Whitehead: "The chief danger to philosophy is narrowness in the selection of evidence." *Process and Reality*, (New York: Social Science Book Store, 1941), p. 512. Cf. also Horace Bushnell: "In one view, faith is grounded in evidence, but it also creates evidence, by the realization it makes of spiritual things. Hence it is declared to be the evidence of things not seen, the substance of things hoped for." *God in Christ*, (Hartford: Brown and Parsons, 1849), p. 301.

[9] A systematic recognition of this point is to be found in David Hume's theory of the imagination. See Appendix III below, "The Imagination and Creativity."

reference, either as a limitant on the will's power or desire to modify, or an expression of value or approbation.[10] (Dorothy Emmet reports Eddington's exclamation: "Reality! Loud Cheers!"[11] The same understanding passes through the American slang expression, "That's for real!")

The distinction between reality and Being is to be prosecuted initially where its dynamics are manifest, in the human will. If we turn to this radix of ontological thinking, we should do so in full awareness of the temptations that lie in wait, and forearm ourselves against them with a recollection of the western intellectual tradition. One of the major temptations in that tradition has been to construe Being exhaustively and without remainder from "reality." Rigorously pursued, such an extrapolation would lead to Being as the *deus ex machina* of man's reality-sense. A flirtation with this temptation has been carried on in many if not all the grand metaphysical systems; and has been estopped (where it has been estopped) by the check on an imperious reality-sense afforded by a philosophical theology that, at once, was an internal development of the system and abutted a viable religious tradition. When that check fell away, because metaphysics was reconceived and because the religious tradition lost its concrete viability in the intellectual community, the temptation secured full submission. This is nowhere more apparent than in that alliance of philosophy with historicism which yields metaphysics as ideology.[12]

The other major temptation in the western tradition has been

[10] See Bertrand Russell, *The Analysis of Mind,* (New York: The Macmillan Co., 1949), p. 186; also Julian N. Hartt, *Being Known and Being Revealed,* p. 9.

[11] Emmett, *The Nature of Metaphysical Thinking,* p. 16.

[12] "Historicism" is to be distinguished from "historicity." The central claim of the doctrine of historicity is that the very being of man is historical. Historicism is *one* possible deduction from this claim, viz., that "human being is exhaustively described as a naturally and historically situated self-making." (Emil Fackenheim, "Metaphysics, Historicity, and Historicism," *The Personalist,* Vol. 46, No. 1 [January, 1965], pp. 47–48. For a fuller discussion, see *idem, Metaphysics and Historicity,* [Milwaukee: Marquette University Press, 1961], *passim.*) In our terms we may say that for historicism no factors transcending man's historical self-making pertain to his being, and therefore that man's being in no way transcends his reality-sense.

to construe reality exhaustively and without remainder from Being. Rigorously pursued, such an extrapolation would make of the reality-sense the self-consciousness of Being, a diremption of Being, or an alienation from Being. A flirtation with this temptation has been carried on in many if not all the great Christian theological systems (especially in the doctrines of the Trinity, Creation and Fall). This siren was resisted (where it was resisted) by virtue of theology's ability to think Being *through* a prevailing reality-sense (and not only as a prescription for the reality-sense) without confusing them. Philosophy made the prevailing reality-sense conceptually available to theology, and so served as a check on theology's temptation to think from Being to reality *senkrecht von oben*. When theology could no longer think Being through the prevailing reality-sense, it could only lay its claims for Being heteronomously and legislatively upon that reality-sense. Here the temptation is fully subscribed, and reality is accommodated altogether to Being. This is nowhere more apparent than in Neo-Orthodox theology.[13]

With these remarks we approach matters more properly considered under "revelation" below. Before turning to that head, a reminder and a summary. The reminder: the phrase "toward an ontology of revelation" is before us, and for some pages past "ontology" in that phrase has been our concern.

The summary (and some anticipation): If theology thinks what it means to be human for and before man and God in the world, it cannot avoid ontological thinking. The basic problems in this thinking are *what* it thinks and *how* it thinks. Ontological thinking frees itself from a fixed subject and a fixed object. The object is no self-standing thing, is not even an object, except by courtesy of habituated perception. Its multi-faceted participation in Being is disclosed only to a thinking that swirls on conventions secured in the will. If these conventions are broken, that can only mean that the will is turned against itself; for the object perceived under the dictates of an habituated will, will hardly

[13] This point was recognized by Dietrich Bonhoeffer in his astute analysis of early Neo-Orthodoxy: "Revelation is its own donor without preconditions and alone has the power to place in reality. From God to reality, not from reality to God goes the path of theology." *Act and Being,* trans. Bernard Noble, (New York: Harper & Row, 1956), p. 89.

118

turn thought back. This will mean as well that fully reflexive thinking involves the turning of imagination upon itself. Imagination, we have said, is the medium through which the will registers in mentality. The habituated will works through an imagination that is stocked by means of historical-social accretion. Reflexive thinking rests in a will whose imaginative prehensions are not fixed, but rather are attuned to the modulations of Being. That goes to say, as well, that the tortured question of activity and passivity in man is raised anew. Passivity toward Being could be counted a virtue in man, as in Heidegger, only if his activity were not ingredient in his own being and disclosure of Being. But activity could be counted a vice, if it lay an imperious reality-sense upon Being; just as passivity could be counted a vice, if it entailed submission to Being that had no "real" voice in human language.

Will against itself, imagination against itself, activity against passivity and vice versa: these name problems with which we shall be dealing in this and especially in the following chapter.

B. Revelation

Our bearings on the phrase "toward an ontology of revelation" must now be gained from the vantage point of the other major component, revelation. These bearings may be achieved rather more swiftly, for two reasons.

(1) The first is the modest scope of the phrase as "revelation" is used in it. In Chapter III it was said that an ontology of revelation would be undertaken for theology's account; thus, while properly ontological, it would not be ontology proper. If theology attains a formal understanding of revelation as fundament, it will do so in connection with the ontological fundamentals of human being and thus in prosecution of a "regional" ontology of man. (Ontology proper doubtless has other regions under purview, and exposes much in a regional ontological anthropology with only indirect claims on theological interest.) For theology's own account: theology intends to think "founding" revelation through the fundamentals as seized within their temporal horizon. That does not mean *primarily*

that we have to think of temporality abstractly, have to think "Being and Time" and "Process and Reality," but rather that we have to think "founding" revelation through the historic situation of man today. Theology is compelled to think its foundation in this way not by books of such title that happen to be in philosophical vogue (however much help they bestow upon the enterprise), but by the matter of the Gospel. Theology may perform the *epoché* upon its matter in order to gain a formal circumscription (as by and large we undertake throughout these pages), but as with every *epoché,* it is the intention of *that* matter that is steadily in view.

But the modesty claimed above is not yet fully in view. It is abstractly conceivable that "ontology of revelation" could refer to an enterprise conducted in the house of theology alone, e.g., by dogmatics. That enterprise would be given over to speaking of such things as God in relation to Being or Being-itself, of God to the being of the world in various modalities, generated and re-generated, etc. Such an ontology would be no ontology proper, although it might abut one or be reared on one (if luck brought the "right" one along), but rather would be the ontological trans-position of a symbolic tradition. Christian theology in the past has managed a lively traffic in this enterprise. And theology will find its tongue to speak of these things or their hermeneutical equivalents again, or else stutter past the expiration of its license. We prescind from a flatfooted judgment on whether an ontology of revelation in the grand old manner is any longer actually possible in any of theology's self-appointed divisions of her task. But it is the claim here throughout that theology's most fructifying relation with ontology is not in this arena sized for epic produc-tions. One has not to enter the drama of a life-giving symbolics by submitting to the admission price of a grandiose metaphysic that, from a position far from the klieg lights, looks like a thing of fancy.

Fundamental theology plays on softer ontological registers. (a) It worries the point of revelation's insertion in man's being and reality-sense. For example: if the revelation-tradition says, in one of its modes of saying, that man is "new" in Jesus Christ, it remains to say this new man eventfully; it is still the problem of *logos,* of bringing the dynamics of manhood to a speech in

120

which man can recognize himself. With that, we have the problems of "old" and "new," of continuity and discontinuity in the creation and self-creation of human being. (b) An ontology of revelation does not seek, as in the older fundamental theologies of Roman Catholicism, to justify revelation before a neutral ontological bench, or to bring suit against another system for metaphysical malpractice. It seeks rather to surprise theological meanings at their place of birth. What pertains to the *generation* of theological claims—and the modalities of theological claims: that, rather than the adjudication of claims, belongs to an ontology of revelation. One could even say that we take recourse to "nature," not in the modern but in the etymological sense (*natura* comes from *nasci,* to be born), to the things being born.[14] The genesis of meaning which theology turns toward fundamentally is that in connection with the genesis of human being.

(a) and (b) chasten the approach to an ontology of revelation. Both aspire to a formal circumscription of the locus of revelation as fundament, the one directed upon the ontic locus, the other upon the cognitive.

(2) A second reason for winning perspective quickly is the fact that "revelation" has been under discussion in previous chapters, and that discussion needs here only to be called forward. That may be done through some propositions serving here both as summary and prolepsis. They are summary by virtue of pulling previously drawn threads together; and prolepsis by virtue of presenting a draft on intelligibility yet to be worked out in succeeding sections. They may therefore be stated with economy.

(a) To stand in a revelatory relation is to stand in a *modifying* relation. Revelation pertains before all else to the dynamics of being and becoming.[15] Before it is a matter of knowledge

---

[14] See Thomas Aquinas, *Quaestio disputata de unione Verbe incarnati,* art. 1; and *Summa Theologica,* IIIa, q. 2., a. 1. See also Matthias Joseph Scheeben, *Nature and Grace,* trans. Cyril Vollert, S.J., (St. Louis: B. Herder Book Co., 1954), pp. 20ff., for a discussion of the fortunes of the word "nature."

[15] "Becoming" is added here for the benefit of those inured to thinking that "being" refers only to something "static," "changeless," or "timeless."

(noting, however, that the "before" is logical not chronological), revelation is a matter of being and becoming.[16] "Revelation" is therefore deracinated when force-grown by restriction to the epistemological sections of theological systems (something well known by pre-nineteenth-century theology).

(b) The study of the dynamics of being and becoming is the work of ontology proper. Theology makes contact with that work, usually indirectly (through hermeneutic of symbols) and always for its own account. Theology's main entry in the account of revelation is: God's solicitation to be (a solicitation effected concretely not in an ontological language tradition but by courtesy of the historio-deiform imagination).

(c) Revelation as "the solicitation to be" is directed to *man* in the situation he inhabits. An ontology of revelation therefore queries the dynamics of being and becoming human.[17] The situation whose dynamics require descrying is not one to which man has to be brought; it is one which he already inhabits, and which must be "derecondited," be brought under re-cognition.[18]

(d) The being to which man is solicited is his own, man's, not God's. Concrete revelation does not situate man within the standpoint of God, but rather *coram Deo* in respect of his (man's) being human.[19] An ontology of revelation in our modest sense therefore cannot bring the being of the divine term under formal circumscription.

(e) The formal locus of revelation is man's ontological instability. If revelation is first of all an affair of modification [(i) above], an affair of the realization of one's being, the notion of ontological instability is endemic to that of revelation. (Being

16 This means, negatively, that revelation does not proffer information about an antecedent state of affairs.

17 "Being human" is used here instead of "human being" for the same reason as given in note 15 above, to avoid the suggestion that man's being is an antecedent and fixed state of affairs about which revelation informs us.

18 If it were not an even more grotesque word, "dereconditization" should replace "demythologization." The latter term has meant, in the Bultmann school, the attainment of a pre-recondite view of man and world.

19 Adequate preparation for this claim would require extensive recourse to the dogmatic and symbolic tradition of Christian theology, a project well beyond our limitations here.

122

perfectly coincident with itself could not be spoken of as revealed; rather it could be said to be revealed only in the sense of "disclosed" or "known" in its perfect coincidence; and material theology knows such a coincidence only in Jesus Christ, whose "presence" is established only in a situation of ontological instability.)

Man's ontological instability refers to his simultaneous coincidence and non-coincidence:

    (i) with himself,

    (ii) with the *polis* and his neighbor, and

    (iii) with the "world."

In the most general terms, the locus of revelation is the coincidence and non-coincidence of man's being and his reality-sense.

(f) What revelation formally *intends,* and in concreteness accomplishes, is the expansion ("maturation") of the self toward its ownmost good, toward the neighbor's weal, and toward the glory of God.[20] A formal understanding of what revelation intends will therefore involve a formal grasp of the dynamics of personal being.

Major stations in this dynamic have already been marked and may be brought forward here in capsule. As gathered into the intention of revelation, personal being

    (i) is constituted, founded, emergent;

    (ii) is interlocked, *qua* personal being, with interlaced regions of being both personal and impersonal; and therefore its noemata are multidimensional;

    (iii) is possessed of a noetic scale anchored in lived experience of the world;

    (iv) both in respect of being and knowing, is qualified by the modalities of time.

These matters were framed in a preliminary way in Chapter III.

(3) From the consideration of "ontology" and "revelation" in the phrase "toward an ontology of revelation" a convergence of themes is now apparent. The former led into the problematic of the *radix* of ontological thinking, the will. The latter identified the intention of revelation as the expansion of human being,

[20] "Toward the glory of God" means fidelity to that Faithfulness with which God steadily solicits man to be.

and named in pertinence to that expansion the whole problematic of man's ontological instability. This convergence brings
us to the threshold of more detailed inquiry and sets its subject
matter: human selfhood, the trajectory of personal being. As
well, this convergence (together with subsequent inquiry) establishes the method for construing the cognitive modalities of
revelation. In thinking about the self, as Bergson never tired of
urging, "object" and method must be strictly commensurate.[21]
"Knowledge" in revelation is construed from the genesis of
meaning that goes hand-in-hand with the genesis of human
being. If imagination is settled upon as the mode of concrete
revelatory knowledge, that is owing to the role of the imagination in the constitution and expansion of human being.[22] As
knowing follows being (logically, not chronologically) in revelation, so the examination of the cognitive power of imagination
follows on the elucidation of its ontological reach. In order to
illuminate the ontological reach of the imagination it is necessary to elaborate this reach not in connection with psychical
states, not even "images," but rather in connection with that

[21] Cf. Henri Bergson, *An Introduction to Metaphysics,* trans. T. E.
Hulme, (New York: The Liberal Arts Press, 1955), pp. 34–37. With
respect to the analysis of the self, Bergson sees modern philosophy as
strewn with the wreckage of systems in which a psychological method
was trained upon a metaphysical object or in which a metaphysical
method was directed toward a psychological object. The latter,

> . . . seeking the unity of the ego in the gaps, as it were, between
> the psychical states, is led to fill the gaps with other states, and
> so on indefinitely, so that the ego, compressed in a constantly nar-
> rowing interval, tends towards zero, as analysis is pushed farther
> and farther; . . . [while the former] making the ego the place where
> mental states are lodged, is confronted with an empty space which
> we have no reason to limit here rather than there, which goes
> beyond each of the successive boundaries that we try to assign to
> it, which constantly grows larger, and which tends to lose itself no
> longer in zero, but in the infinite.

[22] As noted earlier, material theology has an anterior reason for
construing the cognitivity of revelation under the imaginative mode,
viz., because it is given its subject matter to think by the route of
imaginative discourse (scripture, hymn, sacrament, etc.). But this discourse is opened to *thought* only as we grasp the connection between
historic-imaginative discourse and historio-personal being.

124

dimension of the self's life which they express.[23] Only in this way can the engagement of imagination in the exercise of personal being come under compelling recognition.

II. THE AGENT-SELF

A mere inner aliveness or a mere external world is never given to us. Both are not only always together but are bound to each other in the most vital relation: only the development of the intellectual structure increasingly dissolves this connection. And our viewing, perceiving, and thinking are never completely disengaged from this relation.[24]

A. The Self vis-à-vis Itself and World

The scent of revelation is to be tracked on the trail of human being, the "way" of the agent-self. Of revelation we can say, *mutatis mutandis,* what Aristotle said of the being of a thing.

There are many senses in which a thing may be said to "be," but all that "is" is related to one central (or starting) point, one definite kind of thing, and is not said to "be" by a mere ambiguity.[25]

Aristotle also remarks what "one starting point" may mean in this connection; it is that juncture at which a thing is first if not fully comprehensible.[26] From the standpoint of theology, revelation too bears many senses; and it is rescued from mere ambiguity by reference to the *arche* of its initial comprehensibility, the framework of the historical self.[27] Within a restricted

[23] This judgment is backed with precedent in the history of the development of the concept of imagination. See Appendices I–III below, and my article, "The Imagination in Plato," *loc. cit.,* pp. 436–461.

[24] Dilthey, *Gesammelte Schriften,* Vol. VII, p. 16.

[25] *Metaphysica,* Book Γ, Ch. 2, 1003a; in *The Basic Works of Aristotle,* ed. Richard McKeon, (New York: Random House, 1941), p. 732. (Cited hereafter as McKeon.)

[26] *Ibid.,* Book Δ, Ch. 1, 1013a; McKeon, p. 752.

[27] I emphasize *initial* comprehensibility. Material theology claims a

125

understanding of "starting point," then, the human self is the starting point for a formal grasp of revelation. These restrictions bear repetition. The first is the limited sense in which reflexive thinking can be said to have a starting point, discussed earlier in this chapter. The second, noted just now, is that "starting point" refers not to a temporal beginning but to the juncture at which the thing to be understood becomes initially comprehensible.

With the recollection of these restrictions we put ourselves on notice and guard against misunderstanding. In taking the self as the framework for ontological thinking about revelation we purpose neither to elide "world" nor to view the self as the transcendental subject of world-consciousness. Such partitionism falls away with steady resistance to both pejorative Cartesianism and pejorative idealistic Husserlianism.[28] For Descartes the world generally and the body specifically were diversions of the self, thwarting its self-intuition. Only by isolating, contracting, and intensifying itself through a studied suspension of the world could the self grasp its own being.[29] The disappear-

fuller if not final comprehension of revelation. These claims, properly speaking, are human proposals about the self-revelation of ultimately mysterious Being.

[28] "Pejorative" is used advisedly, although more strictly in the case of Husserl than with Descartes. With Descartes it was a matter of ontological as well as methodological principle to elide the world from all reflection on the self *qua res cogitans*. Husserl's preoccupation with world *qua* intended set him in the *tendency* of transcendental idealism, of absolute self-representative world (à la Hegel). But Husserl, the perpetual *Anfänger*, was his own best critic; and his commendation of rigorously reflexive thinking led (especially in the later phenomenological tradition) to a quashing of what might be called "world-idealism," (as opposed to Fichtean "self-idealism").

[29] It is interesting to note that Descartes' recusion of the imagination and *res extensa* go hand in hand in his reflection on the self *qua res cogitans*. Descartes found the imagination to be exercised only in relation to the world, i.e., in relation "to a body . . ." (*Meditations*, Ch. VI; in *Philosophical Works of Descartes*, trans. Elizabeth S. Haldane and G. R. T. Ross, [New York: Dover Publications, 1955], Vol. I, pp. 185–186.) He says explicitly that imagination is dispensable so far as the *cogito* is concerned. ("I remark . . . that this power of imagination which I possess, in as far as it differs from the power of conceiving, is in no way necessary to my (nature or) essence, that is, to the essence of my mind. . . ." [*Ibid.*]) Descartes was able to bring the imagination back into the larger reaches of the self only after elaborating his meta-

ance of the world is thus made a condition of the appearance of the self in its unique nature. This could only lead to the "angel within the machine," or more aptly to what Kierkegaard called "inwardness with a jammed lock," to subjective being cut off from the world. Husserl, on the other hand, meant to neutralize both the reified self and the reified world as they preside over the natural attitude. With him it was not a question of gaining access to the self in its being, but rather of rendering patent the intention of the world that precedes such reification in lived experience.[30] His preoccupation with "world" at this level drove him to the problem of world-constitution, to the self as the underside of world. This leads to an "outwardness" in trans-cendental subjectivity that is so universal as to be attributable only to an absolute ego, and effectively collapses finite selfhood into absolutely self-representative world. Only the alliance of existentialism with phenomenology has managed to stay this reversion to world-idealism.

To evade partitionist schemes is not to banish "otherness" to outer darkness, or inner darkness for that matter, but rather to allow otherness to come forward in its rich modalizations. That "otherness" obtains only between subject and object is one of the more inscrutable prevailing fictions. No catalogue of otherness is called for here, but several types may be mentioned to score the point. (1) There is an otherness internal to the self, an otherness between the modalities of the single self's being: between myself *qua* continuant and myself *qua* ingressed by discontinuous realities. (2) There is an otherness between myself and other selves, themselves not myself or things. (3) There is an otherness between myself and world: things that are no modality of myself nor other selves. In gen-

---

physical doctrine of God as guarantor of the existence of world, *res extensa*. With that he found himself with an acute problem: imagination must have reference to world, yet as a power it inheres in mind. His solution was finally a theological one. His approach was quite the opposite of our own: he sought to understand imagination out of theology, whereas we seek to grasp the intelligibility of theology out of the imagination precisely as the imagination reflects the co-inherence of self and world.

[30] An exceptionally subtle discussion of self and world in Descartes and Husserl will be found in Thevenaz, *What is Phenomenology?*, pp. 93-112.

eral, otherness depends upon power expressed in relation. Anything possessed of being is thereby possessed of power, minimally the power to present itself, the power to appear. As Schleiermacher said, ". . . being posited for itself can only exist where there is also power, just as power always exists only in activity."[31] And to exegete "activity" we may call upon John Locke: ". . . power includes in it some kind of relation, a relation to action . . ."[32] The power to appear is the power to relate, and nothing relates except by establishing itself as other to that to which it relates.[33] All concrete commerce is founded on this elemental point. Apprehended in a response-situation, the self is related to world; grasped as the limitant and provocateur of consciousness, the world is related to the self. The self is not a discarnate spirit, but an embodied, world-intending power; the world is not Dr. Johnson's stone, but a contingent self-representative complex (in which, to be sure, sticks and stones "mean").

My embodied selfhood is something I not only apprehend but *am*. Attending to myself in continuity of act, the "object" of attention is not something viewed *ab extra:* I *am* the span of process under view and review. The self I am is both a one and a many. But the *unum* I grasp with primitive interiority is not abstract; my unity is neither abstracted nor abstractable from something more original, is no species of the class "identity." Moreover, the identical being that I am is a being that is becoming.[34] That is, my *unum* is nourished on the many. *Qua* actual I am an *acting* being; I am possessed of being that requires *enacting* in order to be. So when I seize myself from the

[31] Schleiermacher, *The Christian Faith,* p. 176.

[32] John Locke, *An Essay Concerning Human Understanding,* (London: William Tegg & Company, 1849); Book II, Ch. XXI, Sect. 3; p. 147.

[33] "Internal" relations might be thought an exception. No doubt *absolutely* internal relations would be an exception. But it is contradictory to speak of two things being absolutely related internally; two things so related would be not two things but one. *Absolute* internal relation is therefore an unintelligible notion. "Relation" intrinsically signifies "other" in some mode of otherness.

[34] Cf. Gabriel Marcel, *The Mystery of Being,* Vol. I: *Reflection and Mystery,* trans. G. S. Fraser, (Chicago: Henry Regnery Co., 1950), Ch. IX.

128

inside out as an irreducible *unum,* it is not as a bare nonhistorical unity. ("Know a man's table, know the man," the saying goes.) What is grasped is a center of order uniting the multiple historical-worldly ingredients of my being. Here I gain my original sense of the "power" of being; here I inhabit—and am —the nucleus of an order that puts background and foreground together in such a way that a being (the being I am) is brought forward, appears, presents itself.

No reified quiddity, the self is without tidy boundaries. No delineated object, it is more nearly an operation.[35] It is an integral operation by virtue of its *unum,* that center of order which unites disparate ingredients with the range of its being. In relation to its modal ingredients the self as the center of order has a privileged position; for it precedes and succeeds them, instancing them (i.e., enriching them and being enriched by taking them up into its unity) without being identical with them. The life of the self cannot be passed off as a case of mere sequence or as an instance of the empirical coinherence of qualia.[36] *I* recognize myself as one who is, in a sense, the identical if not entirely the same self who was party to that past occasion now lost as an ontological litter for my being. I succeed what bore me, and I precede what will bear me. The force of this reflection is not lessened by the fact that I cannot grasp myself between litters (that would amount to transcending finite existence). I am always borne by an ontological situation larger than myself, but my selfhood so borne is not merely a subphenomenal feature of that situation. Insofar as I am not only situated but also situate, I have an interior understanding of passing from phase to phase and of the transition from situation to situation.[37]

[35] See Thomas Aquinas, *Summa Theologica,* I, Quest. LXXVI, Art. 1.
[36] Hume to the contrary notwithstanding. See below, Appendix III, "Imagination and Creativity."
[37] Whitehead thought this point so secure as to be fraught with cosmological significance. ". . . If we hold . . . that all final individual actualities have the metaphysical character of occasions of experience, then . . . the direct evidence as to the connectedness of one's immediate present occasion of experience with one's immediately past occasions, can be validly used to suggest categories applying to the connectedness of all occasions in nature." *The Adventures of Ideas,* (New York: The New American Library, 1959), p. 222.

B. The Will as Clue to the Ordering Power
or Principle of Selfhood

While the self embraces generic features of an ontological scale larger than itself, it also comprises a special concatenation of its own. One of the most durable problems in the western metaphysical tradition concerns itself with what the authentic self comprises in its own order. Classical candidates and consortia of candidates have been brought forward: body, soul, spirit, will, intellect, libido, etc. Among these candidating "elements" that the self comprises, which offers the primal clue to what the self is? It has been typical of recent theology to pocket this question with the exhortation to keep the "whole self" in view. But the "whole self" is essentially an eschatological concept. Were a limpid view of the whole self phenomenologically accessible, the ontological problem of selfhood would never arise. The self, like its ordering principle—the will, is neither whole nor entire at any point at which we can surprise it. As St. Augustine said, ". . . if the will were whole and entire, it would not even command it [i.e., itself] to be, because it would already be."[38] If to the will is attributed primacy in the self, that is in part owing to the fact that the will in its own life reflects the dialectic of what is unfinished and finished in man.

In reflecting on what to take as the primal clue to the dynamics of selfhood, it is necessary to remember that our grasp of ourselves is not clear and distinct. It is not so much that all apprehensions are obscure, but rather than the self as a unique order is obscure in apprehension of it. The ontic self is obscure not only because it is unique, the center of its own field, but also because in apprehension the *limits* of its field are nebulous. The self is the center of radii extending we know not how far, yet their extremity is part of what the self is and means. At the social level, for example, who knows how far the selfhood of Mao Tse Tung extends, or that of Lyndon Johnson? And to what extent and to what extremity the outermost limits of these selves *limit* the selfhood of countless others? At the individual level, for another example, in the apprehension of

[38] *Confessions,* VIII, IX, 21; Outler, p. 171.

130

his own active selfhood who can draw a clean line between adopted purposes and biological instinct? (In Peking one must eat; and in order to eat one may have to adopt purposes laid down by the incursion of Mao's selfhood, the latter as the foreground of every self's concentration into act.) The self, in short, is always seen by "the tail of the eye"; we grasp the self in connection with its activity, although it is not exhausted in its projects. And in elaborating an ontology of the self, we attend to its ordering principle, the will.

The attribution of primacy to the will has been a poorly kept secret in preceding pages. We have now only to press the rationale of this attribution to the point at which distinctions may be drawn that will have a fair chance of securing conviction.

As noted earlier, our very sense of reality is never without will-reference.[39] This fact is on display in every crib, as a baby attains a sense of his own reality and that of things about him as they set limits upon his own velleity. Even the *nature* of reality so apprehended is not without reference to the will. The "response" of the crib-side to the baby's movement is not that of his mother against whom he nuzzles. Slowly he comes to distinguish the world by the ways in which it satisfies or frustrates his wants. Even the wildest display of sheer "wilfulness" in a tantrum, the shaking of the fist at all restraint, is not without effect upon a developing sense of reality.

The self therefore does not have its concrete sense of reality all at once. The recognition of this truth has been made difficult by the influence of Descartes's *cogito* upon modern philosophy, or rather his general way of conceiving the self. As Austin Farrer has said, Descartes confused self-evidence of fact re-

[39] Cf. Max Scheler, *On the Eternal in Man*, trans. Bernard Noble, (New York: Harper and Brothers, 1960), *passim* but espec. pp. 191ff. and 220ff; also Scheler's *Der Formalismus in der Ethik und die materiale Wertethik*, 4th revised ed., ed. by Maria Scheler, Vol. II, (Berne, 1954), pp. 143ff. and 154ff.; Wilhelm Dilthey, "Beiträge zur Lösung der Frage vom Ursprung unseres Glaubens an die Realität der Aussenwelt und seinem Recht, in *op. cit.* 4th ed., Vol. V, (1964), pp. 90–138, *passim,* but espec. pp. 90ff. and 131ff., also *ibid.,* 3rd ed., Vol. VIII, (1962), pp. 15ff. and 142; Austin Farrer, *Finite and Infinite,* (Westminster: Dacre Press, 1943), p. 230f. On the role of feeling and feeling-qualities in the formation of the reality-sense, see Whitehead, *Process and Reality,* pp. 267 and 516, and John Dewey, *Experience and Nature,* (New York: Dover Publications, 1958), p. 96f.

garding the existence of the self with clarity regarding that in which the reality of the self consists.[40] From and in my acts I indubitably grasp my *existence;* but from no one of them (in Descartes' case, "thinking") do I glean an equally indubitable concept of what I am (for Descartes, "thinking being": *res cogitans*). What I am emerges as my active existence takes its situating course through those situations comprising my destiny. This is to say that the indubitable conviction of existence, of the *thatness* of the self or anything else, is a function of the will. Only in modifying and in being modified do I grasp myself as an existent being. One can never convince another of the *existence* of something, whether of God or of three-dimensional space, unless that something "causes" him to bother about it. The indubiety of existence is not the indubiety of a concept. An absolutely indubitable proposition as such never has indubitable existential reference.[41] Cases in point are the purely analytical judgments of pure mathematics and self-enclosed systems of symbolic logic. The existential intelligibility of a proposition depends upon its power to focus attention upon a situation that "makes a difference."

It is one of the marks of a thing possessed of being that it communicates itself, that it "presents" itself, or "appears."[42] (That is why the threshold of ontology is rigorous phenomenology.) But nothing presents itself, as Farrer lightheartedly suggests, together with a tray of colors and a set of instructions, with which the mind is called upon to paint its portrait.[43] The thing is *there,* but already in transaction with our being. *Cognitive* transaction is one among others and is always based on transactions more fundamental than itself. What we know *concretely* is not a thing as it presents itself from interior principle but the self as modified by its appearance or the thing in our transactions with it: the thing as intended. In simplest terms, there is no apprehension without *response.* Primal response is

[40] *Finite and Infinite,* p. 98.
[41] Or as Farrer puts it, in an indubitable proposition ". . . the reference is not included in its indubitable content." *Ibid.*
[42] Cf. Hartt, *Being Known and Being Revealed,* pp. 11–15.
[43] Farrer, *The Glass of Vision,* (Westminster: Dacre Press, 1948), p. 87.

132

an affair of the will (as we recognize when we take our "feelings" as a responsible clue to what is before us). Concerning this response two things must be said: that we respond to entities according to their natures (in the grasping of which a system of "representations" is always at work), and according to our freedom. The range of my possible responses to an oncoming bullet is rather more circumscribed than that with respect to my sick child. In either case, any transaction that falls out will have will-reference; although in the first case I may not be around to transpose it into a cognitive key. But someone else can do the job, insofar as that transaction becomes a term to which he responds. The moral is that, in elaborating the ontological order of the self, we cannot attend to mere rationality or intellect: neither a pure theoretical reason, setting up a one-to-one correspondence between concepts and their objects; nor a pure practical reason, legislating responses to objects irrespective of their natures.

It is appropriate to point out that, in departing from the will as the core of agent-selfhood, we are under no necessity to posit access to a pure instance of will, or better, an instance of pure will. [44] Were that the case, the language of ontology would

[44] Even the most radical of metaphysical voluntarists, holding that will is the principle of all reality, have realized that there is no reified will available to rational insight. Jacob Boehme wrote, "Seeing then the first will is something ungrounded (*ein Ungrund*), to be regarded as an eternal nothing, we recognize it to be like a mirror, wherein one sees his own image; like a life, and yet is no life, but a figure of life, and of the image belonging to life." (*Von sechs Theosophischen Puncten*, I, 7; in *Six Theosophic Points,* trans. John Rolleston Earle, [London: Constable and Co., 1919] p. 6.) We hold that the will is grasped in the response-situations of our active existence, whereas the extreme voluntarist depends upon *objectifications* of the will. Boehme and Schopenhauer furnish an interesting comparison at this point. For Boehme the phenomenal world is an objectification of imagination, itself the "centering" power of chaotic will. In Schopenhauer's view the phenomenal world is at an even farther remove from the will, since Ideas are objectifications of the will, and the phenomenal world is an objectification of Ideas. The only quasi-direct *Vorstellung* of will Schopenhauer recognized was in the Arts, especially in music. He wrote, "Music is as *direct* an objectification and copy of the whole *will* as the world itself, nay even as the Ideas, whose multiplied manifestation constitutes the world of individual things. Music is thus by no means like the other arts, the copy of the Ideas, but *the copy of the will itself,*

be indistinguishable from that of psychoanalytic metaphor. No, the grasp of the will is always in a response-situation, and no situation is ever a simple objectification of will itself. This brings to light the most remarkable feature of the will's operation, that in virtue of which it is the clue to an irreducible ontic order. *It is both a term and a relation; and neither is ever had without the other.* It is the one agent-order we know that is both externally and internally related to its field of operation.[45] The will ever engages a fluctuating range of activity; yet its *being* cannot be limited to or identified with any one of its projects. For example, in its creative relation to an object the will is a *term*inal reality: my will is an integral reality in relation to the statue I am carving. But my will is not just a term; it also weaves a relation between all sorts of contents which bear upon the emergence of the finished statue. Without my relating activity the granite would be indistinguishable from the igneous mass out of which it was hewn. And the relating process goes on from the moment that I first intend the act until the moment when the statue is finished, until it is fully "other" than my willing of it, taking on its own "life" or terminality. Moreover, my terminal will did not view this relating process quiescently from some disinterested point of vantage. As an artist I have to carve the statue in order to become what I am. Still, the whole of what I am is not instanced in this statue (and not alone because it now has a "life" of its own); I shall in due course carve another, and between statues I shall not cease to be.

In the perduring terminality of the self, seized in its relationality with world, and in the fluctuating relationality of the self, imbued with "power" to make the terminal self *appear,* we have the dynamics of finished and unfinished man. To retail these dynamics in an ontological coin will scarcely be to sell the

---

whose objectivity the Ideas are. This is why the effect of music is so much more powerful and penetrating than that of the other arts, for they speak only of shadows, but it speaks of the thing itself." (*The World as Will and Idea,* trans. R. B. Haldane and J. Kemp, Vol. I [London: Kegan, Paul, Trübner and French Co., 1906], p. 333.)

[45] Ricoeur shows in great detail how the self is both internally and externally related to its "fault." *Fallible Man: Philosophy of the Will,* trans. Charles Kelbley, (Chicago: Henry Regnery Co., n.d.), xxvii.

secret of anyone's individual historicity: that is for him to say.[46] (Dante evisaging Purgatory is not Bonhoeffer contemplating execution at the hands of Nazis; Paul on the Damascus Road is not Napoleon on his bloody Russian campaign; Moses before the burning bush is not John Kennedy in Dallas.) Ontological analysis comes in aid of individual historicity by furnishing a conceptuality through which that historicity can be "seen," and thus "said." (In roughly the same way that learning a new word lets us see something that has been there at the fringe of consciousness all along and can now be said.)

Before passing to those discriminations through which personal being may be caught at the joints, it may be useful to offer another summary and prolepsis. The ontological reach of the imagination is spied in connection with that in virtue of which the self is both finished and unfinished, viz., the will as the self's principle of order. Thus imagination is construed from an order irreducible to the structure of abstract/rational consciousness. The notion of order which the primacy of will provides is neither that of a static term nor that of a dangling relation, but rather that of term-and-relation unceasingly in dynamic act. While structural features of the will's operation are subject to analysis and therefore abstraction (the whole of our present project, an ontology of selfhood, depends on that!), we hope to show how the fuller scale of the will in various modalizations is embodied without loss of concreteness in the imagination to the enrichment of rationality beyond its (reason's) analytical and abstractive power.

Lest these comments seem over-wispy, let us pull out the carrot. The "ontological reach" of the imagination refers to the order upon which it opens and in which it participates. Imagination intends, and extends, the realm of "coming to be." Stated abstractly, the domain upon which imagination opens is ontological incompleteness, being aborning, unfinished dominions whose finishing is not a matter of rightly reading a blueprint of formality. By this is meant, among other things, that imagination is more than a mental medium for bodying forth in lively figures

[46] Cf. Joseph de Finance, "For each subject the verb in the 'I am' has an incommensurable value." "Being and Subjectivity," *Cross Currents,* Vol. VI (Spring, 1956), p. 170.

the vibrancy and process of existential happening. Imagination is both a cognitive and an ontic power, participating in the very being of dominions it opens upon. One could say that imagination engages those levels of being in which our creativity is involved, which require human *response* for the maturation of their kind and act of being. It is the mental power of that agency whereby the self puts more into the world than it takes out of it; it is the mental medium of the one ontically active and passive power we grasp from the inside, viz., the will. To this extent, imagination is actively effective in those emergent levels of reality in which the will is ingredient and modified.[47]

[47] To associate imagination with the will in this intimate way may appear odd, for imagination is a mode of intellectual process that is sometimes consciously "voluntary," but more often is not. One might challenge the association by making two claims: (i) the activity of will is not that of an intellectual process. (ii) Will is the voluntariness of any mode of the self's act, any mode of the self's act which is itself voluntary. Now if these claims are accepted in the unqualified form in which they are stated, it would indeed hardly be worth the candle to construe imagination in relation to will-centered selfhood. For at best we should increase our understanding of imagination only in its connection with consciously voluntary activity, and thus of a small and perhaps the least significant range of imaginative activity.

But I do not accept the claims as stated: (i) assumes a false view of the relation between will and intellect. It is true that will is not a surrogate of intellectual process or something merely under the dominion of intellectual process. But the relation between will and intellect cannot be an absolutely external relation. The activity of will has some expression in intellectual processes, else reason could not mark its (the will's) structural phases (the entertainment of possibilities, the marshalling of background toward envisaged ends, the concentration of all ingredients into act), issue directives to it, or receive directives from it. Moreover, concrete knowledge, which certainly involves intellectual processes, is never without an implicit will-reference: of that we have said enough.

Concerning (ii), will cannot be restricted exclusively to that aspect of our activity which is "voluntary" in character (however odd that may sound semantically). The will is the ordering power or principle of our active being. In its ordering the will both situates and is situated; without either it is not the will of a human self but that of an angel or a beast. In its voluntary situating the will has always to reckon with an involuntarily situated base; and in some contexts, at least, the involuntarily situated base can be voluntarily qualified even if not removed. (The will has, in Austin Farrer's phrase, "a bodily bias." But men do fast, even unto death, toward some end. Is the situated base, the bodily bias, thereby removed? No, only qualified in concert with a "voluntary" end. What is removed by death is the human will itself.) The will does not become the will to the extent that its ordering is voluntary; that is

It is not enough to say simply that the self is a continuous operation, for precisely the complexity of the self *qua* continuant is the subject under study. "Faced with the complexity of continuous reality," William H. Riker rightly notes, "humans understand it by breaking it up into pieces."[48] The "pieces" are not literal pieces, of course, but rather analytical abstractions; they are rational discerptions of lived selfhood. However sharply cut and thinly drawn, they are threaded to the operation we are. As Plotinus said, ". . . we separate, the better to understand; there is nothing illegitimate in the verbal and mental sundering of things which must in fact be co-existent."[49]

The one self has its life through the overlay of two modes, "continuous ingredience" and "discontinuous ingression." (I use these labels—pinched from Austin Farrer—as rough equivalents, respectively, of "term" and "relation.") Neither mode can be understood without the other, and the self cannot be grasped without both.[50] Both modes embrace the moment of *potency* in the self's operation: the entertainment of what is possibly and compossibly ingredient in the self's coming to be. Fields of potency would however remain merely abstractly compossible

---

a mode of its being but not its being as such. Its being ordered is as much a part of it as is the spontaneously generated order it applies. Thus in the classical controversy over the will we can side neither with the determinist nor the indeterminist. Each bifurcates the will as we know it in active existence, the one settling upon being ordered, the other attending to its intrinsically generated order.

[48] William H. Riker, "Event and Situations," *Journal of Philosophy*, Vol. LIV, No. 3 (January 31, 1957), p. 59.

[49] *The Enneads*, IV, Tractate 3, 9; in *Plotinus: The Enneads*, trans. Stephen MacKenna, 2d. ed., rev.; with a Foreword by E. R. Dodds and an Introduction by Paul Henry, S.J. (London: Faber and Faber Ltd., 1956), p. 268.

[50] To look at the internal conditions of continuity alone (i.e., without adverting to exterior objects and agencies) would be to assume that the cause and the effect of the self's operation are entirely immanent. Not even the subtlest of 19th-century German idealists (I have Fichte in mind) are persuasive that this assumption has merit: we never grasp ourselves without modification from a source that cannot be set down to a species of self-limitation. Nor is the hardy naïve realist more persuasive when he admonishes attention to discontinuous operations alone, for nothing can be said of the interiority of something that bears upon us, or of its passing from phase to phase, without analogizing from our own experience of continuity. Positively, world cannot be refined out of self, as self cannot be filtered out of world.

were they not reduced to eventful conjunction. For the moment of "activity" or actualization we shall use the term "concentration."

These discerptions must now be pressed for their sense. We shall turn first to that entertainment of potency which transpires in the self as it continues out of its *background* and *foreground*.

C. The Self and "Continuous Ingredience"

To continue is not to perdure in a state of undifferentiated quality. Descartes had good ground for reviewing his dialectic: it was not the work of a malevolent demon that beclouded its results, but rather the fact that "I am" (*sum*) possesses a different content in successive affirmations. It is still *I* that "am," not only as the logical prius of dialectic but also as the immediately given identity from which succeeding phases are viewed and by which succession itself takes on meaning. Yet the being that I *am* is differentiated from the being that I *was* by a dialectic that is not only logical but ontic as well. What I am now was then a penumbral *foreground* of what I was, and what I was is a more or less delimited *background* of what I am now. What I am in any given episode of my being is an ontic concentration of background and foreground, a concentration that will itself fund a new background for succeeding episodes.

Adapting one of Bergson's metaphors to the purposes at hand, we may picture the self in its continuity as two balls of string, two ends of which are attached and concealed from view.[51] The balls roll in tandem on the same plane, but one is unrolling while the other is rolling up. I feel myself coming to an end as an enormous backlying mass of biological, cultural and familial heritage concretizes itself; the end is the petering out of this line of heritage, and so of myself. But I also feel myself coming to the beginning as long-intended but distant purposes heave into view, attracting my accumulating selfhood into shape by their sheer finality. In one ball is seen a background that is shrinking and a foreground that is shortening

[51] Bergson, *An Introduction to Metaphysics,* pp. 25-26.

138

with every revolution of concrete act;[52] whereas in the other ball, foreground takes on freshly delineated reality with every revolution that builds background afresh. Under analysis the metaphor gets out of hand. It rightly implies that background and foreground are relative moments in the self's continuity, the "mass" of one relative to that of the other, and so that one is never considerable without the other. (Memory without intention, for example, is nothing.) On this point there is no problem as long as we look at one ball only. There's the rub: how are the two balls related? Unrolling and rolling up, each expresses something of my continuity. But my continuity is not divided between two parallel, noninteracting lines. Of course, in the metaphor the balls are connected. The ball rolling up is rolling up not only the string that lies before it but also string from the center of the ball unrolling; and the point will be reached at which it will roll up the string that is unrolled. But this "point" is not one juncture alone in my life-history, say some moment on my 38th birthday. This "point" is every concrete act that instances my continuity. Here the single metaphor breaks down: we cannot tie the strings together at every revolution without a hopeless tangle. (That says: analysis must have perpetual recourse to lived continuity, where background and foreground are concretely bonded.)

What is involved in the self's entertainment of ingredients with respect to its own continuity? (In so entertaining the self is not idling its engine, is not bemusedly toying with abstract possibilities. It is in gear, reckoning with potentiality for its own forward motion.) The metaphor above points the direction: entertainment comprises the appropriation of background to foreground, and of foreground to background. When entertainment passes into concentration, two vast fields of potentiality (the self's background and foreground) are actualized in specificity; they are existentially appropriated to each other in the concreteness of an act.

(1) *Background*. No one can peep into his background without standing in awe of its size, configuration, and variegation.

---

[52] Cf. Augustine: "The past increases by the diminution of the future until by the consumption of all the future all is past." *Confessions,* XI, xxvii, 36; Outler, p. 266.

Any map of the self's background as a whole, mind-boggling in its enormity, would be like those maps charted by ancient mariners: the most frequently used legend would have to be "presumed and unexplored." Modern means of transport have worked their wonders on topography and cartography. But these wonders pale by comparison with that exploration of the background of the self's continuity which is in many ways co-extensive with modernity itself. Biology, psychology, and above all the historical sciences, to name only a few of the major expeditionary forces. Yet even at this late date in modernity, the revolutionary implications of self-consciousness with respect to background have scarcely more than dawned.

Consider that dimension of the self's background which, in Farrer's phrase, can be called "the bodily bias of the will."[53] I am hungry: shall I finish writing this paragraph before having lunch? I may complete the paragraph, possibly the chapter, before having something to eat; but not the whole book. Bodily bias does not lay a pattern ready-made upon every act, but it does set a limit upon those patterns through which the will effectively entertains. We cannot through introspection discern the point at which this limitation becomes absolute. That does not mean it is not there. Suppose I heroically determine to finish the book before taking food, ignoring everything but the continuity of my project (e.g., the anxiety of my family, my grocer's declining sales, etc.). If my entertainment is effective, do I thereby kick away the ladder of bodily limitation and scale the heights by dint of sheer volitional energy and intention? No, one of two things will happen. (1) I will complete the book before eating and before expiring, but not as I intended it. The grandiose plan was appropriated to an abundant store of energy; now it is accommodated to a dwindling supply. I thought I was denying the power of background, but it ap-

[53] For a perceptive study of human being-in-the-world as *embodiment,* centering on the thought of Marcel, Sartre, and Merleau-Ponty, see Richard M. Zaner, *The Problem of Embodiment,* (The Hague: Martinus Nijohff, 1964); see also Alphonse de Waelhens, "The Phenomenology of the Body," *Readings in Existential Phenomenology,* ed. Nathaniel Lawrence and Daniel O'Connor, (Englewood Cliffs: Prentice-Hall, 1967), pp. 149-167.

pears afresh in the shrinking of foreground. If I do not appropriate foreground to background, background will establish its own foreground; destiny will yield to fate. The thing I accomplish is not my own, which is all the more ironical because I set out on a path of self-determination. Or, (2) I will not finish the book before expiring. By supreme effort of will my foreground remains throughout a fixed constant and everything concerning my being is adjusted to it. I ignore the fact that background and foreground are polar elements of my continuity, I interrupt dialectic in favor of foreground. I do not correlate intention with available bodily energy but exhaust available energy in pursuit of a fixed intention. (The body be damned, I'll write the book as I intend!) This joust with background is no less fateful than the one described above; to fate is added tragedy (or at least, a rather considerable inconvenience). Bodily background exercises its limitation upon volitional pattern finally, if in no other way, by the removal of itself as the internal condition of personal continuity. In the case above, my ignoring of background got me a book of sorts but not the book I intended; in the present case, I keep the pure intention for a while but I lose myself in the process.[54] In either case my continuity suffers (not to mention the poor book) from inattention to the polarity of background and foreground.

With considerations such as these the bodily background of personal continuity only partially comes into view. My body is the community of my being with organic and inorganic being, full of the joys and terrors of that community (full of microorganisms: some sustaining each other, some feeding on each other, some mayhap destroying me). Biological science may intervene upon this community to allay certain episodes of terror, e.g., may arrest the deleterious action of certain microorganisms. But it does so to preserve this community as the internal condition of personal continuity. Moreover, body is not only the submerged base of community with organic and inorganic nature. By the route of *perception,* it is the organon

[54] Perhaps in the interest of temperance it should be said instead: with the removal of bodily background I lose myself *qua* dependent upon bodily support, and specifically I lose myself *qua* writer of books!

of "presence." I am inserted in the world and receive the presence of others by a perception that is always embodied.[55]

"Body" is only one dimension of the background of the self's continuity. One could mention as well the "unconscious," that dark compound of *soma* and *psyche,* in which so many subsidiary backgrounds are secreted. Or one could turn to "language" and the way that, with every word sliding from the tongue, centuries of human spirit supervene on expression.[56] With every word I disgorge my historical background. The use of every word involves an entertainment of my historical destiny.

So to speak, the self bears on its back its bodily nature, its personal history, its cultural inheritance, its national heritage. Shifting the load forms an indispensable part of the self's passing into a new phase or act: something must be brought to the top of the heap as appropriate to the intended act. "Continuous ingredience" depends upon a reservoir of backlying mass that is not fully shaped in any one phase of act, to be sure, but which nonetheless is postured toward (rendered compossible with) any act that is aborning as its (the act's) internal condition; a reservoir which then receives into itself that act when it has died to the present, and in which that act will be held in potency for some new occasion.

From these remarks on background three generalizations may be evoked:

1. Formally, background refers to *recalcitrant limitation upon what can be genuinely entertained.* In the self's concrete continuity such limitation is always material: what I can say depends upon my appropriation of my language tradition, what I can do that requires bodily support (and what does not?) depends upon my body, etc.

2. Limitation by background is exercised in relation to fore-

[55] Cf. Merleau-Ponty, *The Phenomenology of Perception,* Part I, pp. 67-199.

[56] Cf. Owen Barfield ". . . In our own language alone, not to speak of its many companions, the past history of humanity is spread out in an imperishable map, just as the history of the mineral earth lies embedded in the layers of its outer crust." *History in English Words,* Foreword by W. H. Auden, (Grand Rapids: William B. Eerdmans Publishing Co., 1967), p. 18.

142

ground. (For example: the limitation of bodily nature upon a paramecium's "contemplation" of a food particle is not the limitation of bodily nature upon my perception of a Picasso canvas. Bodily background limits in both cases, but the *kind* of limitation varies with intention.)

3. To construe a cognitive scale from a base in the self's continuous ingredience (and thus from background as a polar element in entertainment) is to face the problem of *memory* in acute form, and especially the connection between memory and intention. For only through the inner workings of memory do we have access to the historical dimensions of background, yet the reliability of memory vests in the certitude of continuous ingredience. This matter must claim attention in the following chapter.

(2) *Foreground.* Neither the self nor any act to which the self is party has its being by simply "being there." To be is to "be toward" (Dilthey: *Fortgezogenwerden*).[57] To be a self is to be ordered by the will toward a certain direction, a certain perfection, a certain "finishing" (Aristotle: ἐντελεχέια); it is to be both a "something" in every present moment and a *policy* for being something that transcends the present moment in intention.

The meeting of strangers is commonly marked by smalltalk about their respective pasts, which is understandable for two reasons. (1) No present act can bear the full exposure of the self, to oneself or to another. One's background, however, is not one act but many; strictly speaking, background is not act at all, but a field of potency that is the residue of past acts. (2) The recapitulation of this background serves to show how the self organized, and was organized by, its former field. Yet in the latter point is found the reason why smalltalk about the past alone does not lead to real meeting. From another's background we can discern only in small measure the peculiar quality of his transcendence; we err to say he *is* the residue of past contents and circumstance. "Getting to know a person" means getting beyond smalltalk about past and present, to the intention he casts upon the future. Whoever does not meet a man at this

---

[57] Cf. Nietzsche: ". . . whoever discovered the land called 'mankind' also discovered the land called 'human future.'" *Zarathustra,* p. 253.

143

level of his being knows nothing deeply significant about him. Having met him "there," everything else about him is stamped with the unique quality of his own transcendence. He is seen no longer as a simple prolongment of his background, but rather is known in his surpassingness.

No doubt the world teems with men in whom the demands of vital background are so intense that any thought of foreground extending beyond a satiated stomach must appear a fatuous luxury.[58] Aristotle said that some leisure is essential to the contemplative-moral life. To this extent he was right: some transcendence of background is necessary in order to grasp the enormity and significance of foreground. The circularity of this problem has taken on vast cultural magnitude among overly leisured people in contemporary western societies. For many, wealth and psycho-analysis have conspired to reveal that despair of foreground is owing to a false appropriation of background, that repression of background leads to foreclosure of foreground, that the reflexive relation between foreground and background is tampered with or ignored only at the cost of personal disintegration. By personal disintegration is meant, among other things, the loss of transcendence afforded by "being-toward," the loss of thrust toward ends believed enactable and thus the withering of power to mobilize backlying resources.

Man has his being vouchsafed to him not as a possession but only as being-toward. The child offers perhaps the purest example of being-toward. His being is anticipatory and recollective, hardly one more than the other. His wild impatience for the next phase is matched in intensity only by the reliving of the past phase. Upon both he casts a spell of fancy, sometimes of imagination, augmenting the actual—and himself—by play. In due course he falls prey to the demonic fiction that being-toward has a datable, social and cultural terminus. He becomes a "man" and merely *is;* he loses the treasures of ontological "play." Thereafter background looms larger and foreground

[58] Gandhi is reported to have said: "To the millions who have to go without two meals a day the only acceptable form in which God dare appear is food." Quoted by Bernard E. Meland, *The Secularization of Modern Culture,* (New York, Oxford University Press, 1966), p. 113.

144

diminishes. *Senility* names the horror attaching to a virtual loss of foreground, and the ontological significance of *death* lies precisely in the shock it lays upon our sense of being-toward. Ontology cannot avoid the problem of being-toward the threatened end of being-toward.

Few notions, if any, have such variegated effect upon the sense of personal continuity as that of death. It may serve to shrink foreground, in which case it is correlated only with the bodily aspect of background. Or it may provoke the expansion of foreground, in which case background is opened afresh and seen in its extension beyond the bodily. We said that background exercises recalcitrant limitation upon our being. Yet in the notion of death there is a remarkable example of the power of foreground to amend limitation as well as to instance it. It is true that no intentional response can set aside the limiting force of bodily nature. However forceful and constant my intentions and whatever they may be, I shall die. Still, "being-toward" is not *eo ipso* a being-toward bodily continuity alone. With that we do not incant bodiless spirit *obenrecht von unten*. The shrinking of foreground by the "ontological shock" (Tillich) of death may serve to modify background and thereupon work reflexively upon a commensurately expanded foreground. And this may occur in several ways. One thinks of Pascal's "grandeur of misery": though crushed by the universe, man leans into a transcendence of what crushes him and of what is crushed (bodily continuity) by virtue of *consciousness*.[59] One thinks as well of that situation in which moral decision legislates the death of the decider, the situation in which one can save his "real" self only by perishing.[60] If we have our being in being-toward, that being-toward cannot—vis-à-vis background—be incapable of corruption or enhancement.

By these comments we hope only to suggest the vastness of man's potency of foreground, and also why the sense of this vastness is often weak. To speak in a grander ontological manner of "being-toward structures which expand backlying limitation" would be to strike a standpoint which the self's continuous

[59] *Pensées,* ed. Leon Brunschvicg, (Paris: Hachette, n.d.), Nr. 347.
[60] Cf. Erich Frank, *Philosophical Understanding and Religious Truth,* (New York: Oxford University Press, 1949), pp. 10ff.

ingredience affords less than full access. What we need to turn to now is the matrix of being-toward, the intentional life of the will. No tropistic feature of background, no mere nisus surviving the self's previous phase, intention is that act of man's will whereby he projects his being toward the future.

Intention is a term with a rich history, as it is an act with a rich reference. In scholastic realism "first intention" was understood as a thing's signification of its own real structure, and "second intentions" were held to be the modes of thinking about first intention. In Descartes the intentional object of the mind was no longer the "first intention" of the object but the object mentally intended. For Descartes this was an "objective" intention, without *being* the intention of the object. In subsequent idealism just that transition was made: the intention of the mind *qua* ideational was held to be the being of the object intended. It was Franz Brentano who returned intention to realistic footing,[61] and Edmund Husserl who made it a key-concept in phenomenological analysis. For both, intentional experience is experience in which one is conscious *of* something.[62]

"Consciousness of . . ." for Husserl indicated the essentially centrifugal direction of consciousness and thus its orientation to "world." To evade mere living of the world and thinking the world in the merely natural attitude, it is necessary to perform the *epoché,* the "reduction." The reduction seeks to make the lived world yield to reflexion, and thus is a process of putting the natural (customary) attitude "in parenthesis" (i.e., of robbing the world of the "theses" under which it is thought in the natural attitude). Thus the "objective" intentionality of consciousness is not so much a particular object as it is the outreach of consciousness beyond any apprehended particularity toward the larger field it (the particularity) is taken to adumbrate. In short, the intentionality of consciousness is "meaning."

[61] See Franz Brentano, *Psychologie du point de vue empirique,* trans. M. de Gandillac, (Paris: Aubier, 1944); Iére Partie, Livre II, Ch. 1, Sec. 5; pp. 101-104.
[62] See Edmund Husserl, *Ideas: General Introduction to Pure Phenomenology,* trans. W. R. Boyce Gibson (London: George Allen & Unwin Ltd., 1952), pp. 242-253; also *idem, Cartesian Meditations,* trans. Dorion Cairns, (The Hague: Martinus Nijhoff, 1960), pp. 31-33 (sec. 14).

The consciousness before which world is deployed, in *epoché*, is "pure consciousness." Only from pure consciousness, vested in transcendental Ego (which however is never immediately conscious of itself but only of its intentionality), can claims be made for the generalizability of meaning.

In common with some of the French phenomenologists (Thévenaz, Ricoeur, and to a lesser degree Merleau-Ponty), we agree with Husserl in the beginning and find ourselves quarreling with him at the end. For him the Archimedean point from which intentionality is construed, before which world is deployed, is pure consciousness. Passionately concerned to establish the centrifugality of consciousness in triumph over prevailing subjectivism and psychologism, he tended toward the opposite extremity: an objectivism of world secured in consciousness. For ourselves, we have rejected pure consciousness as the ". . . pure reference point for intentionality, to which the intentional object is present," in favor of active will.[63] Husserl ignored the fact that whether or not the *epoché* is performed is owing to the exercise of will. As we said earlier, one must *will* a radical beginning out of the *radix* of human selfhood itself; otherwise one is left to the linear centripetalism of subjectivism or the linear centrifugalism of objectivism. And one must take account too of these linear motions as themselves rooting in a modality of will, the ossified will, sedimented by custom and "everydayness" (Heidegger: *Alltäglichkeit*). That serves to remind us that, if pure consciousness is to be rejected, no less is "pure will."

In another context, when we come to discuss *symbol* (Chapter VI), Husserl's view of intentionality will be found useful indeed (intentionality: the outreach and inreach of a thing, the "something more"—than itself—that it focusses, symbolizes, or adumbrates for consciousness[64]). Presently *intention* is used to cover the self's complicity in the entertainment of incipient act; more generally, it refers to the "direction" in which the self's foreground lies. As the aim of incipient act and as the direction

[63] Cf. I. M. Bochenski, *Europäische Philosophie der Gegenwart* (Bern: A. Francke AG Verlag, 1951), p. 149.

[64] Cf. Philip Wheelwright, *The Burning Fountain*, (Bloomington: Indiana University Press, 1954), p. 18.

in which the self's foreground extends, intention is the work of envisaging and enacting will. The dynamics of intention in this sense must be examined before we can play upon the registers of symbolism.

When I genuinely intend an act, e.g., to open my office door, I thereby impose a pattern upon the environment in which the act is to occur. "Impose" implies "choose," for although backlying *vital* pattern (my need for air or exercise) may give a negative unity to the act when it occurs, the vital pattern does not necessarily specify the positive pattern through which the act is intended (e.g., I could open the window, or jump up and down, instead of opening the door).[65] With Austin Farrer we hold that intention *qua* intention operates at the level of "super-pattern," recognizing fully that limits to teleological pattern are set by the body, by nature, and sometimes by reason. Intention at this level is the aim of incipient act discretely entertained, or the teleological concentration of environing foreground, specifically focused.

If we look not at a specific project but at the broader field of intention, at something like the total environing foreground of the self's forward thrust, our attention is made possible only through an act of imagination. This is so because the greater is the need to convert the vast potentiality of an intentional field into some mode of actuality: to give some concrete representation of what is intended. Assuming then the at least partially "free" and teleological character of intention and its orientation toward the future, one can discern two quite different but related modes of operation whereby it carries our being-toward. The one can be called "the intention of dominant direction," the other "the intention of the specific project." These two modes of intention will be considered separately even though in concrete entertainment they are inseparable.

(a) The intention of dominant direction. It seems that no one intention can embrace the whole of a man's foreground, the whole of his being-toward. Are we to say then, that human intentions are atomistic spasms, referring only to the immediately

[65] Farrer deals at great length in Part II B (2) of *Finite and Infinite* with the relation of "vital" and "super" pattern in the self's unity. See especially Chs. XV and XVI.

148

next phase of operation? No, there are intentions that extend beyond the oncoming phase, and that function differently from those intentions which in part are bringing the oncoming phase into being.

At the beginning of this section we said that to be a self is to be ordered in a certain direction, to be both a something in every present moment and a "policy" for being something that transcends the present moment in intention. Dominant intention embraces "policy." Dominant intentions are not intentions in the sense of envisaging or purposing specific acts to be enacted; rather they constitute the policy for so intending. They are not formal objects of the will, as specific projects are. They are not in any ordinary sense "values," "ideals," or "principles," that we think *about*. Doubtless, they embody the self's sense of "importance," but in a non-discursive way. When we speak unstudiedly of a person's *self-image,* we refer to his dominant intention.[66]

Intention functions in many dimensions of the self's coming to be, not in foreground alone. There is however but one 'place' where intentions of dominant direction serve to concatenate specific contents, and that, in a reflex action, is in memory. Such concatenation is possible because the environing elements of memory are relatively fixed, both by their attachment to the self's personal history and by the "already happened" character of past events. But the environment of intentions of dominant direction in their reference toward the future is none other than the self's own internal life, so that the solicitation of these intentions into a policy of finality bespeaks a broad patterning of the will's directionality, of its being-toward. This means that intentions of dominant direction reflect 'master' concentrations of the will's directionality, of being-toward, alone. This judgment does not mean that the will can concentrate itself absolutely by supplying both *content* and form for its next phases. (If conceivable at all, that would require a-historical pure will.) But it does mean that I do not intend my being-toward *überhaupt* as I intend my next act (say, the writing of the following sentence), even though the next act must embody in some measure my being-toward.

[66] See the discussion of "master images" below, Ch. VI.

149

It is obvious that much remains to be said about intentions of dominant direction. Few dimensions of personal being display so directly (as this aspect of being-toward) the operation of what the Christian understands as revelation. Before that operation can come more directly into view it is necessary to examine the cognitive form which intentions of dominant direction assume in the mind, and the way in which they exert unremitting pressure upon the will's particular intentions and active existence. Moreover, we have yet to reckon with discontinuous ingredience and so the re-directing power of events and other agencies upon the will's directionality. We have our being in being-toward, but other beings have their being-toward towards us among other things; and "meeting" in the community of being-toward cannot leave our being-toward unaffected. When all these matters have got into the picture we will be in a better position to ask the question that is crucial for an understanding of revelation, how the self's being-toward is informed when it is not altogether self-informed.

(b) The intention of the specific project. The explication of intending a specific project calls for much less elaboration since this mode of intention is more directly in evidence. What is not so commonly appreciated is the fact that every specified or specifiable project is preceded and made possible by a multitude of lesser projects which, at least in relation to the analytical equipment possessed by the mind, have insufficient isolability to be called "specific" projects. For example, if I intend to catch the 10:20 train, an innumerable host of lesser projects are set in motion, which is true as well of the immediately succeeding (isolable) act, viz., reaching for my hat. No real light is shed upon the "least" project by our bio-psychological friend, who tells us it is the sending of brain signals along nerve-routes of motor response, or whatever. He does tell us something valuable (although we already knew it), that our intention of a specific project involves other projects that we do not specifically intend. That he does not tell us more is owing to the radical relativity of projects *qua* intended. We spoke of "catching the 10:20" as a specific project, and so it is in relation to lesser projects leading to and compounded in it. But relative to my intention to buy a book in Adler's at 12:30, a superseding specific intention, "catching the 10:20" is a lesser project. My intention to buy the book subserves my intention to read it, my intention to read it subserves . . . However, the relativity of projects is not a simple linear, or horizontal, relativity. They are "vertically" relative as well, since they are related to intentions of dominant direction. Of this relation it can be said that intentions of dominant direction are the motivating intentions of one's specifically intended projects. Hence the truth of Husserl's insight, cast in our terms, that intentions of dominant direction are recoverable only from lived experience.

The distinction we have drawn between the intention of specific projects and intentions of dominant direction shows certain similarities to Husserl's distinction between "intentionality of act" and "operating intentionality" (*fungierende Intentionalität*). "Intentionality of act" he considers as the basis of conceptual (theoretical) judgment and of voluntarily, consciously adopted positions. It is the equivalent, *mutatis mutandis,* of what we have called intention of specific projects, since it concerns the presence in consciousness of discrete objects or projects. Perhaps it could be said that it concerns the correlation of specific consciousness and specified object. In "operating intentionality," however, we have to do (in Merleau-Ponty's words) with ". . . the natural and antepredicative unity of the world and of our life, being apparent in our desires, our evaluations and in the landscape we see, more clearly than in objective knowledge, and furnishing the text which our knowledge tries to translate into precise language."[67] So described, "operating intentionality" is similar to intentions of dominant direction in two respects. (1) The self's dominant being-toward is "antepredicative"; what is dominantly intended is both logically and temporally prior to explicit qualification. The only manifestation of intention in this mode is what one is able to derive, or reduce, from an exegesis of lived experience. (2) Intentions of dominant direction have two-fold reference, opening to each other two vast fields of potentiality: the self's quasi-patterned memory contents and its quasi-patterned envisagement of the future.[68]

[67] Merleau-Ponty, *The Phenomenology of Perception,* xviii.
[68] Paul Ricoeur (and before him, Max Scheler) sees in the consciousness of "fault" the profound personal unity of the two temporal

Of the "moment of potency" in the self's continuous ingredience enough has been said for the time being. Our being is active being, but activity depends upon a reservoir of potentiality made ready through entertainment. "Making ready" refers to the focussing of the self's background and foreground upon those acts aborning that bear the self. Such entertainment is by no means always conscious; but then, no one supposes his ontic continuity to depend entirely upon conscious attention. No doubt, full continuity harbors within itself a commensurately full entertainment of which, in the nature of the case, we cannot become fully conscious. Full self-consciousness of full entertainment would require the postulation of an a-social, a-historical self. We have called attention to the function of *limit* in entertainment, but we have not developed a sociology of entertainment, a politics of entertainment, etc. Rather we have emphasized what pertains to the self's *unique* onticity. Without engaged entertainment, the marshalling of pertinent foreground to relevant background, no "event" emerges as the bearer of the self's unique continuity. To be sure, the self may deliver its background over to custom and instinct and its foreground over to ideology or phantasy; in that case the self continues, in a weak sense, but it relinquishes the distinctively human mode of being by refusing to enact its own uniqueness.

Having marked the structures of entertainment, we have taken care to note that consciousness flags at the point of what *fills* the structures: from background only memory and from

---

ecstasies (Heidegger's *Ekstasen*), past and present. "The forward *élan* of the project becomes overlaid with retrospection, while the distressed, remorseful contemplation of the past is combined with the certitude of possible regeneration; the project, enriched by memory, re-emerges as repentance . . . the future attempts to encompass the past, self-discovery shows itself as a recovery, and consciousness uncovers in itself a thickness or destiny which would not be recognized by a reflection attentive only to the forward *élan* of the project." Moreover, this joining together of the temporal "ecstasies" in the core of freedom ". . . manifests the total and undivided casuality of the self over and above its individual acts." "While it is a question of a reflection attentive to projects alone, this causality divides itself in bits and fritters itself away in a disjunctive inventing of myself; but in penitent retrospection I root my acts in the undivided causality of the self." *Fallible Man*, xxvi-xxviii. Cf. also Max Scheler on "Repentance and Rebirth," *On the Eternal in Man*, pp. 33–65, *passim*.

152

foreground only intention have been discriminated for attention and further study. From these phases of the moment of potency we turn now to the active moment of the self's continuous ingredience.

(3) *Concentration.* If entertainment brings two vast fields of potency into ever sharper compossibility, with respect to an envisaged event, "concentration" specifies (we might even say, incarnates) foreground and background by bringing the event to actuality. Concentration refers to the active process whereby phases of the self's continuity are unified or embodied in concrete act. Concentration must not be confused here with rigorous advertence of mind. It refers not to a marshalling of mental faculties for purposes of attention or appreciation, but to the focusing of diverse contents in a unifying, actual pattern. (However, just such a pattern is the basis of all rational abstraction). As the term itself suggests, concentration signifies the bringing together of elements around a common center.

The self, we said, is a one and a many. What ontological thinking attains in considering the self's unity is its structural complication, its manyness, whose formality we have cataloged in part. Yet, as Plato concluded in the *Parmenides,* rational consideration of the "many" is possible only on the assumption of its infusion by a "one," even though the unity may be minimal and the discernment of it may be imprecise. The forward thrust of the self's continuity embraces a scale of concentrations, ranging from near chaos of contents (for example) in the lowest grade of memory and in the furthest reach of intention to a fully actual pattern of contents in any present act.[69] (a) There is the continuous concentration of selfhood into unity. (b) There is the concentration of the self's act by which its unity is borne. (c) And there is the concentration of *events,* the meeting and instancing of the self's unity in concert with that of objects. Concentration thus occurs in different ontological modes, differing according to the dimensions of being concentrated, and no one can serve for all.

We have already implied that (a) above can be approached only by means of (b) and (c). When we think about *the* concentrated unity of the self, we catch it only with the tail of the

[69] Cf. Austin Farrer, *Finite and Infinite,* espec. Chs. XVII–XIX.

eye. We cannot think abstractly the ontic *unum* of the self, only its structural complication.

Here is a truth about the self inexhaustibly profound in its implications. The being of the self is such that it cannot be concentrated in any one existential phase. If we look at the existential phase, we can do so in two fundamentally different ways. With Kierkegaard one can call attention to the rational impentrability of such a concrete phase. Or one can take distance on the phase by analysis and abstraction, elaborating the structural nexus in which it occurs. The former way, if not made the first rung in an "existentialist philosophy," relies on the "indirect communication" of concentrated selfhood in the arts. The latter way, if not made the first rung in an "essentialist philosophy," saves concentrated selfhood from evaporating into a merely abstract concept of existence detached from the essence of the self, viz. freedom. We have opted for the latter in order to cast light on the former—in a way that it cannot illuminate itself. Specifically, we seek access to the imagination in the constitution of personal being as a prelude to understanding the bodying forth of concentrated selfhood in the imaginative prehensions of the arts, scripture, etc.

Concentration, then, is not a *structure* at any level; it is the making actual of the unity of structures in any act or event to which the self is party and in which the concrete being of the self is made manifest. Insofar as a vast background of potency is narrowed (and likewise foreground) in pertinence to an emerging event, concentration is already at work. Thus what can be said of concentration in continuous ingredience has already been said; what more can be said will be the underside of the structure to come shortly in view, the self and discontinuous ingression, specifically in connection with "the other," and "event."

It has been our concern to elaborate the ontological truth that the self's concentration of its active being it not a closed affair. The concentration of re-enacted past and intended future in the self's present act is not the long-distance pastime of a remote and static nature; it is the act of a being whose life is just such activity. Our being is not handed us as a piece of cloth with a stamped pattern, to be stitched in according to in-

154

structions: to be rewarded, out of funded ontological largesse, with the right to embroider a curlicue of our own. (One thinks of those hideous, soul-destroying color-books for children, with pictures divided into sections and a color designated for each.) Man concentrates and is concentrated, situates amidst situations. The elaboration of this point will lead us into discontinuous ingression.

The self situates itself through concentration, but into any concentrated act enter factors that are themselves situated. The relevant aspects of the past are re-enacted in the enactment (concentration) of a present act; but the re-enacted past is ontologically distinct from the actual past, and concentration has to join actual past with my re-enactment of the past, else present act loses its continuity and historicity. Intended future is cast upon present act through concentration, but intended future is ontologically distinct from the future that will fall out. The actual future will fall out in ways I cannot now intend, and when it falls out in enactment it will have "background" to which even now I and countless others are contributing. Thus the concentration of present act can neither bear the full weight of the future nor hold in tow the whole train of the past. The background and foreground of the self exceed any of its concentrated existential phases; which means that any present act, in which the self is concentrated, is in principle incapable of bearing selfhood entire. As every present act takes into itself some of the strivings of the past, so it strives itself for "more," so far as the self is concerned. It furnishes no abiding place or permanent time for the being of the self, which must ever concentrate itself afresh. As Emil Fackenheim has written of present act: "Its return-upon-itself is never absolute, but fragmented by the loss of a past which it cannot recapture, and by the refractoriness of a future which refuses to be subdued into presentness. It is, in short, a returning-upon-itself within the limits of a *situation*."[70]

It is to the *situation* of the self that we now turn.

[70] Emil L. Fackenheim, *Metaphysics and Historicity*, p. 42. In the matters under consideration I am greatly indebted to this profound and tightly argued essay.

155

D. The Self and Discontinuous Ingression

Ontological thinking cannot uncover or recover a moment when the self is unsituated, as it cannot find a moment when the self *is* a situation. The being of the self is always enacted and thus discovered in a situation of interaction. We may consider the situation of the self, its in-formation, under two heads, that of the "other," and that of "event."

(1) The "other." I may indeed bracket the "other" out of view, refuse it my complicity, regard it *ohne mitzumachen* (as Husserl said). Thus we have attempted to see the self's procession from an internal vantage, from the standpoint of continuous ingredience. But reflexive attention to such continuity disclosed that, while complicity with world was evaded at one level, the "other" reasserted itself at another. The background of personal continuity could not be discussed without recourse to what fills background up: nature, history, language, etc. While any one "point" in the self's being yields a plurality of dimensions to analysis, and while access to these dimensions will require the rational use of brackets, we can gain no purchase on a point at which our being is only being *pour soi*. Our being is ceaselessly *pour soi* and *pour autrui:* we enter ingrediently into the being of the other, and the other enters ingrediently into our being (Heidegger: *Mitsein*). Moreover, being-for-itself and being-for-the-other cannot be simply juxtaposed, as though being human were split into two parallel tracks on the cross-ties of fate. Continuity is not exclusively a function of myself *pour soi* nor is discontinuity exclusively a function of myself *pour autrui*. I *am* toward myself and toward the other.

Again, the self's sense of concrete reality is owing both to the power of the will to modify and its power to suffer modification. The suffering of modification, the *situation* of the will, is our present concern. The will encounters limitation not of its own making; not all limitation is reducible to self-limitation.[71]

---

[71] German idealism was obsessed with the program of construing the other as a species of self-limitation, a program that becomes understandable only in the light of its historical setting. (In German metaphysical idealism, notably in Fichte, limitation as essentially self-limitation was accounted an achievement of transcendental imagination. For an elaboration of this theory, see Appendix III below, "Imagina-

In order to walk I must concentrate numerous possibilities into act, but I do not concentrate the wall that sets a limit upon my walking.

In respect to its limiting or situating power, under what form does the other "give" itself? This is an exceptionally complex question; it involves, as we shall see shortly, the order of events. For the moment we distinguish two ways in which the "other" gives itself.

(a) Delineated or focal actuality. By an object or "other" we commonly mean in Husserl's phrase, "the embodied self-presence of an individual object."[72] The other in this sense is sharply delineated and concretely given. My immediate field of otherness is narrowed and focalized in the typewriter before me. Without some such focalization of field the will has no stuff on which to work concretely and by which to be limited concretely, the senses have no thing in and of which to grasp a pattern. No field of otherness makes a concrete difference without focalizing itself, without narrowing itself into some delineated actuality.

---

tion and Creativity.") Romantic philosophy was out, at all costs, to remove the tyranny exercized by the merely natural "other" over moral selfhood in Enlightenment naturalism. According to romantic idealism, what the self makes cannot pose an ultimate threat to moral selfhood; thus the world is posited (situated) by the ego as the stuff on which moral agency is exercised, and in relation to which the self achieves consciousness of its own being. (Cf. *J. G. Fichtes Sämtliche Werke*, hrsg. I. H. Fichte, [II Vols.; Berlin: Veit und Comp., 1845–1846], Bd. I, pp. 171–175; also Bd. V, p. 185.) In this program there reposes, I think, an egregious ontological misapprehension and a profound ontological insight. An error, because it robs the "other" of that intransigent resistance whereby the self is brought toward *ontological* maturation (or disintegration, as the case may be), and not merely toward *consciousness* of being already in principle complete. A profound insight because, when the other enters into the ontological constitution of the self it loses some of its otherness. Terms that are really related cannot, *qua* related, be absolutely "other" to each other. (This point should be set in correlation with note 10 above.) If the other absolutely situates all self-making, if the will's situating in no way situates the situation, man is simply an episode of environment. The error of idealism was to break the dialectical relation between self-situating and the situation of self-situating in favor of the self's absolute transcendence-of-situation. It was correct only in disallowing the breach of relation in favor of the self's absolute immanence-in-situation, such as obtains in naturalism. (Cf. Fackenheim, *Metaphysics and Historicity*, p. 45)

[72] Husserl, *Ideas*, p. 127.

(b) Dormant or penumbral actuality. Notwithstanding what has just been said, common sense empiricism errs in its assumption that a concretely delineated "other" exhausts the field of otherness.[73] In apprehension a focal object is girt about with a zone of actuality that is dormant or penumbral. One cannot so sharply apprehend any delineated object as to be free of the marginal zone that surrounds it. The typewriter before me is focalized, but not without reference to its "zone." If I shift attention to the zone of the typewriter, it is no longer that zone or even a zone at all, but the book lying on the table, which in turn is girt about by another field of dormant actuality. This means that any concrete actuality is given to the self against the backdrop of actuality undisclosed and unasserted in the mode of focal actuality. Every delineated "other" concentrates a field that exceeds it in actual range, yet the excess operates as a disturbance to and limitation upon my active concern only through the focalization that the delineated other affords. In some focal objects the "opening" upon fields of otherness may be so small as to escape notice. In other focal objects the size of aperture may pose no problem, but the quality of otherness may be such as not to modify the will. (The typewriter before me hardly propels me toward intercourse with *omnitudo realitatis!*) Not all focal objects function symbolically or metaphorically;

[73] The temptation to cite Bergson and Whitehead in support of this judgment probably had best be resisted. It is true that Bergson mounted a powerful attack on the 'simple location' of actuality; and that Whitehead was no less trenchant in his rejection of that "vacuous actuality" which is the space-time of putative "actual entities." (On the latter see *Process and Reality*, p. 43ff.) In our own terms we can agree too that delineated actuality by itself is "abstract." (i) However concrete the perception, it is grasped under figurations (e.g., I perceive blood under certain scientific models, not as fluid mana). (ii) It is abstract in relation to its environing field of penumbral actuality. But of course Whitehead had a great deal more than this in mind, as did Bergson.

A distinction similar to the one drawn here between delineated/focal and dormant/penumbral actuality will be found in Husserl, who develops the matter in the course of explaining his special use of the term *cogito*. (*Ideas*, pp. 116–22.) ". . . The stream of experience can never consist wholly of focal actualities. . . ." (p. 118). "If one is turned toward some matter in appreciation, the apprehension of the matter is no doubt included in the total attitude; but it is not the *mere* matter in general, but the matter of *valuation*. . . . Not merely the *representing of the matter* in question, but also the *appreciating* which includes this representing, has the modus of actuality" (p. 122).

at least, the symbolic function of some is minimal. Whenever symbolic reference is cognitively rich, the imagination is actively at work; for imagination 'cracks' the focalized boundaries of the delineated object, gaining access to a field of actuality that was, from the perspective of the closed object in rational or sensuous apprehension, merely dormant, but now is, through the active reflexivity of imagination, a vivacious stimulant to and limitant upon the will.

Let us consider an example of the interlacing of delineated and penumbral regions. Ordinarily the Olivetti typewriter on which I write these words affords a very small opening upon its backlying field; it is rather just a component in that concrescence through which my thought enters the public domain. Ordinarily it makes no difference to my will (save when, often enough, it consorts with demons in conspiracy against composition!). I can of course piece together bits of information and personal observation, connect them to the typewriter, and make projections. I read of miners killed in a Ruhr mine disaster: do I type on a spadeful of ore from the hands of one of the stricken, and so does my typewriter concentrate in some minimal fashion the tragic loss experienced by those dear to him? Or do I type on the carcass of a carbonized mastodon, perhaps the trunk of a primeval tree, and so have before me the concentration of millions of years of natural process? I see passing through Rome boxcars of peasants fleeing unspeakable poverty in the land of the *Mezzogiorno,* bound for the industrial north. Did some wind up in Ivrea to work in the Olivetti factory, and do I type on a concentration of their aspirations? We may as well call a halt: fanciful rumination will yield at most only a slightly greater respect for the typewriter, hardly any alteration of volitional pattern. Still, everything depends upon the particular focal actuality and the power of consciousness to grasp it as the spearhead of its penumbral field. One thinks of Proust's lowly tea cup in *Swann's Way*! Or one thinks of the Negro child stealing coal along a railroad track—and the enormous field of familial-social-economic degradation held in tow by such an act, a field that is binding on any moralist worthy of the name.

Some conclusions emerge. First, deeply significant thought

159

is occasioned in the modification of the will by focal actuality. The grandest systems rest on such delineated incursions of the "other" as the wailing of a hungry child, the eruption of a volcano, the rise of a demagogue to power, an act of human compassion, the blooming of a flower. Second, while no limiting "other" can perspectivize the whole of Being, it can lead the mind, shaken from its customary attachments, to a field of otherness exceeding itself in quality and power. This is better known by artists than philosophers, and best of all by poets. Third, as we have already noted, the limiting other is by no means limited to such things as Dr. Johnson's stone. The command of a sentry at the Brandenburg Gate, my children's trust in me, cannibal cells in my bloodstream, the loss of economic fortune, God's intention for my existence: otherness is a many-splendored, if splintered, thing.

In addition to the distinction between delineated and penumbral actuality, we may note two characteristics possessed by the "other" in either mode. Whitehead puts them succinctly: "Two conditions must be fulfilled in order that an entity may function as an object in a process of experiencing: (i) the entity must be antecedent, and (ii) the entity must be experienced in virtue of its antecedence; it must be given. Thus an object must be a thing received, and must not be either a mode of reception or a thing generated in that occasion. Thus the process of experiencing is constituted by the reception of objects into the unity of that complex occasion which is the process itself. The process creates itself, but it does not create the objects which it receives as factors in its own nature."[74]

(2) "Event." Whitehead's "the unity of that complex occasion which is the process itself" is very close to what was discriminated earlier as the third level of concentration, viz., "event." An event (strictly, an *historical* event) to which the self is party is itself a concentration of subsidiary (or antecedent) concentrations; it is a concrete interaction of the self's various phases brought into focus and (who knows how many?) objects with their various phases brought into focus. An event does not constitute or generate these ontologically antecedent (subsidiary) phases, even though events are the bearers of

[74] *The Adventures of Ideas,* pp. 180–181.

160

these phases. Rather the event is constituted, *qua* event, by the interaction of ontologically antecedent concentrations. Events therefore have not the ontic continuity, say, of the self (i.e., an event is not a term). Events instance the "life" of the self (and that of objects too, for that matter); but what continuity they have is coextensive with the novel potentiality they open up: with their residue being taken up into the continuous ingredience of the self, into the background and foreground of the self as these will constellate afresh in some new event. [It will be noticed how we diverge from the Thomistic-realistic scheme here. To be sure, in its subsidiary concentrations the self progressively reduces potentiality to an act. But full-blooded act, the event in which the self brings its being (and likewise that of objects) to public manifestation, replenishes potentiality anew. The continuity of the self in connection with events is thus a lived dialectic between the reduction of new potency to act and the reduction of new act to potency.]

Let us consider the simplest event we can conceive, the interaction of two parties, the self and an object—which of course may be another person. (An ideal case to be sure: no event is so simple.) Such an event is like the meeting of two icebergs; the first and most extensive contact is between the masses below the surface of the water. The visible peaks remain at a distance from each other. Now we commonly take the intercourse of the "peaks" to exhaust the event; i.e., the intercourse of the two delineated actualities. That is because we are commonly given over to ratiocination (specifically, abstraction) and sensation under the dominion of ratiocination. The side-by-sideness of discrete actualities is, if not *ens rationis,* at least in part an achievement of rational abstraction.[75] The real order of an event is not however side-by-sideness, but interaction, the entering of each into the other under the form of ingredient. This too is a matter of common experience. We commonly go through substantial stretches of time and space, in Cudworth's phrase, with "only half a cogitation."[76] Our experience frequently is un-

---

[75] I shall deal with this in the following chapter under II., C., 3.
[76] Ralph Cudworth, *The True Intellectual System of the Universe,* (3 vols.; London: T. Tegg, 1845), Vol. I, p. 247. Cf. also Leibniz's doctrine of "petites perceptions": G. W. Leibniz, *New Essays Con-*

marked by the delineated presence either of ourselves or discrete objects. Our experience is no less eventful for that; we might even say it is more properly eventful for that. For an event is the interaction of the submerged mass (in our extremely simple case) of the self and that of the object, the 'background' and 'foreground' of both self and object as they are presented (in the double sense: pre-sent and pres-ent) to each other.

E. Manhood Finished and Unfinished, and the Classical Ontological Categories

Earlier it was said that the self is borne by an ontological situation that exceeds itself, but that selfhood so borne is not, owing to its own situating activity, a merely subphenomenal feature of that situation. What the self concretely is, we said, emerges as the self's active existence takes its situating course through those situations comprising its destiny. Subsequently these judgments were expanded by way of reflecting upon structural features of the will's continuous ingredience and discontinuous ingression. These reflections may now be brought to a head by developing them in relation to certain classical ontological categories, as these categories pertain to being man.

(1) "Form." What in human being is finished; is not open to decision, but rather is the foundation on which all decision rests?

To attempt an answer to this question is to join the venerable controversy concerning the status of 'form' and 'essence' in human being. Aristotelian realism has an answer ready to hand. Within the order of time, according to that tradition, actual entities change because they are complexes combining a "nature' and a matter that can express it. While the actual entity changes, its nature, or form, does not.[77] Change means the instantiation

---

cerning Human Understanding, trans. A. G. Langley (New York: The Macmillan Co., 1896), pp. 47–48.

[77] Aristotle says explicitly of substance that ". . . its form does not come to be." ". . . Form or substance is not produced, but the concrete thing which gets its name from this is produced, and . . . in everything which is generated matter is present, and one part of the thing is matter and the other form." Metaphysica, Book Z, Chs. 8–9, 1033b, 15–1034b, 10; McKeon, pp. 794–96.

of form that is possible in connection with a certain matter. The condition of change therefore is something unchanged and unchanging, which is form. Aristotle says of a concrete substantial entity that ". . . there must exist beforehand in complete reality another [primary] substance [i.e., form] which produces it."[78] By this Aristotle does not mean that form exists as self-subsistent substances in a separate sphere,[79] but rather that in informed things form is the unmodifiable (primary) nature in relation to which things are modified. In the *De Anima* he expresses this by saying that form has "two grades of actuality," the one referring to the "essential whatness" (fixity of nature) of a thing and the other to the employment or operation of "essential whatness" (comparable to knowledge and the exercise of knowledge).[80] All activity in the thing, therefore, is an illustration of the scope which its form permits; it is ". . . in the direction of fixity or nature."[81]

It will be apparent that we are at loggerheads with this tradition, and indeed with all classical ontologies in which the primary being of the self consists in a form secured against expansion and contraction. Unquestionably, every structure of selfhood is presided over by a certain formality, else structure would be nothing to which reflexive consciousness could gain access. But personal form as such is no mere structure; it is rather only the *limit* on a phase or dimension of the self's being. "Limit" is of course a metaphor for an aspect of the phase; and doubtless other metaphors need to be invoked, according to what the phase is, in order to express what classically has been called "form."[82] "Rhythm," "habit," "situation," "destiny;" all refer to aspects of continuity and ingression.

[78] *Ibid.*, Book Z, Ch. 9, 1034b, 15–20; McKeon, p. 797. The brackets are mine.
[79] *Ibid.*, Book Z, Ch. 8, 1033b, 28; McKeon, p. 795.
[80] *De Anima,* Book II, Ch. 1, 412a, 10–412b, 15; McKeon, pp. 554–55.
[81] *Ibid.*, Book II, Ch. 5, 417b, 10–15; McKeon, pp. 565–66.
[82] Of course, "form" itself is a metaphor in the root usage of the realistic tradition. If I think like an Aristotelian I say: "There is a chair. What does it mean to know it? Obviously, I can't get the chair itself into my mind: the wood won't translate into consciousness. So I will take in what is incorporeal about it, its 'form.' With its form in mind, I will *be* the chair *metaphorically,* i.e., know it."

163

All these metaphors have the ring of "limit" in them. Yet "limit," detached from any ontic phase of selfhood, is intrinsically ambiguous. Consider the limitation of the will by its natural situation. What nature limits is not myself simply *qua* natural being. Nature limits my historicity; paralysis of limbs would limit not only my bodily movement but all my historical attachments, family and friends, all "doing" that involves me. Nature is experienced under the aspect of historicity, and is to that extent *qua* limitant not "purely natural."[83] Even so, the limitation of nature cannot be refined out of historicity.[84]

Or consider the will as limited by its historical situation, narrowed, for purposes of exemplification, to the way one is situated by his own past. Youth was rich with possibilities of development in many directions. Some were chosen, some excluded, and in it all there was limitation by personal aspiration, family circumstance, the counsel of elders, etc. *Now* I cannot will that state of innocence into being as my being; even when I "remember" such a state I cannot leap over the intervening developments that have actually fallen out. I am increasingly situated by my past situating: and there is no way in which I can absolutely situate my past situating. Decisions count for the decider beyond the moment in which they occur, they limit the field of subsequent decision for the decider. This does not mean

[83] One may satisfy himself on this score by studying the history of the concept of "nature" in Western thought. R. G. Collingwood is only partially correct in his judgment that only in recent times has nature been construed on the model of history. (See *The Idea of Nature,* [Oxford: The Clarendon Press, 1945].) If history refers to the order of human act *qua* human, this judgment must be qualified. In the predominant Greek view nature was construed on the model of a gigantic vital organism of which God was the Soul, but this model itself was extrapolated from the human psycho-physical organism. In early modern times nature was construed on the model of a cosmic machine of which God was the retired inventor and mechanic; but this model itself was patterned on man as a mechanical body inhabited by an alien spirit. Nineteenth-century voluntaristic idealism viewed nature as the cosmic sounding-board of moral action, and God as the harmonizer of its discordant tones; but this model was extrapolated from man's alleged situation of reality in the interest of moral freedom and maturation.

[84] Evelyn Waugh's *The Loved One,* (Boston: Little, Brown and Co., 1948), is a biting satire on that special form of wasted human ingenuity which expends itself on denying the limitations of nature.

164

that the development of personal being is accompanied by a steady decrease of freedom, but rather that in the temporal constitution of personal being freedom is modalized.[85] The formation of dominant intentions, of a policy for the use of freedom; the exercise of such a policy upon possibilities; the specific patterning of actuality resulting from such exercise: all are modalities of the self's freedom. But my freedom limits my freedom; past exercise limits present exercise. My be-coming cannot ignore what I have become. "Character" may be shaken, dominant direction may be challenged and re-directed, but not without reference to background; there is no starting again from scratch.

Even so, my historical situation limits me in a way different from the way my natural situation limits my historicity. For my former self does not lie there in the past as a stone lies in geological history. The past self thought is somehow also the present self thinking. Goethe reminds us that what is inherited must be re-earned in order to be possessed.[86] What lies there in the past, my own and that of the race, is human action; just as re-earning and therefore situating that past is itself human action.[87] The past limits, but not as an object "back there"; it limits both in the way of historical fate, and in the way of my re-earning it through my own act. History, both before and after me, can only be said to have a flexible form.

We are unable, then, to find a "founding charter," a fixed form for being human. There doubtless are limits, to transgress which takes one out of humanity (and into, say, bestiality). These limits are not however codified in a charter secured against time. Even if there were such a charter, we would not know ourselves from reading it, anymore than one could know the contemporary United States from reading its 18th century Constitution. Only in bestiality does man live under the power of fixed form, of rigid limit, of unchanging rhythm, of un-

[85] Cf. Farrer, *Finite and Infinite,* Ch. XVI.

[86] *Faust,* Erster Teil, lines 682–83: "*Was du ererbt von deinen Vätern hast, Erwirb es, um es zu besitzen!*"

[87] Cf. Emil L. Fackenheim, *Metaphysics and Historicity,* 52–53; also Erich Frank, *Philosophical Understanding,* p. 117, and p. 133, n. 2.

modified charter; which is to say, only insofar as he fails distinctively human being.[88] The higher entities stand in an ascending scale of finitude, the more impossible it is to account both for the richness of their being and the knowledge we have of them on the basis of their forms alone. For inanimate things and the lower forms of life perhaps the Aristotelian-Thomistic doctrine may be adequate: to know a thing is to be, in an intellectual way, the form of its operation (thus "concept" is "intellected form"). But this formula cannot obtain without remainder for human being, in which form assumes an open-endedness and thus cannot be known under the "concept" alone.

(2) "Essence." It might be said with some justification that the account so far neglects the classic intentionality of "essence." To form, essence adds the notion of teleological or valuational scope. Form as limiting pattern indeed cannot embrace all that will actually fall under its limitation. But it can refer *qua* essence, some voices will be heard to say, to the reservoir of possibilities, to all *possible* existential embodiments that can be described in universal terms.[89] Thus essence would refer to "the aggregate of all that really pertains to the inner structure of a thing,"[90] to that in an individual thing which can also be instantiated in another individual thing and in "the broadest generalities of essential being."[91] Thus essence would be a fund of possible characters, as appropriate to given form; it would refer not to what I am actually but what I can be actually.

[88] It would be interesting to pursue the thesis that the "discovery" of the open-endedness of human being and the "discovery" of human sexuality have been coincident discoveries in late modern times. In subhuman animals there is a strict formality, and therefore an absolute periodicity, about the sexual instinct: a formality that goes with a severely limited mode of being. In man, sexuality is not limited to built-in periodicity. To be sure there is in man (and not alone in woman) a vestige of periodicity in sexual instinct; but it is there only as a bodily bias to the will. Because sexuality in man is subject to importuning and restraint beyond the demands of periodicity, it is a vehicle of his open-ended being—whether in an enhancing or in a pathological way.

[89] Cf. Thomas Aquinas, *Concerning Being and Essence,* trans. George C. Leckie, (New York: Appleton-Century-Crofts, Inc., 1937), pp. 7–15; also Farrer, *Finite and Infinite,* p. 250.

[90] Scheeben, *Nature and Grace,* p. 31.

[91] Husserl, *Ideas,* pp. 53–54.

166

As we have taken form as "limit," in the case of human being, so essence has been taken as 'historical freedom' (with the special connotation of 'goal'). That requires a severe qualification of the account of essence immediately above. My own acts, and the acts of others upon me, are not simply actualizations of pre-established possibility; the formation of personal *character* is not reducible to the instantiation of universal characters. From the concrescence of background and foreground, in personal being, ontologically novel possibility emerges. For personal being, possibility has a history. Essence, then, is in a state of constant refunding. This is to say that in the concrete course of historical existence form and essence exert a modifying relation upon each other. As Farrer has put the matter, ". . . in the process by which essence gets its blanks filled, further enduring characters are added." But this means as well that form is expanded; ". . . the charter of our being receives additional clauses."[92] When we say then that man is in one respect unfinished, we mean that his *being* is unfinished, and not merely that no moment of his existence can bear the full freight of his essence (although that is meant too).

Of course form and essence are not entities. They are "heard" as "overtones" (or as Professor Urban says, "co-implicates") of any concrete phase of the self's being. To play the metaphor out, they are tones of the eschatalogically "whole" self, the self that survives and precedes the discrete notes from bar to bar. But in gaining access to this larger reference there is no expunging the concrete phase, no overtone without the striking of a note. Thus there is no deducing of essence from form, or *vice versa*. Were this not the case there would be no accounting for centuries of ontological reflection on the problems under study. The form and essence of selfhood have to be apprehended ever anew in relation to the self's expanding ontic environment.

(3) "Essential form." If we grasp ourselves as ontologically unfinished, we do so in relation to the self's situating and being situated, as described hitherto.[93] Likewise, we grasp ourselves as

[92] Farrer, *Finite and Infinite,* p. 251.

[93] In recent paragraphs I have laid a heavier emphasis upon the unfinished character of human being (than upon the finished) because this is the character classical ontologies have tended to ignore or deny.

finished; for we are finished by whatever situates us radically; by tongue, national heritage, social position, genes, metabolism rate, etc. However, the ontological instability of man, his being unfinished, has just now been under consideration at another level, that of the mutually modifying relation between form and essence. Is there a sense in which man's being can be spoken of as finished at *this* level? If man's being is both coincident and noncoincident with itself at every level, the answer must be affirmative; i.e., that, in any phase of the self's being, there is a finished relation between form and essence appropriate to the phase, but with which the self is noncoincident. Let us lay aside the phenomenological clarification of this affirmation for subsequent investigation, and turn to the issue it raises, that of 'essential form,' of being finished in a transsituational sense.

One might distinguish two ways of apprehending essential form, the one primarily negative, the other primarily positive. (a) Metaphorically, essence may be seen as the outer boundary of freedom and form as the sentry patrolling this boundary. To ignore the sentry's call for identification and step across the boundary would be to fall out of human being into some other kind of being. Much has been made in existentialistic philosophies of those "boundary situations" that turn the self in upon itself; but much more significant is that *transgression* of boundary that forces the self into recognition of noncoincidence with itself. The apprehension that one has ceased to be what he is, to know the filling only from the void (hence the importance of "nothingness"), is a powerful though *via negativa* witness to self-transcendence as founded on essential form.[94]

(b) No philosopher of note has ever been able to state the positive way without entering upon metaphysical theology. The positive way is the apprehension of the fully actual ground of the unity between form and essence, God. How such an apprehension comes about, how augmented, supported, and commended: these are all functions of a particular metaphysical system. Since

[94] Nietzsche: "I am under more obligation to thank my failures than any of my successes. . . . I know more of life because I have so often been on the point of losing it. . . ." *La Gaia Scienza,* IV, 303; in *Joyful Wisdom,* trans. Thomas Common, (New York: Frederick Ungar Publishing Co., 1964), p. 238.

the development of a natural theology is not embraced in our present purposes, we will not give this way the weighty consideration it doubtless deserves under other circumstances. But it can be indicated how metaphysical theology would typically build on what we have said so far. The apprehension of deity, as the actual ground of unity between form and essence, would be based on (i) the will's aspiration to Infinite Will, or (ii) the recognition of the human will as reduced instance of Infinite Will.[95] In the first case, the will aspires on the basis of its own situating power to a Will that situates merely and is situated not. In the second case, the will grasps itself as a reduced instance of absolutely situating power, and rationality clarifies the apprehension by refining out what situates the will. With ingenuity of dialectical maneuver, the two cases can be gotten together. The prosecution of such a dialectic is not our present business. It was important only to indicate how 'essential form' has been and still is positively approached, and for that the present example suffices.

What *is* of moment is the fact that, in the reckoning with 'essential form' that goes on in metaphysical theology, the intentionality of that phrase is made to shift from human being to divine being. Yet it is by no means apparent that to apprehend the being of God is to apprehend, without remainder, what we are. Between the unity of form and essence in the being of God and the unity of form and essence in our being there is a gap, a gap that classical Christian theology has held in view through the doctrine of *creation*.[96] An ultimate acosmism lies in wait if human being is "finished" alone by that unity of form

[95] Virtually the whole of Farrer's *Finite and Infinite* is devoted to the exploration of finite will as a clue to Infinite Will.

[96] Exegeting Exodus 33:20, Calvin remarks: ". . . Although the angels are said to see God's face in a more excellent manner than men, still they do not apprehend the immense perfection of His glory, whereby they would be absorbed. . . . For it must needs be that that incomprehensible brightness would bring us to nothing." *Commentaries on The Four Last Books of Moses*, (Edinburgh: Printed for the Calvin Translation Society, 1854), Vol. III, p. 381. Cf. Also Luther, for whom doctrine ". . . commandeth us not to search out the nature of God: but to know his will set out to us in Christ, whom he would to take our flesh upon him . . ." *Commentary on St. Paul's Epistle to the Romans*, (Westwood, N.J.: Revell Co., 1961), p. 43.

and essence which constitutes the divine being.[97] While Christian theology may have avoided "acosmicizing" man by refusing to see his finished being laid up in the divine, it has often enough understood his "essential form" in an atemporal frame. That is, it has detemporalized humanity by identifying its very being with the divine communication of the essential form of humanity in originating creation. Thus history becomes the story of divagation from suprahistorically finished manhood.

Our attempt to think human being in relation to certain classical categories has yielded a largely negative harvest; we have had to winnow certain connotations out of them in order to use them. With respect to human "essential form," it is clear that this cannot refer to anything other than man as somehow "finished"; and that it can so refer only in such a way as not to give up what has been secured in the revised understanding of "form" and "essence" themselves. Our next step must be a phenomenological clarification of what "man's 'essential form'" wants to say, and then say it another way.

F. *The Self* qua *Finished and* Potentia Obedientalis

In a way that is strange—nay, hauntingly mysterious—it is out of a situation which reflects my being both finished and unfinished that I aspire to being finished in a way other than that in which I am finished in the situation from which I aspire. My situation is mine; I have made it and it has made me: my condition is narrow, my information is limited, my encounters with other persons for the most part are brief and thin, my reading has been in these books rather than those; those and countless other things are not just things I have done but rather what I have become. Even if I reject these things, the things rejected and the fact of rejection are my situation of being no less. Now just out of this situation, a complex of situating and being

[97] One remembers Kierkegaard's remark that the awful thing about pantheism from a human standpoint is *boredom*. "Boredom," he said, "is the demoniac side of pantheism" since ". . . pantheism is, in general, characterized by fullness." *Either/Or,* trans. David F. Swenson and Lillian Marvin Swenson, (Garden City, N.Y.: Doubleday & Company, Inc., 1959), Vol. I, pp. 286–87.

situated, I aspire to express something that is valid for all yet uniquely for me, something (in Ricoeur's words) "that stands out on the background of my situation as something universal. . . ." "From the very roots of my situation I aspire to be bound by being."[98] I am unfinished as no one else is, not even those in closest proximity to my situation. I put the question of being and truth which no one else can put for me; there is something about myself I have to discover (and thus has to occur, since dis-covery is occurrence[99]), and since no one can do this in my stead, my own *potency* is the framework of ontic constitution.

What potency designates in the self is originally specified in the exercise of "situating," in the experience of influencing oneself or one's environment to pass from one state to another. Formally, potency is the capacity to remain the same or become other. The self's potency is remarkable for being simultaneously active and passive: it accedes both to intrinsic and to adventitious determination. Such potency pertains to the very ontological constitution of selfhood (as we have already recognized, in speaking of the will as simultaneously terminal and relational); it is the possibility of my becoming something I was not before and yet remain "I."

In order to bring the point into focus, we may ally with the notion of potency that of "obedience." The aspiration to be 'finished' from and through the self's situation, yet in a trans-situational sense, is an aspiration rooted in the self's *potentia obedientialis*.[100] Obedience in this connection suggests accession

[98] Ricoeur, *History and Truth*, trans. Charles A. Kelbley, (Evanston: Northwestern University Press, 1965), p. 50.

[99] Cf. Julian N. Hartt, "Some Metaphysical Gleanings," *loc. cit.*, pp. 259ff.

[100] The use of this *terminus technicus* from Roman Catholic theology in this context is not without risk, especially in view of its profound revivification in the writings of Karl Rahner, S.J. While my thinking has obviously been stimulated by Rahner's treatment, it will be apparent that I depart from him at several crucial points. For Rahner, the *potentia obedientialis* is that constitutive feature of the "natural existential" in man whereby he can receive God's self-communication as unexacted grace (the "supernatural existential"). Thus man's *potentia obedientialis*, while allegedly construed in an ontological anthropology as such, is developed in strict correlation with the "supernatural existential" of grace. An ontology of revelation, in my modest sense, cannot have recourse

to an adventitious influence that lures the self toward another mode of being that is however already harbored in its ownmost potency. Without potency, situationally funded, obedience would be empty; without obedience, potency would be blind. Blind potency would make of the self a windowless monad. Empty obedience would make of the self an acosmic moment in Being (or, in whatever the self accedes to).[101]

Already, as used here, the term "obediential potency" is distinguished from its use in classical Thomism. In classical Thomism, man *qua* natural is potentially but not actually ordinated to immediate community with supernatural Being, God. Potency is in man ". . . in two ways: either naturally, that is, with respect to perfections that can be reduced to act by a natural agent; or else with respect to perfections that cannot be reduced to act by a natural agent but require some other agent."[102] The potency in man for immediate communion with God is actualized only "obediently," i.e. in the second of the two ways just mentioned. The potency that goes with obedience is there-

---

to the residual supernaturalism that I see operative in Rahner. In worrying these themes, I have benefited from conversation with my colleague Professor Peter C. Hodgson (who, however, disagrees that Rahner despite his language remains within a supernaturalistic framework). The reader generally unfamiliar with Rahner's central ideas may be referred with profit to Professor Hodgson's essay, "Karl Rahner," *New Day*, ed. Wm. Jerry Boney and Lawrence E. Molumby, (Roanoke, Va.: John Knox Press, 1968). Rahner treats *potentia obedientalis* explicitly in *Theological Investigations,* Vol. I, trans. Cornelius Ernst (Baltimore: Helicon Press, 1961), pp. 171, 184, 313; Vol. II, trans. Karl H. Kruges (Baltimore: Helicon Press, 1963), pp. 240, 243–44; and in Karl Rahner and Herbert Vorgrimler, *Theological Dictionary,* trans. Richard Strachan, (New York: Herder and Herder, 1965), p. 367. For St. Thomas's discussion of obediential potency see *Compendium Theologiae, (Compendium of Theology,* trans. Cyril Vollert, [St. Louis: B. Herder Book Co., 1958]), Ch. 104; *De Veritate,* Q. XXIX, a.3; *Summa Theologica,* Ia, Q. CXV, a.2; IIa IIac, Q II, a.3; IIIa, Q. I, a.3; Q. XI, a.1.

[101] We might say: one would be in Being without being *a* being.

[102] St. Thomas Aquinas, *Compendium Theologiae,* Ch. 104, p. 109. It should be recognized that, in this context, "supernatural agency" is relative to the nature involved and thus does not refer invariably to God. Lumber has potency for being a bench, St. Thomas says, but it becomes a bench by "supernatural" agency—i.e., by human act. We might say that lumber has a natural potency for resin, but an "obediential potency" for benchhood.

fore not a potency *of* nature but a potency *in* nature. "Obedience" locates actualizing power in an exterior agent; thus through "obedience" a potency for immediate communion is actualized in the self-communication of God (the profferment of which Karl Rahner calls "the supernatural existential," "unexacted grace"[103]).

Now if we resort neither to explicit metaphysical argument nor to dogmatic theological statement but hold ourselves to the phenomenon in question in a phenomenological way, a different account is required. Let us remind ourselves of the phenomenon designated by "obediential potency' as we have used the term: from, through, and toward its situation, the self experiences limitation or "finishing" that is irreducible to any situational moment, yet which is inseparable in its conceivability (and thus in its linguisticality) from the situational moment. (It is this trans-situational "finishing" that "essential form" wants, with poor success, to express.)

In a *strict* phenomenology of obediential potency, the matter would be approached through its specific phenomena, through the data of lived historicity. Obediential *potency* is never suprised in living men as an *empty capacity;* nor is *obediential* potency ever descried as a *suspended accession.* Any man's potency has a history, is concretely delimited in its appetition for act not in hand; his range of potentiality has not been communicated to him transcendentally but rather has been established by the diversity of his being in a historical continuum. Any man's obedience will have "character" specified in projects (projects, say, of "the American Way of Life," "Black Power," "White Supremacy," "Flower Power," the "classless state," etc.). The specification of individual character in personal projects involves one's community of being, one's concert with discontinuous agencies and dominant intentions, themselves actualizing limitants on individual being-toward.

No doubt, phenomenological access to obediential potency in man is most striking in the case of the experience of "fault," in the experience of disproportion between what I have become

---

[103] Cf. *Theological Investigations,* Vol. I, pp. xv–xvii, pp. 297–317, *passim,* but esp. pp. 310–313; also *Lexikon für Theologie und Kirche,* (Freiburg, 1959), Vol. III, col. 1301.

and what I have my being-toward.[104] This old Augustinian point[105] is scarcely robbed of its force in contemporary manifestation even when, as in much modern theater, the disproportion is largely internalized or made a matter of blocked communication.[106]

Obediential potency, then, refers to the dimension of man's being out of which we are to think that reciprocal action of 'limit' and 'goal' which lays claim to man's being as a whole in a given situation. In obediential potency so far construed there is nothing especially favorable to theology. To be sure, revelation in the formal Christian sense occurs as the actualization of obediential potency; but then obediential potency is always actualized in one direction or another (we are never just the same; we are always becoming something else). Short of an acosmic account (in which God is the subject as well as the object of revelation), the conditions of revelation are identical with the conditions of idolatry. Paraphrasing and agreeing with Schleiermacher, we may say that if revelation is given to man outside the experience of his own being, it is then something on which he can exercise his own action and thus nullify or modify

---

[104] No such phenomenological project is undertaken here. The reader cannot do better than turn to Vol. II of Ricoeur's monumental phenomenology of the will, the first part of which has appeared in English as *Fallible Man* (cited earlier) and the second part as *The Symbolism of Evil*, (New York: Harper & Row, 1967). It should be noted that Ricoeur uses "fault" not necessarily as "moral culpability" but rather as a metaphor drawn from geology, as a "cleavage" or "crack" in human being.

[105] ". . . So long as a being is in process of corruption, there is in it some good of which it is being deprived. . . . But if it does not cease to be corrupted, neither can it cease to possess good of which corruption may deprive it. But if it should be thoroughly and completely consumed by corruption, there will then be no good left, because there will be no being. Wherefor corruption can consume the good only by consuming the being . . . then the corruption itself must cease to exist, as there is no being left in which it can dwell." *Enchiridion,* XII; in *Basic Writings of Saint Augustine,* ed. Whitney J. Oates, (New York: Random House, 1948), Vol. I, p. 663.

[106] Quentin says: "I think now that my disaster really began when I looked up one day—and the bench was empty. No judge in sight. And all that remained was the endless argument with oneself—this pointless litigation of existence before an empty bench." Arthur Miller, *After the Fall,* (New York: Bantam Books, 1965), pp. 4–5. Here it is clear that the bench is not empty; the litigation goes on. The bench has been moved inside the self, and placed across the self's internal chasm.

174

it.[107] But if it is given as the solicitation into act of his ownmost potency, it is not something against which he stands, but in and out of which he is (i.e., it is Word of God to him and for him).

G. The Structure of Revelation: The Historio-Personal Existential

Let us recollect, collect, and move toward an end for this phase of our investigation.

In the history of western Christian theology there is a long tradition which elaborates the fundamental problems of soteriology and revelation in relation to the split between essence and existence that is taken to characterize human being in time. Within this tradition an analysis of the relation between essence and existence (in "creation") precedes an account of how their split (in "Fall") is overcome in revelation. The cognitive media of revelation would then have their "ontological reach" elaborated in connection with those structures of human being said to be "healed" in revelation.

This tradition is our inheritance, but we have found it difficult to turn into cash. That owes not only to an unfavorable rate of exchange in the marketplace of current conceptuality, but also and especially because it is (to change metaphors in mid-sentence) the "backdrop" of our present self-understanding only indistinctly. So we have established ourselves in the vortex of human reality as directly as ontological language (which is itself a tradition lying on the tongue) allows. There in the "eye of the vortex," by what Bergson called "intellectual auscultation," we have tried to hear the swirling genesis of human being. The arcs were marked (the major discriminations of C. and D. above) and then brought into conjunction with the tradition or a portion thereof. Terms such as "form" and "essence" are there in our language, and we had to see what we could say through them, and also what we could not say that we do see—and for which seeing, require our expansion of language.

The trajectory of genesis has been followed into the complexity of man's ontological instability with no intent of showing

---

[107] Cf. Schleiermacher, *The Christian Faith,* pp. 17–18.

175

that revelation is the next step of an unclouded reason. It is not that, ". . . when we get to the end of human beings," we require ". . . a belief in God, like a gourmet who demands more complex sauces with his food."[108] No doubt it is the case that in understanding how man reckons with his ontological instability on his own—his ingenuity in devising ways of being "finished" —we understand something formally similar to the processes of revelation; and thus gain the possibility of an authentic theological iconoclasm, a war on idolatry.[109] But the crucial point is that, since man's ontological instability is the arena of revelatory address, the pressing of that instability through an interlacing of personal regions discloses wherein the revelatory call to "finished manhood" must be formulated in order to chime with and thus be meaningful for his concrete existence (ie., in connection with his "background," "foreground," "dominant intentions," etc.).

It will be useful to recur to man's *potentia obedientalis:* the vantage from which we saw what we could not say through man's "essential form." Two levels of man's non-coincidence with himself have been discriminated. The first is a largely internal non-coincidence: the unstable relation between the self's finishing and being finished in any immediate situation (event) as the bearer of its being. This could be called the non-coincidence occasioned by the self's diversity of being. The second is a largely external non-coincidence: the unstable relation between particular situations (themselves comprising the first level of non-coincidence) and the trans-situational term ("finishing") that supervenes upon them. (Thus, if I am a Marxist, I am coincident or non-coincident with myself in the events of my immediate field in a way that is different from the way those events are coincident or non-coincident with "the classless state"—and my being is distributed in both ways.) This could be called the non-coincidence occasioned by the self's community of being. Personal being is thus stretched between two

[108] Graham Greene, *The End of the Affair,* (New York: The Viking Press, 1951), p. 125.

[109] A task current American theology has all but forgotten, and to which it is summoned anew by Gabriel Vahanian, *Wait Without Idols,* (New York: George Braziller, 1964); *No Other God,* (New York: George Braziller, 1966).

distributions, two "finishings," each of which in extremity claims all: the monadicism of total self-making, and the acosmism of totally being made.[110]

Obediential potency, when not disjointed, bespeaks that openness in the ontological constitution of selfhood for the harmonious distribution of its being, between its diversity and its community of being. As such, man's obediential potency is that point in man's reality-sense at which revelation inserts itself, the point indeed at which reality-sense and Being are conjoined. It is the point between man and man, the "same" man, wherein he avows at once (in the words of Buber) "it depends on me" and "I am given over for disposal."[111] (Here is the classic

[110] Man situates himself in part and is perpetually tempted to think he situates himself totally; hence atheism. Man is situated in part and is perpetually tempted to think he is situated totally; hence theism. Because man is both finished and unfinished, both theism and atheism are permanent features of human history. It is a profoundly Christian view of man, I believe, which sees atheism as a positive historical assault on rampant theism (since egregious theism always becomes pantheism); and which sees theism as a positive historical attack on wild-flowering humanism (which, unstunted, always amounts to panhominization of the world). Christian theology, as I conceive it, avoids egregious theism and humanism by thinking God's revelation between man and man, the "author and finisher of faith" between man *qua* unfinished and man *qua* finished. That is to take a position against Gerhard Ebeling (to whom on so many counts I am deeply indebted), who apparently wants to think man between God and God, between God *qua* principium and God *qua* finis of human being. Cf. "Der Hermeneutische Ort der Gotteslehre," *loc. cit.,* pp. 283–326; "Existenz zwischen Gott und Gott," *ibid.,* Bd. 62, Heft 1 (Mai, 1965), pp. 86–113.

[111] Martin Buber, *I and Thou,* trans. Ronald Gregor Smith, (New York: Charles Scribner's Sons, 1958), p. 96. Cf. Emil Fackenheim: ". . . Human being must be understood as something more than a mere product, and yet as something less than a self-making. Instead of a self-constituting, it must rather be the accepting or choosing of something already constituted, and yet also not constituted, because the accepting or choosing is part of its essence." *Metaphysics and Historicity,* p. 83. Cf. also Kierkegaard on the self's "absolute" choice of itself; "This self did not exist previously, for it came into existence by means of the choice, and yet it did exist, for it was in fact 'himself.' In this case choice performs at one and the same time two dialectical movements: that which is chosen does not exist and comes into existence with the choice; that which is chosen exists, otherwise there would not be a choice." *Either/Or,* trans. Walter Lowrie, (Princeton: Princeton University Press, 1944), Vol. II, pp. 179ff. A remarkably perceptive and informative discussion of this passage from Kierkegaard and its fuller context, in relation to themes in Hegel, Sartre, Jaspers, and Heidegger, will be found in Fackenheim, *op. cit.,* pp. 84–88.

antinomy of grace, the old point which however cannot with any claim to meaning be made in the old way.) It is the point of "turning": where the self as ". . . the trembling of a unity exposed to contingency and tirelessly recreating itself" accedes to being constituted out of community with Being—care-fully refunded for its good out of its ownmost potency."[112]

There rings through obediential potency something hardly heard and scarcely speakable as "essential form." Let us bring this structure (which in actualization, to be sure, is no mere structure) forward as man's *historio-personal existential*. Since much that follows will be trained on the meaning of this notion, we may content ourselves presently with a few sublating characterizations. Most generally, the *historio-personal existential* is the actualization of man's obediential potency for God's grace: indeed is nothing other than God's universally and endlessly proffered grace, the gift by God of man to himself *qua* finished *coram Deo*.

(1) "Historio." What 'finishes' me, not only situationally but also trans-situationally, is emergent. That does not mean that however history heaves, my "existential" bobs afloat on the next wave. It means, negatively, that what I fail in my situating acts is not a norm antecedently fixed. Failure owes not to a primeval past that has been lost but to an eschatological future that has not been gained. Thus "Fall" is an inadequate metaphor for ontic distance from one's ownmost "existential"; such distance is more like vertigo before a future proleptically present. Positively, *history modifies what I am finally modified by*.[113] Only so can I be obliged to live the "existential's" claim in an historical field.

(2) "Personal." Enough has been said concerning the self's singularity and unsubstitutability of being. The personal dimension of one's authentic "existential" brings that singularity from solitary to political and social manifestation. In a paraphrase of

[112] The quotation is from an allusion to Heidegger by Merleau-Ponty, *Signs,* p. 97.

[113] This can only mean that God's intention for my being is historically qualified; that not only "distorted" but also "authentic" human being has a history. But it also means that revelation can never be confused with "historicism"—the latter meaning that history is the final modification of man.

178

Nietzsche (whose praise of solitude is always misunderstood, like everything else he wrote, without grasping its irony): solitude grows only the beasts brought into it, and the beasts brought in for the most part are "I and myself too deep in conversation." Only the neighbor ". . . is the cork which prevents the conversation from sinking into the depth" of sub-personal existence.[114] Thus to be a person is to be given to a dialogical relation with the *socius* in the *polis* ("the people of God").

(3) "Existential." By now it will be clear that the word "existential" does not refer to a static essence of human being that has to be discovered, nor to some private intention of my own being. It refers to that constitution of human being out of which I comprehend myself and in relation to which I comport myself ontically. Thus in the phrase "historio-personal existential," "existential" has nominative, verbal, and adjectival overtones: it names a structure, instances a state of being and a manner of doing, and describes the quality of comprehension.[115]

[114] Cf. *Zarathustra*, pp. 54–71, *passim*.
[115] Is the "historio-personal existential," as the bearer of God's intention for man's being, always there? If there, always actual? How there, and how actualized? These questions will be taken up in the following chapter under the rubric of "The Imaginative Existential."

V. Imagination and the Scale of Mental Acts

Outline

180

I. INTRODUCTION

A. Recapitulation and Prolepsis

In the preceding chapter we looked at man *qua homo viator,* man ontologically "under way." In the present chapter we are to look at the same man *qua homo cogitans;* man as he grasps himself in the world, cognitively, "on the way." The former project was delimited, and the present is no less so.

Personal being was pressed in order to disclose the where and how of its ontological instability. Since revelation addresses just this instability, it was deemed crucial to delineate those dimensions of personal being engaged in this instability. Only so could it be understood how revelation formulates itself: the genesis of revelatory meaning, we have implied, marches with the genesis of human be-coming *coram Deo.*

The task immediately ahead is to describe the spectrum of mental acts as personal being, in its various modulations, passes through the prism of the mind.[1] It is imagination within that spectrum that we intend to focus upon, with a view to seeing how the imagination is engaged in the constitution and cognition of human being, and finally with a view to understanding the putatively revelatory character of certain kinds of imaginative discourse. Thus the project ahead is not that of a general epistemology, as the preceding project was not that of a general ontology. Even so, we have no recourse to special pleading; the tub must stand on its own bottom. While what is ahead is not epistemology proper, it must be properly epistemological. It is part of the larger aim to show that a hermeneutic of revelation shares in, and is formally coextensive with, a hermeneutic of human being. That means that revelatory solicitation to be man out of a certain horizon must be interpreted in such a way that man can recognize himself as the one so solicited; and can also recognize that what he is solicited *to* is framed out of his ownmost potency, but from which he is debarred as his own in actuality, for want of an actuating horizon that gives him lived access to it. In short, material revelation is Word of God "for us men and our salvation"; it is Word so spoken and heard as to eventuate the expansion of our manhood toward wholeness of being.[2] The formal explication of the dynamics of human expansion (and contraction) has been our concern for many pages past, and we have now to construe the imagination in relation to these dynamics. Such explicating and such construing are independent pieces of anthropological analysis: they are not revelatory. They show us rather how material revelation connects formally with the human modes of being and knowing, and thus how the "meaning" of revelation takes shape in our active existence.

[1] The spectrum-prism metaphor is not without limitations. Personal being is not like light emitted from a luminous body, already fully constituted before entering the prism. The "dispersions" of consciousness are certainly part of what we mean by personal being. Thus the metaphor would be adequate only if we could picture the self as a series of prisms, the light entering each successive prism being a "re-banding" of the preceding spectrum, a "re-banding" that also absorbs light inserted between the prisms from other luminous bodies (i.e., discontinuous ingression).

[2] The root meaning of "salvation" is health, wholeness. Thus salvation is "well-being."

182

Many of the problems prosecuted ontologically in the preceding chapter recur here in connection with the study of imagination. Just enough of these problems may be mentioned to set recollection in motion. To stand in a revelatory relation is to stand in a *modifying* relation (modifying and being modified); and "modifying relation" was pursued through the continuity and discontinuity of personal being. How is the imagination involved in the continuity and discontinuity of man's being? How is the self's being-toward in-formed (trans-formed, expanded) when it is not altogether self-informed? How is thought turned from the "given" in one mode to the "given" in another mode; i.e., how does thought gain new presentiment of the given? How is the given cognitively dispersed and diversified in my transaction with it?

These questions, and others they are meant to recall, will be taken up in the study of imagination that follows. The framework of that study is afforded by those dimensions of unfinished manhood singled out previously as decisively connected with the imagination, viz., memory, intention, and event. There are additional reasons, however, why these dimensions are crucial in a study that intends to explicate revelation in Christian theology. As will be noted in Appendix IV, Christianity was marked in its origins and has been so marked ever since by revelation as doubly featured: in revelation man is placed in immediate intercourse with God in respect of his own being; and he is so placed by virtue of God's intercourse with Jesus Christ, an event somehow ingredient in my own authentic being before God. That is, Christian faith has to do with "event," simultaneously with the immediacy and mediacy of historical event, and therefore with memory and intention. After the imagination has been discussed in some detail in relation to memory, intention, and event, we shall be in a position to take up the relation between image and event, in the following chapter.

B. The Manner of Approaching Imagination Here

But before proceeding, some additional introductory comments may prove useful. In view of the many ways in which the imagination has been approached and can be approached, the following procedure needs to be made clear. For although imagination is here treated within the spectrum of mental acts, it is not alone a mode of cognition but also and fundamentally a way of being human.[3] Imaginative being is accelerated being-toward, the projection of oneself toward his ownmost potency. Thus the "truth" of imagination is not mere cognitive truth, but rather is as well a matter of participation in emergent be-coming. These comments, obviously, race ahead.

Whoever aspires to make the subject of "imagination" his meat and drink for an extended period should first ponder the menu. That menu, which for sheer size would make Maxim's look like Krystal's, might well be mottoed with the words of Samuel Johnson, which resemble nothing so much as a sigh of exasperation: "Imagination, a licentious and vagrant faculty, unsusceptible of limitations, and impatient of restraint, has always endeavored to baffle the logician, to perplex the confines of distinction, and burst the inclosures of regularity."[4] Few subjects are so complex, even bewildering. Indeed one could almost take the simplicity of a theory of imagination as evidence against its truth, or at the very least, as evidence of failure to make contact with the phenomenon itself. It is fair warning that one should not put "imagination" in his conceptual diet if he has little stomach for circularities, for the tendency of one thing to be led into its opposite and back again endlessly (e.g., activity-passivity, intension-extension, memory-intention, immediacy-wholeness (mediacy), construction- destruction, etc.). Every important theory of the imagination has had to reckon with its mediational or schematic character, its role in putting "unlikes" in contact with each other. But equally significant is its divisive character, its role in splitting "likes" apart. Of these things more anon.

[3] The imagination is not unique in this regard. In addition to being media of cognition, all integral mental "powers" are ways in which man *is*. Perception, for example, is the mode of concrete bodily presence, as reason is the mode of maximum community with the world (and thus the mode of abstract presence).

[4] Samuel Johnson, *The Rambler,* 125; in *The Works of Samuel Johnson,* (12 vols.; New York: William Durell, 1811), Vol. V, pp. 321–322.

In the usage of "plain men" (who are just ourselves when we are not thinking carefully) imagination is a term applied to many mental activities, the relation between which is often difficult to make out. A few of these uses may be mentioned. "He merely imagined it"; whatever took place, took place in his head alone. In this case imagination is trained upon the "imaginary." "Imagine that . . ." reflects a number of uses, the core of which is *supposing*. "Imagine that" may mean: suppose a condition obtains that does not in fact presently obtain (for us in this moment), but which could in fact possibly obtain, e.g., "Imagine that it is not raining." Or "Imagine that" may mean: suppose a condition obtains that does not in fact presently obtain and which could not in fact possibly obtain, e.g., "Imagine that you have four wings," or "Imagine that you stand by Caesar's side before the Rubicon." Or, to make an end of supposing-type imagination, "Imagine that" may mean: suppose a condition obtains that, although it in fact possibly or actually obtains, is intrinsically inaccessible to us. (Here it is difficult to give an unequivocal example. Not long ago it would have done to say: "Imagine that you are on the back side of the moon." Perhaps our best choice is: "Imagine that you see the sweep of time through the eye of God.") In addition to the "imaginary" and "supposing" usages, imagination is often used as a term of commendation, as when one says "That lad shows imagination in his work." If one says of another's thought or the work of his hands that it is imaginative, one usually means that it is creative and original, that it shows taste, flair, and substantiality out of the ordinary. How this laudatory sense of imagination squares with other senses in common usage is something about which the plain man rarely if ever troubles himself.

If one turns to the history of western philosophy, he will find that the concept of imagination has had an even more checkered career in the past than obtains in current popular usage.[5] Two reasons may be given for the greater diversity of meanings in the past. First, some of the classical views of imagination have actually been sophistications of one or more

[5] See Appendices I–III below, which comprise a limited typological-historical study of the concept of imagination.

of the common sense views (e.g., in classical realism imagination is seen as the mental power by which objects absent to sense are held before the mind). Second, some of the classical doctrines have simply ignored the common sense views. They have proceeded constructively by construing the imagination in relation to general principles, whether ontological or epistemological (e.g., Kant's doctrine is elaborated in connection with his understanding of the mind's *synthetic* activity). In so far as the first way achieves a *sophistication* of a common sense view, which is to say that in so far as it yields a philosophical view of imagination, it tends finally to take on the features of the second way.

As distinct from the spontaneous use of the term "imagination" in everyday life, and as distinct from the linguistic analysis of diverse uses of the term in everyday life, our procedure will be to determine the function of imagination in the spectrum of mental acts.[6] This way of putting the matter is important. One's study of the imagination would rightly be thought cheap and naïve if it merely exploited the ambiguity of a term. The study is justifiable only if it reduces the ambiguity where that in fact is possible; and only if it exposes the peculiar complexity of the activity to which the term is applied, and therefore exposes why the removal of all ambiguity is impossible. Nothing has contributed so much to the ambiguity of the term in the past as the supposition in some quarters that imagination refers to a single power or faculty of the mind. The falsity of this assumption is now a commonplace of philosophy and psychology alike.[7] We can assume only that "imagination" stands for a

[6] One may conjecture that "imagination" has such diverse uses in contemporary standard English because it has become a catchall word for functions previously discriminated in the language by a plurality of words, e.g., phantasy, fancy, wit, the common sense, interior sense, speculation, etc.

[7] The mind's experience of itself is that of a primordial, immediately given unity. Consciousness is not derived from parts or simpler elements, and so cannot be reduced to any or all of them in mere mixture or combination. No one has emphasized this point with greater rigor than Wilhelm Dilthey: "The psychic life-process is originally and everywhere, from its most elementary to its highest forms, a unity. The life of the soul does not coalesce out of parts; it is not constituted out of elements; it is not a composition, not a result of co-operating sense-atoms or feeling-atoms; it is originally and always an overarching

186

wide region in the spectrum of mental acts, within which many distinctions can and must be made. We will be justified in referring hereafter to imagination as a "mental power" only because the mind in fact focuses itself in distinguishable and distinctive ways. The mind works with now one ordering activity at the fore, now another. But it is not as though one region in the mental spectrum wanes into absolute irrelevance as another waxes: imagination without sensation and reason is nothing, at least nothing recognizably human. If one draws distinctions in one region of the spectrum he will therefore, implicitly, be assuming and pointing toward distinctions in other regions as well.

With respect to that broad and ill-defined region in the scale of mental acts which the imagination comprises, how shall we set about drawing proper distinctions? One can hardly do better than return to Plato, to his program if not its results. If one wishes to understand a mental power (*dunamis*), Socrates is made to say in the *Republic,* it is necessary to ". . . look to its field of objects and the state of mind it produces, and regard these as sufficient to identify it and distinguish it from powers which have different fields and produce different states."[8] Undoubtedly Plato was able to execute this program with greater sureness in the case of some mental powers than others. For example, reason comes out more carefully delineated than imagination. That is owing not to any limitation in the program, however, but to the fact that Plato was unable to find a final resting place for his conception of the "field of objects" upon which imagination trains itself. This reduced ultimately to a problem in his metaphysics, the ontological status of *eikōnes* (images) as the object of *eikasia* (imagination), a problem about which he became increasingly uncertain in his later years.[9] If we dare to speak where Plato thought he had to remain largely silent, by advancing an ontology of unfinished man in

unity . . . whose expression on the highest level is the unity of consciousness and the unity of the person . . ." *Gesammelte Schriften,* 4th ed., Vol. V, pp. 211–212.

[8] *Republic,* 477; in *The Republic of Plato,* trans. F. M. Cornford, (Oxford: At the Clarendon Press, 1955), p. 181.

[9] See my article, "The Imagination in Plato," *loc. cit.,* pp. 436–61.

which the "reach" of imagination figures prominently, there is no reason why we should not take up the Platonic program afresh.

Having distinguished various phases of the will's operation whereby it is concentrated into act, whether as situating or as being situated, we shall seek to determine the role of the imagination in these phases, to see how the imagination is involved in the self's situating and being situated, to understand how some kinds of being depend upon the prehensions of imagination; in short, to construe the operation of imagination in connection with that of the will.[10] As a term standing for a broad range of mental acts, imagination is to be construed by reference to the ontological domain intended by those acts, viz., the "unfinished." The one place where we understand (heaven knows, without perspicacity) the dialectic between the finished and the unfinished is in our active existence, in our experience of agency and modification. The analysis of this dialectic was restricted by the ends our study is expected to subserve, as is the elaboration of "imagination" in relation to that analysis. Thus for further study we singled out *memory* from "background," *intention* from "foreground," and *event* from "concentration."

II. THE IMAGINATION AND HISTORICAL TEMPORALITY

Temporality is contained in life as the first categorical determination of it, fundamental for all other determinations.[11]

A. The Imagination and Memory

". . . We have no time until
We know what time we fill,
Why time is other than time was . . ."[12]

10 On the connection of imagination with will, see above, Ch. IV, footnote 47.
11 Wilhelm Dilthey, *Gesammelte Schriften*, Vol. VII, p. 192.
12 W. H. Auden, "We're Late," *The Collected Poems of W. H. Auden*, (New York: Random House, 1945), p. 26.

The past is "dead and gone"; its spilt milk is not worth crying over. This piece of intelligence is a mixture of wrong information and bad advice. If my past is dead and gone, I have neither a present nor a future. My being-now is in part a being-from the past and a being-toward the past; I cannot isolate any moment of now-being that does not involve the past's projection of itself upon the occasion of that moment.

"The past's projection of itself" should not be understood as though there were something constant we might call "past" which could in fact altogether determine the present activity of the self. The past, we have noted, serves as a limit on the future and as the construct of its possibilities. To be sure, the past is in one respect finished: back there, in another "present" and in another place, possibilities were actualized eventfully for persons who were party to their concentration. Some of those events (indeed, we may say, *all* past events in which we take any interest) happened in such a way as not alone to actualize possibilities; their occurrence established structures of possibility for persons in succeeding times and at other places at an incalculably great remove. What was involved in their happening was of such sort as to continue happening. Therein lies the foundation of the claim that the meaning of an historical event belongs to its future.[13] For that reason, the intelligibility of a past event owes not to its sheer onticity, to its merely having happened, but to its constitutive reverberations in our being. The death of Jesus on the Cross, French peasants storming the Bastille, a small band of new-world patriots signing the Declaration of Independence, six million Jews systematically exterminated, the Watts-Newark-Detroit race riots: these are events that are finished, yet live in the constitution of our being. "Since . . . the total efficacy of an event is, in the texture of life, bound up with its *full* significance and *final* value," wrote

[13] Cf. Rudolf Bultmann: ". . . Historical phenomena are not what they are in pure individual isolation, but only in their relation to the future for which they have importance. We may say: To each historical phenomenon belongs its future, a future in which alone it will appear as that which it really is—to speak precisely we must say: the future in which it evermore appears as that which it is." *History and Eschatology*, (Edinburgh: The University Press, 1957), p. 120. Cf. also *Existence and Faith*, p. 295.

189

Max Scheler, "every event of our past remains *indeterminate* in significance and *incomplete* in value until it has yielded *all* its potential effects."[14] In one respect the past is *made,* and we are made with and by it. But in another respect the legacy of the past is precisely the challenge: what are we to make of it? For one of the things made in the past is a fund of possibilities bearing upon our emergent being. To the extent that we are situating beings, we are disposers not only of our future but of our past as well. To quote Scheler again, " 'Historical reality' is incomplete and, so to speak, redeemable."[15]

One cannot seriously suppose that the ontic past (the fully "happened," actual past) and the recollected (or even recollectable) past are one and the same thing. To argue for or against the supposal is to conjecture from present experience, since access to the ontic past is gained by means of a species of recollection based on "evidence." From present experience we know that events, equally ontic, establish differing ranges of future-projecting potency. Some events open up a negligible field of potency, others establish a field of appetence quickly satiated in act, while still others broach a field that is in turn overlaid by the supervening fields of subsequent events: I throw my dog a

[14] Max Scheler, *On the Eternal in Man* (*Vom Ewigen im Menschen*), p. 40. (The emphases are Scheler's.)

[15] *Ibid.,* p. 41. Scheler continues: "I grant that everything about the death of Caesar which appertains to the events of nature is as complete and invariable as the eclipse of the sun which Thales prophesied. But whatever belonged on that occasion to 'historical reality,' whatever is woven of it as meaning and effect into the fabric of man's history, is an incomplete thing, and will not be complete until the end of world-history." It is only fair to point out that in the context from which these quotations are drawn Scheler is concerned to make a point somewhat different from the one under consideration here. I wish to emphasize those mnemonic processes whereby the self "actualizes" the unfinished business of the past. Scheler's interest in the effect which the past exerts upon present existence is motivated by his doctrine of "repentence." For him, repentance is freedom from the covert power of the past. While this interesting doctrine cannot be pursued here, it can be noted that it rests on a mistaken conception of the relation between historical knowledge and historical being. "Memory . . . is so far from transmitting the effect of our past upon our present life that on the contrary it liberates us from the determining power of that effect. History comprehended frees us from the power of the history we live. Likewise the *knowledge* of history . . . is first and foremost a *liberator* from historical determination."

190

bone, pet my child on the head, and write a book on historical being and the imagination.

The *merely ontic* past is no concern of my present and anticipative being.[16] But then neither does the recollected past exhaust the concern of my present and anticipative being with the past. That part of the non-ontic past which is ontologically relevant to our present and anticipative being, but which is not included in the recollected past, is the potentiality of the past for "fate." For decades the War Between the States was not an item up for conscious recollection in the popular mind. The power of that crucial event in our national life was not stayed, however, by inattention, indifference, and repression. It precipitated eddies in the Deep Well of national memory that, working their way at last to the surface, have brought on among plain men no less than among technical historians an effort to recollect that is almost frantic in nature. Indeed, we cannot understand Selma or Watts without recurring to the "future" of the Civil War that is now our past and present.

These roughly hewn distinctions (between the ontic, recollected, and ontologically relevant past) point to another and more fundamental, the distinction between historical being and historical knowledge. The nature of this distinction and indeed its very justifiability have been the subject of controversy between philosophers of history and historians for a long time, and the end is not in sight. By taking up the problem of memory and the role of imagination in it, we involve ourselves in this controversy, like it or not. Memory in personal being is not exhausted by reference to the ontic past, to what is finished in the past; is not exhausted by reference to the past that is subject to instant recall (and so is not mere "recollection"); and it is not exhausted by reference to the past whose total efficacy is indeterminate and incomplete. As the condition of personal being, memory involves *all* of these references.

[16] This is, no doubt, a poor way of speaking. By "ontic past," I mean the past that actually happened. But of course the establishment of possibilities of a certain sort actually happened too; with what was ontically actualized, novel structures of possibility came into being. It is a question whether possible being can have onticity, or only ontologicality. At all counts, I am suggesting that there is historical ontologicality, established by the onticity of events.

191

To see the problem of memory in this way is to affirm that, methodologically, an understanding of historical being takes precedence over an understanding of historical knowledge.[17] (The understanding of historical being, in broad outline, was the burden of effort in the preceding chapter.) The knowledge of history is made possible and restricted by an understanding of what it means to *be historically*. Applied to our topic, this means that one has to understand how imagination enters into the occurrence of events and the shaping of their field of potency and how events enter into the expansion and modification of imagination in order to speak meaningfully of the cognitivity of historical imagination.[18]

We cannot take up memory in the grand manner which these introductory comments invite, but only in such a way as to illuminate certain functions of the imagination. Of especial importance for theology are those functions of imagination which preserve and actuate the force of the "paradigmatic event" in historical selfhood. In quasi-Whiteheadian language, a paradigmatic event is a "special occasion" in its constitutive and elucidatory power for other and subsequent occasions. It is the event that "keeps on happening" in the deepest ranges of the self and society, that makes possible other events of a certain sort and so gives direction to personal and political destiny, and that illuminates other events by giving them a "hub" or center of reference.[19]

Some of the areas in which we may expect illumination are as follows. The first is the role of imagination in the activity and

[17] Cf. Wilhelm Dilthey: "We are first of all historical beings before we are contemplators of history, and only because we are the former do we become the latter. . . . The first condition for the possibility of historical knowledge lies in the fact that I myself am a historical being, that he who investigates history is the same as he who makes history." *Gesammelte Schriften,* 4th ed., Vol. VII, p. 278.

[18] We should not forget that as the background-past is not the sole dimension of personal being, so memory is not the sole mode of historical knowledge. Equally indispensable, both to historical being and historical knowledge, is the foreground phase of intention, to which we will turn next. The functions of imagination we may mark in connection with one phase require to be augmented by those discernible in another.

[19] "Paradigmatic event" is discussed below in Chapter VI.

192

passivity of memory, the mutual configuration of imagination and memory. The second partakes in the first: how imagination de-structs (not destroys) the past, gains passage from one mode of the past to another, and con-structs what it gains with forward-running selfhood. (E.g., how imagination "turns" the recollected past toward the ontologically relevant past, fate, and thus makes fate re-enactable, destiny.) Third, we may expect to see how the mutual configuration of imagination and memory serves to shape the range of apprehension in the present. Fourth, we may expect to gain a first approximation on the fullness of referential range that goes with an authentic "symbol," since in memory objects perdure with plurisignative reference as does the signifying self.

(1) The passivity of mnemic imagination in classical realism. Aristotle considered memory to be simply retentive, a "state or affection of . . . [perception or conception], conditioned by lapse of time."[20] As for memory of sense, one could say that for him it is the extension of sense perception from the past into the present, or from the present into the past. Memory is the presentational medium whether of past perceptions or of past conceptions.[21] Belonging essentially to the perceptive rather than to the intellective faculty, memory requires the aid of imagination to mediate between these faculties; for perception has no way of storing itself.[22] In the service of memory, imagination is neither less nor more than a passive receptacle of fully fashioned sense impressions and conceptions (the figure used by Aristotle is that of stamping by a seal); and as such, it admits of no *activity* whatsoever. Aristotle thought his argument was shored up by the alleged fact that memory is poorest in children

[20] *De Memoria et Reminiscentia,* Ch. 1, 449b, 25; in *The Basic Works of Aristotle,* ed. Richard McKeon (New York: Random House, 1941), p. 607. (Cited hereafter as McKeon.)

[21] *Ibid.,* 450a, 1–15; McKeon, p. 608. Cf. also Spinoza's treatment of memory in *On the Improvement of the Understanding.* "It (memory) is nothing else than the actual sensation of impressions on the brain, accompanied with the thought of a definite duration of the sensation." *The Chief Works of Benedict de Spinoza,* trans. R. H. M. Elwes, (New York: Dover Publications, 1951), Vol. II, p. 31.

[22] Cf. Thomas Hobbes: "Imagination . . . is nothing but 'decaying sense.'" *Leviathan,* with an Introduction by Henry Morley, 2d. ed., (London: George Routledge and Sons, 1886), p. 17.

193

and the aged, which fact he ascribed to the intense activity of their imaginative powers.[23]

But if imagination serves memory only as a passive receptacle of past perceptions and conceptions, one may ask how memory can err, since a purely passive imagination would leave intact what it has received. Moreover, as Plotinus shrewdly observed, if the mnemic imagination is merely the repository of fully shaped sense data and concepts, we may be astonished not that the mind remembers but that it is able to forget.[24] Plotinus suspected, and many a plain man with him, that the imagination is privy to changes of meaning which memory contents bear.

If the imagination is so involved, Aristotle might counter, it has abandoned the passive for an illegitimately active role. *Qua* veridical, the mnemic imagination merely records in sensa and concepts not only the likenesses of their objects but also the objective *relation* ("the movements") between objects themselves. Because these impressions are retained in the holding-operation that is the passive imagination, Aristotle can speak of recollection as a "mode of inference."[25] Recollection, of course, is not the same as memory. Recollection is an intellectual act whereby a mnemic content is brought into the light of present consciousness. Furnishing the data from which recollecting in-

[23] But cf. Vico: "In childhood memory is most vigorous, and therefore imagination is excessively vivid, for imagination is nothing but extended or compounded memory." *Scienza Nuova,* Book I, Sect. II, Par. 211; in *The New Science of Giambattista Vico,* trans. Thomas Goddard Bergin and Max Harold Fisch (Ithaca: Cornell University Press, 1948), p. 67.

[24] "Are we . . . to refer memory to the perceptive faculty and so make one principle of our nature the seat of both awareness and remembrance? . . . If memory resided in [such a faculty] . . . forgetfulness could not be." *The Enneads,* IV, Third Tractate, 28–29; Mac-Kenna, pp. 284–86.

[25] "When one wishes to recollect, this is what he will do: he will try to obtain a beginning of movement whose sequel shall be the movement which he desires to reawaken. This explains why attempts at recollection succeed soonest and best when they start from a beginning of some objective series. For, in order of succession, the mnemonic movements are to one another as the objective facts from which they are derived. Accordingly, things arranged in a fixed order, like the successive demonstrations in geometry, are easy to remember (or recollect), while badly arranged subjects are remembered with difficulty." *De Mem. et Rem.,* Ch. 2, 451b, 30–452a, 5; cf. also 453a, 10; McKeon, pp. 613–16.

194

telligence infers the thing it seeks to remember, imagination is related to memory and recollection as it is to present sensation and present conception. In either case, the imagination serves as a retaining lock in a canal of impressions.[26]

(2) The totally passive character of mnemic imagination disputed. We must depart from the tradition of classical realism in the degree that, in that tradition, the function of imagination in memory was viewed as a totally passive operation.

Whatever else memory is, it is not alone the simple retention of discrete and fully formed wholes, together with such "objective relations" as obtained between them in original acts of perception or conception. No doubt we do remember (recall) such integral wholes without major intervening modification, and of such Aristotle's is an acceptable account. The learning of geometrical axioms through sensible models, and the recollection of them, is a case in point. Having forgotten the axioms we may call up one of the models impressed in the mnemic imagination and, recalling one obvious relation between the model's parts, proceed to "remember" (i.e., infer) associated axioms. Such force as Aristotle's theory of memory has stems from taking such an example as typical of memory in the round.

But such an example is not typical of memory as it functions in man's historical continuity and discontinuity, as it is not typical of mnemonic processes in moral action and in the fine arts. The classical realist has supreme confidence in the power of the mind to grasp things as they are and as they were. He thinks that, because things are as they are and were as they were, the mind must be essentially passive in order to take them into itself. So simple a summary would of course be a caricature of any of the great realists. Nonetheless it remains the case that realistic emphasis on passivity of imagination owes to ontological fixity in the "object." We, on the other hand, have emphasized that there are orders of being in which the very *is-ness* of some things depends upon (among other factors) our participation in them, upon our simultaneously active and passive

---

[26] This brief exposition manifestly does scant justice to the conception of imagination in classical realism. A fuller account will be found in Appendix I below, "Imagination and Conformation."

existence as their inheritor.[27] Sheer fixity of object confronted by sheer passivity of mind is a situation rarely if ever encountered. The *activity* of mind is a divagation from Being only if Being is a finished whole apart from the self's concern with and constitution in it, or if the meaning of Being does not require active response in order to be understood.[28]

If we are to understand the role of imagination in memory, it is necessary to press further back, to the relation between perception and memory. It is a psychological commonplace that memory retains in pattern only those things which we endow with significance in perceiving or thinking them. Figuring in their concatenation into memory complexes are not alone the intrinsic natures of things, but as well the values with which they are charged by the percipient self. George Santayana, writing of the philosophical stimulation afforded by his travels, says that he constantly and consciously cultivated his powers of percipience. Were one to be "... a mere sensorium, without his own purposes, moral categories and points of reference," his percipience might serve some immediate vegetative purpose but there would be neither reason for, nor possibility of, remembering it.[29] Memory rests then on percipience shaped by the self's inclination, by "postures" of the will. As the intellectual organon of the will, imagination is actively involved in the constellating of data whereby memory contents are formed.

[27] Thus Heidegger: "Perceptive retention of an assertion about something is itself a way of Being-in-the-world; it is not to be interpreted as a 'procedure' by which a subject provides itself with representations of something which remains stored up 'inside' as having been thus appropriated, and with regard to which the question of how they 'agree' with actuality can occasionally arise." *Being and Time*, p. 89.

[28] The poet's poem is an example of an object whose very being depends in part upon the poet's active memory. Moreover, the meaning of the poem depends in part upon the activation of the reader's memory.

[29] George Santayana, *My Host the World* (New York: Charles Scribner's Sons, 1953), pp. 35ff. This view of percipience and memory accounts for much of the artistry of Santayana's autobiographical volumes. In Santayana's descriptions of his friends one is reminded of what Coleridge said of Shakespeare's characters, that they "... were drawn rather from meditation than from observation, or to speak correctly, more from observation, the child of meditation." "Lectures of 1811–12, VII," *Coleridge's Shakespearean Criticism*, ed. Thomas Middleton Raysor, (2 vols.; London: Constable and Company, 1930), Vol. II, p. 131.

The total passivity of imagination in memory must be discredited on another ground as well. Earlier it was said that memory is not simple retention; but it is not the retention of simples, either. We have already called in question the view that, even in the *ordo essendi,* a thing *is* just itself, without ontological intercourse with its field. Likewise in the *ordo cognoscendi,* notwithstanding necessary acts of mental abstraction, the knowledge of a thing requires knowledge of its penumbrae too. (My friend, Sam, is an integral being; I recognize him for himself and no one else. But I know him as qualified by a host of things: his relation to Ted, his crippling disease, our feeling for each other, etc. "He" is in my memory neither as a simple object nor as a simple datum, but as the center of these and other complexities, and as valued by me.) In memory, consequently, a thing is held not in its simplicity but in the complexity of its relations. Moreover, some things are held in memory whose complex relations are not lived out: through memory they lay possibilities upon the present. We could say, figuratively, that a center is retained together with major radii emanating from it, although how far they extend and with what they connect is a matter of the mystery of full historical existence and not to be resolved by attention to memory alone.[30]

As a continuous operation the self is no passive substance; it has no empty space into which objects and events, as soon as they are "past," can be placed without danger of jostling and breakage. The past preserved in memory is the backlying personal condition (not the only one, to be sure) of acts under entertainment and concentration. As such it is constantly being shifted, now one thing now another being called up in new associations, in ready relevance as a limitant upon the emergent novel phase of personal being. Memory contents unceasingly enter into new image-complexes in this process. Few acts of the mind are more remarkable than this, that, whereas in present

[30] Cf. William James: "Every definite image in the mind is steeped and dyed in the free water that flows round it. With it goes the sense of the relations, near and remote, the dying echo of whence it came to us, the dawning sense of whither it is to lead. The significance, the value, of the image is all in this halo or penumbra that surrounds or escorts it—or rather that is fused into one with it . . ." *Principles of Psychology,* Vol. I (New York: Henry Holt & Co., 1890), p. 237.

apperception an object discontinuous with one's being presents itself (*qua* delineated actuality) without any blurring of distinctions, in memory the discontinuous object is profoundly blended with the continuity of the self. It is as if mnemic contents were logs in the "sacred river," Coleridge's figure for memory in its depth. Far from suggesting that the object of memory becomes through active mentality an epiphenomenon of subjective interest, I want only to emphasize that the self in its continuity draws upon its complex past by means of complex memory images; that "in-coming" impressions have their life by ingressing constellations already formed or forming; and that the process of constellating mnemonic contents is the work of (to that degree) active imagination, itself reflecting the life of the will.

(3) The activity of the imagination: the "loosening" of the mnemonic "given" so as to integrate its potency with expanding selfhood. The activity of imagination is by no means limited to its role in memory, but the workings of memory do afford insight into that activity, and especially into one crucial phase of it. Theories which construe the activity of imagination as exhaustively "conformative," "creative," or "synthetic" overlook this phase and are in fact impotent to explain it.[31] I refer to that function of the imagination which involves the piercing, rending, and disjointing of the mnemonic given which prepares it for appropriation to expanding selfhood; the act whereby the meaning of my past changes as I change. The term "mnemonic given" already signals the problem: an object is not given in memory in the way that the typewriter before me is presently given. For example: a particular arroyo in the northwestern Texas Panhandle, in which I herded cattle for weeks on end in my youth, remains in my memory as a region of wild joy and abandoned reverie. When I visit now this shrunk phenomenon in its delineated presence through immediate perception, there is no comparing it in that mode of presence with what it is in my mnemonic mass. For in my memory it is the endless space of the voices of silence that speak from the peripheries of absolute solitude. This paradigmatic space has bespoken different regions

[31] See Appendices I–III below, "Imagination and Conformation," "Imagination and Synthesis," and "Imagination and Creativity."

198

at different times in my accumulating selfhood; and no doubt just before death, somewhere in my being, I shall still be in transaction with what went on in that place of (for me) maximal youthful exposure to the earth's mysterious litany of silent sound.

A few paragraphs back we said that in memory the discontinuous object is profoundly blended with the continuity of the self; it is this blend that is the mnemonic given. And in reckoning with that given we have the circularity of active and passive imagination in evidence. Imagination is passive toward a piece of its former activity: the mnemonic given is a former accommodation of the self and its ingressing constituents. Present appropriation "loosens" the former accommodation in pertinence to new occasions; imagination actively turns on its own passivity, on its own stocked ways of receiving the past. Renewal is not an alteration of the past, but rather the perpetual formation of images through which to receive the depths of its potency.

No doubt the most dramatic instance of this process occurs in connection with the so-called "crisis of images" in a particular individual or in a society at large. In such a crisis, existence is brought into question by a competitive set of "master images"; experience, as it were, is extended over a broader phenomenological range by virtue of more intensive categories. While a less dramatic form of this crisis goes on continually in selfhood, it has burst on the public consciousness and with unprecedented public effect by reason of modern media of instant and "whole" communication. For an American Christian to see via satellite television the life-style of a self-immolating Buddhist priest in Saigon is for him to see another human being whose existence is ordered by radically different self-images: a seeing that, in a sensitive nature, will not be without reflexive effect. No previous crises of images, in the pockets of western intellectual history, have prepared us for the revolution of images (of which we have now only the merest foretaste) that will come with an emergent world culture, made possible by the refinement of world-encompassing communications media. Could we see a history of the world written five hundred years hence, we likely could not understand a line. But we need not turn to times so remote in order to understand the reflexive activity of sundering imagination. Looking to the "long hot summer" violence in the ghetto riots, we see that the reflexive activity of imagination is not a matter of mere abstract importance. The aetiology of this violence is extremely complex. But it owes in no small measure to the ghetto imagination in the face of American television. Seeing there not only the necessities but also the luxuries of middle class white abundance, the ghetto imagination turns in rage toward the re-ordering of the world, starting in the streets.

The activity of imagination in concatenating memory contents is *analytic* in the etymological sense (ἀναλύειν): it "loosens" or "dissolves" the mnemonic given so that the potency of the past may fund, and be appropriated to, the present.[32] In speaking of the power of active imagination to break up the given—more exactly, to increase the phenomenological range of the given—as a prelude to its creative work, I am aware of bringing together emphases that are Coleridgean and Augustinian in origin.

In the *locus classicus* of his theory of imagination Coleridge says of the secondary imagination (the "primary" being for him the creative): "It dissolves, diffuses, dissipates in order to re-create. . . . It is essentially *vital,* even as all objects (as objects) are essentially fixed and dead."[33] By tracing out the process of which the dissolving act of the imagination is the incipient phase, we may achieve some illumination of what John Livingston Lowes called "the very alembic of creative energy."[34]

[32] The sundering activity of imagination can of course become essentially catabolical in a pathological self. Writers on artistic genius rarely fail to point out that the line between genius and the merely pathological, in concrete achievements of active imagination, is notoriously difficult to draw. It is no accident that practicing artists are the source of much testimony about the divisiveness of creative imagination; they witness to the acute agony and disorientation accompanying it, and in extreme cases exhibit in their personal demeanor its destructive aspects.

[33] Samuel Taylor Coleridge, *Biographia Literaria,* Ch. XIII; in *Selected Poetry and Prose of Coleridge,* ed. Donald A. Stauffer (New York: Random House, 1951), p. 263. Coleridge's scant two sentences about the "diffusing" imagination concern the operation of imagination as such and not its connection with memory.

[34] John Livingston Lowes, *The Road to Xanadu: A Study in the Ways of Imagination* (Boston: Houghton Mifflin Company, 1927), p. 44.

Mnemonic contents, as they issue from and exercise pressure upon historical existence and artistic vision, are never simply identical with the givens of present common sense. Indeed Coleridge distinguished imagination from fancy on just this ground. Whereas imagination sunders and re-creates, fancy re-arranges experienced givens in novel patterns;[35] thus the centaur, a conjoining of man and horse, is a fanciful image. The imagination has deep symbolizing power,[36] while fancy can achieve only a skillful piece of photographic editing.

[35] "Fancy . . . has no other counters to play with, but fixities and definites." *Op. cit.* Coleridge would have the support of Sigmund Freud in his view of fancy. Freud writes: " 'Creative' phantasy can, in fact, invent nothing new, but can only regroup elements from different sources." *A General Introduction to Psychoanalysis,* trans. John Riviere (New York: Garden City Publishing Co., 1943), p. 153. Cf. also John Ruskin who claims that (a) fancy has to do with the "outsides of things," does not penetrate their "internality"; (b) fancy, being of externals, cannot feel and so is not directed to the will; (c) fancy is not contemplative, does not brood over the whole, but rather flits from part to part. *Modern Painters,* (Philadelphia: Reuwee, Wattley, and Walsh, 1891), Vol. XXI, pp. 419–21. In direct contrast to such a view as that advanced by Coleridge, Avicenna held that fancy is the fundamentally divisive power of the mind. See Murray Wright Bundy, *The Imagination in Classical and Medieval Thought* (Urbana: University of Illinois Press, 1927), pp. 182–83.

[36] Cf. Eric Unger: "The wider scope of . . . systematic imagination compared with that of reason or rationality in the traditional sense . . . lies in the circumstance that traditional reasonableness tends to follow the lines indicated by the compound facts as they happen to occur or to be given in experience, while reasonable imagination tends to increase the phenomenology which the given represents by either breaking up the compounds into components and connecting them in a different way, or between facts and components which the known experience does not show. . . . In an ultimate sense, imagination too is bound by what is given in experience; but not by the order of composition in which it is given." *The Imagination of Reason* (London: Routledge & Kegan Paul, 1952), p. 106. The context of this passage is a discussion of the imagination as the power through which the mind is related to that which is unknown and eternally unknowable in the scientific sense. Since it is impossible for the All (reality as a whole) to be given to a finite existent, the argument goes, the mind in imagination extends the phenomenology of the givens it has, dividing and recombining them in symbols of the All.

Cf. also Whitehead's discussion of "the fourth grade of actuality" (viz. ". . . the actual occasions which are moments in the life-histories of enduring objects with conscious knowledge"): ". . . [It] is to be identified with the canalized importance of free conceptual functionings, whereby blind experience is analysed by comparison with the

201

The simultaneous diffusion and constellation of the given by imagination in the depths of memory is largely below the surface of consciousness. We are largely unaware of those subtle and far-reaching alliances with which the octopus-like memory enfolds an object perceived or thought. Often it is a matter of mystery why certain events, and therefore certain mnemonic complexes, should exert such affective influence over our continuing existence. T. S. Eliot muses:

Why, for all of us, out of all that we have heard, seen, felt, in a lifetime, do certain images recur, charged with emotion, rather than others? The song of one bird, the leap of one fish, at a particular place and time, the scent of one flower, an old woman on a German mountain path, six ruffians seen through an open window playing cards at night at a small French railway junction where there was a watermill: such memories may have symbolic value, but of what we cannot tell, for they come to represent the depths of feeling into which we cannot peer. . . .[37]

Indeed there is no peering into any particular image-complex as it undergoes constellation in the memory. But when those complexes burst into the poetic consciousness in such a pattern of rhythm as issues in a poem, they open up what Gerard Manley Hopkins called the "inscapes" of things. Increasing the phenomenological range of the "given," mnemonic image-complexes break through the surface of the given to its "in-stress"; they attain a perspective on its wider reach which is inaccessible through such hints as its mere giveness affords.

In connection with the emergence of the work of art, two processes may be discerned: (a) that in which the given object is penetrated and the perception of its broader field is constellated with the self's mnemonic mass, and (b) that in which the memory is "seeded" by a rhythmic intention—issuing in an

imaginative realization of mere potentiality. In this way, *experience receives a reorganization in the relative importance of its components by the joint operation of imaginative enjoyment and of judgment.* The growth of reason is the increasing importance of critical judgment in the discipline of imaginative enjoyment." *Process and Reality,* pp. 269–70. (Emphasis mine.)

[37] *The Use of Poetry and the Use of Criticism,* (Cambridge: Harvard University Press, 1933), p. 148.

integral pattern of images that is the work of art. In the two processes artists (and critics for them) continually testify that memory and imagination are virtually indistinguishable. One recalls in this connection the famous words of Wordsworth:

... Poetry is the spontaneous overflow of powerful feelings: it takes its origin from emotion recollected in Tranquillity: the emotion is contemplated till, by a species of reaction, the tranquillity gradually disappears, and an emotion, kindred to that which was before the subject of contemplation, is gradually produced, and does itself actually exist in the mind.[38]

And again:

... The processes of imagination are carried on either by conferring additional properties upon an object, or abstracting from it some of those which it actually possesses, and thus enabling it to re-act upon the mind which hath performed the process, like a new existence.[39]

When an object re-acts upon the mind like a new existence, when it opens upon the vast field of potency of which it is the focal token, then active mnemonic imagination "hath performed the process."

The poet and biblical prophet make professional capital of what Philip Wheelwright has called man's "threshold existence." Living on the "borderland of a something more" of which the focal given is a token, they build "restlessness into a metaphysical principle," seeking to cross the threshold and yet to return with more, but not less than the numbing mystery of the beyond upon their lips.[40] The act of "distancing" an object, the act of stripping away the forms of its familiar face, is the first stage of the process whereby the active imagination seeks to penetrate the threshold it presents. No less than Wordsworth, Coleridge

[38] William Wordsworth, Preface to *Lyrical Ballads,* (1800); in *The Literature of England,* ed. George B. Woods *et al.,* Vol. II (Chicago: Scott, Foresman and Co., 1941), p. 340.
[39] William Wordsworth, Preface to *Lyrical Ballads,* (1815); in "Essay Supplementary."
[40] Philip Wheelwright, *The Burning Fountain,* pp. 8–16.

bonded this kind of imagination with memory in that deep, unconscious act in virtue of which an object perceived or thought "reacts upon the mind which hath performed the process, like a new existence."[41] Without the "hooks and eyes of memory" man has only the objective givens of a present continuum.[42] And the "hooks and eyes" cannot work unless, as Coleridge said, ". . . imagination, . . . the true inward creatrix, instantly out of the chaos of elements or shattered fragments of memory, puts together some form to fit it."[43]

[41] Cf. also Henry James: "I dropped it [the idea] for the time being into the deep well of unconscious cerebration: not without the hope, doubtless, that it might eventually emerge from that reservoir, as one had already known the buried treasure to come to light with a firm iridescent surface and a notable increase of weight." *The Art of the Novel: Critical Prefaces by Henry James,* with an Introduction by R. P. Blackmur (New York: Charles Scribners, 1937), p. 23.

[42] Coleridge, *The Friend* (London: Printed for Rest Fenner, Paternoster Row, 1818), pp. 25–26. Cf. also John Livingston Lowes, *op. cit.,* p. 43. Eschewing psychological competence and interest, Lowes sets out to show, on the basis of the poems themselves ("The Rime of the Ancient Mariner" and "Kubla Khan"), the contents in Coleridge's memory ("the sleeping images") as they became patterned in his poems. Lowes' performance is only slightly less remarkable than that of Coleridge himself; for in Coleridge, Lowes had to do with ". . . one of the most extraordinary memories of which there is a record, stored with the spoils of an omnivorous reading, and endowed into the bargain with an almost uncanny power of association."

[43] Coleridge, *Anima Poetae,* ed. Ernest Hartley Coleridge, (London: William Heinemann, 1895), p. 206. Among some contemporary poets and critics the relation between imagination and memory is generally thought to tap the very nerve of creativity. The conception of the relation varies from one of simple association to one of virtual identity. Representative discussions will be found in the following: Stephen Spender, *World Within World* (New York: Harcourt, Brace and Company, 1951), pp. 53ff. ("Memory is the root of creative genius"); George Whalley, *Poetic Process* (London: Routledge & Kegan Paul, 1953), pp. 76–94 ("Memory is the central factor in the process of image-making: without memory there can be no poetic creation . . . I cannot see any reason for separating imagination from memory, any more than I can see any reason for separating value and feeling from the elementary states of perception. . . . Imagination as a process of image-making may profitably be described in two modes: first, in its direct relation with perceptual experience, as an unconscious and unwilled process of fusion working upon the sleeping images in the deep well of memory; and then as selecting and fashioning the images of memory into the luminous arresting patterns called poems"); and T. S. Eliot, *op. cit.,* pp. 69–70.

204

If we look more closely at the role of the will in the processes under examination, the Augustinian roots of the present view become apparent. Earlier it was said that perception and memory are structured by the values of the percipient self as well as by the "nature" of the perceived object; Augustine would say the mind bestows attention as it wills.[44] Sensa cannot storm the mind by irrefragable force, he thought; they can only appeal their case, hoping the mind will attend to their claims.[45] By the bestowal of attention in perception and memory, of course, Augustine understood the action of will to be much broader and deeper than that described by conscious volition. Especially is this the case with respect to those percepta and intellectual contents that have gained admission to memory. Once within the retaining walls of memory, they become fair prey for imagination as reflecting the life of will.[46]

As the will is related to the vision of the outward man (viz., in the focusing of attention), Augustine writes in *De Trinitate,* so is the imagination in internal vision the expression of the will and its desires.[47] No passive power of reproduction, the imagination sets to work refashioning the contents of memory along the lines of the will's interest. It is true that Augustine was discussing the nature of error by means of these judgments, since for him all error, as well as all truth, has will-reference. However, error lies not in the imagination but in the will directing imagination as its principle of activity. Nor is it the case that conscious reason can cut in and direct otherwise when the will mis-cues imagination, for two reasons. First, reason itself is

[44] See *De Musica,* 6, 9; also *De Trinitate,* XI, 1–9.

[45] *De Genesi ad Litteram,* XII; 27, 33.

[46] To a Neo-Platonic view of sensation Augustine added a basically Aristotelian theory of memory. He was concerned to show how overwrought active imagination ("phantastical memory") turns on memory for purposes of self-aggrandizement, in short to show how original sin is operative even in memory.

It should be clear that I am not here accepting or commending Augustine's exceptionally crude theory of sensation: If someone sneaks up behind me and gives a blast on a trumpet, I scarcely take counsel with myself before jumping out of my skin. With memory the case is different, however. Horns do not blast in my memory, although I may remember blasting horns. If I do so remember, it will be because that content has been taken under intentional pattern.

[47] *De Trinitate,* XI, 2.

affected by the states and desires of the will;[48] and second, the retained datum becomes so reconstituted by imagination that reason cannot distinguish between the "original" datum and the resultant image. Writing of that internal vision wherein volitionally directed imagination functions, Augustine says:

But if that will which moves to and fro, hither and thither, the eye that is to be informed, and unites it when formed, shall have wholly converged to the inward phantasy . . . then so exact a likeness of the bodily species expressed from the memory is presented, that not even reason itself can discern whether the body itself is seen without, or only something of the kind thought of within.[49]

From this passage it is not difficult to see how the imagination could with great virtuosity play the sycophant to a flatulent will. Certainly Augustine himself spared no rhetoric in his descriptions, drawn largely from personal experience, of how the imagination reconstitutes the data of perception and memory so as to feed the fires of concupiscence. This onanistic preoccupation of the will, through imaginative self-aggrandizement, illuminates the biblical "evil imaginations of the heart."

Having brought into the picture Augustine's view of the relation between conscious reason and will-through-imagination in the ordering of mnemonic contents, we should go on to comment upon the status of intentional pattern with respect to memory, although an extended inquiry into the relation between imagination and intention properly belongs to the succeeding section of this chapter. No doubt it would be foolish to contest the fact that one consciously and effectively imposes intentions upon mnemonic contents. For example, over a number of years I have consigned to memory under various purposive patterns the research upon which this essay unceasingly draws. Occa-

[48] This emphasis is to be found in most of Augustine's middle and later writings. Cf. *Confessions,* XIII, 9; *De Trinitate,* XIV, 6, and IX, 12; *De Magistro,* XI. Otto Zänker summarizes Augustine's position as follows: "If man does not attain a knowledge of truth, the reason for this lies, from the moral point of view, in his impurity of heart, from the religious point of view, in his fundamentally false relation to God." *Der Primat des Willens vor dem Intellekt bei Augustin,* (Gütersloh: C. Bertelsmann, 1907), p. 149.

[49] *De Trinitate,* XI, 4.

sionally, however, an insight bubbles to the surface of the Deep Well whose origins in conscious consignment I cannot fathom, but of whose connection with past learning, in whatever mode, I cannot doubt. It is the form of activating intention at this level with which we are concerned, with the level from which and by means of which the human mind puts more into the world, in terms of meaning, than it takes out of it. (If "creativity" means anything, it means just that!) Coleridge rightly said that ". . . there is in genius itself an unconscious activity; nay, that is the genius in the man of genius."[50]

The deeper the sublimity of a mnemic content the more completely does it approach pure potentiality and thus passivity: the more open is its field of possible alliance with other mnemonic contents. If mnemonic contents at this depth of sublimity are included, there is no reason against supposing that the self, in its forward thrust, carries the totality of its past experience (and in a sense yet to be explicated, the archetypal experience of the race). The crux of the matter, however, is the metaphor "carries"; for the metaphor implies that even in the deepest reaches of the subliminal mind a mnemonic content never eludes activity or activation, however minimal. If this point seems too banal to be emphasized, one does well to recall that the notion of the mere potentiality of mnemonic contents, together with the imagination as their passive receptacle, all but dominated philosophy as near dogma for a millennium or more.[51] Not until the

[50] *Biographia Literaria,* ed. J. Shawcross, (Oxford: The Clarendon Press, 1906), Vol. II, p. 258.

[51] In Albertus Magnus one sees the near-dogma beginning to crack. Albert perpetuated the medieval theory which held that the imagination is the passive receptacle of sensa and so indispensable to memory. But he added the notion that what the imagination retains of the object is its *form* alone. Also, he spoke in a vague way of the imagination as the retainer of "intentions" which were not in the original impressions, and of the necessity for "opinion" to rule on the validity of such intentions. While he did not recognize the imagination as the source, or purveyor, of these intentions, the fact that he considered them (as irreducible to original impressions) to be operative in memory was a giant step in the direction of modernity. See *Alberti Magni Opera Omnia,* (38 vols.; Paris: Vives, 1890–98), Vol. V, pp. 577–81. Discussed at length by M. W. Bundy, *The Theory of Imagination in Classical and Medieval Thought* (Urbana: University of Illinois Press, 1926), pp. 187–95.

207

seventeenth century did such thinkers as Cudworth and Leibniz, having in common the stimulation of Platonism in something like its ancient form, point the direction for a theory of memory which in the recent past Bergson and his followers have developed with far-reaching subtlety. Much that Cudworth said of the unconscious can be found directly applicable to memory as we presently understand it. He wrote:

It is certain our human souls themselves are not always conscious of whatever they have in them; for even the sleeping geometrician hath, at that time, all his geometrical theorems and knowledges *some way* in him; as also the sleeping musician, all his musical skills and songs: and therefore, may it not be possible for the soul to have likewise *some actual energy in it, which it is not expressly conscious of?* We have all experience of our doing many animal actions non-attendingly, which we reflect upon afterwards; as also we often continue a long series of bodily motions, *by a mere virtual intention of our minds,* and as it were *by half a cogitation.*[52]

Applied *mutatis mutandis* to memory, the underscoring in this quotation suggests the point requiring emphasis. A mnemonic content perdures through the ordering power of a "virtual intention," of a "half a cogitation," a pattern that is not always consciously conceived but rather is often unreflexive and non-deliberative.[53] What is the *form* of intentions as they function at this level of mnemonic organization, and as they form the background of personal continuity?[54]

[52] Ralph Cudworth, *The True Intellectual System of the Universe,* (3 vols.; London: T. Tegg, 1845), Vol. I, p. 247. (Emphasis mine.)

[53] Cf. Leibniz's doctrine of "petites perceptions": "There are a thousand indications which make us think that there are at every moment an infinite number of *perceptions* in us, *but without appreciation and reflection,* i.e., changes in the soul itself of which we are not conscious, because the impressions are either too slight and too great in number, or too even, so that they have nothing sufficiently distinguishing them from each other; *but joined to others* they do not fail to produce their effect and to make themselves felt at least confusedly in the mass." G. W. Leibniz, *New Essays Concerning Human Understanding,* trans. A. G. Langley (New York: The Macmillan Co., 1896), pp. 47–48. (Emphasis mine.)

[54] The Stoics rightly estimated the *moral* gravity of this question. Epictetus observed that human deeds take their origin from imagination. Cf. *The Discourses,* Book I, Ch. 28; in *The Stoic and Epicurean Philoso-*

A preliminary answer to this question may be formulated in the following way. Apart from a specifically intended act upon which memory is focused,[55] memory contents are constellated at a subliminal level by *active* imagination (i) as it probes the potential outreach of those contents and (ii) as it orders them according to the dominant intentions of the will. Through these processes novel *ententes* among the contents of past experience emerge; as the depth of past events is increasingly exposed to the expanded and altered directionality of the self, the past, in its "meaning," changes. In the *passive* mode of its operation, the mnemic imagination preserves these *ententes* likewise subliminally, and affords an obscure representation of them at the fringes of consciousness. This representation occurs through "archetypal images" and "master images," which come up for study later. Far from being separable phases, the active and passive modes are polar moments in the functioning of mnemonic imagination. We should not be particular selves with a sense of enriched personal continuity without the simultaneity of these operating modes. Some hint of what near-total personal disintegration would mean is afforded by the common act of recollection. For when one attempts to recall some object, event, or name—especially if it exerted some powerful commerce with his values—he is dimly aware of the deep swelling, shifting, and knocking about of images as the desideratum forces its way to luminous consciousness.

(4) The imagination and the modalities of the past; and mnemonic imagination as limitation of the range of present apprehension. Let us pause to take note of two impressions that may have been forming in the reader's mind. First, it may appear that we have been exploring only the first of the four areas mentioned above (pages 192–193), viz. the activity and passivity

---

phers, ed. Whitney J. Oates (New York: Random House, 1940), pp. 272–75.

[55] When one specifically intends a project, mnemonic contents are specifically focused in relevance to that project. This means that mnemonic contents are torn out of older and larger alliances and established in new and specific configurations. Thus when I genuinely intend to give a lecture on Plato's theory of "becoming," all that I have learned in the past about Plato on other counts ("Forms," soul, errant cause, etc.) becomes patterned in a new and actual constellation.

of imagination in memory. The imagination *qua* active and passive, however, is nothing in itself; imagination is always active on or toward something, as it is passive in the reception of something. Thus the other three areas have been submitted to indirect exploration. Now it will be useful to concentrate rather more directly on the second and third of these, the role of imagination in the transit from one modality of the past to another in memory, and the way in which mnemonic imagination serves to fix the range and quality of apprehension in the present.

Second, it may appear that we have begun to stray from memory as the locus of reflection on the imagination. That impression, indeed, is at least half correct: the offices performed by imagination in connection with memory are performed elsewhere as well, and one will inevitably keep these "elsewheres" in mind when looking to the region of memory. But the impression is half incorrect, too. For one cannot stray from memory so long as he is considering anything involving interpretation. In considering the dissolving, diffusing character of active imagination, we moved imperceptibly from the mnemonic given to the present given. Subsequently it will be necessary to take up the relation between imagination and the "given" as such, but that sort of frontal assault would be meaningless apart from a prior analytic of the modalities of the given and the function of imagination in the shape of these modalities. Consider, for a moment, the complexity of the mnemonic given. Memory "presents." It does so in the double sense: something from the past is "brought forward," made to appear; and the time into which that something is brought is "the present." Here is something odd when we say it: conscious memory is *the presence of a given that is absent*. Something no less odd occurs when we restrict ourselves, or attempt to restrict ourselves, to a present given (i.e., a given shorn of mnemonic reference). That is, there is no given I can grasp in its sheer temporal presence. By the time I can think/say it, it has infiltrated memory: the "present given" is therefore the youngest "mnemonic given." Immediate perception or intellection therefore involves *the absence of a given that is present*. There is no immediacy without the wholeness made possible by memory; there is no wholeness of memory without the immediacy of presence. The offices of

210

imagination are to be marked primarily in connection with the execution of wholeness, wherever wholeness is executed, largely in memory, intention, and the potency of events for expanding and contracting selfhood.

That is not to say that imagination sustains no relation to immediacy, but rather that imagination delivers us from the immediacy of the pure temporal present into the historical unity of the modes of time. Of the *purely* immediate temporal present it can only be said that it is the unintelligible ground of historical time. The purely immediate temporal present is in fact a radical abstraction, the most abstract of all modalities of time (in quite the same way that Being-itself, apart from all beings, is the most abstract of all ontological modalities). The *actual* historical present is always ambiguous, because of its conjunction of immediacy and wholeness; but it is never totally unintelligible to an imaginative mind. Were the actual historical present totally unintelligible, we would be faced with an impossible problem of schematism, as Kant saw with unparalleled genius. That we never surprise a mode of historical time uninfected with the other modes of time is evidence that the schematism is actual; and from actuality to possibility, the old philosophical adage goes, the chances are good. (We may note in passing that Kant, in his doctrine of the transcendental synthesis of schematizing imagination, was one-sidedly concerned to ground the intelligibility of the present continuum: for him, Enlightenment science. He thus lost sight of the intrinsic ambiguity of the historical present, and so short-circuited the implications of his own position on the imagination for the historicity of human being.)

Because of the interpenetration of past and present, it is impossible to consider the role of imagination in gaining transit from one modality of the past to another without at the same time taking up the way in which mnemonic imagination limits the range and shapes the quality of our apprehension in the present. Let us consider the latter first.

Whenever imagination remains fundamentally passive toward its former activity, the range of apprehension becomes fixed in that degree.[56] We are born into a firmament of images; with our

[56] This point will be pursued below under the "stocked, lignified, ossified" imagination, pp. xyg.

mother's milk we drink in a universe of images in which an accommodation between common objects and mental processes already obtains. As the body takes its basic health from an ancestral line and initial food, so the mind takes its prehensions of Being-in-the-world from an endemic cultural inheritance. Of course there is no living the whole of one's life off the initial nurture of one cultural breast; the infant cannot store up strength against the needs of manhood and the plastic mind cannot be prepared for everything by which it will be impressed. The more literate a person becomes, the greater distance he gains on the present in which he lives, the more prolific are his sources of cultural nutrition. Nonetheless, his proliferated nutrience is largely of an intellectual sort. The western *savant* of world religions or the percipient American world-traveller may learn a great deal about southeast Asian Buddhism, but neither will be able to apprehend his Being-in-the-world as a Hinayana Buddhist does, standing (say) in a centuries-old tradition in Burma. It belongs to the historicity of human being to be "oriented," to be inserted into human being according to the ways of previously active, historical imagination, i.e., according to tradition. At the present juncture in history it is simply absurd to speak of a "universal history," a common history out of which all men everywhere have their being. A telling point against the actuality of such a history is the fact that there is no universal language; and nothing is sillier, *pace* George Bernard Shaw and all forms of *Esperanto,* than the effort to create a universal language in advance of a universal history. The time may come, as we have noted, when man will stand out of a universal history. But for the time being, we "see" as our several and radically different historical imaginations let us "see."[57] This is a matter of no small moment for a doctrine of revelation: revelation solicits us to be, out of our own historicity, before God the Lord of the Ages. It does not lay my western historicity upon a Vietnamese peasant as the condition of his being authentic man before God, nor does it subjugate our two historicities to some primordial or even eschatological universal history.

[57] Only "fated" human being remains content with the sedimentations of traditional seeing, to be sure. We shall turn to this shortly.

It is no part of our task to show how imagination is specifically lignified in large or small geographical cultural areas on the contemporary scene.[58] That were an enormous phenomenological project, although it is prosecuted daily in the marketplace, especially by Madison Avenue men, who contribute themselves to lignifying imagination anew (so soap is to be *seen* as enhanced sexuality, and coffee as conviviality). Such a project, for western man, would begin with the root metaphors of the Greek and Judeo-Christian streams of heritage, and end with the confluence of familial and immediately environmental images that go into the apprehension of a present situation. Apart from the "crisis of images" to which we have referred, mnemonic imagination limits apprehension in a largely subconscious way. The unreconstructed white man nurtured in the social and cultural climate surviving the Old Confederacy is hardly aware of adjusting his relationships with Negroes through the power of such images, say, as that of antebellum white southern womanhood or that of the white man as the benign patron of ignorant, ineducable, and basically happy primitives when "in their place" and with a wagonload of watermelons on hand. Or consider the ancient class struggle in its contemporary form in Europe (not to mention its counterpart in the American "status symbol" gaggle). In Italy, for example, where the class lines are perhaps as rigidly fixed as ever, there is a passion to negate the public *appearance* of these lines through what is called the *bella figura.* Thus the Roman cleaning woman will go hungry and move about in tatters in her one-room quarters if by such denial she can join the *dopo siesta* parade tricked out in the latest fashion. The greatest calamity is not to fail to advance from a lower to a higher class, but to *appear* to belong to a lower class. To see at first hand what denial of "natural" instinct is involved in this prosecution is to understand what astonishing power prevailing images exert over personal existence.

Now a life whose sentient and conceptual ambience is handed over to lignified imagination is a life handed over to fate. The foregoing analysis of memory has exposed a basis for under-

[58] The reader who would understand the history of the ossification of the imagination in the west should go, sell what he must, and buy Owen Barfield, *Saving the Appearances,* (London: Faber and Faber, 1957)!

213

standing the role of imagination not only in enriched historical selfhood but also in unhistorical selfhood; the counterfeit is understood from the precious. To grasp the counterfeit is no less important than to know the precious, since the market in human selfhood is flooded with counterfeit coin. For the most part, our *de facto* existence is more heavily freighted with unhistorical, fated memory than with historical memory; we exist, for the most part, in the power of a *custom*arily finished past and so are in bondage to a future that is only more of the same. We refuse to the past our active complicity, thus refuse the potency of its rich modality, and as a consequence abjure responsibility for the present.

So it is necessary to turn to the function of imagination in gaining access to the past in its plural modality of potency. In doing so, the co-inherence of the modes of historical time is once again encountered. The present upon which the past projects itself is itself the recoil of "dominant intention," the "kick" of "dominant intention" when discharged on the future. We live out of the future, understand out of the past. The kind of life had out of the future determines the modality of the past that is accessible to understanding. Thus if the future is effectively closed off, the past will be understood only in its modality as fate. Active imagination evades a fated rendezvous with an object by means of indirectness and circumambience: it seizes the whole background and foreground, the penumbral field, of the object, and overlays that field with the self's own background and foreground. In this way the object is cheated of its "literal," i.e. fated, meaning in advance. Torn in advance from its moorings in jaded vision, the object *appears* in its native historical habitat, i.e., *qua* event.[59]

The modalities of the past, discriminated earlier, may now be brought forward: the ontic, the ontologically relevant, and the

[59] These remarks are pertinent to the fourth area mentioned above (p. 193). They indicate how active imagination achieves fullness of referential range in connection with a delineated object—which object, by virtue of instantiating that range is called a symbol. But I am claiming that active imagination of this sort is by no means limited to what we normally consider as the realm of poetics; that it is involved in the perception of our historical reality.

214

recollected past.[60] I prescind from a discussion of the transit from the present and the recollected past to the ontic past. One has only to mention the name of R. G. Collingwood and the huge body of literature he spawned in order to be made aware of what a responsible inquiry on this topic would require. It is a topic about which Christian theology cannot be indifferent, as prosecutors of "the new quest of the historical Jesus," and notably James M. Robinson, have driven home.[61] While theology shares in a general and generalizable hermeneutic of historicity, it has perpetual recourse materially to a particular fund of ontological potency that was presented or re-presented in the ontic past. In Jesus Christ—including his background and foreground—, by ontic word and deed, an integral potency for human being in the world was established. If I understand them, the "new questers" propose to gain access to the ontological potency of the Christ-event from the side of its onticity in Jesus.

I am presently concerned with transit from another direction, and in a larger or at least more generalizable frame. It is the transit from present onticity "back" to the ontological potency that sleeps, that has not been made compossible with the being I have emerged to be: rather, has been made actual without my complicity, as fate. Fate, I have said, is the ontologically relevant past made to pertain to the present by previous appropriations of it to which I do not accord my active complicity. Fate in fact reduces the ontological potency of the past by making prior appropriations of the past constitutive of the past. To say the same thing another way, fate destroys the eventfulness of the past.

Wherever presentations or re-presentations of Being, whether Being in potential or actual mode, are conjoined with man's reality-sense, i.e., wherever the experience of being man in the

---

[60] These discriminations are rough, as noted before. They are not categorial equivalents; positively, to include "the recollected past" with the other two is very likely to make a "category mistake." For what one recollects will be one of the other two, or some discrimination within one or the other or both.

[61] Cf. especially James M. Robinson, "Kerygma and History in the New Testament," in *The Bible in Modern Scholarship*, ed. by J. Philip Hyatt, (Nashville: Abingdon Press, 1965), pp. 114–50.

215

world is eventful, imagination is actively at work. Likewise, wherever the heteronomous ossifications of man's reality sense are under siege, active imagination will be found leading the charge.

These comments may be expanded by attending to active imagination as it functions in revelation. By revelation in this context I understand the solicitation to "see" myself as existing out of the ontological potency established in the Christ-event, as that potency pertains to reckoning with my own historical temporality. This potency is held captive in the sedimentations of my history and in the ossification of my reality-sense, as it is bound in the traditions of the west in which I share. Whence comes the impulse to imagination? What *activates* imagination, turns it against its own ossifications, its passive perduration in business as usual? These questions are no less complex than crucial for an understanding of revelation, since they raise the question of "constraint" upon imagination as it functions in the revelatory process. We cannot assume that imagination in and of itself will invariably evade the *cul-de-sac* to which its passive office conducts man, unless we can also assume that the will, of which it is the intellectual organon, is invariably oriented to the self's ownmost potency. These matters must be treated more extensively hereafter.

But let us say what we can now. Imagination is turned, made reflexive in the sense described in Chapter IV, in a state of "imaginative shock." Imaginative shock is the mental correlate of "ontological shock" (Tillich). The latter is a jarring of one's reality-sense, the conviction that one's disposition is cheating himself of his ownmost possibilities of being. By that act, active imagination is thrown into gear in quest of just what those potencies are. This gearing up and gearing down is none other than the hermeneutical spiral.

Two points in the spiral may be isolated. (a) Imagination is put in shock only by language spoken in its own tongue. (b) The ontological potency established in the past yields itself in unsedimented form only as its original nondiscursive embodiment (i.e., the interaction of image and event) is re-enacted in the first-order language of presently active imagination. These two interconnected points obviously bear elaboration.

216

(a) Imagination is put in shock only by language spoken in its own tongue: since our recondite perceptions owe to a mode of imagination (i.e., the passive), only an "imaginative" appeal will turn the imagination into another mode (i.e., the active). Only first-order language will invoke the imagination to do first-order, fully reflexive, work. This is the case not only with imagination as it functions in revelation, but also generally, and especially in the arts. Imagination is activated in the reader by the first-order language of the poem: the poem so dis-locates him that he can only think in a non-recondite way.[62]

It is at this point, in our context, that "Word of God" is of decisive importance. Whether in preaching, sacrament, or whatever mode of worship, the sole intent of proclamation is to lay the ontological potency of the Christ-event upon the hearer as his ownmost potency of being man in the world, and that in first-order language. Word of God holds in itself an initial circumspection of ontological potency which the hearer is called to make his own through the re-enactment of his own historicity. It is the sole rationale of the church to speak the first-order language of this initial circumspection in a contemporary idiom. Both the proclaiming church and the activated hearer stand under the constraint of what both are summoned to re-enact. Nothing works against that constraint so much as the church's repetition of its own sedimentations.

(b) Activated imagination sets about to dismember the self's history; it harks back to those potencies excluded by actualizations, and seeks to bring them forward as the frame out of which the self may have its future. Having been shocked into act by first-order language in the present, imagination interrogates the

---

[62] "Language" in "first-order language" is by no means limited to a verbal system. Gesture, line, color, etc., are equally media of first-order language. Having confronted the New Mexico landscapes of Doel Reed, a contemporary artist of great visual power, I am unable any longer to see the "sky" in a recondite way. Even as I write these lines, I have just had a similar experience. A fellow hotel guest, David Burliuk—the so-called "Father of Russian Futurism" and one of the original group of "Blaue Reiter" —has made me see (in part through animated conversation, but more through his rapidly executed sketches) in the craggy masses rising abruptly from the Tyrrhenian Sea at Positano, now visible through my window, not just another heap of fortuitously placed boulders, but a spirited dialogue between Socrates and Schiller.

self's past in quest of those occasions, now bricked over by mythical, conceptual, and temporal distance, in which the self's ownmost potentialities were established and came into first-order expression. With that, personal existence will not have been brought under the power of the Christ-event, except insofar as that event lies in a heritage freshly appropriated. Rather the self is made ready to speak (and hear) in first-order language about its own past, and thus is readied for participation in the illuminating and constitutive power of the Christ-event, itself "de-reconditing," without category mistakes (i.e., one's ownmost potency and that presented or re-presented by Jesus Christ are conjoined in the same mode of discourse, that of first-order expression).

The "de-reconditing" of the Christ-event is a complex affair, to say the least. It is altogether comparable to the way in which active imagination sunders a present given in order to gain access to its penumbral field. And it would be foolish to claim that active imagination works on its own to deliver the Christ-event over to present re-enactment: a lot of plain technical historical labor is involved. All sorts of historiographical means are used to gain distance on present recollection, precisely in order to gain proximity to the event itself in its ontological potency. Technical historiography will disclose unifying concepts, myths, narratives, chronicles, ecclesiastical structures, art forms, etc., as the bearers of the event across the bridge of time. In all these "bearers" active imagination seeks the fundamental language of avowal or confession, that language in which the event is incarnate or "inverbalized." An event in the past which gave rise to no surviving first-order language cannot be re-enacted.

Here we have only sketched the hermeneutical *field* of revelation in respect of memory and the past: a field that "begins" out of a presently spoken first-order language that dimly circumspects the thing intended, a language that invokes its own check and expansion by exciting recourse to the backlying first-order language it intends, which in turn is brought forward in re-enactment out of one's own history in a first-order language that surpasses the "beginning." This process has no term; the hermeneutical spiral is endless. Finished manhood in Christ, as the

218

potency to be re-enacted as one's ownmost, has ever to be appropriated by unfinished man.[63]

B. The Imagination and Intention

The tragedy of life is, it must be premature, inconclusive and inconcludable, in order to be life; it must be before itself, in advance of itself, to have been at all.[64]

In order to show how orientation to the future involves once again and from another perspective the co-inherence of the modes of historical time, it will be useful to bring forward the pertinent discussion in Chapter IV. There two modes of intention were discriminated. The first was called "the intention of the specific project," the purposing to accomplish a discrete task or to bring into being (or presence) a discrete object. Such a specific project was said to cast before it a wave of lesser and even more specific projects, and to leave behind (i.e., ahead, as its future) a wake of larger and less specific possibilities. In addition to a lateral relativity to wave and wake, the specifically intended project was shown to be vertically relative to the second mode of intention, that of "dominant direction." In the mode of dominant direction, intention is not the entertainment of *a* project but rather the projection of the self's dominant directionality as that directionality evades fixation in any past or present point-instant. Thus intentions of dominant direction reflect the self's projective being as a whole. As such they reflect

[63] This point may be set in a larger frame by quoting from an unpublished manuscript by Professor Robert W. Funk, tentatively entitled *Prolegomena to New Testament Theology:* "The Christ-event gives rise to innumerable futures just because it is a historical event and has to be appropriated historically. The meaning of the Christ-event is disclosed only in the faith to which it gives rise. Like the Christ-event faith too is historical. It follows that the Christ-event can be appropriated faithfully only in relation to particular contexts. A single monolithic tradition would yield ahistorical faith and an ahistorical Christ. A historical Christ and historical faith necessarily give rise to a multiplicity of traditions and interpretations." For further development of this theme, see Appendix IV below.

[64] William Faulkner, *The Town*, (New York: Random House, 1957), pp. 317-18.

219

that totality of concern (Heidegger's "Care") out of and through which the self's specific projects are intended; at the same time, they are that upon which specific projects are projected. Through projection in the mode of dominant intentionality, possibility funded in the past is disclosed, and so the past is recuperated; the present is given that quality in which the specific project will "appear." Obviously, it will be necessary to expand these comments, as they gather up the previous discussion but move beyond it.

(1) The form which the two modes of intention assume in the mind. For the moment, let us compare the two modes of intention as regards their mental form. For the most part, neither mode can be said to assume the form of discursive propositions; the mode of the specific project, rarely; the mode of dominant direction, never (i.e., never without distortion). Paraphrasing Farrer, one could say that intention in the mind is the analogue in the will of discursive propositions purporting to describe what is projected.[65] Since intending in both modes, but especially in the second (dominant directionality), is fundamentally non-discursive, it should also be said that intention in the mind is the imaginative analogue of discursive propositions purporting to describe what is intended. There is another reason why intending is an imaginative act. Intending pertains to what is not, rather than to what is coming to be; and imagination is always found to be active in the interstices between non-being and being, in coming to be. Not even the dominant directionality of the self can be said to *be,* without remainder, else it would not need projecting forward. Such constancy as the self has is what it wins from the future, viz., the "form" for recuperating the content of the other modes of historical time. (That is why, at the present perilous moment in the United States, the ghetto Negro can view his death in a riot with apparent equanimity: he has no future out of which to gain constancy.)

Before proceeding, we should take note not to be misled. In looking to the mental form of intention we are not inquiring after that medium through which the future is known. Neither through imaginative intention nor any other mental act is the

65 See Austin Farrer, *Finite and Infinite,* (Westminster: Dacre Press, 1943), p. 122.

220

future known as it will fall out. Anticipatory imagination in the mode of dominant intention does not transform the future into the present, i.e., does not predict. Rather it brings the future toward us in the sense that it garners from our dominant intentions the horizon of the present in which the specific project, in enactment, appears. It is not alone human being that is unfinished; the horizon or framework in which that being is to be grasped is also unfinished. Only where the question of horizon is radicalized can the modalities of the self's becoming be radicalized. In effect, we are attempting to see how the imagination qualifies the horizon of the historical present out of the historical past and the historical future, that present in which the *intentionality* of consciousness functions.[66] Thus we are treating the temporal dimension of *Horizontverschmelzung,* broached in Chapter II.

A few pages back it was said that the present is the recoil of dominant intention, the "kick" of dominant intention as discharged on the future. Now it can be noted that vis-à-vis a specific project the imagination functions in two ways that differ according to the "present" in which that project will appear in its enactment.

(2) Imagination and the specific project.

(a) In one way, imagination is initially active in the envisagement of a specific project, while it is finally all but quiescent as the project, no longer intended, heaves into the present as reality. Suppose I intend to tear down my garage and build a study in its place. I formulate this intention in a discursive way, but not before imagination has played with other and far-reaching possibilities. In direct proportion to distance from enactment, the discursive formulation surfaces rarely; the project is prosecuted intentionally in the imagination. When I go to the garage, it is not the garage I "see." Where the old tires hang on the wall, I see bookshelves; no, not there, a fireplace there. I do not see a garage door but a window. I back the car out the window, drive off, and give the matter no more "thought." I return from a day at the university and park the

---

[66] By "intentionality of consciousness" I mean the openness of consciousness to the given in its referential totality and thus to the given in its plurisignative value. (See above, Ch. IV.)

car in my study; more specifically, in the fireplace. While I have not been "thinking," the fireplace has shifted from the wall and has become free-standing in the middle of the room. In short, the garage has entered a new intentional totality of reference. It is the spearhead of a whole range of possibility, the "point" of which I see through the range.

As the study comes abuilding, the range contracts; and with that imagination wanes, faced increasingly as it is with mounting focalized constraints. Imagination jousts with proliferating discursive thought, but every nail in the study is a nail in the coffin of imagination. Finally the study is a delineated actuality, an object no longer of intentional imagination. It inhabits the sort of "present" the garage inhabited before the garage was an intended study. Of the study as a delineated object we could say what Whitehead said of "percepta in the mode of presentational immediacy," viz., that ". . . they are distinct, definite, controllable, apt for immediate enjoyment, and with the minimum of reference to past, or to future."[67]

Now I have described this way of intending a specific project in the indicative mood. It is however a deficient way of intending; and it reflects an arrestment rather than an atrophy of imagination. It is less the case that the actuated project (the finished study) has nosed imagination out of the picture, more that reason has decreed a present, without reference to future or past, in which the study can only appear as a sharply delineated thing, no longer serving to beckon the imagination to a larger field of reference.

(b) In another way, imagination is no less active initially in the envisagement of a specific project. But rather than being reduced and narrowed by oncoming enactment, imagination in this way is renewed by the irrefrangible relativity of intentions as they reflect the constancy of the self's being-toward. Intentions of specific projects, we have said, are both laterally and vertically relative: no sooner does a project come toward us in fulfillment than it spawns other intentional projects, in renewed imagination, both fore and aft (to consider only lateral relativities, for the nonce). Thus a fulfilled project reaches a

[67] *Process and Reality,* p. 271.

"present" trailing clouds of reference, a present made possible by the future it anticipates and the past it gathers up. So I do not establish myself in the study-chair in the way I parked the car in the garage. When I am in the study in the mood of study, the study is not there in the mode of delineated presence; it is not an isolated "object," except as reason freezes the eventful experience of it. That the study is now actual does not mean that it is the terminus of intentional imagination, but rather that its meaningful actuality is presented by virtue of the future it subserves and on which imagination is at work. I am thinking on a topic; across from me a wall of indiscriminate colors and shapes appear as books; several titles leap out, as though shoved forward in the shelf; from each certain ideas pop out; I take down a copy and am led. . . . In every step, imagination is renewed as the present is made thick by anticipation.

(3) Imagination and dominant directionality. As regards its mental form, the intention of dominant direction needs now some explicit attention. It is in the mode of dominant intention that the imagination is to be found in the nearest thing to a pure state. That is so because in the mode of dominant directionality the will projects forward its patterns of concern without specificity of content; or perhaps one could say, projects the will's patterns with respect to wholeness of value rather than in connection with the immediacy of particular acts. The historical future has no environment, and thus no contents upon which directionality may exercise itself. (As noted earlier, in the discussion of memory, intentions of dominant directionality order contents reflexively. The historical past is instaurated through the reflex application of projected form upon mnemonic legacy.) In the intention of dominant directionality the imagination projects something like the pure patterns of the will's teleological drive. Indeed in this form of intention is to be found the nearest thing to the coalescence of imagination as modality of mind and the will as potential ontological power. In a life given over *entirely* to intending in this mode (if such a thing is conceivable), the will's power would be limited to the "imaginary," and the imagination would be constrained only by the endogenous appetition of the will. Perhaps the nearest thing to

223

this extremity (common in the mentally ill) in average experience is "day-dreaming."

It follows from what has been said about lack of specific contents that intentions of dominant direction themselves are never fully concentrated into particular acts.[68] In themselves they are intentions without intensification or concentration. As there is no action in the "pure" mode of intentional directionality, so there is no knowledge in the "pure" mode of imagination.[69] This is the foundation of the commonplace that one is ignorant of nothing so much as his own deepest motives. Rather than fulfilling all righteousness by making *instant* theological capital of this point, let us prosecute the question of how we know the self's dominant directionality, insofar as we do know it.

(4) Dominant directionality, world, and interpretation. If what has been said so far possesses merit, that knowledge can only be circumambient. One's dominant directionality is known indirectly only through the "world" that recoils from it. By world I mean the reality-frame in which entities appear as the intentionality of experience. World is indeed coextensive with the horizons of the historical present, with the added note that it is that fusion of horizons which disposes us to receive or see whatever appears in the historical present in a particular way.[70]

[68] Cf. Austin Farrer: "If one particularises the intention of the will *a priori,* the will contains implicitly and potentially all that it will ever do, and therefore an implicit knowledge of its own destiny, and its history is ony the unwinding of this, and is logically independent of any bit-by-bit determination by its environment—the extreme form of Leibnitzianism." *Finite and Infinite,* p. 138.

[69] Positively, imagination is cognitive only in respect of the *intentionality* of consciousness, i.e., out of the concert of mind with a given in plurisignative mode.

[70] It will be noticed that I speak of the *historical* present, not the temporal present. In this I follow Fackenheim generally and Heidegger obliquely. Cf. Emil Fackenheim: "The temporal present is a vanishing point of passage. The historical present is an act of integration in which anticipated future possibilities are integrated with past actualities into present action." *Metaphysics and Historicity,* (Milwaukee: Marquette University Press, 1961), p. 40. (On Fackenheim's distinction between the temporal and historical past, and between the temporal and historical future, see pp. 37-40.) Cf. also Heidegger, *Being and Time,* Sections 32, 64, 65, and 74; and *idem, Einführung in die Metaphysik,* (Tübingen: Max Niemeyer, 1953), p. 34f.

224

As Heidegger never tires of saying in *Being and Time,* world for the most part is shaped by environment in the temporal present rather than by procession from the historical future. In the terms developed earlier, world for the most part is dominated by the environing things of passive, ossified imagination, the things of "common sense" (the medieval seat of the imagination!). But the anticipatory world of dominant directionality has no environment (save an instaurated historical past); it is won in liberation from a hardened temporal present, and so breaks the vicious circle between environment and world. In a reverse spiraling recoil, an authentic world is afforded in which "things" may appear in the concert of their background and foreground with the background and foreground of the self. In short, a world of symbolic, eventful intercourse is wrested from the modalities of time.

Imagination is therefore ineluctably bound up with the historical possibilities of human being. With that imagination is not a license to invent *ex nihilo;* it cannot, in an undemented self, intend a world that is not bound to the historical past it renews; indeed, renewal means the disclosure of ontological possibility funded in the ontic, temporal past, that now must be brought forward historically. Moreover, insofar as imagination reflects not alone the self's endogenous will to power, it is impelled toward anticipatory world as toward mnemonic re-enactment, viz., by *shock.* This shock need not be Heidegger's all-embracing being-toward-death. It may be *A Communist Manifesto;* a hand reaching over the Berlin wall; a parable of Jesus spoken in a parabolic way. Take the last: a parable of Jesus, parabolically spoken and parabolically heard, activates the imagination. For the parable shocks the intention of a world (precisely not an "otherworldly" world) in which, and only in which, one can see what the parable says.[71]

That is, world (and so dominant directionality) is known only by *interpretation.* It is not that we know world by interpreting it, but rather that world is circumspected in the interpretation of whatever is presently at hand. As Heidegger says, interpretation ". . . is grounded in *something we have in advance—in a fore-*

[71] Cf. Funk, *Language, Hermeneutic, and Word of God,* pp. 124-222.

having. . . . in *something we see in advance*—in a *fore-sight*."[72]
All interpretation involves the projection of those possibilities
of a being which it is. The possibilities of a being make projection possible, and it is projection that discloses possibilities.[73] In
the case of the self, its specific projects are interpreted in relation
to that upon which they are projected; and the "upon which" is
the self's dominant directionality, the world circumspectively
fore-seen and fore-had. Our dominant directionality is disclosed
circumambiently as we track our common interpretations
(interpretations of the common) to their lair. That is why the
parable shocks. It presents itself initially as "sensible," as packed
with common interpretation. But when we follow the signal of
what is there interpreted commonly, we are led into a peregrine
world, an "upon which" that cannot bear the projections of
common interpretation. If our own dominant intentionality is
infiltrated by that peregrine world, so that it becomes our ownmost as well, we are led into the parable as the disclosure of
our possibilities; i.e., we are interpreted by it.

Let us pause to take our bearings. In the development of a
theory of imagination, as the matter is viewed here, two things
are of crucial importance if the function of imagination in the
intentionality of experience is to be descried. (i) It is required to
see how imagination yields "food for thought" by allowing the
background and foreground, and thus the penumbral field, of
a given "entity" to preside over its apprehension. (ii) It is
equally necessary to see how imagination constellates the self's
background and foreground as the historical present, as the
horizon in which an entity-field is given for apprehension.

Under the rubrics of memory and intention, we have been
concerned with (ii); and the discussion of imagination under
those rubrics has disclosed certain items in the problematic of
imagination that bear directly on (i),[74] indeed upon the conjunction of (i) and (ii). We do not have (i), then (ii); or (ii), then
(i). We have both if we have historical event known in the
historical mode of knowledge.

[72] *Being and Time,* Section 32, p. 191.
[73] See my "Heidegger's *Being and Time* and Phenomenology," in
loc. cit., pp. 309–29.
[74] These items are enumerated below, note 80.

And we have both in the event issuing in a work of art. Such an event, as will be developed more fully later, does not first occur, then is known, and then finally gives rise to a work of art. The poet's grasp of the event and his verbal articulation of it are indistinguishable: he knows in expressing. Here is an analogue of the role of imagination in revelation: the poet's imagination discloses that by which it is finally solicited. The imagination gives rise to an event that cannot be concentrated *qua* event except as the event gives rise to imagination. The event may have been potential and immanent in the poet's being; but it occurs actually and transcendently (i.e., it becomes possible for others—and for him—to participate in it) only as incarnated in his rhythmic pattern of words and images.[75]

[75] Before leaving the subject of intention I should say that I do not suppose the two modes of intention discriminated here to cover every human act in which intention is involved. For example, there appears to be some form of intention in all poetics, some "seeding" of the clouds of experience that precipitates the work of art. Such intending seems to have neither the specificity of a project nor the generality of a dominant direction. From artists themselves we have testimony that an invoking intention of some sort goes together with the evocation of diverse elements into an art-form. While this claim could be illustrated from a great variety of sources, there will be some merit in staying with those cited earlier on the role of mnemonic imagination in poetics.

Coleridge notes that beyond "that state of nascent existence in the twilight of imagination and just on the vestibule of consciousness" there must be, in the poetic process, "a confluence of our recollections" through which "we establish a centre, as it were, a sort of nucleus in [this] reservoir of the soul." (*Collected Letters of Samuel Taylor Coleridge,* ed. Earl Leslie Griggs, [Oxford: The Clarendon Press, 1956], Vol. I, p. 377; *Biographia Epistolaris,* ed. A. Turnbull, [London: G. Bell and Sons, 1911], Vol. II, p. 182.) Elsewhere (*Anima Poetae,* ed. Ernest Hartley Coleridge, [London: William Heinemann, 1895], p. 206), Coleridge writes of "the streamy nature of association, which thinking curbs and rudders," in commentary upon which John Livingston Lowes has written the following: "Grant all you will to the involuntary and automatic operations of the Well [of memory]—its blending and fusings . . . there still remains the architectonic imagination, moving, *sua sponte,* among the scattered fragments, and discerning, latent in their confusion, the pattern of the whole. And the shadow of a sail in an old travel-book and the rude parallelism of a pair of sketches of porpoises and dolphins—themselves among the recollections tumbling over one another in the dark—may through an act of imaginative vision gather up the whole chaos into consciousness as a poised and symmetrical shape of light." (*The Road to Xanadu,* p. 72.)

In the same essay in which he describes poetry as "the spontaneous overflow of powerful feelings," Wordsworth says that ". . . poems to

227

We turn now to imagination and event, the conjunction of (i) and (ii).

C. The Imagination and Event

Earlier examination of "event" in various contexts must now be advanced. An historical event to which the human self is party, it was said, is itself a concentration of subsidiary concentrations. The simplest historical event conceivable would be the concrete interaction of oneself's various phases brought into focus and one object with its various phases brought into focus. Not only is so simple an event rare to the point of non-existence; the description of it is a discerption. Only from a vantage in rational distance is an event broken into constitutive concentrations. That sort of distance is required, to be sure, in the degree that the event is complex, ambiguous, and important. Indeed, without a scale of cognitive responses we very likely should not discriminate events at all, not to mention discriminations within an event. Were the flow of reality experienced exclusively in the

---

which any value can be attached were never produced on any variety of subjects but by a man who, being possessed of more than usual organic sensibility, had also thought long and deeply." However much a poem embodies and evokes the feelings, he continues, it does so worthily only in relation to the *purpose* it incarnates. (Preface to *Lyrical Ballads, op. cit.,* p. 333.) For something of the same emphasis upon the balance of "inspiration" and intentional organization, on the contemporary scene, cf. T. S. Eliot, *The Use of Poetry and the Use of Criticism,* (Cambridge: Harvard University Press, 1933), p. 146.

An uncommonly fresh and exhaustive treatment of this issue will be found in George Whalley, *Poetic Process,* Chs. V and VI, *passim.* Whalley writes: "Without the poet's collusion, the poem cannot make itself; but the poet must wait until what was known and forgotten makes itself known afresh in a new and singular light, constellated in secret, enucleated out of the black fire of memory. . . . The poetic germ is not the subject or the theme of the poem; its function is to crystallize, to 'seed' the images of memory into a pattern which is felt to be significant even though the significance cannot be known until the poem has been fully extricated. By insemination the germ generates an event of reality which is compact of numerous instants of reality, remembered and forgotten, and with none of which it can be identified. One mark of poetic genius, I suspect, is the knack of recognizing the germ and fostering the process of parturition, by a dainty poise between passivity and concentration, between astonished acceptance and critical severity, between stimulation and selection" (pp. 84–86).

228

mode of feeling, for example, the flood would be without boundary. Experience would not be episodic. To be sure, in the rush of feeling there are whirlpools, rapids, and eddies; what might be called "gathered ambiguity." Reason as well as imagination responds to gathered ambiguity in the continuum of feeling; and so it can scarcely be said that an event is a merely subjectively differentiated portion of the action or motion of reality.[76] In response to gathered ambiguity, just so that ambiguity may be rationally arrested, the mind sets an *a quo,* an initial situation, and an *ad quem,* a terminal situation; peoples the space-time between, i.e., identifies movers, actors, sufferers, and audience; and calls the whole unit "event." It is an infallible sign of intense and far-ranging ambiguity when the mind has acute difficulty with placing its boundary markers and with making out the *dramatis personae.* Where feeling (as distinct from sentiment) refuses to submit to rational arrest, it is a sign that the *ad quem* of an event has been posted but not observed. It was an understanding of event as felt, gathered ambiguity that led Durrell (through Balthazar) to say, ". . . I love to feel events overlapping each other, crawling over one another like wet crabs in a basket."[77]

It is a stunning fact that history, as that discipline is prosecuted for the most part, is the story of mental arrest or catalepsis. In the ordinary writing of history a felt concretum of ambiguity is circumscribed by boundaries and peopled with actors, i.e., is relieved of ambiguity. Given a name, the event calls up the boundaries and the actors, only rarely the felt ambiguity which gave rise to episodicity. Thus long-named events become "facts"; in effect, natural quanta. If the assassination of President Kennedy is still something that chews on the outer edges of our consciousness, that owes to the fact that we have not sufficient distance on it to make it a quantum.

[76] William H. Riker to the contrary notwithstanding: "The motion and action in an event are objectively existent, but the boundaries are subjectively imposed." ("Events and Situations," *Journal of Philosophy,* Vol. LIV, No. 3 [January, 1957], p. 60.) While I disagree with Riker on this point, I think his examination of *ambiguity* in an event extraordinarily perceptive.

[77] Lawrence Durrell, *Balthazar,* (New York: E. P. Dutton & Co., 1961), p. 125.

Long-named and quantified, the assassination of President Lincoln is something else. Safe to say, school children a hundred years hence will "know" the event of John Kennedy's death with greater certitude than we who have lived through the ambiguous continuum (and that whether or no any new "evidence" is turned up!). Of course there is something right about that if, as hitherto urged, an event is significant by virtue of its call on the future. But that means that the *ad quem* of an event is a relative boundary, relative to the gathered ambiguity working itself out as ontological potency. The recognition of this is made difficult, I'm afraid we must say, by the delusions of natural grandeur fostered in the social sciences. For the social scientist, ". . . long named events become 'natural' quantums of action."[78] No doubt science of any sort depends for its possibility upon a reasonable stability of subject matter. "Reasonable stability" is, however, just the kind of reference scientific generalizations have. While this recognition obtains more broadly in the natural (oddly enough) than in the social sciences, it is fundamentally in the arts that something like a systematic protest against the rational sedimentation of eventful reality is prosecuted.

Earlier discussion of the hermeneutical spiral must likewise be brought forward if the elaboration of the spectrum of mental acts vis-àvis historical event is to be advanced. The mystery of every significant event, for the hermeneutical mind, is that it gives and withholds its field of being simultaneously. Historical reality does not proceed through the mind, givingly or withholdingly, as water through a conduit. Responses of mind are geared into the giving and withholding of historical being. Thus both the intension and extension of an event are unintelligible apart from appropriate cognitive acts.[79] That the relation between intension and extension is inverse means that an event cannot be grasped in a single mental act, and so that the inter-

[78] William H. Riker, *op. cit.,* p. 69.

[79] Intension should not be confused with intention, as the latter term has been used hitherto. The intension of an event refers to its inmost privacy, particularity, uniqueness, that which resists its subsumption under a class. Extension refers to an event's publicity, its "character" in relation to its field of enjoyment. See above, Ch. II.

230

pretation of it cannot proceed in a single cognitive mode. Shortly we shall see how knowledge in the mode of imagination occurs, in the scale of mental acts, in closest proximity to the event itself, and so aims to embody the intensional wholeness of the event without loss of significant feeling-tone. Knowledge in the mode of reason occurs at farthest remove, on the other hand, and aims to embody the extensional wholeness of the event without regard to its claim on feeling. The simultaneity of intension and extension in and of an event is the foundation of what will be called hereafter the "imaginative existential," the claim of an event upon the mind to harken to its unitary ontological range. Suffice for the moment to say that so long as consciousness remains vitally hermeneutical in respect of an event, a spiraling relation obtains between event and mind.

In order to unpack these introductory comments, which both gather up and anticipate, it will be necessary to bring forward previous claims about the imagination and establish them in a rather more systematic framework.[80] Initially it will be useful to state some general propositions about knowledge, which likewise do not appear here for the first time.

(1) Cognitive relations.

(a) Cognitive relations do not exhaust relations and are founded on relations more primitive than themselves. (I have various kinds of knowledge of and about my wife, but all are founded on relations that are not in the first instance cognitive.) Primordial relations beckon cognitively as food beckons appetite (likewise cognitive appetite is satiated only by primordial food).

(b) The previous point can be stated otherwise and with some advance: there is no knowledge without *distance* from the event known. While this point is to be pressed in some detail later, some preliminary reasons can be stated here as to why there is no knowledge without distance.

(i) The first is the logical generalization that the relation between extension and intension is an *inverse* relation. The

---

[80] I refer to the discussion of imagination under the rubrics of memory and intention in respect of its activity and passivity, its relation to immediacy and wholeness, its dissolving character, its plurisignative reference, its connection with ossification, its role in the modalization of the given, etc.

extensive meaning of a term is gained in distance on its intensive meaning, and *vice versa.*

(ii) There is no apprehension without *response.* Kant and others have taught us that the response of mind is geared into apprehension at every level.

(iii) The distance that goes with response is a divagation from being only if being is finished without our concern for and openness to it. Thus a radically conceptualistic or intellectualistic philosophy must view the intercalation of "response" between mind and event as the source of error. What is wrong with this is its assumption that mind and event are two fixed quantities and that anything which prevents the one from getting inside the other likewise frustrates knowledge. The standard realistic account of the scale of mental acts suffers from the assumption that the event to be known is "there" without our complicity. The standard idealistic account suffers not because it affords no "otherness," as is commonly charged, but because it reduces this otherness to a transcendentally regulative function: more strictly, it *standardizes* the self's response.

(c) The full range of cognition cannot be accounted for in relation to fixity of form. Most epistemologies in the history of western philosophy have been geared to the fixity of form, whether in the object, in the mind, in some noumenal realm, or in "custom." But an event does not have a fixed form, however much it may comprise parties having some internal life of their own and so a certain formality. As noted before, the confrontation of a fixed object by a fixed mind is much rarer than we suppose, and is always achieved by high abstraction from concrete events. Aristotle saw that this could be accomplished continuously only as "thought thinking itself," a kind of thought he reposed in the mind of God (in which, more's the pity, he has been followed by many a theologian).

(2) Feeling and the reproductive imagination. Primary responses are behavior-responses. Behavior-responses are those of *act* rather than knowledge, or of the preponderance of act over knowledge. They reflect the non-attending, pre-predicative, non-deliberative interpenetration of self and environing objects that goes with an eventful existence that is however not made episodic by ratiocination.

232

Primary behavior-responses do not exhaust the life of feeling. Feeling is a continuum of "suffering" (*pathos*) and responding that underlies every mental act so primordially as to be the precondition of each. It is no accident, as Heidegger rightly notes, that Aristotle refused to consider this continuum under the rubric of psychology, preferring instead the framework of rhetoric, i.e., hermeneutics.[81] Philip Wheelwright has recently refurbished this framework with the central claim that feelings have ". . . distinctively ontological bearings of their own."[82] That is to say that in the wholeness of vital pathos-response, a wholeness which includes activation of the total affective, conative, and emotive machinery of the self, one achieves a perspective upon the reality in and with which he is engaged that, if not itself cognitive, furnishes the base for cognitive insight inaccessible on any other grounds.[83] As a form of prehension, feeling is far removed from the pejorative meaning that passes among us, that of sensory titillation; it cannot be separated from *concern* and *value,* from the way we insert ourselves into the world and bear in ourselves the infiltration of the world. Feeling, like imagination which perpetuates it, has always a double character: it is a feeling *of* something, and so has centrifugal force; and it is a feeling *for* something, and so a centripetal motion to receive it.[84] In closest proximity to such

[81] *Being and Time,* p. 178.
[82] Cf. *The Burning Fountain,* pp. 30-51, *passim.* I should note that Wheelwright prefers the term "emotion" for what I term "feeling."
[83] Cf. Shakespeare, *A Midsummer Night's Dream,* Act V, Scene I:

Lovers and madmen have such seething brains,
Such shaping fantasies, that apprehend
More than cool reason ever comprehends.
The lunatic, the lover, and the poet
Are of imagination all compact: —
One sees more devils than vast hell can hold;
That is, the madman. The lover, all as frantic,
Sees Helen's beauty in a brow of Egypt.
The poet's eye, in a fine frenzy rolling,
Doth glance from heaven to earth, from earth to heaven;
And, as imagination bodies forth
The forms of things unknown, the poet's pen
Turns them to shapes, and gives to airy nothing
A local habitation and a name.
[84] Cf. George Whalley, *op. cit.,* pp. 66-69, 105-106.

233

feeling, artistic imagination surprises (in Gerard Manley Hopkins' phrase) "the inscapes of things."

It were presumption of the grossest sort to claim that these brief remarks suffice to describe, let alone explain, the continuum of feeling. There are at least two complexities over which we can only glide. The first is the so-called continuum itself, whether "feeling" is the proper name for it, and whether it admits of internal discrimination. By the continuum of feeling I have in mind the phenomenologists' *Lebenserlebnis* ("lived experience"), Scheler's and Wheelwright's "emotion," Heidegger's "mood" or "disposition" (*Stimmung, Befindlichkeit*), and what in average American talk is connoted by "experience." A full phenomenology of the life of feeling would disclose, I think, an internal modalization of feeling. These modes doubtless would include apperception, instinct, emotion, and mood.[85] Even to glance at these modes of feeling in passing is to see that the imagination is not *uniformly* reproductive in relation to each and all of them. Vis-à-vis instinct, for example, imagination does seem bound to the stimuli which it affords. But with respect to mood, imagination may be either reproductive or productive. If I am bored, say, with a particular book, imagination may extend this boredom to a total mood, a general *ennui,* reproducing particular stimuli in a total field. But imagination may, as it were, produce its own stimuli, directing attention away from the boring book, and thus permutate feeling.

The second complexity sets us in the feeling-imagination nexus even more directly. I refer to *generic feeling.* The very phrase jars, and strikes incredulity in the heart. How can something nearer to us than hands and feet be *generic?* Yet the thing slides out of our unstudied speech: we get the feel of a place; we seek the feel of the Greek mind, the Renaissance in Italy, etc.; the Irish have a feeling for politics, the Jews for money, the Russians for the earth, Southerners for place, Northerners for time, etc. If language is the surest clue we have to the primal schematization of experience, there is no denying to feeling a generic reproduction of itself along cultural and racial lines. And along lines that transcend race and culture.

85 Cf. Milton C. Nahm, *Genius and Creativity,* (New York: Harper Torchbooks, 1965), pp. 239ff.

234

Why does the heart leap in felt recognition to metaphors of the hunt and the chase; of martiality, victor and victim; of spring and winter, grass and snow; of fertile sow and voracious bull; of sirens, wind, and stormy deeps; of water, water everywhere, and not a drop to drink?

In the following chapter we will return to the life of generic feeling, the repository of recurrent symbols and home of archetypal images (the "old and universal arousers"). And shortly the matter will come again into view under the "ossified imagination." For the moment it is enough to remark on spontaneous and generic feeling.

Spontaneous feeling has as little to do with the "subjective" as with the "objective." It is in fact the spontaneous *epoché* of all such distracting abstractions in favor of participating being in its immediate, overwhelming presence. (Thus it is that level of experience which phenomenology has sought to reproduce at a methodological level by means of self-conscious *epoché* or "reduction.") Yet spontaneous feeling is rarer than we suppose, because the continuum of feeling is overlaid by reproductions of feeling in generic schematisms. In simplest terms, we are told how to feel "spontaneously" by generic reproductions of feeling. That is why we can feel with authentic spontaneity only through an education or reformation of taste. For the most part, even our feelings are recondite; they are typically an interdiction between us and the immediate presence of being.

In the de-reconditing of feeling and thus in the education of taste, works of art are the true schoolmasters. That is why average feeling stands in terror, say, of modern painting: such terror vests in anxiety for the veracity of average feeling. If a Jackson Pollock canvas so shakes the average equilibrium of feeling that not only the painting's intentionality but also environing objects are spontaneously felt, the generic feeling of the perceiver is brought into question. "Shock" in a work of art is the breakdown of equilibrium in average feeling and its re-establishment at another level; in every great work of art, the felt world is at stake.

As distinct from that imagination at work in the production and appreciation of a work of art, imagination operative purely within the continuum of feeling is pre-cognitive. Vital pathos-response is shot through with imagination, but with imagination that produces no "images," as Kant said of the "pure synthesis of the imagination."[86] In the modalities of feeling imagination embodies altogether schematically the concrete intercommunion of the self and the other that constitutes an unepisodic continuum. These schemata afford a merely adumbrative prehension (or "precursion") of the continuum, and therefore are pre-

[86] The name of Kant is difficult to pass over here, yet dangerous or at least confusing to include. Difficult to pass over because it is Kant above all who deals with the schematic character of imagination at this level (which of course he calls the level of apperception, not feeling, while I have identified apperception as a *mode* of feeling). But dangerous or confusing because Kant held this sort of imagination to be purely *productive,* and precisely that which makes all reproductive imagination possible. (On this point and on the brief remarks that follow in this note, see the discussion of Kant's theory of imagination below, Appendix II: "The Imagination and Synthesis.")
    A host of issues in connection with Kant's account of the pure synthesis of productive imagination cry out for the sort of extensive discussion upon which I cannot enter here. Briefly, I should be more attracted to Kant's account (i) were I persuaded that Heidegger's understanding of that account is correct (viz., that pure or primary imagination forms *transcendence* within the horizon of time) and (ii) were I equally persuaded by Heidegger's claim that by this account Kant meant to establish the conditions of proper ontological knowledge. (Martin Heidegger, *Kant and the Problem of Metaphysics,* trans. James S. Churchill [Bloomington: Indiana University Press, 1962], pp. 133-208.) But I am not persuaded of either. For it seems to me that Kant was concerned in the first *Critique* with transcendence of only a cognitive sort; and that he wound up there saying in effect that only that transcendence is *cognitive* which is achieved by virtue of the concept. I cannot escape the judgment that the *terminus ad quem* for all imaginative activity, for Kant, is the categorial fixity of the understanding ("the unity of apperception in relation to the synthesis of imagination is the *understanding.* . . ." *Critique of Pure Reason,* trans. Norman Kemp Smith [London: The Macmillan Co., 1953], p. 143). Categories of the understanding remain constant, while all manifolds are adjusted to them by rule through the imagination. On this view imagination can serve only a mediational role, i.e., cannot possess a cognitivity insusceptible of translation without loss into another and superior mode of cognition. Still, I am hesitant to claim that this is Kant's final word on the subject. Certainly in the *Critique of Judgment* he veers away from any final indentification of imagination and the understanding. ("By an aesthetical idea I understand that representation of the imagination which occasions much thought, without however any definite thought, i.e., any concept being adequate to it; it consequently cannot be completely compassed and made intelligible by language." Sec. 49; in *Immanuel Kant: Critique of Judgment,* trans. J. H. Bernard, [New York: Hafner Publishing Company, 1951], p. 157.)

236

cognitive. In so far as schemata permutate one mode of feeling to another, imagination is reproductive; and imagination is reproductive above all in the formation of generic feeling. Active, productive imagination gains distance on feeling in its reproductive modalities. Effecting "symbolic extrication" from the event by incarnating the self's feeling for and of it in an explicit paratactical structure, productive imagination assumes cognitivity through the form of an interlocking network of images.[87] It is to symbolic extrication that we now turn.

(3) Productive imagination and symbolic/metaphorical extrication.

To withdraw from things until one no longer sees much of them, until one has even to see things into them, *in order to see them at all*—or to view them from the side, and as in a frame—or to place them so that they partly disguise themselves and only permit of perspective views—or to look at them through coloured glasses, or in the light of the sunset—or to furnish them with a surface or skin which is not fully transparent: we should learn all this from artists, and moreover be wiser than they. For this fine quality of theirs usually ceases with them where art ceases and life begins: *we,* however, want to be the poets of our lives, and first of all in the smallest and most commonplace matters.[88]

The sole cognitive permutation of feeling, without loss of feeling-tone, is achieved in symbol or a pattern of symbols. (Symbol here is used as a class comprising metaphor, image, and to some extent, simile.) To understand formally the cognitivity of symbol is to understand its distribution in a triad. The first is *poetics* in the classical sense (recovered in the eighteenth century as "poesy"), the process whereby the event is generated and nurtured in the modalities of feeling to the point of intolerable ambiguity. The second is the work of art itself, simultaneously an extrication from the event *qua* chaotic feeling and an embodiment of the event *qua* potentially proportional feeling. The third is the actualization of that potency, or some fragment thereof, in "appreciation"; i.e., having one's feeling

[87] The phrase "symbolic extrication" is George Whalley's, *op. cit.* pp. 104–115.
[88] Nietzsche, *La Gaia Scienza,* IV, 229; in *Joyful Wisdom,* p. 233.

actually proportioned by the work of art so that one is drawn knowingly into the eventful reality it discloses and constitutes. While all three "parts" of this triad are in view wherever imagination is the script, the first has been to the fore in preceding sections of this chapter, the second comes now rather more directly frontstage, while the third whispers cues from the wings and prepares for entrance.

That imagination lays claim to knowledge in symbol or metaphor goes to say that there is no imaginative knowledge in the mode of sheer temporal immediacy.[89] The reason for this are complex and varied, although some of them have already come in view. The historical present, and thus the context of all immediacies, is an achievement of imaginative circumambience and so of the wholeness of the self's historical temporality. Moreover, an event would yield to immediate intuition only if its essence were delivered up to an unvarying form. But an historical event yields its importance to the "expanded form" it instantiates, to the potency it lays on those who participate it

---

[89] A fascinating study of the relation between imagination and "immediacy" will be found in Kierkegaard's *Sickness Unto Death,* trans. Walter Lowrie, (New York: Doubleday Anchor Book, 1954). Describing the form of despair attaching to the man of "pure immediacy," Kierkegaard says that he is a person devoid of imagination, living passively and unreflectively in the undifferentiated continuum which concrete existence affords. It is a life without envisagement of possibility; for "possibility" requires a breach with immediacy through imagination (pp. 184–194). This is not to say, on Kierkegaard's lights, that one is delivered from despair through imagination *eo ipso*. For through imagination the despair of the immediate concrete may be transformed into a despair of all particulars *in toto,* i.e., into a despair of the totality of earthly existence (p. 194). Still, the essence of imagination is thereby advanced as Kierkegaard conceives it: "Generally speaking, imagination is the medium of the process of infinitizing; it is not one faculty on a par with others, but if one would so speak, it is the faculty *instar omnium* [for all faculties]. What feeling, knowledge, or will a man has, depends in the last resort upon what imagination he has, that is to say, upon how these things are reflected, i.e., it depends upon imagination. Imagination is the reflection of the process of infinitizing. . . . The self is reflection, and imagination is reflection, it is the counterfeit presentment of the self, which is the possibility of the self. Imagination is the possibility of all reflection, and the intensity of this medium is the possibility of the intensity of the self" (pp. 163–164). These remarks on imagination assume added weight when it is recalled that for Kierkegaard the self is composed ontologically of infinity and finiteness (p. 162).

238

in maximum cognitive mode. Thus knowledge is *metaphora* (μεταφωρά) or *translatio* in the etymological senses of these terms: "carrying over."[90] That precisely does not mean that Shelley on occasion immediately perceived a skylark, on another intuited "blithe Spirit," and on still another sat down to effect a *tertium comparationis* in his poem "To a Skylark." Skylark is not a paraphrase of blithe Spirit, or *vice versa*. What Shelley saw he could only see through the skylark, yet what he saw was not the skylark ("bird thou never wert"). Indeed Shelley's vision was consummated in the "carrying over," the poem itself.[91] Now cut loose from such immediacies as lay in Shelley's history, the poem as an independent imaginative whole constitutes a call on my felt perception of the world. Imagination ever works in spiraling circuits: in the instance at hand, whether in artist or appreciator, from the schemata of immediacy, through the wholeness of symbol and metaphor, to instaurated presence, and over again. By "wholeness" I refer to that symbolizing act of imagination whereby the penumbrae of the given are conjoined with the depth structures of the self in unitary vision.

The work of art takes its rise (to revert to the first of the triad) from a complex state of heightened feeling on the part

[90] For an exceptionally astute review of metaphor as *translatio* in modern literature, and especially of the animus against metaphor as logical comparison, see Beda Allemann, "Metaphor and Antimetaphor," *Interpretation, the Poetry of Meaning*, ed. Stanley R. Hopper and David L. Miller, (New York: Harcourt, Brace, & World, 1967), pp. 103–123.

[91] The artist does not know in advance of representation but through representation. Cf. Max Scheler: "It is as if the mind's eye were fixed to the tip of the drawing crayon or painting brush and saw for the *first time* that part of the total project which the brush or crayon was on the point of representing." Scheler finds a strict parallel in religious experience: "Similarly, the religious experience is not rounded and complete until it is expressed in forms of worship and receives ritual representation. . . . Ritual and the concrete idea of the religious object are mutually interdependent variables. . . . They who pray kneeling have not seen God in the same light as they who pray standing." *On the Eternal in Man*, pp. 265–266.

One is reminded of an exchange in *The House of the Seven Gables*. Having heard from Holgrave an impassioned speech of near oracular tone, Phoebe exclaims: "I hardly think I understand you." "No wonder," replied Holgrave, "for I have told you a secret which I hardly began to know before I found myself giving it utterance." Nathaniel Hawthorne, *The House of the Seven Gables*, (Boston: Houghton Mifflin Company, 1952), Ch. XIV, p. 257.

of the artist. Feeling is heightened by virtue of total immersion in ambiguity that gathers on itself intolerably. "I tell you," said Nietzsche, "one must harbor chaos if one would give birth to a dancing star."[92] So highly refined a capacity for pathos-response (Wordsworth's "more than usual organic sensibility") is not of course average feeling. It rather accompanies imagination as imagination actively cracks the focalized given to disclose its inner stress. So Coleridge spoke of having become accustomed from childhood to ". . . as it were, unrealize whatever of more than common interest my eyes dwelt on . . ." and thence to find his way into it. Gerard Manley Hopkins spilled into his journal the towering terror he felt at the felling of an ashtree in his garden: "It was lopped first: I heard the sound and looking out and seeing it maimed there came at that moment a great pang and I wished to die and not to see the inscapes of the world destroyed anymore."[93]

The work of art is not a description of heightened feeling but an embodiment of it; and an embodiment of it in extrication from it. Nietzsche's dancing star has no umbilical cord into the womb of his chaos; and Hopkins' "Sweet fire the sire of Muse" has no charred path into the holocaust of his felt world. In the same act by which the artist extricates himself from an intolerable ambiguity of meaning, the work of art is extruded from his own imagination. No less for the artist than for the appreciator, the work of art is an achievement of discovery, integration, and catharsis. Of discovery, because random feeling is brought under proportion; ambiguity is made to signify under the guidance of word, line, color, gesture, etc.[94] Of integration,

[92] *Also Sprach Zarathustra,* Prologue 5; in *Zarathustra,* p. 10.

[93] Quoted by Whalley, *op. cit.,* p. 73. Whalley comments: "The more clearly and intensely an artist perceives, the less is he like a camera. For his intense perception engages the whole person in a flow of outward-turning response to his world, the world being grasped as a delicately poised and intricate texture of feeling. And a human being in a state of wholeness is a great deal more complex and energetic than any photographic emulsion" (pp. 73–74).

[94] Cf. Dilthey: "We are dependent on the interpretation of the creations of the mind in order to say what is in it." *Gesammelte Schriften,* Vol. VII, p. 319. "Neither in its temporal flow nor in the depth of its content is the self fully accessible to us in lived experience. For the small area of conscious life rises like an island from inaccessible depths. But expression lifts something from out of these depths: It is creative.

because what is discovered is an expansion of very selfhood in chime with deepened world. And of catharsis, because an older frame of feeling is sloughed in favor of a new insertion in being, an insertion vivified and proportioned by the work of art itself.[95]

Because the work of art is a symbolic extrication and a symbolic extrusion, it has a life of its own apart from the event of its incipience in heightened feeling and apart from the event of its extrusion in the personal history of its creator. Thus it cannot be said that a work of art holds an identical event in view; but rather that it holds a watching brief for a certain range of being, to conduct us knowingly into which it is richly suffused with potency. To this remarkable matter, how an independent non-discursive articulation of a certain range of being (owing to events far removed) can engage and expand my own being, we will return when we consider the "imaginative existential." Suffice for the moment to say that while "a certain range of being" is not an event in the sense of a discrete episode, it is coextensive with what we have called "paradigmatic event," the event that recurs in its illuminating and constitutive power.

The processes of imagination under inquiry here are by no means restricted to the creation and appreciation of works of art. Symbolism and feeling proportioned to symbols shoot our existence through and through, from old wives' tales to the celebration of the Eucharist. *Every* mode of articulation is a form of embodying event and at the same time a form of extrication from it: that is the root meaning of the hermeneutical spiral. Language itself, even bodily gesture, is a form of distance on the reality it brings to expression. We *know* no reality without this sort of distance. Cognitive distance occurs at different lengths

And thus, in the process of understanding, life itself becomes accessible as a reproduction of creative activity" (p. 220).

[95] For the artist there is another sort of catharsis, that of being freed from the torture of immersion in an all-consuming feeling-complex. Nietzsche said he did not write in order to think, but rather in order to get rid of his thoughts, and that this riddance was a necessity of his sanity. (*Joyful Wisdom,* II, 93; in *op. cit.,* p. 127.) He also spoke of revenging his feelings by giving them publicity. (*The Use and Abuse of History,* trans. Adrian Collins, [New York: The Liberal Arts Press, 1949], p. 11.) Anyone who has ever been impelled to write will know what is here at stake: there is something inside one must bring to speech if he is to have any peace. Like a pregnancy at full term, the word must cry flesh in a life its own.

and thus in different modes, one mode checking another, and all being checked by being rebanded through the prism of event, freshly "apparent" in another revolution of the hermeneutical spiral. In the scale of cognitive acts, imagination remains nearest the event, elaborating its feeling-tone in a universe of non-discursive discourse: it brings the event to expression as language-event, as gesture-event, as line-and-color-event, as plastic-form-event, etc.

(4) Imagination and the modalities of the given. At the beginning of this chapter questions were posed concerning the modalities of the given and the scale of mental acts. How, it was asked, is consciousness turned from the given in one mode to the given in another mode; how does the given attain proliferated presentiment in and to the self? How is the given cognitively dispersed and diversified in my transactions with it? Because these questions have been pursued in several contexts in this chapter, we need now to touch home base and tote up the score. Since it is a matter of summary for the most part, we may proceed swiftly and with economy.

(a) The given as focal actuality, and ossified imagination.

We get used to it. We get broken into it so gradually we scarcely notice it. But if we could shake off custom and descend on to the world without any conception of what we were going to see, we should be like the old woman who looked at the giraffe in the zoo and refused to believe a word of it . . . I mean the reality we have made for ourselves by 2,000,000 years of getting used to it, the domestication of the enormous miracle, the reality in which we no longer see a moving, articulate, thinking shape, of quite extraordinary design and substance, across the breakfast table, but something which, by a long process of getting-used-to, we have subdued into a gentler image, our wife. . . . If we stop pretending for a moment that we were born fully dressed in a service flat, and remember that we were born stark naked into a pandemonium of most unnatural phenomena, then we know how out of place, how lost, how amazed, how miraculous we are . . . Our difficulty is . . . to see through the windows which are so steamed over with our daily breath. . . .[96]

[96] Christopher Fry, "A Playwright Speaks: How Lost, How Amazed, How Miraculous We Are," *The Modern Theatre,* ed. Robert W. Corrigan (New York: Macmillan Co., 1964), pp. 1042–1044.

242

Like sleeping beauties, they lie there prone and rigid in the walls of Castle Logic, waiting only for the kiss of Metaphor to awaken them to fresh life.[97]

What active, symbolic imagination has first to step over, in its rendezvous with the delineated given, is its own corpse; i.e., itself in lifeless, reproductive mode. To be sure death, petrifaction, and ossification touch all mental acts, perception and conception no less than imagination.[98] "Seeing," writes R. N. Hanson, "is a 'theory-laden' understanding."[99] The phrase is tautologous if "theory" ($\theta\epsilon\omega\rho\epsilon\hat{\iota}\nu$) be held to its root meaning: seeing or beholding. Thus "seeing" is "seeing-laden"; our seeing is laden with the way we have come to see. Imagination in reproductive mode builds up a frame for seeing, including a frame for what we can see as "fact."[100] The same is true of language: one wants to say his unique thing, and comes immediately up against language as a communal, reproductive deposit.[101] His

[97] Owen Barfield, *Poetic Diction*, 2d. ed., (London: Faber & Faber, 1952), p. 115.

[98] On the "ossified imagination" see Nicholas Berdyaev, *The Beginning and the End*, trans. R. N. French (New York: Harper & Brothers, 1952), pp. 175ff.

[99] *Patterns of Discovery*, (Cambridge: Cambridge University Press, 1958), p. 18.

[100] Cf. J. W. Swanson: "What we allow to count as a fact is a function of antecedently accumulated conceptual machinery—of a system of categories, explanatory principles, concepts, and labeling rubrics which somehow manage to sort, sift out, and arrange what we get from our nerve ends into a coherent conceptual pattern permitting of extrapolation to future experience." "Religious Discourse and Rational Preference Rankings," *American Philosophical Quarterly*, Vol. IV, No. 3 (July, 1967), p. 249.

One may observe too that even when an older framework is discarded and thus its "visible" facts, the older framework often continues to exert a holding action against newly "visible" facts. Cranly says to Stephen: "It is a curious thing . . . how your mind is supersaturated with the religion in which you say you disbelieve." (Cf. W. Y. Tindal, *James Joyce*, [New York: Scribner's, 1950], pp. 12–13). Thus Stephen, throughout *Ulysses*, intones fragments of the Mass—precisely in his bitterest attacks on the church.

[101] Cf. Ludwig Wittgenstein: "An image (*Bild*) held us captive. And we could not evade it, for it lay in our language and our language seemed to repeat it to us inexorably." *Philosophical Investigations* I, trans. G. E. M. Anscombe, (Oxford: Basil Blackwell, 1958), #115, pp. 48–48e. (I have altered Anscombe's translation slightly.)

243

fight *for* the thing is a fight against language. The poet is one who will not duck this fight on either front; he wins a renewal of perception through a renewal of language, and vice versa.

One could illustrate the "stocked, ossified" imagination at random. But it is nowhere more obvious than where in average sensibility it is thought most absent. I refer to "nature" and its "representation," and the claim of average sensibility that "real art" is "realistic." But what is "realistic nature"? To the most casual observer of art from diverse cultures that includes "nature" in its subject matter (say, Chinese landscapes from any epoch, contemporary Congolese representations of jungle life, the Altamira Cave paintings, and Frederick Remington's land-scapes of the western American frontier), it is immediately apparent that "nature" is not the "same" in all representations of it. Oscar Wilde grasped the point fully in his witticism, "nature imitates art." Bernard Berenson has written:

Rightly interpreted, the phrase ("nature imitates art") is nothing if not exact. It means simply that the public now sees and feels, in what it had previously regarded as nature, things that hitherto it had seen and felt only in recent works of art, paintings, narratives, music. As the public is inclined to believe the work of art to be a product of mere imitation or mere fancy, it is overcome with aston-ishment to discover correspondence between recent masterpieces and what *these* masterpieces have taught *this* public to see and feel for itself. After not too long an interval this accretion to the public knowledge is so integrated with the previous notions regarding "nature" as to form an indissoluble whole, and the public remains little more aware that it is by similar connections that our ideas of both "nature" and "human nature" have been framed. This process goes on and will go on while mankind flourishes on this planet.[102]

Thus works of art have at least this public residue, that they lignify anew the common imagination. (In this connection it should be said in a loud voice that the history of art and the history of theology and philosophy are ridiculously truncated subjects when pursued separately.) But the time lag is notorious, and historical being does not stand still: we cannot know the historical present out of Gainsborough. Moreover, however

[102] *Aesthetics and History*, (London: Constable & Co., 1950), p. 37.

244

helpful the merely formal studies of schematizing imagination may be (monumentally, in Kant), they are not the supremely needful thing. It is the historicity of schematism that needs to break upon us, that we may have eyes to see and ears to hear and hearts to understand. For the "time" to which Kant's manifold of the given was adjusted in the schematism of imagination is not an ahistorical constant, but rather is that co-inherence of the modes of time in which our expanded being is put to us as a possibility, and indeed a possibility in concert with and arising from the historically given.

(b) Focal actuality and active, productive imagination: the achievement of symbolic range. We need now to attend to those impulses in active imagination in execution of which focal actualities are "carried over" symbolically.

(i) Imagination and the dissolution of the given *qua* delineated.

> ". . . Alpha continues to begin.
> Omega is refreshed at every end."[103]

> "Ourselves in the tune as if in space
> Yet nothing changed, except the place
> Of things as they are and only the place
> As you play them, on the blue guitar."[104]

For the actively imaginative mind, the given focalized object is first of all an occasion for break in plane.[105] Imagination's "blessed rage for order" (Wallace Stevens) is initially expressed in disordering, dissolving, dissimulating the object of average, ossified sensibility.[106] (Of imagination in the exercise of this

---

[103] Wallace Stevens, "An Ordinary Evening in New Haven," *The Auroras of Autumn*, (New York: Alfred A. Knopf, 1950), p. 121.

[104] *Idem*, "The Man with the Blue Guitar," *Poems*, selected by Samuel French Morse, (New York: Alfred A. Knopf Vintage Books, 1959), pp. 73-90.

[105] Cf. Lawrence Durrell, *Balthazar*: "A true work of art never shows a plane surface . . ." (p. 226); "Art . . . 'reworks reality to show its significant side' " (p. 147).

[106] Recall the lines from Coleridge quoted earlier: "It dissolves, diffuses, dissipates in order to re-create. . . . It is essentially *vital*, even

245

function one could say what Nietzsche said of the mind, that it is "more like a stomach than anything else.") Indeed in its negative impulse active imagination regards the given object of average sensibility as a gross superficiality. "Counter to this will to illusion, to simplification, to the mask, to the cloak, in short this will to surfaces (for every surface is a cloak) operates that sublime impulse of a man of insight, that spirit which takes and *wants* to take things deeply, complicatedly, and thoroughly. This is the cruelty characteristic of the intellectual conscience and taste." Such a man, Nietzsche continues, will have "sharpened his eyes" and will have subjected himself "to rigorous discipline and to rigorous words as well."[107]

What active imagination dissolves is the "givenness" of the delineated object with respect to the focalized limits of its putative self-presentation. It wrests the "thing" out of its customary context, taken for granted by the perceiver or reasoner, and puts it in an alien (to everyday mentality) context that is however its natural habitat, viz., the context of interaction-event. Active imagination falls upon the given of average sense or conventional logic as the spearhead of a whole active background and foreground, seeking by its dissolving action upon the "point" to gain access to that background and foreground in something like full scope (the "penumbral actuality" of earlier discussion, or the event *qua* paradigmatic). Symbolic imagination "cracks" the delineated actuality to see what it is the spearhead of, if we may put it so. This is the "conferring additional properties upon an object, or abstracting from it some of those which it actually [I should say: in the mode of delineated actuality] possesses" mentioned by Wordsworth, whereby the delineated object may react upon the mind "like a new existence."

In the dissolving action of imagination the world is not destroyed or displaced but rather is allowed to appear in its primal rapport with the self. In the thetic or natural attitude of average sensibility (for modern western man), a thing is just *a being*.

---

as all objects (as objects) are essentially fixed and dead." *Biographia Literaria,* Ch. XIII.

[107] Nietzsche, *Beyond Good and Evil,* trans. Marianne Cowan, (Chicago: Henry Regnery Co., 1955), p. 160.

246

Paul Ricoeur has described such an attitude as ". . . the positing of each being absolutely without relation to a consciousness." It is to make of world an "in-itself." "This in-itself is nothing but the absolutizing of the ontic, of the 'this' of 'beings.' "[108] In such a world, language would be without metaphor, since we use metaphor to bring into speech that which is no mere in-itself.[109] Metaphor and symbol serve to carry over into consciousness the carrying over between things, and between things and the self, in their very being.

Thus we may hazard (and it is a hazard) a generalization: the universal negative impulse in all active imagination is distrust of the "given," a stern doubt that the objects of jaded perception and arrested conception give what is "there." Moreover, it is inadequate to say symbolic imagination is unconcerned with the being of what is there; that concern with "meaning" suffices. Skepticism of meaning is skepticism of presentiment of being; and skepticism gives way only as meaning is recommensurated with deepened presentiment of being, as the thing is endowed symbolically.[110] In its own mode, imagination does not of course

[108] Paul Ricoeur, "Kant and Husserl," *Philosophy Today,* Vol. X, No. 3/4 (Fall, 1966), pp. 148–149.

[109] Cf. Arthur C. McGill: "It [metaphor] serves to break up the static and objective character which things have when they are considered from a distance and securely identified. It frees the mind from the illusion of names. It recalls it to that realm . . . where nothing is just itself but keeps turning into other things, where every moment is alive with objectively impossible possibilities. . . . It threatens all the logic of . . . practical life." *The Celebration of Flesh,* (New York: Association Press, 1964), p. 26.

[110] It should be clear that I do not mean to make of symbolic imagination, through its dissolving function, an Olympic (or Olympian) pole-vaulter, leaping over concrete beings into Being. Some recent criticism, both literary and theological, has underscored the anchoring of imagination in the external finite object. Thus Allen Tate fumes at art which uses objects as the occasion for evoking gnostic infinitude from the artist's own delicious interiority (See *The Forlorn Demon,* [Princeton: Princeton University Press, 1953], pp. 68ff). Nathan Scott likewise excoriates those who treat the object only as a function of consciousness (Cf. "Prolegomenon to a Christian Poetic," *Journal of Religion,* Vol. XXXV, No. 4 [October, 1955], pp. 200ff.); while William F. Lynch, S.J., labels such a view of the imagination as "Manichaean" (Cf. "Theology and the Imagination, I," *Thought,* Vol. XXIX, No. 112 [Spring, 1954], pp. 61–86; "Theology and the Imagination, II: The Evocative Symbol," *Thought,* Vol. XXIX, No. 115 [Winter, 1954], pp. 529–54; "Theology and the Imagination, III," *Thought,* Vol. XXX,

treat these matters ontologically. In the work of art it controls perspective so as to invite perception and give it a tendency. With that there is an acute formal analogy between the problem of the communication of a work of art and the problem of the communication of revelation: both can only presuppose among the communicants a world of delineated things and a jaded sensibility.

(ii) Imagination and the increase of phenomenological range. A second generalization must be brought forward quickly, one intrinsic to the first and indeed its rationale. The universal positive impulse in all active imagination is the increase of the phenomenological range of the given as it comes to us initially by average sensory and rational presentiment. As Robert Penn Warren has said, imagination restructures experience in the interest of a fresh experience of structure.[111] The dissolving act of imagination is *for* freedom, for the "for us" of the world, and for the "for the world" of the self. Imagination breaks the plane of the ossified given that it may become *imago mundi* in active, symbolic imagination.

Imagination as the increase of phenomenological range works in all the several dimensions of the self, as we have seen; in memory and intention, as well as upon the phenomena of the historical present. The ontological assumption of symbolic imagination is that neither the self nor its proliferated world is a mere in-itself. It assumes, and proceeds to embody symbolically, that the secret of a thing is not located absolutely in itself. Metaphor and symbol bring into consciousness what earlier was

No. 116 [Spring, 1955], pp. 18–36.) (William Lynch, let it be said, has homesteaded the land that must be cleared; he has opened a path into the tangled growth of "theology and the imagination.")

These caveats are doubtless rightly entered against *evocateurs* and *symbolistes*. But it is no good clucking one's tongue at the use of objects to evoke subliminal subjectivity; no good, that is, if the alternative is only a commendation of "real external world," "integrity of the created order," and the like. For the question is still, how full-orbed imagination is to *honor* the being of finite things. I have suggested that active imagination honors that being initially by being skeptical of the way it is ordinarily taken. (The same is true, of course, with respect to the self, which also is taken for the most part as a thing.)

111 Robert Penn Warren, "Formula for a Poem," *Saturday Review of Literature,* (March 22, 1958), p. 23.

called the "interlacing of regions" out of which we have our being in the world. The movement of symbolic imagination is therefore from and through objects toward events. For the imaginative mind, almost anything at all can serve as a temptress to the inscapes of things, as a beacon of the channel deep and broad.[112] This thing is not expendable, in its uniqueness, for symbolic imagination, whatever the depth and breadth of range it affords; but rather is the gate of access, through which imagination must enter and through which it must pass on return, with more on its lips than when it entered in.[113] Withal, symbolic imagination is not a merely demiurgic power, re-arranging a dismembered body; what it achieves is ontological novelty, a fresh insertion of the self in being.

It thus belongs to imaginative utterance that *what* it says is not a self-standing thing, even though the *what* it says is not unlimited, may even be precise. What imaginative utterance says in the work of art is an echo in the communicant, the appreciator. Yet that echo is not an echo of the communicant's own voice, but rather the echo of sounds emitted in the work of art itself. To this we shall have to return below, under "answering imagination."

(c) The "given" and the scale of mental acts. We need to remind ourselves periodically that the "given" and "imagination" are not the hard, unitary things speech makes them out to be when they are used as the subjects or objects of sentences (e.g., "Imagination falls upon the given . . ."). Here is a case

[112] Augustine and his discussants happen upon a cock-fight and "see" there the problem of "order" instantiated, reason beckoning to itself. "For what do the eyes of lovers of truth and beauty not encompass; where do they not search through to see beauteous reason signaling something thence? . . . Whence indeed and where can she not give a signal . . . ?" *De Ordine,* Book I, Ch. 8, 25; *Divine Providence and the Problem of Evil,* trans. Robert P. Russell, O.S.A., in *The Fathers of the Church,* Vol. V, (New York: Cima Publishing Co., 1948), p. 262.

[113] Cf. Paul Ricoeur: "Unlike a comparison that we *look* at from the outside, symbol is the very movement of the primary meaning that makes us share in the latent meaning and thereby assimilates us to the symbolized, without our being able intellectually to dominate the similarity. This is the sense in which the symbol 'gives'; it gives because it is a primary intentionality that gives the second meaning." "The Hermeneutic of Symbols," *International Philosophical Quarterly,* Vol. II, No. 2 (May, 1962), p. 194.

in point of the inverse relation between the extension and the intension of a term: the more generally I use the term "given," the less the term refers to any particular given (or any special sense of "given"). In recent pages, generalizations about imagination and the given have been brought forward in the hope that both terms might achieve greater extensional and intensional range. In summary and as a hedge against misinterpretation, we need now to prosecute this hope even more directly.

Near the beginning of this chapter it was said that imagination stands for a wide spectrum within the scale of mental acts. This spectrum, we have come around to say, is that range of responses in closest logical proximity to the event which engages the mind as a whole. Also it was said that distinctions must be drawn within any range singled out for study. Just such distinctions within the range of the mind's imaginative activity have been our concern for many pages past.

Likewise at the beginning of this chapter the problem was laid out, how thought is turned from the given in one mode to the given in another mode, i.e., how thought gains varied and variegated presentiment of the given. This problem has been one of several problems bearing upon our inquiry into the processes of imagination in connection with memory, intention, the modes of time, etc. *In nuce,* a thing or event is worried imaginatively when the modalities of its givenness is *the* problem. Thus what the imaginative mind seeks in connection with any "thing" is plural and rich presentiment, or as was said just recently, the increase of its phenomenological range.

The "given" is not *simply* given: that has been the emphasis throughout. The datum for knowledge is not exhaustively (i) a sensation-complex that is the effect of an external cause, or (ii) a thing or "other," simply, itself. The concrete datum is an interaction-event, a field susceptible of giving itself variously according to modalities of pathos and response. If the senses, imagination, and reason are identified as the principal spectra of the scale of mental acts, the "given" on which imagination initially trains itself may be so given in and to any of these spectra. There doubtless is an imagination of sense: the smell of a fragrant flower can provoke the imaginative mind in many ways, to an increase of sensory range, to the recollection of associated occasions, etc. No doubt there is also an "imagination of imagination": the "imaginary" can provoke the imagination, as in day-dream and phantasy. An imagination of reason is no less in evidence, formerly in the great metaphysical systems, today more in the theoretical natural and social sciences: a "given" structure is probed for what it subsumes, and from it other structures are extrapolated which will both describe and explain it.

Thus it will be seen that imagination both comprises a spectrum in the scale and transcends its spectrum in the scale. Just because imagination is not bound to a sensory, imaginary, or rational given, it is the disposition of the mind as a whole to the "thing" in plural presentiment, to the intentionality of consciousness in its plurisignification.

We said earlier that distinctions drawn within one spectrum of the scale would require discriminations with respect to the other spectra. Let us consider reason briefly. All mental powers are tethered to the concrete event (or to the continuum of presentiment that is "eventuated"), for what is offered them, but reason has the longest stake-line. Its capacity for universality and fixity is its capacity for most extensive distance. And reason removes from the concrete event, we said in Chapter II, by means of cataleptic pauses or stations. Reason places the event under "arrest"[114]; it assumes that an event is a closed affair, a delimited base from which solid ideas may arise and to which they apply. Reason assumes that the *a quo* and the *ad quem* of an event enclose a fixed significance, that the event does not open or open upon a new field of potentiality. The concepts of reason are abstract just because they are abstracted from a stable referent. In a different metaphor, we may say that reason "freezes" the event in order to be able to chip off its crystallized attributes, qualities, structures, etc.

Every mode of knowledge (and its appropriate form of communication) is a form of embodying the event known and at

[114] Cf. Aristotle: "Thinking has more resemblance to a coming to rest or arrest than to a movement." *De Anima,* Book I, Ch. 3, 407a, 30; McKeon, p. 545.

the same time a form of extrication from it.[115] Put another way, that only has a claim to knowledge of an event which keeps it both intensively and extensively in view. The tendency of reason is invariably toward maximum extension, universality; as the senses bend instinctively toward maximum intension, particular and immediate presence. Imagination tends toward both intension and extension at once, although in any particular cognitive achievement of the imagination one will be more heavily weighted than the other. (Thus the event of perceiving a skylark may issue in Shelley's "To a Skylark" or in da Vinci's treatise on aerodynamics.) As reason extricates itself completely from a concrete event, its concepts become empty; as imagination fails to remove itself from event as mere existential occurrence (i.e., does not submit itself to *discipline:* in poetry, that of rhythm, metaphor, etc.), its images become blind. To know an event in its immediacy and fullness is to know it in a plurality of modes. That is why both the poem and "criticism" are necessary in order to know that for which the poem is a watching brief; likewise with scripture and theology.

Now it may appear that we have made contrary affirmations concerning the cognitivity of imagination. On the one hand it has been said that imagination situates itself in the scale of mental acts in closest logical proximity to the event itself; and this suggests a veering in the direction of immediacy. On the other hand, it has been claimed that cognitive imagination effects symbolic or metaphorical extrication from the event; and this suggests a veering in the direction of distanced wholeness. What the two claims mean put together is that cognitive imagination elaborates the feeling-tone of the event in a universe of non-discursive discourse: it brings the event to expression as speech-

---

[115] What I call the simultaneity of embodiment and extrication has been emphasized by Paul Ricoeur as the simultaneity of "manifestation" and "dissimulation" in language. Applying sociology of knowledge to the great philosophical systems, he sees in the language of the system the reflection of a particular social situation; but at the same time and in the same language he sees a dissimulation of situation, in so far as the system aspires to a *universal* problematic. See "The History of Philosophy and Historicity," in *History and Truth,* trans. Charles A. Kelbley, (Evanston: Northwestern University Press, 1965), pp. 63–77, esp. p. 72.

252

event (or painting-event, etc.). Since non-discursive forms of articulation (to take an example other than the arts, the sacrament of the Eucharist) intend to embody an event "on its own terms," they sustain a more intimate connection with the imaginative perpetuation of it than do discursive modes (e.g., preaching), which transmute and transform response (rather, indicate response in another mode) in the interest of a more inclusive universe of discourse.

Because of its historical character, imagination cannot give itself up to sheer temporal immediacy. This we have sought to show in the investigation of the relation between imagination and the modes of historical time. By the same token, imagination cannot give itself up to a fixity of the whole, an intuition of plenitude. That imagination is exercised with pluralizing and variegating presentiment, with increasing the phenomenological range of such immediate givens as sense and reason may boast of, is evidence that it lacks plenipotentiary powers. Momentarily, under the rubric of the "imaginative existential," we shall look to the ontological matrix of the coincidence of extension and intension, and thus of the commensuration of immediacy and wholeness.

The mention of immediacy-wholeness and intension-extension will perhaps recall the caveat at the beginning of this chapter, viz., that to track imagination is to follow a thing or tendency to its opposite, and around again endlessly. The matter may now be put positively. Referentially, imaginative discourse is plurisignative; in terms of meaning, it is polysemous.[116] Imaginative discourse plays on many registers, and relies on no one of them exclusively for reference or meaning.[117] For everything said

[116] On plurisignative reference, see Wheelwright, *The Burning Fountain,* pp. 61–62, 112–117. (The ". . . symbol tends, on any given occasion of its realization, to carry more than one legitimate reference in such a way that its proper meaning is a tension between two or more directions of semantic stress" p. 61.) The word polysemous (meaningful at many levels) was used by Dorothy Sayers, if I recall correctly, in her description of Dante's *Divine Comedy.*

[117] Cf. John Ruskin: "There is in every word set down by the imaginative mind an awful under-current of meaning, and evidence and shadow upon it of the deep places out of which it has come. It is often obscure, often half told, for he who wrote it, in his clear seeing of the things beneath, may have been impatient of detailed interpretation, but if we

there is a particular unsaid that is essential to imaginative meaning, an unsaid that is not stipulated but rather is iconically signified. For the immediately present, denotated, delineated actuality ("object"), there is a mediate, connotated, marginal background; iconic penumbrity is essential to imaginative meaning and reference. For every object grasped in imaginative symbol, there is a "world" in which self and object are disclosed to each other in polysemous intercourse. To touch an artery of symbolic imagination is always to feel a dicrotic pulse, a double-beating centripetal and centrifugal action.

III. THE IMAGINATIVE EXISTENTIAL

The themes of recent pages lead directly into the problematic of what we shall call the "imaginative existential." This phrase obviously recalls another, the "historio-personal existential" developed at the end of the preceding chapter. Let us pause initially over the connection between the two phrases.

A. The "Historio-Personal" and the "Imaginative" Existential

The "existential" in the two phrases refers to the same ontological structure, viz., the emergence and profferment of my unique being *coram Deo*. "Historio-personal" describes the ontological quality of this structure: it is an "existential" (not an essence) funded out of my historical space-time and that of my political fellows. My disjointed participation in this space-time affords a dim discernment of potencies harbored there, as it affords also the possibility of recognizing and acceding to a proffered refunding of them, a profferment that promises to save my being distended among them. The competition for my accession is

choose to dwell upon it and trace it, it will lead us always securely back to that metropolis of the soul's dominion from which we may follow out all the ways and tracks to its farthest coasts." *Modern Painters,* Vol. II: *Of Truth and Theoretic Faculties,* (Philadelphia: Rouwee, Wattley and Walsh, 1891), p. 415.

acute; and promises are legion. Christian faith enters this competition when and if it knows the name of the game. It claims for revelatory profferment that God offers us ourselves afresh, a graced structure enucleated from what we have made of ourselves and from what we have been made by.

"Imaginative" describes the cognitive character of the apprehension of this structure. That is, "imaginative" qualifies the mode of presence or givenness which this structure has in our unstable humanity, as it also expresses the character of mental response to it. Without the foregoing inquiry into imagination, the word "cognitive" might be thought at once too strong and too weak to associate with the imaginative apprehension of this structure. Too strong, because in the typical contemporary philosophical *Zeitgeist* cognition would be reserved to reason or rationally falsifiable statements. Too weak, because cognition typically would not be thought to be involved in the creative or constitutive modalization of the presence of the thing known. Needless to say, these typical views have been under assault, even if not frontally, throughout this chapter.

Nonetheless, certain questions concerning man's historio-personal existential, as the ontological structure of revelation, were left dangling at the end of the preceding chapter; and these questions must now be taken up with the directness warranted by the position so far developed. As the bearer of God's intention for man's being, is his (man's) historio-personal existential always "there," always present to him? If there, always actual? If not actual, how there and how actualized?

For theology that has not ceased to be theology, the first of these questions is rhetorical (in the pejorative sense of rhetorical): theology explodes its own foundation unless it claims for man the presence of his ownmost historio-personal existential. The claim advanced here is that this ontological structure of revelation is presented and actualizable in historical time in a way that is formally analogous to the presence and actualization of a work of art. Obviously, we need next to attend to the work of art in its modes of being. By no means incidentally, that attention should help to illuminate the claim that full-orbed imagination intends and extends the domain of "coming to be." Preoccupied with being aborning, imagination is more than a mental sensitor for registering in lively figure the vibrancy and process of existential occurrence. As in history so also in art, imagination is an ontic/ontological power, participating in the very being of what it opens up and upon. Imagination is engaged by those dimensions of being which lay a claim upon man's creativity, which require human response for the maturation of their and his act of being.

B. The Modes of Being of the Work of Art

(1) The existence of the work of art. In the ontology of aesthetics two points evoke our interest in respect of the existence of the work of art. The first is the making or production of the art object; the second is its "appreciation," or the apprehension of it as a work of art.

(a) The "physics" of artistic making. To what has been said already about poetics (*poiētikos*) it is necessary only to add some comments about the "physics" of the art object. So long as an art object has an actual potency for becoming a work of art, it is dependent on a physical system, i.e., is dependent upon that physical system continuing in existence.[118] By "actual

[118] There are several problems in connection with such a statement upon which I cannot dwell here. For one thing, it is exceptionally difficult to specify the point at which the physical system of an art object loses its potency for being a work of art. Many art objects survive the classical and primitive periods only in defaced, eroded form, yet manage to retain their potency and thus function as works of art. Other objects survive in such form as only to permit the judgment that they are artifacts. Very likely a circularity of judgment is involved in the borderline cases: where the work of art can be actualized in sophisticated sensibility, the physical system of the art object is judged to be still integrally intact (i.e., to have power over the range of actualizations).

For another thing, it is an extraordinarily complex question whether a reproduction of the physical system of an art object can suffice as the existential continuant upon which a work of art depends. On this point, one scarcely can generalize for all the arts. It would be much more disastrous if Michelangelo's David were destroyed and we had to rely on the David in the Piazza della Signorini than it would be if the original score of Berlioz's *Symphonie Fantastique* were destroyed (if in fact it now exists) and we had to rely on any one of hundreds of reproductions. Indeed I cannot see that Berlioz's *original* score has any important bearing on the emergence of his *Symphonie* as a work of art.

potency" I mean that the physical system is so configured as to delimit the range of possible actualizations of *this* art object as a work of art. Physical system is of course a loose designation in this usage. It refers above all, say, to the supernally configured stone which delimits Michelangelo's David; but it refers as well to the configuration of notes in a musical score; and to words— their order, beat, cadence—in a poem. No doubt "physical system" has larger reference, too. The physical system of Michelangelo's David extends into the quarries of Carrara and aeons of geological process, as it extends to those physical conditions under which the statue may exist *qua* physical continuant. The poem too has a larger "physical" reference, namely the linguistic heritage its words condense. The continuity of the specifically configured words, as an actual potency for a work of art, depends upon this heritage. That is why the "poetry" of an utterly dead language has lost its potency for being a work of art, even though it retain the specificity of a physical system in a narrow sense. The same is true of any image-complex brought forward as the (logically) initial presence of revelation. It is insufficient that an image-complex condense a background; the background itself must have a foreground if the image-complex is to be actualized, i.e., be interpretable.[119]

In addition to its own existentially continuing physical system, the art object *may* embrace some reference to physical objects outside the system that may or may not continue to exist.[120]

[119] Here is another exceptionally subtle matter. While the art object configures and condenses a physical system, and that system is a condition of the emergence of the work of art, the work of art *qua* work of art expands the physical system of the total complex. It is the genius of poetry to use words in such a way that, at once, they condense their history and break that history open to new meanings. Poetry is thus both a conserver and creator of language. The language of poetry and the language of faith are in this respect not just analogous but entirely alike. What revelation wants to say cannot be said in the physical system in which it is presented, although it cannot be a first term without that system.

[120] This point may seem ridiculous today when art has so little or at least so little conspicuous reference to physical objects. But that way of putting the matter concedes too much to those who wish to hog "reference" for "realistic" objects. I suspect there is as much reference in Picasso and Pollock as there is in Gainsborough. (Nonetheless, one can only emphasize the *may* in "the art object may embrace some reference . . ." It is not apparent to me that a musical score can

257

Corot's painting *Coup de Vent* is a physical system (a continuously existing canvas of such-and-such configuration) and ostensibly refers to physical objects: sky, wind, trees, peasants, etc. Both the painting and the physical objects to which it ostensibly refers have a completeness of existence which the work of art does not have. Of physical objects and the relation of a work of art to them Professor Margolis has written:

> They either exist or cease to exist, without reference to the works of art that precariously depend on them. And yet, if the work of art exists in a context other than that of the physical object (let us say, to gain some specificity, in a world of imagination), we are not prepared to say that the work of art exists merely as a potency of the physical system on which it depends; it is a new object created by perceiving certain physical systems in a new way. A physical object is entire, complete. We may fail to see all of it at any one time, but we conceive it as complete. An art object is incomplete until we complete it by beholding it (imaginatively) entire [until we complete it as a work of art].[121]

Unlike the physical system of the art object on which it depends in part (e.g., without the continuing physical system the work of art would have no public dimension), the work of art will therefore have "gaps" in its existence. The intermittence of its existence has nothing to do with the objects to which the art object may have referred in the artist's original vision, and a great deal to do with the way in which the art object is grasped. Professor Margolis may be quoted again: "The work of art is autotelic but its existence must first be seen thus: and that existence is not completed prior to the activity of a certain kind of imagination."[122]

(b) The "appreciation" or actualization of a work of art. The work of art itself, as Roman Ingarden says, is an inten-

---

have any reference to physical objects.) The point requiring emphasis is that the continuity and discontinuity of the work of art are radically different from the continuity and discontinuity of the art object (both as a physical system and such physical objects as it may refer to).

[121] Joseph Margolis, "The Mode of Existence of a Work of Art," *Review of Metaphysics*, XII, No. 1 (September, 1958), p. 32. (Brackets are mine.)

[122] *Ibid.*, p. 33.

tionality of imagination.[123] The art object is a potency, a call on imagination (that of the collaborating appreciator) produced by imagination (that of the artist), a thing inducing the movement of activated imagination in a certain tendency. But the art object *qua* stable existent is a merely necessary, not a sufficient condition for the emergent being of the work of art.[124] The art object is not a sufficient condition because it does not possess in itself the makings of the whole, the completed work of art. Hegel grasped this point when he said that the art object ". . . is . . . not by itself an animated thing; it is a whole only when its process of coming to be is taken along with it."[125]

The art object takes its process of coming to be along with it only as the collaborating, co-operating, answering imagination of its perceiver is thrown into act. The emergent work of art therefore depends upon aesthetic experience that ". . . is a creative act of the same order as the act of artistic creation."[126] Such aesthetic experience, said Schiller, ". . . will endeavor to receive as it would itself have produced, and to produce as it aspires to receive.[127] We may draw upon Keats for a delicate prehension of the same point:

> Poesy alone can tell her dreams,
> With the fine spell of words alone can save
> Imagination from the sable chain
> And dumb echantment. Who alive can say
> "Thou art no Poet—mayst not tell thy dreams?"
> Since every man whose soul is not a clod
> Hath visions, and would speak, if he had loved
> And been well nurtured in his mother tongue.[128]

[123] Cf. Roman Ingarden, *Das Literarische Kunstwerk,* 2d. ed., (Tübingen: Max Niemeyer Verlag, 1960), pp. 14ff. Not only is this book important in its own right for its phenomenological aesthetic; it is a bibliographical mine on the matters under discussion here.

[124] Cf. Hilde Hein, "Intermittent Existence and the Identity of Works of Art," *Review of Metaphysics,* Vol. XII, No. 4 (June, 1959), p. 634.

[125] G. W. F. Hegel, *The Phenomenology of Mind,* trans. J. B. Baillie, 2d. ed., (London: George Allen and Unwin, Ltd., 1949), p. 715.

[126] Cf. Milton C. Nahm, *Genius and Creativity,* (New York: Harper Torchbooks, 1965), p. 248.

[127] Quoted by Nahm, *Ibid.*

[128] "Hyperion: a Vision," Canto I, 8–15; in *The Complete Poetical Works of Keats,* (Boston: Houghton Mifflin Company, n.d.), p. 233.

In short, it is one of the cardinal functions of the work of art to create the creator; to correlate artistic genius and appreciative taste; in Kant's words, to arouse the man of taste "to a feeling of his own originality."[129]

Withal, in reckoning with the existentially incomplete, answering imagination cannot without becoming fanciful "complete" it in any direction whatsoever. The existential intermittence of the work of art will have been seriously misunderstood if that work is thought to be, in nub, a formless challenge to the licentiously evocative imagination. In the art object *qua* latent work of art there are lineaments of provocation: one treasures a particular canvas because its "virtual completeness" exerts a unique pressure on the tendency of its actual completion in imagination. Against the last quotation from Kant must be set another: ". . . in all free arts there is yet requisite something compulsory. . . ." Without the latter, the work of art ". . . would have no body and would evaporate altogether. . . ."[130] Later we shall speak (i) of the way in which a tendency is invited if not compelled through the configuration of archetypes in an art object (especially the poem); and (ii) of the way in which answering imagination is given a tendency by the firmament of master images which is its historical habitat. For the moment it is sufficient to observe that the emergence of the work of art, although the work of free imagination, is strung between two constraints upon that freedom (i and ii). It is the conjunction of these constraints and free imagination that permits the art object to become more in intention than it is in stable existence, i.e., ontologically emergent work of art.

(2) The "what" of the work of art. To speak of the art object being more in intention than it is in stable existence is to question the adequacy of the category of existence to account for the being of the work of art. However it is instructive that we cannot go on to promote another candidate for adequacy, viz., the "essence" of a work of art, but rather must speak of it

---

[129] Cited by Nahm, *op. cit.,* p. 329. Cf. also Wilhelm Dilthey: "The words and sentences of a piece of literature resemble the color spots of a late Rembrandt: only the co-operating power of the hearer's or reader's imagination forms figures out of it." "Die Einbildungskraft des Dichters," Section 4, Ch. 2, 10; in *Gesammelte Schriften,* Vol. VI, p. 220.

[130] *Critique of Judgment,* Section 43; Bernard trans., p. 147.

neutrally as the "what" of the work of art in advance of developing more precise terminology.[131]

Terminology for this "what" has in fact been brought forward, although whether with requisite precision were a problem of analysis and argument too vast to be entered upon here. For Vico the "what" of a work of art is an "imaginative universal"; for Spinoza, the "singular essence"; for Hegel, the "concrete universal"; for Dilthey, "the essential of an actuality" (*das Wesenhafte eines Tatbestandes*); for Milton C. Nahm, the "concrete significant form"; for Merleau-Ponty, the "lateral universal"; and for Philip Wheelwright, the tension of the "archetypal imagination."

As a start on commending the designation "imaginative existential," let us look as simply as possible to the way in which the problems of the "what" arises. The work of art, like anything existent and especially like anything freshly come into existence, appears to be something very concrete. One values a particular painting because from time to time he sees in it something not seen elsewhere. As both fecund and resistant, the truly concrete is the "abyss of cognition" (Tillich), drawing the mind to itself again and again in richly varied presentiment yet refusing to dissolve into either a more primitive or a more encompassing unity.

Of the concreteness of the work of art in this sense, there can be no doubt. But the meaning of this concreteness is established in an aura, an iconic penumbrity, that can scarcely be called concrete itself. Rembrandt's "Aristotle Contemplating the Bust of Homer" doubtless is a concrete occasion in the aesthetic experience of it. Yet it were as difficult to specify what is concrete in this experience as to bring forward what is universal in it, as absurd to say that we meet Aristotle and Homer (or even Rembrandt) concretely as to say that we chance upon "man" (or even "early and late classical man"). Art is never a "you were there" re-enactment of history, as it is never an audio-visual documentary on *ante rem* universals.

Thus if one's first impression of the "what" of a work of art

[131] Such a promotion is not out of the question *a priori*, of course. One might argue that there is an appropriate essence or universal that an art object now and then instantiates, as the work of art is actualized. But it will be clear that such a view is closed off to the position under development here.

261

is that it is characterized by concreteness, that impression is quickly followed by another. It is a concreteness of an odd sort, differing from concreteness outside the aesthetic frame. Outside the aesthetic frame, the more concrete a thing is the more exclusive it is with respect to the reference requisite to its being what it uniquely is. Thus of my wife I never think "animal," rarely even "woman." Conversely, the more I think on these larger references, the less I have of her concrete presence. Logic has a rule ("law") to cover this common experience, one we have had occasion at various points to comment on, the rule of inverse proportions as between intension and extension.

Perhaps this rule of inversion can be stated in terms of "meaning" and "significance." When one has trouble understanding another he will often say, "I don't get your meaning—could you make it more concrete?" Often too one hears the comment after a highly abstract lecture, "I think what he was about was significant, but I'm unsure of the meaning of it all." Meaning and significance are of course dictionary synonyms, but in ordinary usage there is a difference. Significance is meaning, but meaning with weight and extensiveness of reference or applicability. In ordinary communication we try to strike a balance between specific meaning and broad significance, tilting the seesaw so that meaning will not slide off the one end in abstract significance, or significance plummet off the other end in idiosyncratic meaning.

One can only feel not a little ridiculous at attempting a statement to cover all works of art. Yet if *any* statement may be made in the round it is that the "what" of the work of art ignores the logical caveat that intension and extension, meaning and significance, may not be increased simultaneously. The "what" of the work of art, stated formally, is precisely the simultaneous increase of intension and extension, of meaning and significance. For this simultaneous increase or coincidence, the phrase "imaginative existential" is used.

"Imaginative" must be used in the phrase for reasons that should be obvious by now. (a) The art object *qua* existent requires the exercise upon it of negative impulse in order to yield its phenomenological range *qua* latent work of art. (b) In this exercise imagination sacrifices neither immediacy to wholeness nor wholeness to immediacy; neither activity to passivity nor passivity to activity.

"Existential" must be used for similarly obvious reasons. (a) The chief of these is the difference between worlds, and thus between universes of discourse, inhabited respectively by the stably existent art object and the intermittently existent work of art. (b) In specification of (a): an existent has a manner of existing that is irreducible to itself merely *qua* existent. In the work of art, its "what" is not a pasting together of an anterior concrete entity and an antecedent universal character, class-concept, or manner; so that what is concrete in the work of art cannot be an "illustration" of universality, and what is universal cannot be deduced or induced from what is concrete. In short, with emergent existence comes its commensurately emergent "existential," the horizon out of which the existent is to be understood. For that reason the work of art is insusceptible of paraphrase without remainder outside the aesthetic mode of discourse, as it is equally insusceptible of reduction without remainder to private or purely idiosyncratic meaning.

If one is given pause at this point, it is doubtless because on such an understanding no small part of our artistic heritage is put in jeopardy; and, if the analogy between theology and art holds, no smaller part of our theological heritage as well. But this is the consequence of taking seriously the formal statement of a norm, whether in aesthetics, theology, or whatever discipline, and is a part of what is meant by unthinking or dismantling the tradition. For example, we can now see why certain kinds of art have been in danger of sliding off the ends of the artistic scale. "Neo-classical" art courts artistic disaster on the end of "nature" and the "universal," degenerating in steady progression to ". . . a standard of . . . objectivity, the average tulip, the average human form, some sort of average," a standard that can only abort in platitude. Radically "romantic" art teases artistic suicide on the end of "particularity" and "originality," burrowing finally in ". . . the idiosyncratic and the unintelligible and . . . the psychology of the author."[132] Analogous

[132] Cf. W. K. Wimsatt, Jr., "The Structure of the 'Concrete Universal' in Literature," *Criticism: The Foundations of Modern Literary Judgment,* ed. Mark Schorer *et al.,* (New York: Harcourt, Brace and Company, 1948), pp. 695–696.

263

jeopardies are rife in the western religious tradition. Preaching has often been a private "meaning-sing" off the existentialistic end of the continuum, as theology has often been an exercise in proportion without regard to concreteness and feeling,[133] off the essence-universal end. No doubt the language of confession is more intensional and the language of theology is more extensional; but each language is bound through the hermeneutical spiral to the emergent "existential," the tensioned coincidence of intensive and extensive man for the present historical time.

C. The Imaginative Existential in Revelation

Rather than detailing the similarities and dissimilarities between the imaginative existential in the work of art and in revelaton, and thus anticipating the following chapter, let us now only point the moral in a few broad strokes.

Recall the questions we proposed to overtake by recourse to the work of art and its modes of being. The first question was: How is revelation as fundament "there"; how is man's authentic historio-personal existential presented to him? The second question goes back to the original statement of the problem of an ontology of revelation in Chapter III. There we denied an actual revelatory noesis of universal scope, at least as a foundation for deducing the formal character of revelation. Then it was asked what it would mean to affirm universally proffered revelatory noemata. Such an affirmation seems essential to the continuity, extension, and publicity of revelation's intentionality. Would not the enterprise appropriate to revelation so conceived then be ontology, not theology? If man's historio-personal existential is universally proffered, is that not all but self-contradictory: the particular interlacing of regions supplanted by a structure of extension?

The answer to these questions, hopefully will be apparent by now. Above all it has been our intention to show how the rhetoric of revelatory discourse closes the distension between intension and extension with respect to man's authentic being

[133] Such theology turns the "local habitation and a name" of scripture into "airy nothing," thus inverting Shakespeare. See note 83 above.

in the world *coram Deo*. In this regard the rhetoric of revelation is formally analogous to the rhetoric of the arts. But the analogy extends as well to the way in which revelation as fundament is proffered and actualized.

Like the art object, revelation as fundament is proffered as an existing continuant. ("God has not left himself without a witness. . . .") This existing continuant is refunded in all the ways described hitherto, e.g., in the way of triadic constitution (Ch. III). But full-orbed revelation is *actually* gappy or inter-mittent. Full-orbed revelation is thereby construed on the model of the process whereby the art object is actualized *qua* work of art: of noema and noesis in the hermeneutical spiral. Because full-orbed revelation is never merely a structure to which we have only to accommodate ourselves, nor yet merely an evocation of private perspective we have only to avow, theology is reducible neither to ontology nor to confession.

In revelation as in the arts the imaginative existential is no passive reflection of an alien form, nor is it the active abstraction of a class-universal. The imaginative existential in revelation adumbrates the quality of transcendence which characterizes the presence of whole manhood for me. "Transcendence" is the better word over "universality" in this connection; at least, transcendence characterizes the quality of universality to be found in the imaginative existential, a quality expressing itself in and through historical time. Such a discrimination is neces-sary because the word universality usually connotes extension over space ("everywhere"). The transcendent quality of uni-versality shows itself in the revelatory imaginative existential, however, in the co-inherence of the modes of time. Where the imaginative existential functions in a revelatory way (i.e., where the possibility of one's manhood is funded anew out of one's own time, and where one "answers" in appropriate mode), man closes up the distention of his own presence in time. My being, deployed and for the most part dissipated through disjointed times, achieves transcendence when through the imaginative existential I encounter my own fully temporal presence. Thus the human imaginative existential is not distributed to abstract instances of "humanity," but rather to the ontic presence of ontologically expanded man to himself. And so it will be clear

265

that the revelatory imaginative existential is not a structure intended through an ". . . activity by which the human spirit reproduces in itself the form and the ideality of an alien or alternate actuality."[134] It is rather an act of ontological generation, an act by which man is offered not without his complicity his ownmost possibility of presence in the world.

[134] Cf. A. Robert Caponigri, *Time and Idea: The Theory of History in Giambattista Vico,* (London: Routledge and Kegan Paul, Ltd., 1953), p. 176.

I should perhaps note that, in developing the notion of the imaginative existential, I owe much to Vico's theory of "poetic character" and the "imaginative universal." (See *La Scienza Nuova Seconda,* [Bari: Guis. Latera e Figli, 1942], paragraphs 374-79, 401-02; in Giambattista Vico, *The New Science,* pp. 104-107, 114-115.) But the view here developed has little in common, finally, with the Vichian account. Reacting against the prevailing Cartesian dualism and the bifurcation of intellect and imagination he took it to suggest, Vico like Fichte long after him developed his doctrine of imagination within the unitary framework of a metaphysics of mind. Within that same framework he worked out his understanding of history, in which understanding his theory of the imaginative universal played as decisive a role as in his theory of art.

And indeed, I could as defensibly have developed the imaginative existential here from a base in the character of historical knowledge (and have chosen not to do so for economy's sake). The reader who wishes to pursue issues under discussion here in that framework may profitably consult Theodor Litt, "The Universal in the Structure of Historical Knowledge," *Philosophy and History: The Ernst Cassirer Festschrift,* (New York: Harper Torchbook 1115P, 1963), pp. 125-136. In fact, the whole of this volume of essays is pertinent.

VI. Tradition, Imagination, and the Theological Task

Outline

INTRODUCTION: SCOPE OF THE CHAPTER

The imagination is not to be used as a dray horse for carrying the lumber of the schools through the gardens of the Muses.[1]

[1] Edwards Amasa Park, *The Theology of the Intellect and That of the Feelings:* a discourse delivered before the convention of the Congregational ministers of Massachusetts, in Brattle Street Meeting House, Boston, May 30, 1850, (Boston: Perkins and Whipple, 1850). Re-

The concern of this chapter will be to see what theology may do to coax from the historical past its potency for expanding the human good. We shall want to know how what was once presented as man's possibility of authentic being can be re-presented through tradition (both as *traditio,* the process of re-presenting, and as *traditum,* the material possibility itself), and thus made a sextant for shooting the present situation. The concern here, as formerly throughout this essay, will be a formal one; it is the intention to descry the formal lineaments of a theological program vis-à-vis tradition, not within the present scope to execute that program upon the material tradition, or even a tiny fragment of it.

It will be useful initially to recapitulate the three-fold problematic within the horizon of which the inquiry has been conducted, and to note especially those points at which each of the major problems has been intersected. Following that, it will be of importance to characterize the need for reliance, by theology with pretensions to systematic traffic with the symbolic tradition, upon a phenomenology of the symbolic tradition. Crucial media for the transmission of tradition will be identified as having primal claim on the attention of such a phenomenology; and they will be developed along the lines previously laid down. Finally, it will be necessary to expose the "position" of systematic theological symbolics, with particular attention to *method.*

I. RECAPITULATION OF THE THREE-FOLD PROBLEMATIC

Of the three areas of problematic under scrutiny in these pages the first two so far have been most directly in view. Reduced to catch-words, these areas were designated as the problem of an ontology of revelation, the problem of revelation and its cognitive scale, and the problem of the re-presentative and cognitive potency of tradition.

"Ontology of revelation" embraced the interrogation of

printed in *American Philosophic Addresses, 1700–1900,* ed. Joseph L. Blau, (New York: Columbia University Press, 1947), p. 649.

theology's ownmost *given* in Chapter I; the consideration of horizon formation and fusion in Chapter II; the deliberation of that constitutive process wherein and whereby the "what" or substantive bearing of revelation is built up, in Chapter III; reflection on the reflexive relation between unfinished and finished manhood, and the historio-personal existential of grace, in Chapter IV; and development of the analogy between the potency and the actualization of a work of art and the potency and actualization of revelation, in Chapter V.

"Revelation and its cognitive scale" comprised the problematic of the cognitive intersections in the traffic between grace, faith, and theology in Chapter I; the description of the hermeneutical spiral in Chapter II; the meditation on fundamental revelation as intending multidimensional noemata and as comprising a noesis at bottom pre-thetic and pre-predicative, in Chapter III; the deployment of the question of knowledge according to our insertion in historical being, in Chapter IV; and the retailing of mental acts and thus of the modes of cognition, in Chapter V.

Perhaps it is worth pausing to emphasize that these two areas of problematic have been entered upon in such a way as to keep in tandem with the contemporary experience of reality. For purposes of general visibility, that experience has been transposed where possible into an ontological medium. No mirrors would be required to show in detail that and how every major doctrine of revelation in the history of Christian reflection has been construed against an ontological backdrop. Indeed, whenever a broad consensus has obtained with respect to the scale of cognitive acts embraced by revelation, it has done so under the aegis of an equally widespread ontological account— especially as that account gathered up and impinged upon the trajectory of human life. So much is not to deny even more; for example, that the ontological account was itself a metaphysicizing of archetypes prevailing in the mythological organization of experience.

By the same token (if the past is any clue), the collapse of an ontological backdrop—itself telegraphed by the arts—signals imminent decay for the doctrine of revelation that leans into it. In a hermeneutic of revelation that has a chance of purchase

269

in viability today, just those problems are most pressing that arise in connection with the crisis in contemporary ontological meditation, a crisis that reflects the cross-currents in our experience. Modernity in this respect, to be sure, has been shaken not by one tremor alone but rather by a series of worldquakes: by seventeenth-century conceptions of "substance," by eighteenth-century doctrines of "nature," and by nineteenth-century theories of "spirit," "history," and "classes" (to mention only a few that have set theology's seismographic needle aflutter). The most shattering quake of all, the one in the wake of whose reconfigurations we are seeking the formal contours of revelation, goes back to a fissure that appeared at the dawn of the high civilizations and comes to the apogee of fury in our contemporary technology. With a plethora of anthropological detail, Joseph Campbell has argued that the high civilizations were preceded and made possible by a human leap of quantum proportions, viz., the transition from man the hunter to man the agrarian.[2] Central to this transition (although Campbell does not put it so) was the emergence of man *qua* incipient *homo faber*. Through agriculture and the domestication of animals man gathered unto himself power over the perimeters of his

[2] See Joseph Campbell, "The Symbol Without Meaning," *Eranos-Jahrbuch, 1957* ed. Olga Fröbe-Kapteyn, (Zürich: Rhein-Verlag, 1958), pp. 415–475. The title of this essay is a poor clue to its richly provocative content. Campbell's thesis, lifted out of his style and therefore shorn of much of its force, is that we are presently at the end (indeed, past the end) of a 6,000 year age. This age found its social form in the hieratic city state, a form that was at the same time religious because it was a mirror image of a mythological order. Within that form religion was a cohesive force and priests a function of the community. With the dissolution of the requisite mythological underpinnings, both these social and religious forms have effectively vanished. While the thesis itself is scarcely novel, Campbell's mounting of evidence in support of it from the history of religions is stunningly impressive. So much cannot be said, I think, for his systematic counsels. He proposes recourse to the human stream shunted aside by the high civilizations, to a religion of shamanistic rather than priestly mentality. He nonetheless scores a point (whether or not he intended to do so) eminently needing to be made, that theology may no longer be prosecuted as an academic discipline without closest proximity to the study of the history of religions (something known in the nineteenth century, and above all by Troeltsch). I gratefully acknowledge my indebtedness to Professor David L. Miller of Syracuse University for introducing me to Campbell's thought.

270

experience; his tools made him a maker. For primitive man and for man in the high civilizations of antiquity, indeed through the high Middle Ages, human making was however a subordinated making. His making was scored on a celestial model, and so was informed by archeypes set to a mythological music for which metaphysics supplied the program notes.

With the Renaissance and the Copernican revolution, *homo faber* receives a new ordination: that of *humanitas* itself. The mythological frame of human making and being made, even so, was sloughed but slowly. No doubt the nineteenth-century stands as a watershed, largely for its conjunction of theoretical and practical consciousness that this idea was bursting into the fullness of time. Without the germinal notion of man as maker, the theoretical work of the nineteenth-century idealists can only appear bizarre. But if allied as in Marx with the practical intuition afforded by the Industrial Revolution proceeding apace, viz., that around the corner lie the technological means for extending human making in limitless directions, that work accounts in large measure for the political and social reality of the twentieth century. Wallace Stevens, at once a practitioner of free enterprise business and an incomparable poet, was surely correct to say that imagination is visible today on the grandest public scale not in the arts but in world communism.[3] That may be taken to mean, in the terms developed here, that the dialectic of human making and being made has been accepted as the frame for construing man's experience of reality. When it is considered that over half the earth's population has been won to this frame in only a few decades, not to mention the fact of its pressure upon alternative economic-political philosophies (as in the United States), one can only conclude that a latent tendency in modern man has found thereby its means of public expression.

At all events, this frame has been risked here as *the* frame in which and out of which to think the formal contours of revelation. Whether this frame is itself in process of dissolution, as claimed by Martin Heidegger and Joseph Campbell on different evidence or on the same evidence differently read,

[3] See *The Necessary Angel: Essays on Reality and the Imagination,* (London: Faber & Faber, 1951), p. 143.

271

is no doubt a possibility to which theology and every other humane discipline must be alert. We are surely nearer the *ad quem* of an epoch of human existence ordered by an integral bundle of archetypes than its *a quo*. But authentic faith has ever conceived itself between the times, between the decay of the old and the emergence of the new. It cannot honor the call for recourse to that juncture in primeval time when man took a false turn, to return to which is to be given one's possibility of being.[4] Nothing is more central to the Judeo-Christian circumspection of revelation than that God gives us our humanity in concert with the course of historical reality. Because that humanity is not merely coextensive with or an epiphenomenon of the course of historical reality, it is given (constituted) between the times; or as has been claimed here, through the co-inherence of the modes of historical time. But because that humanity is constituted as a possibility in *concert* with the course of historical reality, the course itself cannot be gone back on; cannot, that is, except in the way of understanding. *Understanding* out of the past and its potency may indeed open the future out of which we are to live; but *living* out of the past on the basis of an understanding putatively won from the future (say, the imminent end of an age), the end-run tried

---

[4] Perhaps it is well to strike a note for theological independence at this point. Just as faith does not go out on loan, neither does philosophical meditation that advances the theological task (oh, hard truth for today's theologian, so willing to pay usurious rates of interest, so quick to bid up the price for second-hand philosophy!). The phenomenological meditation of revelation as fundament may indeed coincide with a philosophical project when prosecuted in certain ways; but if the full range of what renders revelation problematical in the first place is to be kept in view, that meditation must be carried through for theology's own account. We have every right to suspect, and with care to discover, that revelation is not thought through to its ground when its theological formulation is advanced as a grace note, an *appogiatùra,* to Whitehead, Hartshorne, Heidegger, Hegel, *et al.* Simply put, the point is that no question is radicalized until we approach the birthplace of meaning, the meaning of what is at stake in the question. For that rigorous journey no mercenary will do. If we go ourselves we will of course be outfitted from many a source, and will not arrive unless we are. Taking the beat of our meditation from a certain philosophical "style," we will owe thanks to a philosopher or a school of philosophy whom or which we judge to have executed that style in an ideal way. If we hew to the radicalization of our own question, however, we will not deploy that style in a merely manneristic way.

by those moderns who hanker for pre-critical naïveté, is quite impossible. For modesty's sake: so much is quite impossible for Christian theology.

These comments bring forward the third area of problematic, that of the re-presentative and cognitive potency of tradition. As broached in Chapter I, this third area is really the conjunction of the other two areas as that conjunction bears upon the historical past. The question of tradition in a hermeneutic of revelation is therefore two-fold. The first is, how tradition possesses a potency for revelatory intentionality. No doubt the question may be proliferated: how tradition re-presents what was once presented, how tradition enters into the constitution of present reality, etc. The second fundamental part of the question concerns the knowledge value of the tradition. The cognitive potency of tradition refers then neither merely to the knowability of tradition nor to our power to know tradition but rather more to the potency of tradition as a means of knowledge, the potential power of tradition to illuminate our existence in the present.[5]

If the problem of tradition is the conjunction of the problem of theology's given and the problem of theology's modes of knowledge as that conjunction bears on theology's own past, it will be clear that the problem of tradition has been in view obliquely all along. Thus it was emphasized in Chapter II that the hermeneutical spiral is a temporal and not merely a logical spiral (and may not be merely logical without being a logically vicious circle). Chapter III saw the initial development of fundamental revelation as containing in its reference a temporal prius, a reference to past paradigmatic events. Even more di-

---

[5] If the question of tradition is given over solely to the question of knowledge *of* tradition, the imperialism of a unilinear historiography prevails. That is, a self-understanding won from the present experience of reality is packed along as the substrate of understanding what went on in the past. To emphasize the cognitive potency of tradition is not to set that historiographical direction aside but rather is to insist upon its reflex action as well (i.e., to insist upon the hermeneutical spiral). A unit of tradition may not be considered known, consequently, until by its means some segment of present experience is illuminated. The cognitive traffic with tradition is thus not one way: The cognitive potency of tradition is its potency for expanding our self-understanding (i.e., the understanding of our present experience of reality).

rectly related to tradition were the development of the ontological function of "background" in Chapter IV and that of the cognitive functions of memory in Chapter V. The points of contact have in fact been too numerous to recapitulate fully, as a further sample may indicate: the way we are inserted into the experience of our being according to the residue of previously active, now ossified imagination; the role of active imagination in gaining transit from one modality of historical time to another, and especially in gaining access to the past in its plural modality of potency; the perpetual recourse of material Christian theology to a particular fund of ontological potency that was presented (in the Christ event) and re-presented in historical time; the dismantling of tradition to surprise this fund of ontological potency, by "imaginative shock," etc.

II. THE TASK OF A PHENOMENOLOGY OF THE SYMBOLIC TRADITION

Withal, it is necessary to focus attention rather more directly now upon tradition as it bears upon the revelatory nexus. Three foci may be distinguished in the theological task vis-à-vis this bearing. The first comprises those considerations which precede and require a phenomenology of the material symbolic tradition. The second embraces the location and description of those media of transmission to which a phenomenology of tradition will rivet itself. The third describes the task of systematic theological symbolics. Taken up in turn, the second of these foci will receive fullest development. Each, but especially the second and third, can only be sketched in a programmatic way.

A. Considerations which Precede and Require a Phenomenology of the Symbolic Tradition

These considerations need only to be drawn together from the preceding inquiry; where possible, summary propositions will be used with minimal comment.

274

In its broadest sense "tradition" refers to the whole linguistic legacy of theology, and doubtless includes much language that is not specifically theological. Hereafter tradition will be used to refer not to that larger legacy, however, but rather to the language in the larger legacy which theology must assume once to have been viable for the expression of revelation. As it touches the present revelatory nexus in systematic elaboration, tradition refers to those types of language in the past which intended to bring revelation to speech or act as directly as possible. "Types of language" is thus construed broadly to include not only oral and written language but also the discourse of rite, sacrament, etc. In short, it is language put forward as event-inverbalizing language, the language of imaginative discourse, to which a phenomenology of tradition will address itself. That a systematic judgment is involved in the location of revelatory language in imaginative discourse is apparent; and the rationale for this location has been our concern for many pages past. From a quite different systematic standpoint, one locating revelatory language in the conceptualities of technical theology, what would be required would be not a phenomenology of imaginative discourse in the tradition but rather a history of ideas in the tradition. That a "history of ideas" approach to tradition has prevailed, by and large, accounts in part for the lamentable partition which exists today between historical theology and systematic theology on the one hand, and between systematic theology and theology of culture (culture above all has its traditions of imaginative discourse!) on the other.

Language reflects the effectiveness of a tradition in our common life. This is no less true for theological than for any other language in use. Since imaginative discourse is noticeable largely by its absence, at least by its infrequency of use, in the rhetoric of the church today, we must conclude that the effectiveness of the Christian tradition in its imaginative dimensions is weak. Nietzsche's judgment is pertinent at this point: "It is now no longer our reason, but our taste that decides against Christianity."[6] This may be taken to mean that aesthetic taste does not find its theological equivalent in the discourse Chris-

[6] *La Gaia Scienza*, III, 132; in *Joyful Wisdom*, p. 173.

tianity brings forward today, or else finds it but finds it ineffective. Appeal to reason cannot be forgotten, to be sure. Reason that counts, that counts whether it is decided for or against, is reason elevated from presently viable imaginative discourse.

"Presently viable imaginative discourse" is of course the nub of the problem. Were the tradition's symbolic discourse viable, it would be effective in our rhetoric; more, it would exert pressure on theological-conceptual extrapolations. But the *lingua franca* today shows neither this effectiveness nor this pressure. The task of theology as it precedes a phenomenology of tradition is thereby made no less difficult than acute. Such theology must sense the present universe of imaginative discourse in which any symbol or imaginative complex from the past will have to gain its viability of understanding, its possibility of coming into effective language. This sense must then be laid on phenomenology of tradition as its formal principle of selection. A phenomenology of the *whole* symbolic tradition is quite impossible, or at least quite useless.

Theology that precedes phenomenology of tradition runs an enormous risk, the risk of self-defeat. It may put demands upon phenomenology that phenomenology cannot fulfill without ceasing to be phenomenology—demands that remove the phenomena of tradition or their *logoi*. To put the same thing another way: theology may become so enamored of the contemporary horizon of understanding as to direct that what is brought forward shall be not only understandable but also *believeable* and *edifying,* i.e., shall comport materially with the contemporary experience of reality. Here another leaf may be taken from Nietzsche, who warned that the will to translation is often only the will to imperialism—the will, as he put it, to wipe away "the wing-dust of the butterfly moment."[7] Left to himself and his systematic inventiveness, the translator's question is likely to be, "Should we not make the old new for ourselves . . . should we not . . . inspire this dead body with our soul?"[8]

[7] Thus for Roman conquerors, the Greek classical texts were like Greek slaves taken in battle, so many objects for the *imperium Romanum.* See *ibid.,* II, 83; in *Joyful Wisdom,* pp. 115–116.
[8] *Ibid.*

276

If theology evades the translator's temptation to imperialism, it will be for two reasons. The first is that it will not exit from the hermeneutical spiral. Theology does not look to the contemporary frame of understanding without *any* notion of what could count as materially revelatory within that frame. One's historio-personal existential counts *against* himself, however much it is a refunding of self-making, else it is something one makes entirely for himself. Thus the "text" of value in the tradition is the text having the potency to save us from becoming the victim of our own thinking, the text so surcharged with the subject matter that it affords the focal point through which we have to gain access—against our "thinking"—to our range of being. As said before, theology has not to begin but to recommence.

The second and doubtless more powerful check on imperialism in the translator is the rigorous application of phenomenological method upon the designated segments of the symbolic tradition. The phenomenology of symbols, as Paul Ricoeur has said, discloses the comprehension which symbols intend within their native habitat of symbolic reference.[9] In pursuit of that comprehension every instrument of critical method is brought into play. For that reason the comprehension that is gained phenomenologically will be post-critical; it will not be the pre-critical naïveté that went with the symbol as performative hierophany or anthrophany. In short, phenomenology of symbols is hermeneutical: it brings the comprehension of symbols forward in such a way that this comprehension is the post-critical equivalent of their pre-critical performance.[10] The indispensable function of phenomenology of tradition is therefore to bring forward that imaginative discourse through which systematic theological symbolics will take its material

[9] Cf. "The Symbol: Food for Thought," *Philosophy Today,* Vol. IV, No. 3/4 (Fall, 1960), pp. 203–204.

[10] *Ibid.,* p. 204. I cannot agree with Ricoeur when he discriminates the phenomenology of symbols from the hermeneutic of symbols. And it appears that Ricoeur does not agree with himself, for he makes nothing substantive of the discrimination. Indeed he contravenes it by insisting on the inescapability of the hermeneutical circle in all phenomenological "comprehension," viz., by insisting that one cannot comprehend without interpreting and vice versa.

"fix" on the present situation, and to bring that discourse forward in a form that is already hermeneutical. The middle term of theological work is thus inescapably historical-phenomenological.

B. Problem Areas for a Phenomenology of Symbolic Tradition

It is necessary now to indicate certain concerns of a phenomenology of symbolic tradition which the position so far developed can be expected to illuminate. This may be achieved through propositional summaries.

(1) What is given in revelation cannot be referred without remainder to a previous cognitive fixation.

(2) The previous fixation is however a watching brief, in the way that an art object is a watching brief. A complex of imaginative discourse from the tradition possesses potency for cognitive purview of our present being if that discourse is actualizable in answering, contemporary imagination. We may participate the language of tradition only as we participate the genesis of meaning for which catchwords in the tradition ("atonement," "justification," "Chalcedon") stand as fixations.

(3) The "constancy" of the revelatory given poses special problems for phenomenological access. But then, the same problems have their systematic counterpart; and the resolution of the systematic problems point the direction for a phenomenology of tradition. Thus:

(a) There is no absolutely independent, a-historical term or constant that counts in or as the revelatory given. The revelatory given that impinges upon the experience of reality, and verifies that experience as the experience of one's authentic being, is in some sense a successor of past correlations (i.e., correlations in the past between man and his experience of being *coram Deo*). In other words, the "given" in revelation is not absolutely *occasionalistic,* is not born fresh for every experience of reality. Were this not the case, we should have to speak of an historio-personal *existentiell* rather than an historio-personal *existential*. Not to be evaded is the consequence

278

of this affirmation, viz., that revelation is not without remainder *event* (i.e., *occasionalistic* event). The very existence of a revelation-tradition counts as evidence against occasionalism; the tradition itself, through its imaginative discourse, affords connectional tissue between events of concretion.

With that said, more is required. What exceeds event as its connectional tissue is connected with it (*qua* co-presentor and re-presentor of the revelatory given) as its cognitive harbinger and as its cognitive residue, viz., *image*. Without the historicality of images as the key to the cognitivity of events, we should have to speak of the *ideational* rather than the *imaginative* existential. The upshot of these considerations is that a phenomenology of the symbolic tradition can be executed only by close attention to the dialectic between image and event.

(b) To be designated as "paradigmatic" are those events in which all preceding correlations are called into question. In the paradigmatic event, the disclosure of what it means to be man before God *and* man's experience of reality coincide (coincide, i.e., for one man, say Jesus, or for a group, say the disciples). A type case of the complex intercausality between image and event, the paradigmatic event is visible *qua* paradigmatic only by virtue of images surviving the older correlations; yet the older images are put in crisis by the event whose intelligibility they at once afford the first fix on and cannot contain. (The conflict between the Jewish and Gentile Christians over the older messianic images, as affording the framework for the intelligibility of the Christ-event, is a case in point). The paradigmatic event is therefore the spawning spring for the reconfiguration of images.

(c) A phenomenology of tradition that aims to disclose the uniqueness and constancy of revelatory structures, or patterns large and small in the permutation of revelatory structures, will rivet itself to the study of two non-discursive forms as they are fleshed out in the imaginative language of the religious heritage. These forms are (i) archetypes, and (ii) what may be called historical master images.

In sum then, precisely through its reckoning with the material content of the symbolic tradition, a phenomenology of the symbolic tradition must concern itself with four things: (i) the

279

relation between image and event, (ii) *paradigmatic* event, (iii) archetypes, and (iv) historical master images.

Before taking these matters up, we do well to remind ourselves from the earlier discussion of the work of art that the contours and efficacy of symbols require consideration in two contexts. The first is the "initial" context in which and from which the symbol emerges. In poietics this context was seen to embrace both the particular art object in which the symbol makes its appearance and the yet wider matrix of meaning on which the artist draws to focus symbolic vision. For the poet, "wider matrix of meaning" will include the history of the language in which he writes, the body of viable archetypes available to him, etc.

This sense of context has its equivalent in the religious symbolic tradition, and it is of the "initial context" of symbols that a phenomenology of symbolic tradition will speak primarily. In that tradition this context will be found both narrow and wide. Narrow because, however much bandied about as counters and units in "comparative religion" textbooks, images as the stuff of symbols are not found in the tradition as single or isolated things. They survive in symbol-complexes: in hymns, narrative sketches, blessing and thanksgiving formulae, prophetic oracles, dream reports, kerygmatic summaries, etc. Yet a wider context is necessary to the intelligibility of these concretions of images; a context that is laterally wider by reference to environing systems of archetypes, and temporally wider by reference to the history in which available images have come to their present permutation.

As the work of art is "tied" to the art object, and the art object by continuity of existence to its initial context, so a phenomenology of the symbolic tradition is tied to particular symbol-complexes as concatenated in their initial context. But the art object is there on view to the public: say, in a museum; whereas symbol-complexes in the religious tradition have often to be brought out of ghetto hiding, and so through translation, in order to be publicly visible.

The second ("appreciative") context is that of "answering imagination," the context into which the symbol enters in the present. This context also has a wide and a narrow reach. As

280

narrow, it embraces the moving, developing life of the person who is responding, collaborating, participating in the symbolic action. As wide, is comprises the present state of the firmament of images, the universe of imaginative discourse prevailing, the "world" of the individual's collaboration.

Just as phenomenology of tradition is directed primarily toward context in the first sense, and thus toward that "comprehension" intended by a symbol-complex in its initial setting, so systematic symbolics is oriented primarily toward context in the second sense and consequently toward those conditions under which the forwarded symbol-complex may serve as an interpretor of present existence. These conditions are formally identical, in their problematical character, with the four problem areas just now sketched.[11] Positively stated, these "conditions" are the forms through which symbolic tradition (both as *traditio* and as *traditum*) is able to re-present. To them we may turn now in greater detail.

C. *The Forms of Symbolic Tradition*

(1) Image and event. To the long section devoted to this theme in the preceding chapter ("The imagination and event," pp. 228–254), it is necessary now only to add some remarks concerning its bearing on tradition. For many decades a debate has raged in theology over the character of biblical revelation. Hardly at question, in the broad consensus, is the historical character of that revelation. That revelation occurred in and through certain events transpiring in late antiquity is a theological commonplace. What has been in contention is the cognitive character of revelation in relation to its historical onticity. Stated in another way, the revelatory events survive only in various linguistic forms through scripture; events cannot

[11] That is, phenomenology of tradition and systematic symbolics differ by reason of having different time frames in view (although that is not the only difference between these enterprises). For example, both must face the problem of what to make of archetypes, but the archetypal context for a piece of fourth century B.C. prophetic symbolism differs radically from a comparable piece of discourse in mid-twentieth century America.

store themselves (except in the ontological potency they establish), and thus cannot be re-enacted in their uniqueness. The question is, through what cognitive structures can "interpretation" gain access to these events without selling off either their revelatory or their historical character? Biblical theologians tend to be suspicious of this way of stating the question, remembering as they must how cognitive structures have been advanced of such a time-transcending sort as to work against the historicity of the events such structures were called in to adumbrate. In the end these structures rather than the events are made to afford the foundation on which theology builds, and thereby theology wins its license for libertarian constructivity.

This way of stating the problem and the presuppositions of this way of stating the problem render it insoluble. From the presupposed antinomy between event and language it could only have been expected that an *aporia* would develop between revelatory event and "interpretation." From the dichotomy between event and interpretation, and especially from the one-way direction: first event, then interpretation, it could only have been expected that event would be foreshortened into interpretation, especially if uninterpreted event (whatever that might be) were accessible only to an end-run around language.

These antinomies and dichotomies rest on recondite language and a recondite view of historical event. In the understanding developed here, the relation between event and language has been prosecuted at the point of their greatest propinquity, namely in imaginative discourse. Imaginative discourse employs and deploys language at the lowest level of abstraction: it teeters on the boundary between event as sheer immediate presence and event as "frozen" for universal conveyance.[12] So positioned, this discourse is the bearer of the imaginative existential. The matter may also be put another way. If we accept the distinction drawn alike in structural linguistics and in phenomenology of language, viz., that *language* regarded as such is an independent ("synchronic") system of signs and that *speech* is the individual, innovative use of signs, we may say that imaginative discourse

[12] In imaginative discourse, as Max Picard says, ". . . the words are still quivering from their collision with the objects." *Man and Language,* trans. Stanley Godman, (Chicago: Henry Regnery Co., 1963), p. 93.

282

is the overlay of language and event that emerges as *speech*. Imaginative discourse therefore proceeds *from* the speaking subject who participates the paradigmatic event in genesis of meaning. This discourse proceeds *toward* the "speaking hearer" who, if he collaborates in the imaginative mode, participates the event anew.

"Tradition," we have been at some pains to say, is not the same thing as "the past." Not the whole of the past, tradition is that potency established in the past which yet bears upon our unfinished being. It is therefore not just something to be known and left alone, but rather something ever to be brought forward (*traditio!*) into a new historical frame and by means of which in part we are to know our possibilities as established in that frame. In this sense, tradition transcends the merely ontic, unrepeatable past and enters into historical causality; and so, as Troeltsch said, it bears ". . . upon understanding the occurrence of the new and the increase of reality."[13]

Recall now what was said at the end of the last paragraph but one: imaginative discourse proceeds *from* the speaking subject who participates the event in genesis of meaning (say, for some specificity, the Exodus) *toward* the speaking hearer who, if he collaborates in imaginative mode, participates the event anew (say, for some specificity, one's concrete experience of "alienation"). Now "the event" in the two cases obviously cannot be the same event, just as the event of extruding the art object cannot be the same as the event of actualizing the work of art. But neither can the two events be simply discontinuous. Imaginative discourse as contoured by a paradigmatic event holds within itself a watching brief for the range of being embraced by that event (in the case of the Exodus, a range both individual and social). To "participate this event anew" is not to recapitulate the Exodus but rather to eventuate its imaginative discourse, i.e., allow that discourse to interpret the present situation.

The intelligibility of the point being pressed here is grounded in the historical intercausality between image and event. We

[13] Cf. Ernst Troeltsch, *Gesammelte Schriften,* (Tübingen: J. C. B. Mohr, 1913), Vol. III, pp. 48–49.

have spoken repeatedly of revelation as an interlacing of regions. "To intercalate realities," Lawrence Durrell rightly says, "is the only way to be faithful to time . . ."[14] The intercalation or reticulation of background and foreground, and thus the seat of unity in the historical time sense, has been seen to be the function of imagination. This judgment together with the complex intercausality between image and event can be found fleshed out on almost any page of the Bible.

An extraordinarily keen perception of this point is detailed by Erich Auerbach in Chapter I of *Mimesis*. In a comparison between the Odyssey and the Old Testament on the sense of time and the "presence" of the gods or God, he finds the gods in the Homeric poems to be fully present at any point in the narrative. Likewise the Homeric heroes have a crispness of presentation, both to their fellows and to the gods: they ". . . wake every morning as if it were the first day of their lives."[15] In the Old Testament, on the other hand, both God and men are "fraught with background" and surcharged with foreground. Unlike Zeus, Yahweh is never comprehensible from his sheer presence; "it is always only 'something' of him that appears, he always extends into depths." But the same must also be said of men in the Biblical stories. How should one understand Abraham as he accedes to the command to sacrifice Isaac? Here is no isolated "event," nor yet a man whose action is to be explained by his "character." A previous history bursts on and through this man, through what has been accomplished for him and through what has been promised to him. The accomplishment and the promise survive in images of "homeland" and "people"; and these images do not merely *survive*. They serve as the means for understanding the very events which they, in part, bring about. So much is to be observed again and again in the Biblical stories. How should one understand the "search and destroy" mission against Absalom in II Samuel, Chapters 18 and 19? Who is the chief actor on this haunting battleground? The one who is not himself there, but is there in

14 *Balthazar*, (New York: E. P. Dutton & Co., 1961), p. 226.
15 Erich Auerbach, *Mimesis: The Representation of Reality in Western Literature*, trans. Willard Trask, (Garden City: Doubleday Anchor Books, 1957), p. 10. The whole of Ch. I, pp. 1–20, is pertinent.

everyone who is there: David. The father who would and would not destroy his son is there and is not there.

As Auerbach suggests, the Biblical narratives do not so much permit or invite interpretation; they demand it. It is not that the *event* of Absalom's death (in the crook of an oak and at the hand of Joab) is an event that requires interpretation. It is rather that unless we are swept into the interpretive stream "before" we reach the event, we shall scarcely see it in its significance when we do reach it. Indeed, interpretation is not something exhaustively and without remainder that goes on after the event has occurred. (a) Images which precede and enter into the constitution of an event already shape its interpretability: in this way the most specific, concrete occurrences are attached in their understandability to a "world" of discourse. (b) But the converse is also true. Images are themselves collocated and molded by event, and in the process are re-specified. That is, images of a general or archetypal sort are made to take on historical reference. It is the simultaneity of (a) and (b) that is meant by the complex intercausality of image and event.[16]

(2) Paradigmatic event.

. . . Events aren't in serial form but collect here and there like quanta . . .[17]

The Christianity which persists among us is not a philosophy; it is an account of and a meditation upon an experience or a group of enigmatic events which themselves call for several philosophical elaborations and have not in fact stopped arousing philosoph*ies,*

[16] For an illustration at once elaborate and detailed, the reader may be referred to an essay by James M. Robinson concerning the nature and use of "blessing" (Berachoth) and "thanksgiving" (Hodayoth) formulae in both the Old and the New Testament. Robinson emphasizes —and shows—that these formulae in their non-liturgical use were attached to *occurrences* and thus to concrete events; but at the same time, they precisely gathered up the significance of the events. "The occurrence of the formula is thus both a reliable historical hint about the event and itself part of the historic effect of the event" (historical: *historisch;* historic: *geschichtlich*). Robinson therefore finds in these formulae a coalescence of what we have called image and event; in his terms, the coalescence of the historical and the historic. "The Historicality of Biblical Language," *The Old Testament and Christian Faith*, ed. Bernhard W. Anderson, (New York: Harper & Row, 1963), pp. 124–158.
[17] Durrell, *Balthazar*, p. 245.

even when one of these has been accorded a privileged position. Christian themes are ferments, not relics."[18]

Tradition is constituted above all else by paradigmatic events and their ambience in imagination. All events are episodic, it has been noted; but the paradigmatic event is episodic in high visibility, at least it is so in the culture or civilization in whose tradition it stands. An inverse ratio obtains between the clarity of episodicity of a paradigmatic event and the clarity of its meaning. Stated positively, when a civilization's public life is ordered by the clear and obvious celebration of its founding paradigmatic events, those events yet possess an intense ambiguity of meaning. As paradigmatic events gain clear and average meaning their power to render public life episodic is greatly diminished. In that case, celebration becomes merely "traditionalistic;" or it offers an excuse for doing what would be done under one ruse or another. Because everyone knows what they mean, Christmas and Easter have come to function this way in American social ritual.

"Paradigmatic" comes from a Greek verb meaning "to show forth pattern." The paradigmatic event is therefore an event of extraordinary "importance" in that it manifests the pattern by which other events are co-ordinated.[19] As such the paradigmatic event is doubly episodic.

(a) Like other occurrences designated as events, the paradigmatic event is an episode in the sense that it has an initial and a terminal situation. But the intrinsic ambiguity of the paradigmatic event owes at once to the fixity and the mobility of its initial and final situations. Consider, for example, the event of the Sinai Covenant. This event doubtless had an initial situation, since the event itself calls all preceding events in the Exodus into focus. But should the initial situation be called altogether fixed, when whatever is fixed can only be understood through the master images of preceding history? The matter is circular and therefore ambiguous. From Egypt to Sinai is

[18] Merleau-Ponty, *Signs*, p. 134.
[19] Cf. Dorothy M. Emmet, *The Nature of Metaphysical Thinking*, (London: Macmillan and Co., Ltd., 1949), pp. 161ff. Cf. also Josiah Royce, *The Problem of Christianity*, Vol. II, (New York: The Macmillan Company, 1913), pp. 283ff.

a course made intelligible by the event of Covenant: preceding events are thus co-ordinated by paradigmatic occurrence that is simultaneously event and image. No less surely, this occurrence had a terminal situation, else it would not have been an integral episode in the history of a people, a center for enucleating their self-images. Yet that terminal situation, however ontic in history, established a fund of ontological potency out of which succeeding generations were to live in one mode or another of appropriation. The paradigmatic event, we have said, is the event that keeps on happening: its terminal situation is open.

(b) The paradigmatic event is episodic in another sense; it serves to periodize time. In so far as this occurs in a fundamental and not merely conventional way, the paradigmatic event founds time anew; public celebrations amount to renewals of time. If the paradigmatic event is re-enacted and brought forward in public rite, that owes to the conviction that the event embodied in itself a co-inherence of the modes of time, and thus is the key to the temporal unity of the history in which its celebrants stand. As such the paradigmatic event is accorded the right, through public rite, to divide the times.

Paradigmatic events function ritualistically wherever there is tradition: we are speaking of something very widespread indeed. If one wants to know what the paradigmatic events of a cultural heritage ostensibly are, he has only to look to its holidays and festivals. No doubt much sociological analysis of calendar rites would have to be joined with a careful phenomenology of paradigmatic tradition in order to determine just what remains viable out of the tradition. Very likely it is safe to say on the basis of hunch, however, that the modern west and Christendom have permanently parted company on this score. While the official calendar rites in the west are yet officially connected with the official paradigmatic events of Christianity, that means they are only so ritually "observed" as to permit "legal holidays." If one would see paradigmatic events suffusing ritual with dramatic power and proportioned meaning today, he should turn to the incantational folk music of contemporary freedom movements. Here it is known that time stood still at

287

Philadelphia, Mississippi and at Selma, Alabama, and that time waits to be born.[20]

No small consequence of the dissociation between Christendom and modern western culture is the fact that Christian faith has a chance of being formed under conditions *formally* similar to those prevailing at the beginning of the Christian era. Then as now public ritual was essentially pagan. Then as now the common imagination had its hub in paradigmatic events other than those of the Jewish-Christian heritage. Indeed we can learn what monolithic Christendom has suppressed, viz., that there are many strands of imagination in the human story; and perhaps more important, that there are strands within the Christian story itself long since lost to view.

To be sure, this opportunity is not a *material* one: we cannot leap back over 2000 years. The strands of historically formed imagination in whose horizon faith must now frame itself are not those of the *pax Romana,* Hellenistic Gnosticism, etc., but rather those of the contemporary world. Cut loose from a contemporary crutch of ritual support in Christendom, the immediate temptation of theology is to revert to what Nietzsche called "monumental history." Recourse to monumental history, he said, is the return to segments of the past as "effects in themselves," not to the "real historical nexus of cause and effect, which, rightly understood, would only prove that nothing quite similar could ever be cast again from the dice-boxes of fate and

[20] We cannot give this matter its due here. Suffice to say that we would have to switch our model from poetry to drama in order to establish the framework in which to treat of the ritualistic dimensions of "showing forth pattern" today. While poetry moves by metaphor, drama enlivens metaphor by propelling it with agency. Drama articulates the reality in the present tense for which the past paradigmatic event is a watching brief. No doubt in the theater the drama is ". . . a present tense made possible only through semblance." (Cf. Joseph H. McMahon, *The Imagination of Jean Genet,* [New Haven: Yale University Press, 1963], p. 144f.) But with drama in the streets it is otherwise. In the freedom movement today there is almost no prose; and rightly so, for prose is the vehicle for logic accommodated to form. Poetry, more so drama, is the vehicle for logic accommodated to the expansion of form by freedom. Drama in the streets today is present tense and no semblance, but its discourse is no less dramatic for that. Indeed demonstrators in the streets are like the clown on stage: only the body can express what must be said.

the future."[21] If we "return" to the paradigmatic events of faith without attending to the history that intervenes between us and them, they are ". . . always in danger of being a little altered and touched up," and of being ". . . brought nearer to fiction." Indeed, if the paradigmatic events of faith are merely a complex of *effects* to which we have only to go back, the motto of that journey will be Nietzsche's apt twist: "let the dead bury the— living."[22]

As phenomenology of tradition will seek the comprehension of paradigmatic events in their initial cause-effect nexus, so systematic symbolics will seek in the wake of that comprehension the advent of new or renewed human being *coram Deo*. The meaning of our being cannot lie without remainder in past events. The significance of certain of those events, like that of the art object, lies in the potency of surviving imaginative discourse to effect the advent, the present tense, of the range of being for which they stand in the tradition as beacons. With Schleiermacher (and in paraphrase of him), we may say that the very notion of revelation carries with it the notion of founding, original events. Against Schleiermacher, it must be contended that these founding, original events have the potency to operate upon man as a cognitive being; and that this precisely does *not* make revelation "originally and essentially *doctrine.*"[23] The logical integration of revelation reduces to a base in paradigmatic events brought forward in the advent of new being *coram Deo*. That is the reason there is no *absolute* logical integration of Christian faith; the logical integration of faith is itself historical. That is, it is a plurality of events to which Christian faith looks for its logical unity. Even if all logical-temporal units are somehow referred to Jesus, the Jesus-event must be

[21] Nietzsche, *The Use and Abuse of History,* p. 23.

[22] *Ibid.,* p. 25.

[23] "The idea of revelation signifies the originality of the fact which lies at the foundation of a religious communion, in the sense that this fact, as conditioning the individual content of the religious emotions which are found in the communion, cannot itself in turn be explained by the historical chain which precedes it. . . . But I am unwilling to accept the further definition that it [the original fact] operates upon man as a cognitive being. For that would make revelation to be originally and essentially *doctrine.*" Schleiermacher, *The Christian Faith,* p. 50.

referred back and forth for its own temporal logic. The New Testament itself is shot through with a plurality of kerygmata, whose only logical integrity is that of paradigmatic events surviving in imaginative discourse. This imaginative language is the underived language of faith, language in closest proximity to the paradigmatic events themselves.

(3) Archetypal images.

> "God guard me from those thoughts men think
> In the mind alone,
> He that sings a lasting song
> Thinks in a marrow bone."[24]

Imaginative discourse plays on many registers; reads from a palimpsest text; moves at once in the sky, on the surface, and underground. Therewith the reason why the "reference" of imaginative language is so tortured a question. That question is torturous not only because of the diversity of referents, but also because the unity of them is not itself a referent in any ordinary sense of referent. The unity of plural and diverse reference in imaginative language is present only in the language itself, or in what the polysemous language makes present to answering imagination.

It has been our concern not so much to play on the registers but rather to identify them and check their tonal range. With archetypal reference we turn to the lowest registers of the bass clef; to the dimmest ciphers behind and below the legible text; to the underground and the watery deep. It is instructive that the "position" of archetypes can be described only through metaphors of *depth,* a fact that owes perhaps to a minimal survival of etymological meaning. *Archetypos* means "primordial implantation," or "implanted, stamped, engraved from the beginning." To the question, "Where are the archetypes?", one can only reply that they are in the depths; that in themselves they are nowhere; that they are known or rather that we know *by* them only in symbolic conjunctions.

If the spring and goal from and toward which the sciences

---

[24] W. B. Yeats, quoted by Arthur Koestler, *The Act of Creation,* (New York: Macmillan Co., 1964), p. 317.

move is the universal *logos* or concept, the impelling confluence for the arts is the vivified archetype.[25] It is a mysterious thing when the vivification happens, both for the poet and the reader, the priest and the celebrant, the preacher and the listener. One reads along in Donne's "Annunciation" and hears the Angel say to Mary:

> ". . . . yea thou art now
> Thy Makers maker, and thy Fathers mother;
> Thou hast light in darke; and shutst in little roome,
> Immensity cloystered in thy deare wombe."

By the time we reach "wombe," in the words of Arthur Koestler, ". . . some archetypal motif is sounded, the response is much stronger than warranted by its face value—the mind responds like a tuning fork to a pure tone."[26] The images attain their highest vibrational intensity as they strike archetypal chords in the hearer. Indeed the work of art draws upon archetypal reverberations both in its initial and in its "appreciative" contexts.[27] Art has a claim upon man, as Milton C. Nahm has said, because his generic feeling has been worked into, configured with the symbolism of the art object.[28] The prevailing tropes of generic feeling are in fact an inexpugnable limitant upon artistic creativity, since it is they and they alone that the artist and his appreciators have in common. Stated another way, it is a body of typical predispositions that endows the

---

[25] Cf. Wilhelm Dilthey: "Thinking brings forth concepts; artistic creativity brings forth types." *Gesammelte Schriften,* 4th ed., Vol. VI, p. 186. Dilthey's understanding of "type" underwent several mutations. A masterful study of these changes and his mature view will be found in Ludwig Landgrebe, "Wilhelm Diltheys Theorie der Geisteswissenschaften: Analyse ihrer Grundbegriffe," *Jahrbuch für Philosophie und Phänomenologische Forschung,* Vol. IX, (1928), pp. 237–366, esp. pp. 284–297. For an excellent study in English which sets Dilthey's notion of "type" in the context of his theory of *understanding,* one may be referred to the Vanderbilt dissertation of David Linge, *Historicity and Hermeneutic,* (1968).

[26] *The Act of Creation,* p. 353.

[27] For the distinction between "initial" and "appreciative" contexts, see above, pp. 280–281.

[28] *Genius and Creativity,* (New York: Harper Torchbooks, 1965), p. 244f.

291

appreciator with sufficient familiarity with what is presented in the work of art to make insertion in its world possible. Because these archetypes live in the reproductive life of generic feeling, and because this life is the perpetual context of art, the history of art in one of its most important dimensions is the history of the recurrence of symbols.[29]

It were as presumptive as impossible to enter in brief compass upon the etiology of archetypes. A responsible review of viewpoints would take us from Plato to Jung; and the merest glance will show what a distance separates these two. For Plato the archetypes are vestigial remnants of divine perspective, the after-images of the soul's primordial communion with the gods. By virtue of possessing archetypes, men are *theoeidēs* and *theoeikelon,* deiform and in the likeness of God.[30] For Jung, on the other hand, the archetypes are in a carefully guarded sense the achievement of experience. Involving the "collective unconscious," that experience is transindividual and stretches into "the dark backward and abysm of time." The archetypes themselves are "psychic residua of numberless experiences of the same type." Collective in origin, ancient of age, the archetypes recapitulate in the unconscious today the most persistent of the race's mythological themes.[31]

As for what the archetypes bear upon, the implications of the position developed here may be quickly sketched. An archetype

[29] One archetypal motif, stated discursively, is that the sweetness of life is ever abridged by the inevitability of death. Erwin Panofsky has traced this motif through the fortunes of its symbolic expression in the phrase, *et in Arcadia ego.* In a brilliant essay, which he conceives as an exercise in the "history of types," Panofsky follows the phrase through its use in literature, in paintings, tomb inscriptions, etc. In effect, he demonstrates the constancy of the archetypal motif in the symbolic phrase, yet shows that its meaning has varied greatly according to particular symbolic conjunctions. Thus in one tomb inscription it is the voice of Death saying "Even in Arcadia, there am I;" whereas in Poussin's painting bearing the phrase as its title, it is the voice of the interred saying "I, too, lived in Arcadia." "Et in Arcadia Ego," *Philosophy and History,* ed. Raymond Klibansky and H. J. Paton, (New York: Harper Torchbook, 1963), pp. 223–254.

[30] *Republic,* 589c; 50lb. Cf. Robert E. Cushman, *Therapeia,* (Chapel Hill: The University of North Carolina Press, 1958), p. 43.

[31] See Carl G. Jung, *The Psychology of the Unconscious;* in *Two Essays on Analytical Psychology,* trans. R. F. C. Hull, (New York: Pantheon Books, n.d.), pp. 3–117.

is a nondiscursive similitude of *form* in historical manhood. Form itself has been understood as "limiting pattern." Man's being-in-the-world is characterized by two sorts of limitation or relative fixity: the fixity of his appetite and the fixity of cosmic pattern. Archetypal images may therefore be said to be the nondiscursive embodiment of the interaction between man's fixity of appetite and the fixity of pattern in the cosmos. As such, archetypal images open upon the repetitive features of man's being-in-the-world. To be sure, different strands in the human story have their preferential emphases. For example, the intellectualistic and mystical traditions root in the emphasis upon cosmic-natural pattern, and usually employ the *sun* as the organizing pole and central image in their mythologies. Voluntaristic traditions on the other hand root in the human-appetitive or hero mythologies, and usually employ some life function (love, hatred) as the predominant image. As the nondiscursive similitude of form undergoes discursive translation in these traditions, characteristically different metaphysics ensue; in the former, a metaphysics of light (as in Platonism and Neo-Platonism), in the latter a metaphysics of *energeia* (as in Schopenhauer). These two traditions scarcely exhaust the fundamental archetypal strands, needless to say. And one does not have to look far to find integral fusions of these two; Augustine, for example, advances a profound intercalation of a metaphysics of light and a metaphysics of volitional *energeia*. In his case the intercalation owes not to a metaphysical *tour de force* but rather to a remarkable conjunction of Neo-Platonic archetypes with historical master images from the Hebraic-Christian prophetic tradition. In that particular, Augustine was only accomplishing *tradito:* carrying the tradition forward as it had been carried forward on crucial occasions in the past—as Israel, for example, had brought its images forward in the horizon of Canaanite archetypal environment.

With these comments we come directly to the question: what do archetypes have to do with revelation, and especially, what have they to do with the potency of tradition for revelatory intentionality? This question may now be approached out of the understanding of archetype as "nondiscursive similitude of *form* in historical manhood."

One of the things Christian theology took from its contact with Greek philosophy was the de-generate way in which Greek philosophy dealt with the Greek archetypal-religious tradition. Christian theology thus developed a tendency to treat its own tradition in the same de-generate way. In the full bloom of Greek culture philosophy was integrally related to a substratum of mythological-cultic archetypes. But in Hellenistic diffusion these archetypes lost their culturally generative force. They survived in philosophy as discursively translated forms; and in their sheer formality constituted the base of an independent philosophical theology.[32] Metaphysics thus introduced what was to become an *aporía* between the tradition and the clarification of religious conceptuality. For Christian theology abutting philosophy, the problem ever since has been how to avoid this *aporía,* a problem exacerbated by the fact that the Christian tradition includes a far greater plurality and diversity of archetypal strands than the Greek heritage. Where Christian theology failed its uniquely unifying task, the matter was distributed to two parallel tracks. *Traditio,* the vivification of the archetypal and the historical master images, was left to the church's cultic-liturgical life. As regards its conceptuality, the *traditum* was left to the discursive formalities of academic theology accommodated to a philosophical model. This was only to celebrate the *aporía.*

Any further celebration of this *aporía* can only be a *danse macabre* for Christian theology, indeed a "wake" for the Christian faith itself. A broad recognition of this point, accompanied by no little anxiety, has come with the preoccupation of much recent theology with "demythologization." But demythologization cannot be allowed to proceed in such a way as to re-instate the old *aporía,* which is precisely what happens when the symbolic tradition is translated without remainder into an ontological (Bultmann?) or a metaphysical (Ogden?) formality. Beyond that, it needs to be observed that "demythologization" is a poor description of the *contemporary* problem (i.e., unless one leaps back over two millennia of history to mythological systems). In a paraphrase of Paul Ricoeur, we may say that the archetypal

[32] This matter will be developed at length in Appendix IV under the rubric *"Méthodos* and *aporía* in Greek and early Christian 'theology.'"

294

images served a revelatory function discretely, but were ". . . developed in narrative form, articulated within a time and space that cannot be coordinated with critical history and geography."[33] Today, however, the archetypal images are not strung together in a story, nor are they coordinated with space and time, critical or otherwise. They are, in short, already demythologized. No: not quite. Merleau-Ponty put the point perhaps too strongly when he said that ". . . psycho-analysis is our own witchcraft," more defensibly when he said that "neurosis is an *individual* myth."[34] Mircea Eliade grasps the matter exactly in his claim that archetypal organization no longer takes place on the public, ritual level but rather in the imagination of the inner, individual man.[35] But that goes to say that the archetypes are no longer mythologema.

If we object to bringing the symbolic tradition forward solely by ontological or metaphysical translation, that itself owes to the ontology and hermeneutic of revelation developed in these pages. As we could not speak of form in itself, because form in historical manhood is an expanding limit, so we cannot speak of archetypes in themselves. Likewise knowledge was seen to be miscued when directed alone to fixity of form.

Now if the major archetypal strands of western civilization have been effectively demythologized by the course of history itself and if ontological translation brings forward only a cleft surrogate of archetypes in their native mythological habitat, it may well be asked why theology concerns itself with archetypes at all, why phenomenology is turned upon the archetypal heritage.

The answer to this question takes four forms.

[33] Paul Ricoeur, "The Symbol: Food for Thought," *Philosophy Today*, Vol. IV, No. 3/4 (Fall, 1960), p. 201.

[34] *Signs*, pp. 121–122. (Italics mine.)

[35] Mircea Eliade, *Rites and Symbols of Initiation*, (New York: Harper & Row, 1965), pp. 125–135. My thanks are due Professor Byron Earhart of Western Michigan University for much help with the Eliade corpus.

Writing on the archetypal theme of "the Night Journey," the "dark night of the soul" that is "the meeting of the Tragic and the Trivial planes," Arthur Koestler remarks: "Dreaming is for the aesthetically underprivileged the equivalent of artistic experience, his only means of self-transcendence, of breaking away from the trivial plane and creating his own mythology." *The Act of Creation*, pp. 359–360.

(a) In the first place, the analogy drawn between the work of art and revelation suffers at one crucial point. The art object is an actual continuant and therefore exhibits a fixed range of potency. If art object "X" goes out of actual existence, it obviously cannot be actualized *qua* work of art. The "giving" side of a work of art is consequently fixed, and the work of art is in that sense a-historical. But revelation is given in concert with the course of historical reality, although, because actualized only in answering imagination, it is not given *qua* historical reality. That says, in effect, that the giving side of revelation is not an actually existent continuant; in classical theological terms, it is gratuitous. To be sure, scripture is an actually existent continuant, and is the only analogue in revelation to the art object known to theology. So far from being continuously and actually revelatory, however, scripture cannot be said without qualification to afford the giving side of revelation *merely qua continuant*. Only brought forward hermeneutically as Word of God is scripture strictly analogous to the art object. Since the first-order language of scripture is shot through with archetypal imagery, theology cannot avoid bringing the "comprehension" of that imagery forward in such a way that it may be actualized in a contemporary idiom of imagination.

(b) The second reason is the obverse of the first: while the giving side of revelation is not *eo ipso* continuous, neither is it absolutely occasionalistic. Without *some* modality of constancy in the presentation of a revelatory claim, there could be no scripture. (Just as there could be no ontological speech without some modality of form in human being.) If theology cannot avoid archetypes in looking to this constancy, that owes to the fact that paradigmatic events put their tentacles into humanity at large (i.e., into men beyond the circle of original participants) by being brought to speech through language drawn from both a particular history (reflected in historical master images) and an environment of archetypes.[36]

(c) A third reason for theology's preoccupation with archetypes touches the contemporary situation. The difficulty with all attempts to bring faith to speech without any archetypal

[36] This second point was discussed at greater length above, II., B., 3.; pp. 278–280.

connections is that imagination, through which such language is effected, is thereby assumed to act *in abstracto*.[37] The investigation of reproductive, ossified imagination has shown however that imagination never functions in a vacuum; that imagination is stocked out of a particular historical lineage, and is bestirred by the residue of archetypes that may have fallen out of their mythological unity but have not released their fateful hold on our being.

(d) A fourth reason archetypes must be worked over wherever they are met is that, being similitudes of form, they are intrinsically *anonymous* and conceal the problematic to which they are answers.[38] (This problem, incidentally, is only exacerbated by translating them into metaphysical terms.) In their extensiveness of range, archetypes serve the "existential" of the "historio-personal existential"; but their anonymity works against the dimension of the historio-personal. And that they conceal their problematic (i.e., generalize the problematic beyond one's power to see himself uniquely in it) indicates that, cut loose from mythological conjunctions, they are non-hermeneutical. In Chapter II we saw that that only can be hermeneutical grist for the mind whose problematic shapes the course of inquiry. For the archetypal tradition to serve the intentionality of revelation, then, is to have its problematic brought into connection with our own, in ways that are historical and personal.

Let us be sure of the point, by example. If we look to some of the great archetypal "answers," we see such things as the following: Prometheus, the Tower of Babel, Faustus; satyrs and centaurs: Pan and all; dying and rising gods in plenty; the mating of heavenly stars and chthonic earth; the Water of Life, the Light-bringer, the cosmic Vine, and the Tree of Life; the

[37] This point is made by Professor Amos Wilder in a skillful polemic against the "expressionism" of Croce and Collingwood. See *New Testament Faith for Today*, (New York: Harper and Brothers, 1955), p. 69.

[38] Cf. Aron Gurwitsch on the centrality of "the typical" in the social sciences, in his valuable Introduction to the pioneering work of Alfred Schutz on that score: Alfred Schutz, *Collected Papers*, Vol. III, ed. I. Schutz with an Introduction by Aron Gurwitsch, (The Hague: Martinus Nijhoff, 1966), p. xxiv. See also Paul Ricoeur, who treats of "anonymity" and "concealment of problematic" in those histories of philosophy that are essentially *typological: History and Truth*, pp. 46–47.

contest of God and Satan; Paradise; the celestial court; Oedipus Coloneus; the Divine Father and the Earth Mother. If we look to some of the prominent archetypal "problems," we see (with no view to correlating with the "answers" above): wresting power from the gods—fate and freedom; questions of danger, vengeance, retribution; of change, rebirth, old age, death; the passage of time, the revolutions of the seasons; origin and continuity—of man and the earth; food supply and the earth's fertility; the contest of the sexes and its derivatives—masculine concept and feminine intuition; good and evil, innocence, justice; the relations of family and the struggle between generations; ordeal and trial, the test by outrageous onslaught.

What we have in such lists are timeless questions and timeless answers. It belongs to the archetype to run in this direction. The type-image no less than the type-idea would be unable to subsume and absorb more than one individual experience were it shorn of anonymity and made explicit in the range of problematicality it embraces. It cannot be had both ways: extensive organization of experience over the vicissitudes of time *and* particularized problematic in correlation with particularized answer. The archetype runs to extension, not intension; but it sprints to a nondiscursive cadence, since it is energized in the reproductive life of feeling, and so does not have the *kind* of extension that the class universal has.

What the fourth point means when lumped with the other three is that a phenomenology of the symbolic tradition is not an end in itself and cannot be expected to do the work of systematic symbolics. The most to be hoped for—and it is a great deal—is that such a phenomenology will put us in post-critical contact with archetypal symbolic comprehensions. Phenomenology can only bring these comprehensions forward in their anonymity, i.e., in "reduction." To systematic symbolics belongs the task of inserting these comprehensions into the contemporary hermeneutical spiral and thus into a contemporary problematic. Indeed the archetypes are blown out of their anonymity—cease to function merely as archetypes and enter into symbolic compounds with intensional images—precisely by the emergence of new problematic. Thus for example the greatest flurry in creative research on the archetypal tradition has been occasioned in recent time by the problematic opened up by psychoanalysis.[39] One may conjecture that the coming horizon of problematic out of which the archetypal tradition will be brought into new conjunctions will be afforded by the structural linguists (in the train, say, of Ferdinand de Saussure) and the socio-cultural anthropologists (e.g., Claude Lévi-Strauss). At all events, systematic theological symbolics will be unable to assume that the problematic is, so to speak, entirely its own yo-yo.

With theology's recent past in mind, a final comment on its relation to the archetypal tradition is in order. Theology that has majored in "existentialism" will scarcely need exhorting to specify and individualize what lies anonymously in the archetypes.[40] In a time of rampant individualism the opposite exhortation is more to the point. Unique and individual perceptions require to be "grounded," in both the ontological and electrical senses of the metaphor "ground." The self as the conductor of the historio-personal circuit is subject late and soon to the lightning of merely schematic and unproportioned feeling. Along that circuit lies not the shock of revelatory illumination but rather the overload of idiosyncratic image-systems. What the historio-personal circuit requires is the ground circuit of the "existential," the absorptive diffusor and proportioner of energy. The existential-ground, as we have said before, is as much the *polis* and the *socius* as it is the natural cosmos. This ground terminal is not however reflected in the class-concept generalizations of the social and physical sciences but rather in the archetypal world of such sciences (in the reconfiguration of which the particular sciences play an undeniable role). The thinking that goes on in the ground-circuit is therefore, in Yeats' magnificently grounded line, "thinking in a marrow bone." If there is anything to the master Christian images, it is a carnal and dusty bond we have with historical universality; as it is in flesh of our flesh and bone of our bone that God has put

[39] Can it be only coincidental that classicists attuned to the modern "unconscious" have been in the vanguard of this perception? One thinks of Nietzsche, Erwin Goodenough, and Norman O. Brown.

[40] I need scarcely emphasize that "existentialism" in its American sense is the opposite of what I refer to as the "existential" in the phrase "historio-personal existential." It is the "historio-personal" that is existentialistic in American usage.

in potency before us what it is to be before him as his man.
(4) Historical master images.

> The histories and political economy of the present and preceding century partake in the general contagion of its mechanic philosophy, and are the product of an unenlivened generalizing Understanding. In the Scriptures they are the living educts of the Imagination . . . [giving] birth to a system of symbols, harmonious in themselves, and consubstantial with the truths of which they are the *conductors*. These are the Wheels which Ezekiel beheld, when the hand of the Lord was upon him, and he saw visions of God as he sat among the captives by the river of Chebar . . . Whithersoever the Spirit was to go, the wheels went, and thither was their spirit to go: for the spirit of the living creature was in the wheels also.[41]

As the framework of revelation, the apprehension of one's ownmost historio-personal existential owes its cognitive character to the symbolic compound of archetypal and historical images. From the position so far developed, that statement appears to be necessary but also insufficient. It is insufficient because it invites the old split between—or for that matter, the old convergence of—an independent archetypal "general revelation" and an independent, historical, positivistic "special revelation." When the church has followed its instinctive preference for historical master images, that has owed to the fact that, performing in a revelatory way, these images already embraced both historical and archetypal "presences." It is a matter of record, of course, that nothing guarantees the simultaneity of intension and extension in master images over a long stretch of time. They begin to appear not as a compound but as a mixture; the intensional element precipitates out as "fact," as information about some individuals in the past, or as something somehow connected with the past but in itself not re-enactable; the extensional element wafts skyward on clouds of archetypal gas. Master images dissolve, that is, as they cease to exert uniform pressure upon active and cognitive life, as men fail to find through them the intensive and extensive range of their being.

As master images dissolve, others take their place. Men are

[41] Samuel Taylor Coleridge, *Statesman's Manual,* (London: Printed for Gale and Fenner, 1816), pp. 34–35.

300

not to be found, in whatever state of cultural sophistication, who are exempt from the dominion of master images. There may have been a time when the church could take as its chief concern the overlaying of culture with its own master images, and thus give to culture the imaginative form of its unity. This dream is dreamed out, and is a nightmare in retrospect. It is a nightmare in retrospect because in the dream the very historicality of the master images was sacrificed; the earthly was accommodated to a super-historical city. Today the intelligent faithful participate culture out of another problematic, which is *the* contemporary problematic of Christian faith. This problematic may be stated in the form of a shrieking paradox: the master images of faith *solve only in dissolution.* We have lured the intelligibility of this paradox from the "mechanics" of the imagination as it functions in historical manhood. But the paradox itself remains; rather it remains for a non-temporal logic. Faith wins its circumspections from the contemporary experience of reality as that experience is illuminated and configured by past paradigmatic events, yet those events are brought forward by master images which *can* bring forward only with equally high regard to the course of historical reality and the mechanics of imagination. Of dissolving and dissembling in these mechanics, enough has been said. It remains to add what is implicit, that the paradox of solution through dissolution is reduced only in a logic accommodated to the co-inherence of the modes of historical time, a logic that will at the same time be a logic of the historical imagination.

Let us say what we can, *paucis verbis,* about the historical master image. (For less cumbersome language, let "master image" stand for "historical master image.") What is to be said about master images refers to such nondiscursive appellations in scripture as Covenant, Israel, New Jerusalem, Second Adam, Son of Man, Kingdom of God; but also to such things as "black power," la grandeur française, "the Southern way of life," etc.

That master images are simultaneously extensional and intensional in historical manhood goes together with the reflections advanced earlier in the ontological consideration of selfhood. The self, it was argued, is at once terminal and relational.

301

On the one hand, it would be a denial of the self's terminality were the self reducible to a web of universals. Yet the depths of the finitely terminal self are expressed, as Professor Julian N. Hartt has said, in relatively stable character. Archetypal or extensional structures amount to ". . . terminal existents expressing themselves and being themselves in these expressions, relatively to one another."[42] On the other hand it would be a denial of the self's relationality were the self reducible to an incommunicable particular or a particular incapable of communication. One scarcely knows which to emphasize the more: that the self experiences accrual of meaning through communication and so is relational, or that the self relates and so experiences an increment of communication. The two emphases are likely one in the end, and signify that the self is open to expansion beyond the repetitive fixities of interior terminality.

Perish the thought that an understanding of historical master images may be deduced, without remainder, ontologically! No scratching among fundamentals will unearth among the modalities of selfhood "black power," the "success" mania of American business, or the Kingdom of God. But since master images are intensive and thus have relational character, are extensive and thus have unifying force, it is important to see how they lodge in the constitutive and cognitive ranges of the self.

Master images are relational: they open upon the span between person and person and between person and event. Because they are relational in their bearing, master images are temporally "scotched." That is, they cannot roll down to a plain of timeless problematic. What is joined in the relation is so joined in time; and in that master image in which the relation is purviewed "the times are in joint." It can be said with equal merit that master images profuse themselves in time and that they profuse time from themselves. For master images take up the *relata* in their temporality and at the same time, as cognitive

42 Hartt, "The Situation of the Believer," *Faith and Ethics,* ed. Paul Ramsey, (New York: Harper and Brothers, 1957), pp. 242–43. I should note that Professor Hartt is making a somewhat different point in the context from which I quote. In the same volume will be found a valuable discussion of master images by Professor Hans Frei, who sets his discussion in the context of the impact of historical consciousness upon theological method. See pp. 21–32, espec. 25.

vehicle of the paradigmatic event, they periodize the things related or illumined. Here everything said earlier about the relation between image and event comes into play. Ezekiel by the river of Chebar was in the time of Exile, and it was Exile that gave him all the time he had. "Black power" was an aside from the lips of Stokely Carmichael until it entered into historical causality. As the phrase inserted itself into the occurrence of events and became an inescapable "category" through which they had to be understood, it was inserted into actual lived time; and simultaneously it afforded to some persons their first "real time" in which to live. Neither Exile nor "black power," so long as each functions as a master image, rolls back to a timeless problematic of "alienation" or "racial prowess."[43]

Because they are attached to and ingredient in the history of terminal selves bound together in community, master images are interlarded with archetypal influence. This is especially the case in those complex cultures in which men participate simultaneously a plurality and diversity of communities. A man is a Christian, the head of a family, a professor, a Democrat, a western Americana buff, a dry-fly fisherman, a do-gooder, etc., and his being is distributed to the respective communities. Only in primitive totemic and shamanistic cultures is there anything approaching imaginal monoliths; and anthropologists will rightly howl even at that.

As long as master images evade a split between their historical and archetypal dimensions, it is the complex interweaving of paradigmatic event and master images that determines what they take from the environing fund of archetypes. This is no-

[43] Today before our eyes, however, we can see "black power" gathering archetypal nuance to itself. This image has begun to evoke patterns long buried in the American Negro sub-culture totally unknown to whites (apart from nondiscursive manifestation in jazz, "blues," the "spiritual," etc.) and hitherto largely unconscious even among blacks. The extraordinary recourse to African dress and symbolism is perhaps the most striking evidence of the power of this image to enucleate and vivify a somnambulant archetypal tradition.

It should be observed that no one in the history of American theology has devoted more or more careful attention to the stocking and restocking of imagination among the scriptural witnesses than Horace Bushnell in the nineteenth century. Although now "dated," the landmark essay to see is "Our Gospel a Gift to the Imagination," *Building Eras in Religion,* (New York: Charles Scribner's Sons, 1881), pp. 249–285.

where more apparent in scripture than in Hosea, Chapters 1–3. Here is a complex situation and a complex literary text. Hosea makes the master image of Covenant to preside over Israel's habitation among the worshippers of Baal while using the archetypal images of that fertility cult to exegete the master image of Covenant; and post-Exilic editors, through insertions in the text, show how subsequent events and subsequently generated master images (e.g., Exile) are cast back to interpret the past. On Hosea's lips, the Lord's "quarrel with the inhabitants of the land" is no simple piece of apologetics; he does not borrow archetypal images from the fertility cultus and invert the rituals of Baal alone to chastise the enemy with the enemy's own weapons. Rather he anchors the master image of Covenant in the imaginative idiom which Israel has learned to speak, and thus in the historicality of first-order language.

We can now take up with equal brevity the cognitivity of master images. A master image is not an *id quod cognoscitur* (that *which* is known) but rather an *id quo cognoscitur* (that *by* which is known). Without ever becoming the direct object of knowledge, it is the nondiscursive form or horizon through and in which things are known.[44] Master images are "insights" in Max Scheler's sense: they are not bodies of completed vision, but rather they furnish the delimited form in or through which the mind sees.[45] The mind is thereby not so much *informed* by an inflexible context as it is endowed with the *form* of perception and thinking. What is given with the master images is a way of reckoning with the world's givenness. Thus Hosea was not out to fix the Israelite mind upon the image of Covenant; he undertook to vivify that image as the authentic *id quo cognoscitur* of wayward Israel's existence. Vibrant with current language, the image allowed the Israelites to see their existence as a whoring profligance and a denial of conjugal vows made with Jahweh and the earth he had given into their care. It is not Covenant but the violated earth and its frenzied social order that is "known," and known precisely in the presence of Jahweh the faithful

[44] Cf. R. Lazzarini, "Intentionalism and Contemporary Currents in Spiritualist Philosophy," *International Philosophical Quarterly,* Vol. I, No. 2 (May, 1961), p. 327.
[45] Cf. Max Scheler, *On the Eternal in Man,* pp. 201–202.

partner to Covenant. In a paraphrase of Coleridge we may say that Covenant is a living educt of the imagination, conformal with the truths of which it is the conductor.

III. SYSTEMATIC THEOLOGICAL SYMBOLICS

At the beginning of this chapter the bearing of tradition upon a hermeneutic of revelation was divided into two basic questions. The first was assigned to a phenomenology of the symbolic tradition, and preoccupied itself with the way in which tradition possesses potency for revelatory intentionality. Subsequently several segments of the phenomenological task in pursuit of that question were discriminated and developed according to lines laid down in preceding chapters. The second question was distributed to systematic theological symbolics; and concerned itself with the cognitive value of tradition, the power of tradition to illuminate our existence in the present. It remains finally to undertake a comparable if briefer formal account of systematic symbolics. An initial statement on the position of systematic symbolics in the theological enterprise will be followed by the consideration of method. Then an expanded exposition of the task of systematic symbolics will bring us not to the end, but to the end of a beginning.

Systematic symbolics assumes a Janus orientation in the theological enterprise: on the one face, it has a view toward the sedimented, ossified discourse of tradition; on the other, a view toward the emergence of that first-order speech and life of enacted parable that goes with presently vital faith. This formulation will bear expansion after some remarks on method.

A. Method

One of the signal gains from the emphasis upon hermeneutics in contemporary theology is that the problem of method has been removed from an exclusively ancillary position and made to infiltrate every line of theological discourse. A kind of methodolatry was the fruit of theology cut on the older, largely

305

Neo-Kantian model in which the initial concern with method tended to outdistance the concern for what might be achieved through the use of method. On the model of the hermeneutical spiral, however, method is not at any point dissociable from the subject matter on which it is exercised. Since the notion of the hermeneutical spiral is itself a transposition into *methodological* key of the inter-relation between being and knowing, the basis for talk about method is obviously just that inter-relation.[46] The being and knowing of revelation have been the focus of vision for this essay; and latterly the question of tradition has been brought into the focal point of concern. In the light of two conclusions, the matter of method may now be taken up rather more directly. The conclusions are, on the one hand, that theology can neither think revelation nor aid in its coming to speech and act anew without recourse to tradition (both as *traditio* and as *traditum*), and on the other, that theology can neither think nor say the same thing the tradition thought and said without thinking and saying that thing in a different way, i.e., in concert with the course of historical reality and language. These conclusions may now be traced to their ramifications in method.

(1) It is a commonplace that method necessarily implies repeatability; that, as Professor Buchler says, "methodic practice limited to one possible occasion is a contradiction."[47] Theology tends typically to go cross-eyed at this point: if it accedes to repeatability, it chucks its revelatory foundation; if it accedes to the contingency of revelation, it releases its claim to method. We have denied this dichotomy, root and branch. Confidence in the repeatability of revelation is finally, of course, a confidence in the Faithfulness of God: a mother may forget her sucking babe but God will not forget Israel. (Such confidence may afford a methodology; it cannot be the result of method.) The repeatability of profferment is not however coextensive with the repeatability of actualized revelation. That repeatability with which

[46] The distinction drawn between method and methodology in Appendix IV is pertinent here. Method refers to procedure, the "way" of access to subject matter; methodology refers to the rationale of method drawn from the subject matter itself.

[47] Justus Buchler, *The Concept of Method*, (New York: Columbia University Press, 1961), p. 17.

306

theology can have to do is therefore only the harbingers and the residue of revelation in the past, the master images comporting with paradigmatic events. If theology rivets itself to the repeatability of the tradition's master images precisely *through their permutation in history,* that will mean that, unlike the physical sciences, its turn to repeatability is not undertaken in order to predict and guarantee (intellectually) continuous results.

(2) The last point may be put another way. Theology's orientation to repeatability (and thus to tradition) is intrinsically ambiguous. It cannot be concerned exclusively with repeatability, with the "old" in its various structures, and thus cannot be the exercise alone of what Jeremy Bentham called "the *tactic* faculty." The reason for this is simply that *mere* repetition would distort the character of revelation itself. The interest theological method takes in repeatability is an interest that aims at the development of renewed discourse that coincides with renewed insertion in historical being. Theological method is therefore more exploratory than regulative, and hence is nearer to the method of arts and morals than that of technology or any other discipline oriented fundamentally to casuistry. As Tillich put the matter in one of his earliest writings, a method which cannot embrace form-breaking notions and realities is foreign to theology, and that because such a method would amount to an epistemologically formulated renunciation of the very knowledge theology exists to understand and inculcate.[48] On this head theology should cease and desist thinking of itself as a special case and make common cause with others in the same boat of method. Arts, letters, and the whole of the humanities depend upon the repeatability of generic signs; but without novel concretions there would be no new art, no new literature, no renewal of the human story.

(3) The Janus posture of theology may be expressed in the formula: theology understands out of the past, lives out of the future. The order applied by theology in its work is an order emergent from the intersection of these two movements. Let us

[48] Cf. Paul Tillich, *Religionsphilosophie,* in *Gesammelte Schriften,* hrsg. Renate Albrecht, Bd. I, (Stuttgart: Evangelisches Verlagswerk, 1959), p. 309.

consider first the movement of understanding out of the past. The present is understood from loci in the past, from connected aggregations (paradigmatic events) richly suffused with potency for benevolently expanding human life in time; and these aggregations are exhibited in their life-expanding potency through master images as these images undergo the permutations of "answering imagination." This means that for theology there are antecedent complexes of an historical and an imaginative sort that set a limit to its own ordering activity. "Living out of the future" therefore cannot be a starting from scratch: the history that "stands under" limits the future.

(4) "Living out of the future" goes together with an element in method that is as fundamental as repeatability, viz., activity or creativity. The very notion of *methodos* suggests a bustling note: the way to be set out upon, the path to be hacked out. If Professor Buchler may be quoted once again, ". . . it is primarily by reference to the world as influenced, rather than to the world as endured, that method may best be explained."[49] "Men who wish to render themselves more determinate in a particular respect are on the verge of method: they wish to extend or intensify some phase of their being as productive creatures."[50] It is surely a fact of no small significance that the interest in method and the interest in human creativity arose at roughly the same time in the modern west. In the same temporal and cultural climate the imagination came for the first time to be understood as a fundamentally active and creative power, and not merely as a faculty for enduring the world under the impress of "higher images."[51] These developments were to have their effect, to be sure very belatedly, on the Christian doctrine of creation. No small consequence of this effect was the legitimation of human audacity with respect to the future. Now hailed as a recovery of the Biblical understanding of creation, this legitimation owes as well to the "secular" developments just now noted. One of the most important outstanding tasks of contemporary theology is the elaboration of a doctrine of creation in which man's complicity in his own future, and even his

[49] *The Concept of Method*, p. 89.
[50] *Ibid.*, p. 92.
[51] See below, Appendix III: "The Imagination and Creativity."

audacity if not his "duality" of being before God the Creator, receive the kind of attention which *methodos* in theology presuppose.

(5) Theology can no more guarantee that understanding out of the past and living out of the future will intersect in a present revelatory moment . . . than aesthetic "criticism" can guarantee that, through the execution of critical method, the art object will become a work of art. While there is method in theology and criticism, there is no method of revelation or of art. This raises matters best treated by returning to the "position" of systematic symbolics in the theological enterprise.

B. The "Position" of Systematic Symbolics in the Theological Enterprise

The nature of systematic theological symbolics is equally misunderstood by those who would refuse it board and keep in the secular university and by those who would manage with leg irons, if necessary, to restrict it to the divinity school or the church seminary. These misunderstandings have in common the view of systematic symbolics as more or less overt catechesis, proclamation, or (to be done with it) propaganda. But however much founded on revelation, theology *qua* theology never has the full founding of faith *immediately* in view. To theology as systematic symbolics is denied the full remembrance of Egypt *and* the crossing of Jordan into the Promised Land; it is interposed between language in serious if not terminal illness (tradition) and language in pangs of birth (the language of first-order *homologia,* and action toward the neighbor's good).

Interposition is the position of systematic symbolics. This position is sometimes described, as by Ebeling, as a position between the scriptural text and the sermon. While that is true as far as it goes, it is restrictive beyond enduring. On the one hand, scripture and its master images owe their successive exhibition to the church and its continuity of memory; but the tradition to which systematic symbolics turns is broader than the church's memory; it embraces as well the permutations of archetypes in the cultural environment of that memory. Indeed, since (as

James Luther Adams says) ". . . the cohesion of a religious community demands continuity of linguistic usage . . . ," systematic symbolics must often suspect the church of forcing a continuity of linguistic usage as a self-serving device for cohesion.[52] That means that the language of tradition must often be comprehended in its interstices, in its "silence," and from the acoustics of its cultural situation. All this goes to say that, in its orientation to tradition, the purview of systematic symbolics extends well beyond the scriptural text and the church's "inside" language.

But the same thing is to be said, on the other hand, of theology's orientation to the emergence of first-order speech and act. Let us consider first-order speech first. The first-order speech toward which systematic symbolics works doubtless includes the sermon and all other instantiations of the community at celebration of its renewal *coram Deo*. Of interpositional theology in such occasions there is scarcely a hint; such theology is the seed that must fall into the ground and die in order to transfer its life to another, intrinsically imaginative mode of discourse. To sermon and rite belong the invocation and thus the concretion of the content of faith in a viable imaginative idiom.[53] One reason, surely, for the short life of neo-orthodox theology in America was the fact that its seeds not only died but rotted in the ground of homiletics and hymnody. But there is a more significant reason. Neo-orthodox theology was unable, as every interpositional systematic symbolics must be able, to look beyond the gathered church community in order to recognize the first-order speech of human advent *wherever it is being spoken*.[54] As Wallace Stevens said in speaking of religion and poetry, ". . . both have to mediate for us a reality not ourselves

[52] James Luther Adams, *Paul Tillich's Philosophy of Culture, Science, and Religion,* (New York: Harper & Row, 1965), p. 9.

[53] In a paraphrase of Bultmann: Preaching has to make known *what* faith is in the present situation, and is to do so only in the way that what faith is *can* be known. That means, negatively, that preaching is not a lecture on the *how* of faith. (Wir haben die *fides quae creditur* zu verkündigen, nicht die *fides qua creditur*.) "Zur Frage der Christologie," *Glauben und Verstehen,* Bd. I, (Tübingen: Verlag J. C. B. Mohr, 1958), p. 99.

[54] Paul Tillich must be excepted from this judgment, but then his was only in some respects a neo-orthodox theology.

and . . . the supreme virtue here is humility, for the humble are they that move about the world with the lure of the real in their hearts."[55] Wherever language is found to be luring man into what Dilthey called *Daseinssteigerung,* "the expansion of human being" systematic symbolics will be found an attentive listener.[56] It will not assume, to be sure, that any and all *Daseinssteigerungsprechen* will already be the speech it seeks to evoke as the speech of man before God (although that cannot be ruled out in advance). But it will find in the speech of present human advent, at the very least, the idiom in which faith will find its tongue.

In emphasizing that systematic symbolics orients itself to the emergence of first-order discourse *and act,* we mean by the latter emphasis that it orients itself no less to political intercourse. Preoccupation with the cognitivity of faith's language is mis-directed unless it is understood that that cognitivity is rooted in the will and thus is a form of practical knowledge. The requisite distinction was precisely drawn by St. Thomas when he said that practical knowledge "is the cause of what it understands," whereas speculative knowledge "is derived from the objects known."[57] Thus the understanding that goes with faith is bound up with *making* history; or, as I should prefer to put it in this context, is bound up with enacted parable. For this there is high precedent indeed. One scarcely knows whether to say that Jesus' acts among the proud, the lowly, the despised, and the irreligious were already parables, or that his parables were already acts. Then as now, for those with eyes to see and ears to hear and hearts to understand, the decision need not be made; they were both.

[55] *The Necessary Angel,* p. 99.
[56] Cf. Wilhelm Dilthey, *Gesammelte Schriften,* 4th ed., Vol. V, p. 275.
[57] *Summa Theologica,* Ia, IIae, Q. III, art. 5, obj. 1.

APPENDICES

Typological-Historical Studies in the Theory of Imagination

Introduction

It has not been possible within the body of this book to take note of the theory of imagination in the history of western thought. The same must be said, perhaps to a slightly lesser degree, of those doctrines pertinent to the theme at hand in the history of Christian thought. From time to time, however, historical allusions were made, along with the promise of fuller development subsequently. That promise needs now to be made good.

Given burgeoning contemporary interest in the imagination, the paucity of historical studies of its theoretical mutations is a remarkable fact. Perhaps that is just as well, given the *character* of contemporary interest in the imagination. Like any other category in the history of thought, "imagination" can be prosecuted only through a certain body of questions, only out of a certain horizon of problematic. If there were "standard" histories of theory of imagination at hand, they would now or very shortly want rewriting.

In the recent past it has been philosophers of aesthetics who have reckoned most steadily with the tradition, as it has been they who have realized most faithfully that imagination can often be tracked in history only through its surrogates under other names.[1] Nonetheless, it is a restricted range of problems in connection with imagination that typically guides the aesthetician's recovery (e.g., is imagination "mimetic," "expressive," "inspired," etc.,?). Theory of imagination is occasionally traced

[1] See, for example, the following. Bernard Bosanquet, *A History of Aesthetic*, (New York: Meridian Books, 1957); Benedetto Croce, *Aesthetic*, trans. Douglas Ainslie, (London: Macmillan Co., 1929); and Milton G. Nahm, *Genius and Creativity*, (New York: Harper & Row, 1965). Nahm's book was originally published under the title, *The Artist as Creator*, [Baltimore: Johns Hopkins Press, 1956]).

historically in the interest of delineating the "faculties," and so from an essentially psychological base.[2] To psychological interests are sometimes added ethical concerns.[3] Rare to the point of non-existence (to my knowledge), however, is the comprehensive historical study of imagination that is guided by the two problems in theory of imagination held here to be crucial, viz., the cognitivity of imagination and its "ontological reach."[4]

The following studies are by no means the comprehensive work that needs doing. They are advanced here primarily as developments of historical allusions made earlier. But they are presented non-dialectically; that is, without critical rejoinder and without connecting them in either a positive or negative way with the argument of preceding pages. In short, I shall essay an analysis of selected "types" of imagination, an analysis that will be conducted by reference to certain developments in the history of western (largely modern) philosophy. As such, these studies will essay neither an exhaustive interrogation of imagination in ideal "type," nor a complete history of the role of imagination in philosophical systems.

The type to be considered first draws generally on perennial

[2] See Livingston Welch, *Imagination and Human Nature*, (London: Kegan Paul, Trench, Trubner and Company, 1935).

[3] See Murray Wright Bundy, *The Theory of Imagination in Classical and Medieval Thought*, (Urbana: University of Illinois Press, 1927).

[4] There are of course valuable monographs and articles on particular thinkers which hold these problems in mind. A representative sampling would include the following. Émile Bréhier, "Images Plotiniennes, Images Bergsoniennes," *Les Études Bergsoniennes,* Vol. II, (Paris: Albin Michel, 149), pp. 110–28; Victor Basch, "Du rôle de l'imagination dans la théorie Kantienne de la connaissance," *Revue de Métaphysique et de Morale*, Vol. XII, (1904), pp. 425–440; Gerhart B. Ladner, "The Concept of the Image in the Greek Fathers and the Byzantine Iconoclastic Controversy," *Dumbarton Oak Papers*, No. 7, (Cambridge, Mass., 1953), pp. 3–34; Kate Gordon Moore, "Augustine on Imagination" *Journal of Psychology*, Vol. XIII, (April, 1947), pp. 161–168; J. Freudenthal, *Ueber den Begriff des Wortes Phantasia bei Aristoteles,* Göttingen: Druck der Universitäts-Buchdruckerei von E. A. Huth, 1863); J. Fröhschammer, *Ueber die Bedeutung der Einbildungskraft in der Philosophie Kant's und Spinoza's,* (München: Theodor Ackerman, 1879); Jean H. Roy, *L'Imagination selon Descartes,* (Paris: Gallimard, 1944); Edgar Maurice Wolff, *Étude du rôle de l'imagination dans la connaissance chez Kant,* (Carcassonne: Bonnafous et Fils, 1943); and Martin Heidegger, *Kant and the Problem of Metaphysics,* trans. James S. Churchill, (Bloomington: Indiana University Press, 1962).

"realism," and especially upon Aristotle and Thomas Aquinas. The second makes contact with the "critical" tradition out of Kant. The third embraces three sub-types which are traced primarily out of Hume, Fichte and Schelling, and Sartre.[5]

[5] I may mention as a complement to these studies my article, "The Imagination in Plato," *loc. cit.*, pp. 436–461.

I. The Imagination and "Conformation"

Outline

According to the "type" to be investigated first, imagination is an essential phase in that power of the mind in virtue of which modes of being, incommensurable in the *ordo essendi,* are rendered commensurable or "co-natural" in the *ordo cognoscendi.* Through the processes of imagination the mind and other modes of being are "conformed" to or "leveled" with each other. This presupposes that the mind in its own mode of being does not open upon all modes of being, or being itself, but only potentially so. In order *actually* to open upon a mode of being other than itself, the mind must undergo the processes of conformation to such a mode, which means that both the active and passive functions of mind must be exercised upon that mode of being. Knowledge occurs when the act or form of the mind is conformed to the act or form of its object. Since imagination is not identical with the active phase of mental operation, it cannot

318

itself be cognitive: knowledge has to do with act or formal actuality. But neither is imagination identical with the passive or potential phase of mental operation, i.e., with the processes of sensation. Indeed, imagination is the irenic faculty of the mind, mediating between the active and passive phases of mental operation, conforming the mind to the object and the object to the mind.

These summary remarks may be expanded in the following order. First the metaphysical context of the present "type" of imagination will be surveyed. Second, the relation of imagination to other processes of knowledge will be investigated. Third, the role of imagination in knowledge of God, both natural and "supernatural," may be brought into view.

I. THE METAPHYSICAL "FIELD" IN WHICH IMAGINATION OPERATES

The metaphysical underpinning of this view of imagination is palpably realistic. If knowledge requires that modes of being naturally incommensurable be made intellectually co-natural, it is obvious that the mind confronts that which ontologically cannot be reduced to, or derived from, itself. Although realistic, this metaphysic is not *dualistic* in the Cartesian sense. For in the metaphysical context of a dualism of *substances* the imagination serves to *represent* the one substance to the other through an imaginal surrogate,[1] not to conform the one to the other in virtue of that which they have in common, although in different mode, viz., *form*. The metaphysic of the present type centers not in a plurality of radically different *substances,* not to mention one substance with numerous modes, but rather in a plurality of substantial operations. Its "field" is one of differing operations, not quidditative entities. By this is meant that in anything that *is,* a plurality of operations is to be discerned. There is that which receives determination (potency, matter),

[1] A dualistic metaphysic affords a distinct "type" of imagination (classically evident in Descartes, for example), but one which I shall not explore here.

that which determines (form, act), and the complex of the two in its particularity, the *compositum*.[2] One might illustrate these operations, respectively, by saying that they refer to: that *which* is; that which *is;* and *that* which is.

Most of the classical Greek epistemologies accepted the maxim that "like knows like." As is well known, however, there were sharply differing accounts in antiquity concerning the metaphysical underpinning of this maxim. The "participationist," or Platonist, considered the soul to be composed of all the primal elements, and thought that the soul can know its objects because it has the same constitutive principles as they.[3] To this view Aristotle, a classical champion of the present type of imagination, objected along the following lines. How can the soul know an object *qua* determinately composite, i.e., the object as composed of elements combined in a determinate mode or ratio? For the Platonist's metaphysic of "like knows like" to be satisfactory, the soul would have to possess prior to knowledge not alone all the elements but also the formulae of all possible ratios of combination. That would mean however that there would be no actual distinction between the knower and the known; and that knowledge would be only a matter of the soul's introspection or self-intuition.

Aristotle sought to avoid this conclusion by means of the metaphysic underlying the present type. Metaphysical realism always faces the problem, to put the matter simply, how to keep knower and known ontologically distinct yet sufficiently "alike" to permit genuine cognition. According to the present view, they cannot be alike *qua composita* (i.e., in the particular mode of their being); yet they must be alike at some level of substantial operation, else knowledge is impossible. In short, the mind must *be* the object, not in its unique mode of being, but in an intellectual mode. The mind does not transform the object to fit its categories, but is itself conformed to the object, such that it *is* the object in an intellectual way.[4] That is, the mind is

2 Cf. Aristotle, *De Anima,* II, 1; 412a, 5–10.

3 This metaphysic of knowledge is elaborated in my article, "The Imagination in Plato," *loc. cit.*

4 See Thomas Aquinas, *Summa Theologica,* I, Q. LXXIX, art. 3; cf. also Aristotle, *De Anima,* III, 5; 430a 10.

"leveled" to its "like" in the object, to the formulable essence or universal form. The reason or intellect does not intuit some transcendent quiddity and then perceive that this object is "like" it; it is to the form of *this* object that the mind is con-formed, not some third separate or separable thing. And it is worth emphasizing that it is not to the object *qua compositum* but to its form that the mind is con-formed in the act of knowledge.

The object of the intellect consequently is the universal or formulable essence. A phenomenology of the imagination would perforce proceed in connection with the process whereby the intellect attains its universal forms, or principles of order. It will be seen how extraordinarily complex this process is when we recognize that it involves all the machinations included under the classical terms, "passive and active intellect." As noted above, the metaphysic of the present view argues that ontologically the terms of the knowing relation are dissimilar; and the entire program involving activity and passivity of mind, so far as epistemology is concerned, is advanced to account for the assimilation or conformation of the terms to each other.[5] Reality accessible to the "natural" imagination is that in which potentiality passes into actuality. The object of imagination is neither potentiality nor actuality, but the phase of transition between them.

II. IMAGINATION AND THE PROCESSES OF KNOWLEDGE

Having surveyed its metaphysical "field," let us turn now to the workings of imagination itself. Being a mediating faculty, the imagination comes into view in its relation to other moments in the noetic process. In exposition of this process it is important to remember that there are both passive and active dimensions to everything that concretely *is*. The incarnate intellect is not exempt. Although *qua* formal the intellect is the first grade of actuality, only through its simultaneous passivity is it able to be

[5] See *De Anima*, II, 5; 418a, 5.

in contact with other modes of being.[6] That is, the act of the mind must be able to receive the act of the object in a process which we may call "leveling." This means that the very act of the object is potential in relation to the act of the mind; and that the very act of the mind is potential in relation to the act of the object. In sum, finite actuality itself has a potential aspect in respect to other acts. And *knowledge* results when two or more acts have been conformed to each other through the passivity which each bears to the other, such that the coalescence of con-naturalized acts (or forms) achieves conscious intellegibility. One might say that in knowledge of a thing its form becomes self-conscious, which is to say that its form must be intellectualized, or that its form must in-form the matter of the mind.

A. Imagination and the Passivity of Mind

The imagination is indispensable to the process of con-formation and in-formation. If one may state one half of the case (the other half having to do with imagination and *activity*), the imagination is the medium of passivity in active intellect. Imagination is that in virtue of which the mind suffers its objects cognitively. As such it is not to be identified with sensation, however. For although the exterior senses be dormant, as in dreams, the imagination may be fully operative and poignant.[7]

[6] Pure Act, or Pure Form, can be related only to itself, and so can know only itself. Cf. Aristotle, *Metaphysica*, Book Λ, Ch. 9; 1074b, 15–1075a, 10.

[7] That imagination is not simply a species of "exterior" sensation was recognized and insisted upon in the major "faculty" psychologies in the long period from Aristotle to the Renaissance. In those psychologies imagination was associated either with the "common sense" (*sensus communis*), which was thought to be the common ground between the exterior senses (e.g., sight, hearing, etc.) and the interior senses (e.g., memory, opinion, etc.), or else with the interior sense, in which case imagination was thought to hold together the other interior senses, such as memory and opinion. See Aristotle, *De Mem. et Rem.*, 1, 450a, 10; Augustine, *De Genesi ad Litteram* XII, 16, 33; Synesius, *De Insomniis*, in *Patrol. Graeca*, ed. J.-P. Migne, Vol. LXVI, p. 1289; Boethius, *Philosophiae Consolatio*, 5, 4; Thomas Aquinas, *Summa Theologica* I, Q. LXXVIII, art. 4; and Roger Bacon, *The "Opus Majus" of Roger Bacon*, ed. J. H. Bridges, 3 vols., (London: Oxford University Press, 1897–1900), Vol. II, pp. 4–5.

It is like sensation in that it is a medium for receiving impressions ("species") from the object, but unlike sensation in that it gives to impressions a certain permanence. The motion of the object is, so to speak, "frozen" in a *phantasm* of the imagination; but not "frozen" to the extent that its vitality is lost. An image or phantasm is precisely that mental content which grasps the form of an object together with its vital relations. But the imagination as such draws no distinction between form and its vital relations within its images.[8]

An image or phantasm is a mental content produced by the act of an object upon passive intellect. But the imagination is not simply to be identified with passive intellect. Indeed, as it stands between potency and act, perception and conception, so it mediates as well between passive and active intellect. The imagination cannot *be* active intellect precisely because it cannot distinguish the form in the image from what we have called its vital relations (i.e., the relations between form and other factors in the object *qua* a *compositum*). For the image to become an object of ratiocination it must be divested of everything but the form "resident" in it. An image "copies" in the sense that it encapsulates the form of its object, retaining that form until active intellect abstracts it from the image.[9] We may say then that through the imagination the object in-forms the intellect. The imagination is rather like a series of canal locks between two bodies of water not level with each other; through the performance of these locks commerce between the two bodies becomes possible. Through the channels of the imagination all material for thinking must come; there is nothing in the intellect that was not previously in the senses and mediated by

[8] This view of imagination's unique vision of the transition from potency to act opens up several provocative possibilities for a Thomist aesthetic. It is more than passing strange that only recently, to my knowledge at least, Neo-Thomists have awakened to these possibilities. Cf. Jacques Maritain, *Creative Intuition in Art and Poetry*, (New York: Meridian Books, 1953).

[9] St. Thomas: "For the retention and preservation of these forms, the *phantasy* or *imagination* is appointed, being as it were a storehouse of forms received through the senses." *Summa Theologica*, I, Q. LXXVIII, art. 4; quoted from *Basic Writings of Saint Thomas Aquinas*, ed. Anton C. Pegis, (New York: Random House, 1945), Vol. I, p. 742. (Hereafter cited as *Basic Writings*)

way of imagination. But the imagination cannot unload the boats which pass through it: that is a task for active intellect alone.

B. *Imagination and the Activity of Mind*

It has been noted in what sense the imagination is passive; and that it is not, properly speaking, active. But we have still to show in what sense it is active, which is the other half of the case referred to in the last paragraph but one. For the imagination must have affinities with both passive and active intellect if it is to mediate between them. The question of whether or not the imagination may be true or false hangs in this balance as well. If the imagination is fully passive, like the senses it cannot lie. But if the imagination is in some sense active, it is subject to the judgment of that which is properly active, namely the reason.

The question of the *activity* of imagination cannot be considered in isolation from the character of *memory* and *time*. Memory is the repository of images, modified in time through the imagination. One is not to think from the foregoing account that each phantasm is consigned as a discrete package to the "deep freeze" of memory. So far from this, the intimate interpenetration of imagination and memory perpetually effects new alliances between images, forming clusters or wholes of them in virtue of their vitality. Not alone in memory, but in dreams as well is the active character of the imagination to be seen. Indeed, the imagination has a deliberate role in the formation of image-systems. And this is a fact of considerable ethical magnitude, for images—whether mnemonic, dream-, or deliberative—have great efficacy with respect to appetite. Unless the imagination is subservient to reason, ethical chaos is likely. That is, the intellect must abstract from a cluster of images their respective forms and thereby determine whether they constitute a harmony or mere will to vitality or power. This means that although the imagination is indispensable to the intellect (in that through an image an object is presented to the intellect, whether or not the object itself is present to sense), the intellect must hold the

324

imagination suspect in so far as imagination arrogates unto itself an activity proper only to reason. In sum, so long as the passive and active elements in the imagination remain in tension, the imagination is a veredicious faculty; although the truth that it bears is not of its own order of vision but of the order of intellect (viz., substantial form). One could speak of the veredicious imagination only by expanding (or contracting) its images so as to yield their universal forms.

By now it will be apparent why this view of the imagination has been called "conformal." It is the epistemological role of imagination to conform the intellect and its object through "contuition." The processes of imagination involve a two-way action, both passive and active. One might say that imagination is structured from both an external and an internal source. (a) The form of an object enters the mind through imagination, shaping its images, and ultimately in-forming the "matter" of the soul. (b) Through imagination the intellect insinuates itself into the object, becoming its form, or becoming the object in an intellectual way. These descriptions are of course highly metaphorical. In them we have sought to descry the work of the imagination in establishing the conditions of cognitive commensurability between different modes of being.

III. THE ROLE OF IMAGINATION IN KNOWLEDGE OR VISION OF GOD

The discussion of "conformal imagination" thus far has been conducted with regard to its role in that knowledge which finite mind has of finite reality, assuming that both finite mind and finite reality are hylomorphically constituted and that they exist in a scale of modes. What follows for the ingredience of imagination in knowledge if the metaphysical field be extended to include its "power" or First Cause? Here we have an incommensurability of a different sort, such that the mind is, so to speak, the lower term in the cognitive relation. Can the "natural" imagination perform an act of conformation in this instance as well?

A. Imagination and Natural Knowledge of God

Answers to the foregoing questions will vary with diverse speculative possibilities, which are determined by the nature of the relation thought to obtain between finite agent intellect and Infinite Agent Intellect. The speculative possibilities turn upon whether finite mind has an agency of its own or is merely the occasion, in so far as it is active, for the operation of Infinite Agent Intellect.[10] Stated otherwise, and in simplest terms, the speculative possibilities are shaped by whether or not something like the Christian doctrine of creation is affirmed.[11] If, as with Aristotle, God (the Unmoved Mover) is related to the world neither cognitively nor creatively (the one would imply the other), the imagination will be confined in the present type to a naturalistic role, i.e., to knowledge of hylomorphic nature. But if the world is really related to God, as in St. Thomas, the imagination may be seen to perform an ancillary task in rational or natural knowledge of God. This task is no different from the one described above: the imagination presents to the intellect the sensible world in the form of phantasms, from which intellect abstracts universal forms, on the basis of which intellect reasons to their First Cause and its necessary attributes. In both the non-creationist and creationist schemes the imagination is naturalistic, but in different senses. In the one, the cognitive efficacy of imagination is limited to nature as its object. In the other, imagination plays a subordinate role in the natural knowledge of supernature.

One can easily see why the natural imagination in itself, on the present view, cannot conform the Divine Essence and finite

[10] This is a notorious problem of interpretation in Aristotle: the problem, that is, of the status of active intellect in man. St. Thomas argues that there is in man an agent intellect separate from infinite intellect, or God; but that there must be present in and to human active intellect ". . . some power derived from a higher intellect, whereby it [human active intellect] is able to illumine the phantasms." *Summa Theologica,* I, Q. LXXIX, art 4, in *Basic Writings,* p. 750.

[11] We ourselves have had occasion to observe earlier, without developing the point, that the single most important classical theological doctrine, from the standpoint of elaborating a theory of revelatory imagination, is the doctrine of creation.

mind to each other. The imagination can be truly conformal only between those terms in each of which there is a distinction between potency and act, matter and form, essence and existence. Its domain of reality, that to which it refers, is that in which the tension between these polar elements is manifest. It follows that if God is defined as Pure Act or Form, in whom is no potentiality, the divine essence cannot be said to be an object of the imagination as such.[12]

To recapitulate: in a creationist metaphysic underpinning the present type, imagination plays an ancillary role in establishing the existence of God and his necessary attributes. In fine, the imagination is an epistemological presupposition of the cosmological argument.[13] But the natural imagination itself cannot yield even indirect knowledge of the divine *essence,* for the mode of being in the known (God) infinitely transcends the mode of being in the known (finite mind).

Still, anything is knowable according as it is actual; and God being supremely actual must be supremely knowable.[14] But that which is knowable in itself (i.e., intrinsically) may not be knowable by a particular finite intellect because of its infinitely transcendent mode of being, because of what St. Thomas calls ". . . the excess of the intelligible object above the intellect."[15] On the principle that essential act is proportioned to the being whose act it is,[16] and in view of the claim that the being of God is incorporeal, it must be concluded that the *essential act* of God cannot be known either through sense or imagination. Consequently two assertions shape themselves. (a) God is intrinsically knowable, but essentially (i.e., in the internality of his Act) unknown by natural intellect. (b) If God is to be "seen" (not "known", in the sense of comprehended), then God him-

---

[12] In this connection it is interesting to observe that in those thinkers for whom God includes potentiality the imagination plays a dominant role in man's knowledge of God. See the discussion below of Böhme and Schelling in Appendix III.

[13] *Summa Theologica,* I. Q. XII, art. 13.

[14] *Ibid.,* I, Q. XII, art. 1.

[15] *Ibid.*

[16] *Ibid.,* I, Q. XII, art. 3.

self must unilaterally conform natural intellect to himself; which, in St. Thomas's terms, means that *conformal* imagination must become *deiformal* imagination.[17]

B. The "Deiformed" Imagination and Supernatural Vision of God

The transition from conformal to deiformal imagination constitutes *grace*.[18] According to the tradition under examination, God is not by grace rendered intelligible, since he is intrinsically intelligible. Rather by "grace" it is understood that in some sense the known (God) becomes the knower through the derivative agency of finite intellect. This process is effected by divine *illumination* and by deformation of the imagination. The images of the imagination require to be divinely illumined (as in "natural" imagination images require to be acted upon by active intellect) before they can be concretely revelatory of God.[19] In grace God is not "known" in that mode proper to his own existence, but rather in the mode proper to deiformed finite intellect. The knowledge of God in revelation therefore is not the knowledge which God has of himself, but that of a hylomorphic being whose intelligible form has been insinuated or pervaded by divine light. "Therefore, he who sees God's essence sees in Him that he exists infinitely, and is infinitely knowable. Nevertheless, this infinite mode does not extend to enable the knower to know infinitely . . ."[20]

The last point about "knowledge" in revelation can be stated in various ways. Through the deiformed imagination one attains

[17] "The essence of God is not seen in a vision of the imagination, but the imagination receives some form representing God according to some mode of likeness; as in divine Scripture divine things are metaphorically described by means of sensible things." *Ibid.;* in *Basic Writings,* p. 96.

[18] *Ibid.,* I, Q. XII, art. 4.

[19] "It may be said that this light [divine illumination] is not a medium *in which* God is seen, but one *by which* He is seen; and such a medium does not take away the immediate vision of God." *Ibid.,* I, Q. XII, art. 5; in *Basic Writings,* p. 99.

[20] *Ibid.,* I, Q. XII, art. 7; in *Basic Writings,* p. 103.

the knowledge of "sight" rather than the understanding of "comprehension." St. Thomas develops his view of revelation through imaginative "vision" by combining his own doctrine of illumination with Augustine's theory of imagination and "spiritual vision."[21] The relation between divine illumination and deform imagination will be taken up below. For the moment it is sufficient to note that through the "prophetic" or deiform imagination the vision of God combines *immediacy* with *wholeness:* through his images the prophet "sees" God with immediacy and as a whole, not piecemeal. By contradistinction the conformal or natural imagination, with its discrete images and its discursive operation in time, is bereft both of wholeness and of immediacy.[22] The noetic content of "the divinely formed imagination," consequently, is not that of scientific knowledge; for the vision is not that of the believer, but of him who is believed.

In such limited compass one cannot enter upon a detailed account of St. Thomas's doctrine of the prophetic or "deiformed" imagination;[23] a few bold strokes must suffice. Recalling that the *abiding* form of the mind is active intellect, it will be apparent that the deiformed imagination is in the intellect not as its substantial form but rather as a "transitory passion."[24] The case is perhaps not stated too strongly if one says that the natural active intellect is displaced or supplanted by a supernaturally passive intellect, the latter being identical with the deiformed imagination. The absolute passivity of prophetic imagination is indicated by the fact that the prophet cannot

[21] Augustine's theory is elaborated in *De Genesi ad Litteram,* XII.

[22] *Summa Theologica,* I, Q. XII, art. 10.

[23] St. Thomas's doctrine of prophetic imagination is developed at great length in *Suma Theologica,* II, Qq. CLXXI–CLXXV.

[24] "The prophetic light is not in the prophet's intellect by way of an abiding form, else a prophet would always be able to prophesy, which is clearly false . . . The prophetic light is in the prophet's soul by way of a passion or transitory impression . . . Hence it is that even as the air is ever in need of a fresh enlightening, so too the prophet's mind is always in need of fresh revelation . . ." *Ibid.,* II, Q. CLXXI, art. 2; in *The Summa Theologica of St. Thomas Aquinas,* trans. by Fathers of the English Dominican Province, Vol. XIV, (London: Burns Oates & Washbourne Ltd., 1935), pp. 5–8.

distinguish what he says by his own spirit from what he says in the power of divine afflatus.[25] Displacement of natural activity by supernatural passivity is absolutely gratuitous; no man has the gift by right. There is no one natural disposition more favorable to it than others; the giving of divine inspiration creates in the subject the very disposition to receive it.[26] That the presence of the Holy Spirit is thought to be identical with the deiformed imagination, is taken as sufficient evidence of its gratuitous, not substantial character.[27]

While the *goal* of prophetic knowledge is intellective rather than imaginative vision of God, the intellect can achieve its vision only through images "impressed" in the deiformed imagination by divine agency. This process requires two things, acccording to St. Thomas. "The intellect's natural light is strengthened by the infusion of gratuitous light ["illumination"], and . . . also the images in the imagination are divinely formed, so as to express divine things better than do those which we receive naturally from sensible things, as appears in prophetic visions . . ."[28] Thomas maintains that in prophetic revelation new images are impressed upon the intellect, and not merely an intellectual light. He reminds us that two distinguishable things are requisite for knowledge: the representation of things, and

[25] *Ibid.*, II, Q. CLXXI, art. 5.

[26] *Ibid.*, II, Q. CLXXII, art. 3. Cf. the exact opposite in Spinoza's theory of prophetic imagination. Spinoza insists that a mind "given to what is right and good" is the condition of a prophet's receiving revelation through imagination. *Theological-Political Treatise,* Ch. II; in *The Chief Works of Spinoza,* trans. R. H. M. Elwes, Vol. I, (New York: Dover Publications, Inc., 1951), p. 29. St. Thomas, in addition to what was said above, circumvents moral purity as a condition of prophetic imagination in the following way. We may deny that moral goodness is requisite to prophecy on two counts, he says. (1) Prophecy differs from goodness or charity on account of their respective acts. That is, prophecy, even though it occurs through imagination, pertains to *intellect,* whose act precedes the act of the *will.* (2) Prophecy differs from goodness or charity on account of their respective ends. Prophecy is given for the good of the church, ". . . and is not directly intended to unite man's affections to God, which is the purpose of charity." *Summa Theologica,* II, Q. CLXXII, art. 4; in *The Summa Theologica of St. Thomas Aquinas,* Vol. XIV, p. 26.

[27] The raising of "the intention of the mind" to divine things is itself by motion of the Holy Spirit. *Ibid.,* Q. CLXXI, art. 1.

[28] *Ibid.,* Q. XII, art. 13; in *Basic Writings,* p. 110.

judgment of the things represented. The former is the work of the deiformed imagination; the latter is a work of judgment, which is to say, illumination. Thus St. Thomas suggests what every abstractionist says to a pure illuminist, viz., that the doctrine of illumination alone ignores the problem of the formation of concepts and their "stuff." He agrees with Augustine, in other words, that prophetic knowledge pertains most of all to the intellect, but this means for him that it must refer to the divine material first, viz., the "new images" implanted by God in the intellect, and secondarily to the illumination of "intellectual light." "But it is the first of these two [viz., the "new images" impressed upon the imagination] that holds the chief place in prophecy, since judgment is the complement of knowledge."[29]

Prophetic knowledge ("vision") of God comes about through various operations of the deiformed imagination. First, there may be an infusion of new images, the direct impression of images by God upon the mind, ". . . as in the case of those who received infused . . . knowledge or wisdom, such as Solomon or the apostles."[30] Secondly, images of sense may be presented to the mind under divine guidance. That is, natural images, arising through sense, may be concretely revelatory through divine illumination. Thus Daniel's experience of the handwriting on the wall, and Moses' vision of the burning bush. Thirdly, under divine guidance there may be a coordination or restructuring of images already held in imagination, whether of sensible or of divine origin, so as to produce a new constellation of meaning ("thus Jeremiah saw the boiling caldron from the face of the north"[31]). Finally, prophetic revelation may occur through the infusion of intellectual light, i.e., the power of judgment. This takes the form of judging, on the part of the prophet, the imaginations of others (such as Joseph's judgment of Pharoah's dreams). In any event, this infused light is required, as it were, to transpose all images into supernatural key. St. Thomas summarizes the case in the following way. "Intellectual vision is not

[29] *Ibid.,* Q. CLXXIII, art. 2; in *The Summa Theologica of St. Thomas Aquinas,* Vol. XIV, pp. 36–39.
[30] *Ibid.*
[31] *Ibid.*

effected by means of bodily and individual images, but by means of an *intelligible image*. . . . Sometimes this intelligible image is, in prophetic revelation, imprinted immediately by God, sometime it results from pictures in the imagination, by the aid of the prophetic light, since a deeper truth is gathered from these pictures in the imagination by means of the enlightenment of the higher light."[32]

C. Imagination, Ecstasy, and Rapture

In view of this elaborate theory of the deformed imagination, one might well think it to be the last word on knowledge of God, according to the present "type." That this is not the case will be seen if we ask the question, which is more excellent, prophecy accompanied by both intellective and imaginative vision, or by intellective vision alone? St. Augustine inclines to the former option. He writes, "He is less a prophet who sees in spirit nothing but the signs representative of things, by means of the images of things corporeal: he is more a prophet who is merely endowed with the understanding of these signs; but most of all is he a prophet who excels in both ways."[33] But St. Thomas, upon whom we have relied to illustrate the present type of deform imagination, takes the latter option: prophecy aims at pure intellective vision, although the prophet as such is not able to achieve pure intellection of God. The prophet requires the aid of imagination, but ". . . prophecy is all the more excellent as it needs less."[34] The excellence of the means, imagination, is to be measured by the end; and the end of prophecy is the manifestation of a truth that surpasses the faculties of man. "Hence it follows that the prophecy whereby a supernatural truth is seen by intellectual vision, is more excellent than that in which a supernatural truth is manifested by means of the similitudes of corporeal things in the vision of the imagination."[35]

[32] *Ibid.* (Emphasis mine.)
[33] Augustine, *De Genesi ad Litteram*, XII; 9.
[34] *Summa Theologica*, II, Q. CLXXIV, art. 2; in *The Summa Theologica of St. Thomas Aquinas*, Vol. XIV, pp. 48–51.
[35] *Ibid.*

To this point, it has been seen how imagination is involved in natural knowledge of nature, the natural knowledge of supernature, and, through prophecy, the supernatural "vision" of supernature. If man is to *know* the divine essence, and not alone "see" it, he must transcend the prophetic mode. Whereas prophetic vision involves the *ecstatic* imagination, sheer intellection of the divine essence entails a state of *rapture*. The prophetic or deiformed imagination was seen to be ecstatic in that, in prophetic vision or utterance, the simultaneously active-passive "natural" imagination is supplanted by an absolutely passive imagination directed toward the divine operation. In addition to being ecstatic, sheer intellection of the divine essence is *rapturous*. This means, according to St. Thomas, that to ecstasy is added "violence."[36] That is to say that in the pinnacle of cognitive relation to God all human faculties are "violated." Of course the ultimate cognitive relation is through the intellect,[37] but that relation is achieved through a deiformed intellect and not through a deiformed imagination.[38] In winding up at this point St. Thomas embraces a fundamentally Plotinian doctrine of the imagination.[39] Indeed, apart from St. Thomas's association of imagination with abstraction, the present "type" could have been developed from a base in Plotinus as handily as from a base in St. Thomas. Both are finally intellectualists, departing from the fixity of form or structure. With both knowledge con-

[36] "The violent is that which has its principle without, and in which he that suffers violence concurs not at all." *Ibid.*, II, Q. CLXXV, art. 1; in *The Summa Theologica of St. Thomas Aquinas*, Vol. XIV, p. 63.

[37] *Ibid.*, II, Q. CLXXV, art. 4; in *The Summa Theologica of. St. Thomas Aquinas*, Vol. XIV, pp. 70–72.

[38] "For God's essence cannot be seen by means of a phantasm nor indeed by any created intelligible species, since God's essence infinitely transcends not only all bodies, which are represented by phantasms, but also all intelligible creatures. Now when man's intellect is uplifted to the sublime vision of God's essence, it is necessary that his mind's whole attention should be summoned to that purpose in such a way that he understand naught else by phantasms, and be absorbed entirely in God. Therefore it is impossible for man while a wayfarer to see God in His essence without being withdrawn from his senses." *Ibid.*

[39] Plotinus' theory of imagination, especially in relation to memory, is developed in the fourth *Ennead,* Tractate III. He treats of the relation between imagination and intellection in knowledge of God, or the One, chiefly in Tractate IV.

sists in the intellectualization of form, in which process the imagination can play only a subordinate role. For both, revelation finally takes on the form of an intellectualistic mysticism—which means that the understanding of imagination they embrace cannot subserve a doctrine of revelation which is oriented to the historical expansion of form.

II. The Imagination and "Synthesis"

Outline

I. HISTORICAL MILIEU

Before elaborating the view of imagination as an essentially synthetic act of mind, from a base largely in Kant but to some extent also in Coleridge, it may be useful to recall the historical *milieu* in which the problem of the relation between imagination and *synthesis* arose in modernity. The problem emerged as one of undeniable moment when continental rationalistic doctrines of "substance" came under attack at the hands of English empiricists in the seventeenth and eighteenth centuries.[1] In those

---

[1] I certainly do not mean to suggest that, because the category of "substance" was their chief preoccupation, the continental rationalists had nothing of importance to say about "imagination." (That judgment is all too frequently found in the scant literature on the subject. Cf. Edward Charles Kollman, *Studies in the Modern Theory of Imagination with Especial Reference to its Historical Development from the Renaissance to Kant,* [Harvard Ph.D. Dissertation, 1950], Ch. VI.) It is of course true that the major continental rationalists depreciated the imagination, but not by mere dismissal. (1) Descartes depreciated imagination by

rationalistic doctrines "substance" accounted for structure and order, which veredicious intellection was thought to grasp directly. Exercising certain options in Descartes, Locke inaugurated that venerable English empiricist tradition which

---

reason of an ambiguity in his metaphysics. (2) Spinoza's depreciation of imagination rooted in his doctrine of substance. (3) Leibniz depreciated imagination largely by evading the epistemological implications of his metaphysical commitments. These sweeping judgments can hardly be developed here with any fullness, but an earnest can be indicated for each.

(1) Descartes' equivocation on the mind-body relation, and the implications of what relation for the imagination, has already come under notice in Chapter IV, note 29, and need not be repeated.

(2) Spinoza's distrust of imagination results from his own brand of metaphysical monism (although not all monisms have this result, as will be seen in Appendix III). In the *Improvement of the Understanding* (in *The Chief Works of Benedict de Spinoza*, trans. R. H. M. Elwes, Vol. II, espec. pp. 12–41) Spinoza develops in detail the thesis that imagination is the source of error with respect to veridical knowledge of Nature, or Substance. Knowledge of substance is by means of the Understanding, especially through "true" or "standard" ideas. Such an idea refers to nothing extrinsic to itself: ". . . thought is said to be true, if it involves subjectively the essence of any principle which has no cause, and is known through itself and in itself. . . . That which constitutes the reality of a true thought must be sought in the thought itself, and deduced from the nature of the understanding." (*Ibid.*, p. 26; cf. also p. 34) Now imagination (as the source of error) for Spinoza is always associated with ". . . certain sensations fortuitous (as to speak) and disconnected, arising not from the power of the mind, but from external causes, according as the body, sleeping or waking, receives various motions" (p. 32). Imagination is the source of error because it is wholly passive to nature in its aspect of particularity; failing to conceive nature through its essence, it promiscuously accepts such order as particular things present, thus "perverting the [true] order of nature" (p. 28). Because imagination is not controlled by the Understanding, it presents nature to the mind under the aspect of particularity and finitude, so that "things" appear as localized in extension, as well as separate and successive in time (pp. 33 and 40); whereas the Understanding, conceiving nature "through itself," presents nature under the aspects of infinity and eternity. (It is important to note that in this summary I have taken no account of Spinoza's extensively elaborated theory of the "prophetic imagination" in the early chapters of the *Theologico-Political Treatise*.)

(One may mention in passing an ostensible contradiction in Spinoza's theory of imagination, a contradiction besetting every monistic metaphysic which reckons with the problem of "process." As we have said, in the *Improvement of the Understanding* Spinoza implies that nature is particularized and made disparate only in virtue of the imagination. But in the *Ethics* [see espec. Part II, Prop. XVII] he implies that nature is in one respect constituted by existent particular things; and because the body is particular, there must be [so to speak] a cognitional correlate

336

sought after order not in the operation of substantial being but rather in the processes of the mind's operation, chiefly in the "association of ideas." In this tradition imagination came to play an important role in the association of ideas, especially in the formation of "complex ideas." Only Berkeley seems to have discerned that, strictly on empiricistic terms, the associative power of imagination could not be construed as *necessary*. He therefore argued (in his *Siris*) that only those ideas can be necessary which are ordered by and emanate from God. Remove God from the system of Berkeley (or Malebranche) and one has left, as in Hume, the pure association of ideas by an imagination whose propensity is determined not by intrinsic rationality but by mere convention.[2] While empiricism of the seventeenth and eighteenth centuries found a necessary relation

of these particularities, which is the imagination. In short, he implies that particulars "exist" because of imagination and that the imagination exists because of particulars, which is to make of imagination simultaneously both cause and effect. No doubt within the framework of a metaphysical monism a point is reached where the same operation must be both cause and effect, and that point is ultimate "substance." [For a perceptive discussion of this problem in Spinoza see John Dewey, "The Pantheism of Spinoza," in *Journal of Speculative Philosophy*, Vol. XVI, p. 249]. But Spinoza clearly could not allow the operation of imagination to be the ultimate substantial act. In connection with this, however, it is interesting to note that certain other monists do not cavil at making precisely this affirmation, as will be developed in Appendix III.)

(3) Concerning Leibniz, of whom it was said above that his distrust of imagination is due to his neglect to ramify epistemologically certain of his metaphysical commitments, we may suggest only two points. (a) In his doctrine of "substance" as "force" or "activity" and in his provision for the unconscious through his theory of "petite perceptions," Leibniz was a significant precursor of Bergson, although Bergson worked out the implications of these doctrines for a theory of imagination in a way that seems never to have occurred to Leibniz. (b) In connection with "truths of matter of fact" Leibniz undertook a metaphysical expansion only, showing that they are verified through "sufficient reason," itself grounded in the nature of God. Had Leibniz given a methodological, as well as a metaphysical, analysis of "sufficient reason" he might well have anticipated Kant's doctrine of the transcendental imagination. That is, he might have shown that all intuition of matters of fact require the application of categories to sensa through the scheme of time in the productive imagination. There is a hint of this in Leibniz's insistence that there is nothing in the mind not previously in the senses, *except the mind itself,* whose operations are not derived from the senses. (See above, Chapter V, note 52.)

[2] Propensive imagination so understood will be taken up in Appendix III below.

to obtain between imagination and synthesis, it was unable to ground the necessity of judgment in that relation.

For Kant, then, the problem of the relation between imagination and synthesis could not be solved by recourse either to rationalism or to empiricism. With the empiricists, he agreed that synthesis would have to be accounted for from the side of the mind; but with the rationalists he agreed that no account of synthesis would be worthwhile that did not lay bare the *necessary* character of judgment. His doctrine of synthetic imagination was an attempt to transcend and sublate empiricism and rationalism.

According to the "type" now to be taken up, the primary effect of imagination is one of synthesis (Kant), "esemplasy" (Coleridge),[3] or unity, an effect aptly indicated in the German word *Einbildungskraft*.[4] It is the function of synthesis to bring together otherwise disparate ingredients of knowledge. There are three such ingredients, and to each of them corresponds a distinguishable level of synthesis. (The three levels of synthesis will be elaborated below.) These ingredients are the sheer sensuous manifold (i.e., phenomena considered in their material aspect), the pure forms of intuition (i.e., phenomena considered in their formal aspect of intuitability and reproducibility), and the categorial concepts of the understanding.

Already it will be clear that synthesis pertains not to the association of ideas but rather to that to which concepts refer.

[3] Concerning the word "esemplastic" Coleridge writes: "I constructed it myself from the Greek words, εἰς ἕν πλάττειν, to shape into one; because, having to convey a new sense, I thought that a new term would both aid the recollection of my meaning, and prevent its being confounded with the usual import of the word, imagination." *Biographia Literaria*, Ch. X; in *Selected Poetry and Prose of Samuel Taylor Coleridge*, ed. Donald A. Stauffer, (New York: Random House, 1951), p. 191.

[4] Notwithstanding his differences with Kant's use of the term Coleridge remarks in a notebook entry the aptness of *Einbildungskraft* to indicate the leading work of imagination. "How excellently the German *Einbildungskraft* expresses this prime and loftiest faculty, the power of coadunation, the faculty that forms the many into one—in-eins-bildung! Esenplasy, or esenoplastic power, as contradistinguished from fantasy, or the mirrorment, either catoptric or metoptric—repeating simply, or by transposition—and again, involuntary as in dreams, or by an act of the will." Quoted by George Whalley, *Poetic Process*, p. 62.

338

Assuming that order is not imposed upon the mind by the noumenal being of its object, the form which the mind legislates through imaginative synthesis will not yield *knowledge* unless the imagination operates according to necessary rule. In short, imagination can be shown to be indispensable to all knowledge whatsoever only by showing that it is indispensable to *necessary* synthesis, itself essential to knowledge. Utilizing Kant's terms and the context of his thought in the first *Critique,* it can be said that the synthesis which underlies all knowledge is "pure," *a priori,* "transcendental," and hence "necessary." The synthesis achieved through imagination is *pure* because its origin is in the mind alone (in the sense that the *form* which imagination applies to the manifold, whether sensuous or *a priori,* derives from the mind alone[5]); it is *a priori* because it is logically independent of experience; and it is *transcendental* because it is the condition of all experience whatsoever.[6]

II. THREE LEVELS OF SYNTHESIS

Although the synthesis performed by the mind through imagination is essentially one, it has distinguishable dimensions which may be discerned in connection with apprehension, reproduction, and the categories of understanding.

A. Apprehension and Imagination

Apprehension requires for its possibility a synthesis of intuition. Strictly speaking there can be no representations of a manifold (i.e., it cannot be apprehended through intuition) apart from

[5] See *Critique of Pure Reason,* trans. Norman Kemp Smith, (London: Macmillan Co., 1953), pp. 65–66.

[6] Kant's full statement in the "Transcendental Analytic": "By *synthesis,* in its most general sense, I understand the act of putting different representations together, and of grasping what is manifold in them in one [act of] knowledge. Such a synthesis is *pure,* if the manifold is not empirical but is given *a priori,* as is the manifold in space and time. Before we can analyze our representations, the representations must themselves be given, and therefore as regards *content* no concepts can first arise by way of analysis. Synthesis of a manifold (be it given

its being "run through and held together" by the form of time (and in the case of sensuous intuition, space).[7] We may say that space and time are not themselves unities but rather the forms of possible intuition, and that they must be wedded with the content of the manifold in order to yield unified representations. The "synthesis of apprehension" has to do therefore with the receiving, arranging, and connecting of representations.[8] It is the ordering into stable units of what otherwise would be a blind chaos of phenomena. Through its "schemata" the pure productive imagination arrests the chaos of phenomena by imposing upon it the forms of time and space, an *arrestation* which permits as well an "intellectual synthesis" by making possible the application of the mind's categories.

B. Reproduction and Imagination

The problem of the reproductive, empirical, or associative imagination is solved in principle by what was said in the preceding paragraph about "productive" imagination. Without

---

empirically or a priori) is what first gives rise to knowledge. . . . Synthesis is that which gathers the elements for knowledge, and unites them to [form] a certain content. . . . Synthesis in general . . . is the mere result of the power of imagination, a blind but indispensable function of the soul, without which we should have no knowledge whatsoever, but of which we are scarcely ever conscious." *Ibid.*, pp. 111–112.

[7] *Ibid.*, pp. 131–132.

[8] Kant writes: "Appearances are only representations of things which are unknown as regards what they may be in themselves. As mere representations, they are subject to no law of connection save that which the connecting faculty prescribes. Now it is imagination that connects the manifold of sensible intuition; and imagination is dependent for the unity of its intellectual synthesis upon the understanding, and for the manifoldness of its apprehension upon sensibility." *Ibid.*, p. 173.

Further: "Now, since every appearance contains a manifold, and since different perceptions therefore occur in the mind separately and singly, a combination of them, such as they cannot have in sense itself, is demanded. There must therefore exist in us an active faculty for the synthesis of this manifold. To this faculty I give the title, imagination. Its action when immediately directed upon perceptions, I entitle apprehension." In a footnote to this last statement Kant writes, "Psychologists have hitherto failed to realize that imagination is a necessary ingredient of perception itself. This is due partly to the fact that that faculty has been limited to reproduction, partly to the belief that the

some such doctrine both the Humean empiricist and the transcendental idealist, who hold that cognitive contents are not ordered from the side of the object, have the problem that the reproductive imagination has nothing to refer to. According to the present view, this stable reference is furnished by the *a priori* synthetical unity of phenomena accomplished in the productive imagination. In this connection, Kant writes: "If we can show that even our purest *a priori* intuitions yield no knowledge, save in so far as they contain a combination of the manifold such as renders a thoroughgoing synthesis of reproduction possible, then this synthesis of imagination is likewise grounded, antecedently to all experience, upon *a priori* principles; and we must assume a pure transcendental synthesis of imagination as conditioning the very possibility of all experience."[9] Indeed experience presupposes reproducibility; for continuity of representations, whether those of objects or of the self, presuppose their having achieved such stability in "inner sense" as to allow association without loss of identity. But discrete impressions cannot become representations unless the manifold of the intuition of them, be it pure or empirical, is combined according to a rule of synthesis. That is, impressions cannot become ingredient in knowledge unless there is a necessary synthetical unity of them. Therefore the presupposition of the empirical, reproductive, or associative imagination is the productive imagination, or pure transcendental synthesis of imagination: "The synthesis of apprehension is thus inseparably bound up with the synthesis of reproduction."[10]

C. Category and Imagination

A third dimension of synthesis requisite to knowledge, according to the present view, is "the synthesis of recognition in a concept." Knowledge is not possible without explicit consciousness

---

senses not only supply impressions but also combine them so as to generate images of objects. For that purpose something more than the mere receptivity of impressions is undoubtedly required, namely, a function for the synthesis of them." *Ibid.,* p. 144.

[9] *Ibid.* p. 133.
[10] *Ibid.*

that what we think now is the same as what we thought before. Such a "synthesis of recognition" cannot depend entirely upon a "synthesis of sensibility," the schematization of appearances through the forms of intuition by productive imagination. For recognition requires that schemata must be subjected to a "synthesis of understanding," whereby they are informed by the universal categories of the understanding.[11] In other words, the transcendental synthesis of pure (productive) imagination stands between and, so to speak, "introduces" sensuous intuition and the concepts of the understanding.[12] It imposes the universal principles of synthesis contained in the pure categories upon appearances given under the form of time (and in the case of sensuous appearances, space). Therefore an object is recognizable universally and necessarily through the synthetic *a priori* concept of it.

III. SYNTHESIS, IMAGINATION, AND THE TRANSCENDENTAL UNITY OF APPERCEPTION

Having spoken of three dimensions of synthesis we must now consider the absolute transcendental condition of synthesis as such, and the relation of imagination to that condition. Since synthesis does not arise from the side of the object it must, if it is to be universal and necessary, emanate from that which is numerically identical and continuous, and not itself in need of

[11] *Ibid.*, pp. 133–138.

[12] Of pure imagination Kant writes: "By its means we bring the manifold of intuition on the one side, into connection with the condition of the necessary unity of pure apperception on the other. The two extremes, namely sensibility and understanding, must stand in necessary connection with each other through the mediation of this transcendental function of imagination, because otherwise the former, though indeed yielding appearances, would supply no objects of empirical knowledge, and consequently no experience. Actual experience, which is constituted by apprehension, association (reproduction), and finally recognition of appearances, contains in recognition, the last and highest of these empirical elements of experience, certain concepts which render possible the formal unity of experience, and therewith all objective validity (truth) of empirical knowledge." *Ibid.*, pp. 146–147.

synthesis. This something is the formal unity of consciousness,[13] the "abiding and unchanging 'I,' "[14] the "I" of intellectual synthesis, or in Kant's technical phrase: the transcendental unity of apperception. Left to itself imagination (although exercised *a priori*) would yield only a synthesis of sensibility; but apperception is combined with pure imagination, ". . . in order to render its function intellectual."[15] This combination is essential to the claim that imagination is indispensable to all knowledge (and experience) whatsoever.

The relation between the synthesis of pure productive imagination and the transcendental unity of apperception in Kant, or more simply the relation between imagination and human selfhood, is a notorious "metaphysical" problem of interpretation in Kantian studies. In the "type" under development here, perduring self-consciousness takes metaphysical priority over pure imagination. If the relation of priority were reversed, as in the type to be developed in Appendix III below, imagination would assume not only epistemically synthetic powers but also and especially ontologically *creative* powers. Since it is no part of our intention to expose Kant's full doctrine of imagination, not to mention adjudicating its difficulties (the third *Critique* has been mentioned not at all!), the "metaphysical" question may be laid aside. As for the logical relation between the syntheses of imagination and the unity of apperception, it is at all events safe to say that Kant held each to presuppose the other. For he says that ". . . the principle of the necessary unity of pure (productive) synthesis of imagination, *prior to apperception,* is the ground of the possibility of all knowledge . . ."[16]; and only a few paragraphs later that ". . . the objective unity of all empirical consciousness in one consciousness, that of original apperception, is . . . the necessary condition of all perception."[17]

We can now summarize those features of the present type that have come into view. From an undifferentiated field of phenomena the pure imagination selects, arranges and connects, synthe-

13 *Ibid.,* p. 135.
14 *Ibid.,* p. 146.
15 *Ibid.*
16 *Ibid.,* p. 143 (emphasis mine).
17 *Ibid.,* p. 145.

sizing units under the forms of space and time, effecting their intellectual wedding with the continuity of mind. It may be said that the *primary* work of the imagination is to "objectify" objects; to arrest the blind rush of phenomena by amalgamating their contents with the forms of the mind. Neither content nor form are reducible to the creativity of the imagination. Such a view is "realistic" in the sense that imagination *produces* schemata for the understanding only by *introducing* what are otherwise (logically) fixities or "givens." Through this indissoluble combination pure imagination forms the logical base for all acts of knowledge, as it gives to understanding a "stable" referent. By the same token, however, pure imagination has no cognitive efficacy in its own mode of operation. This is so because the synthesis of productive imagination is finally governed by the categories of the understanding. The intention of such a theory of imagination is to explain the "synthesis of understanding," not to afford cognitive content to a "synthesis of imagination," or even to an "imagination of reason." Rather, on this view, pure imagination is made to serve a function of mediating synthesis; to insure the applicability of categories to experience; to guarantee that concepts will not be empty and percepts blind. In short, through all those dimensions of synthesis in which it is engaged, the transcendental imagination mediates order, structure, and regularity to nature.[18]

18 *Ibid.,* pp. 146–149.

344

III. The Imagination and "Creativity"

Outline

The problem of creativity, and a faculty in which to localize it, was not the problem for classical and medieval philosophy that it has been for modern philosophy, expecially since the Enlightenment. In the perennial philosophy nature was so understood as to comprise a dumb creativity. Nature was thought to be constantly informed by the Demiurge, the Prime Mover, or First Act; it possessed the structures in which creativity was going on, but not the *consciousness* of creativity. As for mind or spirit, it was conceived as that special instance of nature in which creativity is envisaged, apprehended, or made self-conscious.

When nature was given over to an absolute regularity of cycle and structure, in the Enlightenment, the problem of creativity in its modern form emerged. That problem was an especially staggering one in the period between the Enlightenment and the emergence of the so-called "principle of indeterminacy" in latter-day physical and life sciences. In that period, the burden of creativity was shifted from "nature" to "mind" or "spirit." Whereas in classical views imagination sustained no integral relation to creativity, now the imagination was advanced as the native habitat of the creative instinct.

The proliferation of theories of imagination in this period has been so great as to defy the sketchiest of surveys in brief compass. We shall therefore consider only three types, or subtypes, under the rubric of imagination and creativity. The first will be developed largely out of Hume and will be concerned with the role of imagination in the formation of *belief*. The second, a radical subjugation of nature to free spirit, will be elaborated from a base in Fichte and Schelling. The third, a radical negation of the absurdity of existents, will be framed from Sartre.

I. IMAGINATION AND THE CREATIVITY OF MENTAL "PROPENSITY"

On the view now to be taken up, the creativity of imagination vests in an act of completion rather than in an act of initiation. While imagination has nothing to do with the *origin* of the mind's contents or the objects to which they refer, it has a great deal to do with the ordering of those contents and consequently with the formation of beliefs about objects. If the creativity of imagination is due to its propensity, that means that imagination has an initial *bias,* inclination, or disposition. Through propensive activity, imagination "completes" the bias by ordering the contents of the mind in relation to it. By the same act of propensive completion the imagination gives rise to beliefs about the objects of mental contents. From this advance summary of the view of imagination *qua* propensive, two matters emerge for first consideration.

346

It is necessary to observe, for one thing, that the ordering of mental contents does not derive from an exterior or non-mental source.[1] For Hume mental contents are "impressions," whether those of sense or those of reflection. Discrete impressions of sense are in the mind as distinct existences;[2] and "simple ideas" correspond exactly to them.[3] The genuine units of knowledge, however, are not these distinct impressions. Knowledge for the most part, and belief altogether, vests in the combination of simple impressions or ideas in "complex ideas." In so far as simple impressions retain their identity and vivacity, they are functions of memory; and in so far as they enter into combination, they do so by virtue of the imagination. (Locke, as well as Hume.)

For a second thing, it should be noticed that the ordering power of imagination is here connected with what has been called "the association of ideas" in the empiricist tradition.[4] That association of ideas which imagination effects is not by *chance* on the one hand nor by *reason* on the other. Not by chance, because the associative power of imagination is guided by certain principles.[5] Not by reason, for the union of mental contents by imagination is neither necessary nor inseparable; and more

[1] David Hume: "Upon the whole, necessity is something that exists in the mind, not in objects; nor is it possible for us ever to form the most distant idea of it, consider'd as a quality in bodies. Either we have no idea of necessity, or necessity is nothing but that determination of the thought to pass from causes to effects and from effects to causes according to their experienc'd union." *A Treatise of Human Nature,* Book I, Part III, Sect. XIV; ed. L. A. Selby-Bigge, (Oxford: Clarendon Press, 1888), pp. 165–166. (Cited hereafter as Selby-Bigge.)

[2] *Ibid.,* Appendix; Selby-Bigge, p. 636.

[3] *Ibid.,* Book I, Part I, Sect. I; Selby-Bigge, p. 4

[4] The view under analysis here could be developed, however, through such a reading of Kant as is found in Hans Vaihinger. See, for example, his *The Philosophy of "As If,"* trans. C. K. Ogden, (London: Routledge & Kegan Paul, 1949), espec. Part I.

[5] Hume: "Were ideas entirely loose and unconnected, chance alone wou'd join them; and 'tis impossible the same simple ideas should fall regularly into complex ones (as they commonly do) without some bond of union among them, some associating quality, by which one idea naturally introduces another." *Op. cit.,* Book I, Part I, Sect. IV; Selby-Bigge, pp. 10ff.

347

especially because "demonstrative and probable reasonings" have to do with discrete impressions and their attendant simple ideas, not with their *relation* to each other.[6] With the association of ideas by imagination, as excluding both chance and reason, we must now deal in some detail.

The guiding principles by which the ordering power of imagination is thought to escape chance association are said by Hume to be resemblance, contiguity, and causation. Resemblance: ideas resembling each other have high valence bonds. Contiguity: those distinct impressions tend to connect in the mind which arise from objects that are ostensibly contiguous in time and space. Causation: those ideas incline to associate with each other which, either in themselves or in the objects from which they originate, display an ostensible relationship of cause and effect. I say "tend" or "incline" because these "principles" are finally only propensities, and require an active power of mind (viz., the imagination) to exercise them in the actual organization of mental contents. To state the matter in this way is to direct attention to one of the most crucial problems in this view of imagination, viz., the logical relation between imagination and its guiding principles. As a convenient way of getting at this problem we may examine specifically the relation between imagination and the principle of causality (or more broadly, "necessary connexion").

It was said that causality is one of the principles guiding imagination's association of ideas, if imagination is to escape chance association. But now it must be remarked that, if we attend only to mental contents and their inspectable patterns of organization, the principle of causality itself seems to be a work of imagination. This will be seen if we reflect that in order for

[6] Cf. Hume: "The word, imagination, is commonly us'd in two different senses . . . When I oppose the imagination to memory, I mean the faculty, by which we form our fainter ideas. When I oppose it to reason, I mean the same faculty, excluding only our demonstrative and probable reasonings." *Ibid.*, Book I, Part III, Sect. X; Selby-Bigge, pp. 117n.-118. Cf. also: "In short there are two principles, which I cannot render consistent; nor is it in my power to renounce either of them, viz. *that all our distinct impressions are distinct existences,* and *that the mind never perceives any real connexion among distinct existences.*" *Ibid.*, Appendix; Selby-Bigge, p. 636.

348

two objects to exist in a cause-effect relationship it is necessary not only that they be related contiguously and successively, but also that ". . . these two relations are preserv'd in several instances," that is, that they be "constantly conjoined."[7] And no amount of experience of their conjunction can necessarily assure us of their *constant* conjunction. Are we to say then that the idea of their constant conjunction arises by means of reason or by means of imagination? Not by means of reason, for in its limitation to discrete impressions and their attending simple ideas reason is ". . . nothing but a species of sensation."[8] So far from accounting for ideas of connection between two objects, reason cannot account for the idea of one object as a continuous existent.[9] Why then do we *believe* that an object remains identically the same, and that in its existential continuity it is always attended by other identical objects as its cause or effects? The answer is a circular one. We *experience* objects as conjoined. The mind associates ideas of objects in perceiving them and manages its association on the basis of previous perceptions of them or objects similar to them. Thus experience depends upon *custom*. But custom obviously depends upon *experience,* since custom is simply the repetition of experience without alteration.[10]

It seems then that ideas of the constant conjunction of objects arise by means of imagination. This does not mean that any objects whatsoever may be conjoined, or more strictly that ideas of them may be associated, just as the imagination fancies. While imagination is the power and the medium for conjoining and associating, both the nature and the direction of its propensity are determined by *custom*. Imagination is a power of the mind for organizing and vivifying ideas in accordance with a direction which is given to the imagination. Thus Hume says that ". . .

[7] *Ibid.,* Book I, Part III, Sect. VI; Selby-Bigge, p. 87.

[8] *Ibid.,* Book I, Part III, Sect. VIII; Selby-Bigge, p. 103.

[9] *Ibid.,* Book I, Part IV, *passim.*

[10] Hume: "Now as we call every thing *custom,* which proceeds from a past repetition, without any new reasoning or conclusion, we may establish it as a certain truth, that all the belief, which follows upon any present impression, is deriv'd solely from that origin." *Ibid.,* Book I, Part III, Sect. VIII; Selby-Bigge, p. 102.

the imagination, when set into any train of thinking, is apt to continue, even when its object fails it, and like a galley put in motion by oars, carries on its course without any new impulse."[11] Because we are accustomed to the conjunction of two objects, to perceive one object is to have imagination fill the blanks of perception with the idea of the other. And to *believe* in the *constant* conjunction of the objects, apart from the mind, is to have imagination give rise to an *idea* of their conjunction, and to give to such an idea a high order of vivacity.[12]

In net effect, the ordering of mental contents (and so the beliefs which follow upon the force of their combination) is not a rational but rather an imaginative process. Imagination is a power for applying order to these contents, but it does not produce the order. Its creativity consists in its part in the emergence of beliefs through the application of order to mental contents. This order has a non-rational base, deriving variously from custom,[13] fictions,[14] disposition,[15] "taste and sentiment,"[16]

[11] *Ibid.*, Book I, Part IV, Sect. II; Selby-Bigge, p. 198.

[12] While I have emphasized the role of imagination in *belief,* especially concerning causality, it should be noted that Hume stresses the *reciprocal* relation between imagination and belief. According to him custom itself is a sort of dumb belief, so that belief in this form gives imagination its initial stimulus. Imagination expands this belief and renders it explicit. But imagination is not merely propensive, i.e., it is not limited to tracing out the lines of accustomed belief. Through its power to vivify ideas imagination has the power to induce belief beyond that which gives imagination its initial propensity. Through this fact we have reason, at best, to accord high status to the arts and, at worst, to suspect the "lively imagination" of the mere rhetorician. Cf. *Ibid.,* Book I, Part III, Sect. X; Selby-Bigge, pp. 122–123.

[13] Hume: "Objects have no discoverable connexion together; nor is it from any other principle but custom operating upon the imagination, that we can draw any inference from the appearance of one to the existence of another." *Ibid.,* Book I, Part III, Sect. VIII; Selby-Bigge, pp. 102–104.

[14] I have in mind here what Hans Vaihinger calls "tropic fictions," which mean essentially for him what "propensities" mean to Hume. According to Vaihinger, these fictions are indispensable to thinking even though they have the logical status of a mere "as if." They provide stimuli to the mind to organize its data in a certain way. Thus Vaihinger considers all of Kant's categories of the understanding (e.g., substance, causality) to be "tropic fictions." Cf. Vaihinger, *op. cit.,* Ch. IV, *passim,* but espec. pp. 27–32.

In his examination of "ancient philosophy," Hume remarks that

and instinct.[17] No doubt the imagination is guided by certain principles in its application of order derived from these various sources, but the point to be underscored is that neither the principles nor the sources are intrinsically rational. This will mean, as Hume said, that ". . . memory, senses, and understanding are, therefore, all of them founded on the imagination . . .,"[18] and that ". . . imagination . . . [is] the ultimate judge of all systems of philosophy . . ."[19]

In summary, imagination renders explicit the order implicit in custom, and does so by connecting that order with the mind's impressions and ideas. In this way, imagination creates *belief*. Neither the propensive tendencies of custom nor the contents of the mind can effect a union with the other. There are gaps in mental impressions which only the imagination, having grasped the regulative ideal of a propensity, can fill. Belief in an external world and a continuing self is dependent on this power to realize fictions, on the power to stuff the interstices of impressions with purposes that are instinctive, cultural, or customary in origin.

II. CREATIVITY AND THE *ONTOLOGICALLY PRODUCTIVE* IMAGINATION

The simultaneity of creation and knowledge was thought to be a prerogative of *God* in scholastic Christian doctrine, but the coincidence of creation and knowledge was ascribed as well to *man* in nineteenth-century philosophical Romanticism.[20]

---

among classical philosophers imagination was under the domination of such "occult fictions" as prime matter, substance, substantial form, etc. Cf. Hume, *op. cit.*, Book I, Part IV, Sect. III; Selby-Bigge, pp. 219–225.

[15] *Ibid.*, Book I, Part III, Sect. VIII, Selby-Bigge, p. 98.

[16] *Ibid.*, Selby-Bigge, p. 103.

[17] *Ibid.*, Book I, Part IV, Sect. II; Selby-Bigge, p. 215.

[18] *Ibid.*, Book I, Part IV, Sect. VII; Selby-Bigge, p. 265.

[19] *Ibid.*, Book I, Part IV, Sect. V; Selby-Bigge, p. 225.

[20] For a thorough study of Fichte's influence upon the early Romantics, especially through his theory of productive imagination as the founda-

Much earlier in modern thought this ascription had been introduced by Vico, but it fell on deaf ears in an atmosphere dominated by Cartesianism.[21] Vico, who taught that imagination is the one power through which man both knows and creates, restricted the simultaneity of creation and knowledge to the order of *history*. Nature, according to him, requires no creativity on the part of man for its very being. In the type of creative imagination to come under review presently, this attitude toward nature is directly contradicted.

Nature itself, including all that the "plain man" considers to be "real" apart from himself, is understood to be a creation of the imagination and so to require imagination for knowledge of its inmost essence. The full elaboration of so large a claim can be seen as a conflation of Romantic and classical Christian thought on the point of creativity. The simultaneity of creation and knowledge would be understood both epistemologically and metaphysically only as the creativity-knowledge "moment" in the divine life were understood in its relation to the same moment in the human ego.

One cannot emphasize too strongly that, in order to understand the central claim of this type, imagination must not be viewed as merely a psychological faculty for the spontaneous creation and association of images. No "free play of fantasy" that is bereft of law and purpose, imagination is to be construed as an ontological power whose force is restricted "not at all to the limits of the empirical," but rather is seen to vest finally "in the transcendental (*übersinnlichen*) world."[22] Of Fichte's theory of productive imagination Julius Drechsler writes that "it serves not only to ground knowledge, but above all to advance that creative, structuring, shaping principle in virtue of which reality is unified and carried forward."[23]

---

tion of man's relation to nature, see E. Gelpcke, *Fichte und die Gedankenwelt des Sturm und Drang,* (Leipzig, 1928), pp. 148ff.

[21] Cf. Benedetto Croce, *The Philosophy of Giambattista Vico,* trans. R. G. Collingwood, (London: Macmillan Co., 1913), pp. 21ff.

[22] Johann Gottlieb Fichte, *Tatsachen des Bewusstseins,* (1813), in *J. G. Fichtes Nachgelassene Werke,* hrsg. I. H. Fichte, (Bonn: Markus, 1834), Bd. I, pp. 499ff.

[23] Julius Drechsler, *Fichtes Lehre vom Bild,* (Stuttgart: W. Kohlhammer Verlag, 1955), p. 65.

It will be useful to clarify the ontological creativity of imagination by means of transcendental analysis as prosecuted by post-Kantian idealists, notably by Fichte and Schelling. Such an effort would have been thought futile by Jakob Böhme, whose view of the imagination may also be located within this type. Böhme thought human creativity to be understandable only from a base in the divine, only from a standpoint in ". . . the centrum of the eternal and temporal nature."[24] According to him, a description of the internal processes of creation through imagination will strike a responsive and affirmative chord only in one who has experienced the "New Imagination," that rebirth by which one is taken up into the center of the divine life.[25]

While the romantic idealists wanted to understand how human creativity is a surrogate of, and sublated in, the creativity of the Absolute Ego, they were motivated by two other reasons to turn to the productive imagination afresh.

(1) The first reason is that Romantic poets and philosophers were terrorized by the possibility of losing the ideal self through its subjection to the necessities of mechanistic (Cartesian) nature.[26] To escape necessity of that sort, Fichte thought, one must discredit the existence of any eternal thing apart from its relation to the ego.[27] Should one be able to discredit existents apart from the ego's productivity he could then claim, as Fichte did, both that "Reason is not for the sake of existence, but existence for the sake of Reason"[28] and that "I do not exist for Nature, but Nature exists for me."[29] How then can Reason legislate the *existence* of nature (not, as with Kant, only its laws)? The answer Fichte and Schelling gave was: through

[24] Jakob Böhme, *Apologia*, I, 23, cited by Howard Brinton, *The Mystic Will*, (London: Allen and Unwin, 1931), p. 109.

[25] Böhme, *Von der Menschwerdung Jesu Christi*, Th. II, Cap. 7, Nrs. 2, 8, 14; in *Sämtliche Schriften*, hrsg. Will-Erich Peuckert. (Stuttgart: Fr. Frommann's Verlag, 1957), Bd. IV, pp. 158–159, 160–161, 164.

[26] Fichte, *The Vocation of Man*, ed. Roderick M. Chisholm, (New York: Liberal Arts Press, 1956), p. 76.

[27] *Ibid.*, p. 96.

[28] *Ibid.*, p. 114.

[29] *Ibid.*, p. 153.

productive imagination. Before pursuing this answer, let us turn to the second reason for its emergence.

(2) The second reason is basically like the first, centering in the fact that the Romantic could not rest in an unresolved *Entgegensetzung* between man and nature, spirit and matter, finite and infinite.[30] He required an ontological power to account for their *apparent* duality and an epistemological power to body forth their essential identity. Great ingenuity was called for to show the oneness of these powers, as will be seen by the following: if the "Not-I" is produced by the "I" through imagination, the *necessity* of a purely objective existent is supplanted; but if the Not-I so produced is to be *known,* it must be produced with a certain necessity. In short, *necessity* must be a function of the ego's productive imagination. From (1) and (2) it is clear that we need to inquire into two central areas if we are to understand the central claim of this "type" of imagination: (a) how imagination creates the phenomenal world, thereby achieving self-consciousness for the ego; (b) how the imagination does this with necessity.

A. Imagination
and the Production of the Self's Objects

The point of departure for this view is that activity of the self whereby it achieves self-consciousness. Expressing its activity in relation to objects, the self attains self-consciousness only through a reciprocal relation to them. An object is neither a *Realgrund* nor a *Ding an sich;*[31] it is a *Vorstellung* of myself (and so a Not-I) to myself,[32] through which I am drawn out

[30] Cf. Drechsler, *Fichtes Lehre vom Bild,* p. 69.

[31] Fichte, *Grundlage der gesamten Wissenschaftslehre,* Teil II, Nr. 4; in *J. G. Fichtes Sämtliche Werke,* hrsg. I. H. Fichte, (11 vols.; Berlin: Veit und Comp., 1845–1846), Bd. I, pp. 171–175.

[32] Fichte, *The Vocation of Man,* p. 94. The same note is found in Böhme, who writes: "If the mind did not flow out of itself it would have no sense perception and if it had no sense perception then it would have no knowledge of itself nor of any other thing and could neither work nor act. But the efflux of the mind which is an object of

of myself and so in a sense determined (*bestimmt*) by it.[33]
The productive imagination is the fundamental ground of the
possibility (*theoretische Grundvermögen*) of this reciprocal
relation (*Wechselbestimmung*) between the I and the Not-I.[34]

The self's activity is simultaneously independent and determined. How is this simultaneity possible? The self's activity is
independent only if it is not conditioned, indeed only if everything is conditioned through it. Therefore the ego's independent
activity is necessarily *productive:* everything is its *product.* Yet
the self's activity is limited (*beschränkt*) by the objects to which
it is related. Because this activity is independent it is *productive;*

---

the mind, in which the mind finds itself, causes it to will and desire.
Hence it introduces the senses into a something which is, as it were, a
centrum of selfhood. Here the mind works through the senses and
thereby reveals and contemplates itself." (*Von göttlicher Beschaulichkeit,*
I, 18; trans. Howard Brinton, *The Mystic Will,* p. 116.) Böhme continues:
"Every spirit is able to see something only in its essential figurability,
i.e., only through an essence figurated in the imagination. By the same
essence spirit brings itself under review and establishes the limits of
self-knowledge." (*Von Christi Testamenten,* Teil I, Büchlein I, Cap. I,
Nr. 16; in *Sämtliche Werke,* Vol. VI, pp. 11–12.)

[33] According to Böhme, nothing can become manifest to itself without
contrariety. (See *Von göttlicher Beschaulichkeit,* I, 8.) This is especially
true of the ego or soul which ". . . is a thing which is without ground,
but seeks and makes a ground in itself and has its origin and dwelling
in the original conception in which it first conceives itself in itself."
Böhme quaintly describes this "original conception" as arising from the
self's "going outside itself" into a "before itself" through a "mirror of
itself." (See *Viertzig Fragen von der Seele,* 11, 1; in *Sämtliche Werke,*
Vol. III, pp. 81–83.) Nature, Böhme continues, is created by the imagination as a mirror to the will. That he thought this activity of imagination
to be a reflection, in reduced scale, of divine creation and divine self-
knowledge is suggested by the following. "The origin of all essential
being consists in nothing else than an Ungrounded Imagination (*Imagination des Ungrundes*) which shapes and introduces itself through an
inclination in particular imagination and so is brought to imageability
(*Bildlichkeit*). In this way the Eternal One is brought to self-contempla-
tion." (*Von Christi Testamenten,* Büchlein I, Cap. 1, Nr. 5; in *Sämtliche
Werke,* Vol. VI, pp. 8–9.)

[34] Of the productive imagination as the ground of the relation between the ego and the non-ego Fichte wrote: "Without this remarkable
capacity one could not account for human spirit. Without it, indeed,
one could ground human spirit entirely in a mechanism." *Grundlage der
gesamten Wissenschaftslehre,* Teil II, Nr. 4; in *Sämtliche Werke,* Bd. I,
p. 208.

355

because it is dependent or limited it is *objective*. It must be both at once; therefore it must be an activity such that its products are at the same time its self-restricting objects. We have to do here, of course, with a problem found in several contexts to be crucial in a theory of imagination, viz., the relation of the active aspect of imagination to the passive. It is a question whether the imagination in its activity applies an order already possessed by the self (reason), or whether through its passivity imagination is subject to structures apart from those of its making. In the present "type" this question is addressed head-on.

Now an *object* is a representation (*Vorstellung*) of that which is distinct or distinguished from me, limiting and defining me, and so a Not-I. That is, *qua* object it appears to be "outside" me, strange and alien. But if I reflect on my *activity* alone, in relation to an object, I cannot be aware of it as being outside me; but only of it as determined by me.[35] Therefore consciousness can only be objective when it is non-reflexive; that is, only when one is not conscious of his activity, or of objects as products of his activity. Only through the *unconscious* productivity of the active ego can an object be strange, alien, or *ausser mir*.[36] As Kuno Fischer has written, expounding Fichte's theory of imagination: "This activity of the productive ego is the imagination; and while it is a spontaneous and independent activity, it is made determinate at the unconscious level by and through the Not-I."[37] So far as we represent the world

35 Cf. F. W. J. von Schelling: "Intelligence is productive in a twofold manner, either hidden and unconscious or free and conscious. It is unconsciously productive in the formation of a view of 'reality' [*Weltanschauung*], consciously productive in the building up of the 'ideal' world." *Entwurf eines Systems der Naturphilosophie*, (1799), 1; in *Schellings Werke*, hrsg. Manfred Schröter, (6 vols.; München: C. H. Beck und R. Oldenbourg, 1927–1928), Vol. II, p. 271.

36 Following the line noted in the preceding footnote, Schelling ascribed both an unconscious and a conscious function to the imagination. "The ideal world of art and the real world of objects are products of one and the same activity. The unconscious confluence of conscious and unconscious productivity yields the real world; the conscious confluence yields the aesthetic world." *Ibid.*, p. 349.

37 Kuno Fischer, *Fichtes Leben, Werke und Lehre*, Vol. VI of

to ourselves without thinking about the act of representation (e.g., in sense perception), so far is the world strange, alien, and *von aussen*. The very possibility of a world therefore depends upon the unconscious productivity of imagination. In Fichte there is no equivocation on this point: "It is held here—and indeed it should not be understood otherwise in a system of transcendental philosophy—that all reality is generated through the imagination."[38] Imagination is therefore the ontological ground of the possibility of consciousness. Consciousness is possible only through reflexion upon its own activity; but it can be *conscious* of its own activity only in relation to the *products* of its *unconscious* activity. This is to make the imagination the source of all order and structure in the world, although the imposition of order in representation is an unconscious act.

If the mind only reproduces consciously in intuition what is produces unconsciously in imagination, one might wonder if the whole program as developed above does not have about it an artificial air. If the ego is truly independent, it would seem to have absolute freedom and so be able to intuit itself and everything else with pure immediacy. To this the Romantic idealist rejoins: Were the self fully *conscious* of its absolute freedom it *would* see the manifold world to be its product; and every distinction between I and Not-I, between Ideality and Reality, would fall away. But the ego does not have full consciousness of absolute freedom: The reason the ego does not have *full* consciousness is the condition of its having any self-consciousness of freedom at all, viz., the limiting and conditioning power of the Not-I. Knowledge depends on a necessary relation between the I (subject) and Not-I (object). If the I is to attain self-consciousness of freedom, therefore, it will have to do so in a way that evades *knowledge*. We shall return to this point after examining the necessary character of knowledge.

Geschichte der neureren Philosophie, (Heidelberg: Carl Winter's Universitätsbuchhandlung, 1914), p. 346.

[38] Fichte, *Grundlage der gesamten Wissenschaftslehre; in Sämtliche Werke,* Bd. I, p. 227.

B. Productive Imagination
and "Necessity" in Knowledge

The Romantic idealist, as noted earlier, was out to exchange the necessity of "nature" for the necessity of "spirit." Assuming now that "necessity" has been enclosed by spirit, how is that necessity which goes with universal knowledge to be accounted for?

Knowledge can be universal and necessary, according to Fichte, because the productive imagination gives rise not only to objects but as well to the categories which are universally applicable to them. In a strongly worded statement, referring presumably to Hume or Maimon, Fichte wrote that "one of the greatest thinkers of our age" had rightly perceived an intimate connection between imagination and the category of causality, but that through his failure to clarify this connection he had ended in skepticism.[39] Kant rightly took the next step by showing the regulative character (*Gesetzmässigkeit*) of the categories, i.e., their universal applicability to objects through the schematism of the synthetic imagination. In Fichte's lights, however, Kant left out of view the *origin* of the categories. If they are to be indisputably applicable to objects, on Fichte's view, they must originate *with* objects and so from an identical source. "Epistemology (*Wissenschaftslehre*) must understand the categories to arise at once with the objects and, in order to render objects intelligible, the categories must be seen as founded in the imagination itself."[40] Because "causality" and "substantiality" (indeed, even the forms of intuition, space and time) are created by the imagination, they are necessarily applicable to all its products. In this way Fichte claims to transcend Dogmatism (with its view of causality and substance as purely objective), Skepticism, and the halfway house of Criticism,[41] and thus to offer a basis for universal and necessary knowledge of the world.

[39] *Ibid.*
[40] Fichte, *Grundriss des Eigentümlichen der Wissenschaftslehre*, 3, VII; in *Sämtliche Werke*, Bd. I, p. 387.
[41] *Ibid.*, pp. 388–89.

C. Imagination, the Ultimate Status of the Self, and the Absolute

On the foregoing account it would seem that the Romantic idealist should be satisfied with the achievements of his *Wissenschaftslehre;* for he set out to supplant a mechanistic, merely natural necessity, having no antecedent relation to the ego, with a necessity produced by the ego itself. But the goal of that doctrine was to assure the ultimate status of the self in its freedom, its status as a *Ding-an-sich.* It needs to be seen now why this goal failed of achievement in the Romantic *Wissenschaftslehren* as such. The "Spirit," Fichte's dialogical partner in *The Vocation of Man,* says to him at the conclusion of their examination of *knowledge:* "Now, when you have seen that all things exist only in and through yourself, you will doubtless no longer fear that which you now recognize as your own creation."[42] Suddenly aware of the corner into which he has been argued, Fichte exclaims:

You have abolished necessity by annihilating all existence . . . by all that you have hitherto said, there is nothing, absolutely nothing but presentations—modes of consciousness, *and of consciousness only.* But a presentation is to me only the picture [image], the shadow, of a reality; in itself it cannot satisfy me and has not the smallest worth. I might be content that this material world beyond me should vanish into a mere picture [image], or be dissolved into a shadow; I am not dependent on it. But according to your previous reasoning, *I myself disappear no less than it;* I myself am transformed into a mere presentation, without meaning and without purpose.[43]

Fichte *believes* that as an "I" he is not simply a mode of consciousness, but also a *will.* His theory of knowledge, however, does not recognize this, and on its basis alone cannot make room for it.

Fichte remarks that, strictly speaking, he cannot say, "I will, perceive, feel," but only, *"The thought appears that I will,*

[42] Fichte, *The Vocation of Man,* p. 76.
[43] *Ibid.,* emphasis mine.

perceive, feel." Summarizing the results of his theory of knowledge, and pointing up the despair to which he is brought by it,
Fichte writes:

I know of no being, not even of my own. There is no being. Images
are: they are the only things which exist, and they know of themselves after the fashion of images; images which float past without
there being anything past which they float; which, by means of like
images, are connected with each other; images without anything
which is imaged in them, without significance and without aim. I
myself am one of these images; nay I am not even this, but merely
a confused image of the images. All reality is transformed into a
strange dream, without a life which is dreamed of, and without a
mind which dreams it; into a dream which is woven together in a
dream of itself. Intuition is a dream; thought—the source of all the
being and all the reality I image, the source of my *own* being, my
own powers, and my own purposes—is the dream of that dream.[44]

If the earlier discussion of the role of productive imagination
in necessary knowledge is recalled, this conclusion may sound
strange. But not if it is borne in mind that the Romantic
philosopher is out to discover the self in its inmost reality and
identity. What has been said about the relation of productive
imagination to knowledge is not rendered invalid by the failure
to find the real self in that relation. But it does mean that the
real self, as an immediate expression of the Absolute Ego, must
be sought in another operation of imagination than that involved
in theoretical knowledge of nature. Let us be clear as to why
theoretical knowledge does not yield the *desideratum* of ultimate
self-knowledge.

The consciousness that the finite "I" attains is always in
relation to *phenomenality,* since by means of theoretical consciousness one cannot get at the fundamental principle of
identity out of which all phenomenality arises. To be sure one
can outline the *presuppositions* of theoretical consciousness
and phenomenality, e.g., the productive imagination, as de-

[44] *Ibid.,* p. 80. "Image" here translates *Bild,* a function of *Bildungskraft*
or *Einbildungskraft.*

veloped above. It is one thing to philosophize about these presuppositions, however, but quite another to know concretely the centers of identity out of which theoretical consciousness (spirit) and phenomenality (nature) arise. Neither knowledge of nature, nor knowledge of the conditions of knowledge of nature, can yield concrete knowledge of the source of all bifurcation. In sum, theoretical knowledge of nature will not afford the self knowledge of its relation to the Absolute Ego.[45]

How then is concrete knowledge of the self as a noumenal *Ding-an-sich* to be had? Two options out of the present type may be sketched, the one from Fichte, the other from Schelling. According to the first, the self knows itself *qua* noumenal through moral action; in the second, through aesthetic creation.

(1) Imagination and moral action. About my relation to other persons two facts are self-evidently true: in my *acts* toward them I am *free,* and at the same time I acknowledge certain constraints to act toward them in certain ways. Free, because my wants, desires, and enjoyments (in short, my *will*) in relation to them are not antecedently fixed. Constrained, because in my acts toward them I cannot regard them as simply "presentations," but rather must regard them as having values of their own.[46] The combination of freedom and obligation, and the immediate experience of their unity in relation to other things, is man's clue to his relation to the Absolute.

[45] The "Spirit" says to Fichte: "You wanted to *know,* and you took a wrong road. You looked for knowledge where no knowledge can reach . . . I wished to free you from your false knowledge; but by no means to bring you the true." *Ibid.,* p. 81.

Contemporary "Christian existentialism" has an important root in this aspect of Romantic philosophy, which is evident in at least three ways. First, in its insistence that "nature" is not only irrelevant to knowledge of God, but positively misleading. Second, in the claim that theoretical knowledge leads to "despairing" of any cognitive relation to God. Third, in the view that cognitive relation to God is possible only through man's freedom.

[46] Fichte writes: "From this necessity of action proceeds the consciousness of the actual world and not the reverse way; the consciousness of the actual world is derived from the necessity of action. We act not because we know, but we know because we are called upon to act: the practical reason is the root of all reason." *Ibid.,* p. 99.

361

"Without the idea of freedom," Fichte writes, "we are . . . without the faculty for another world."[47]

Finite moral action requires imagination, for through imagination is mediated, both to the self and that in relation to which it acts, the absolute unity of freedom and moral law. This absolute unity is God, or the Absolute Ego. As in the processes of theoretical consciousness the "I" posits the phenomenal world and stamps it with categories through imagination, so in moral action the "I" stamps both its objects and itself, through imagination, with the "image of God" (*Bild Gottes*). The self and its objects stand apart in the natural attitude. If they are to be re-united consciously in a moral act it must be in virtue of that which is simultaneously free (corresponding to the self) and lawful (corresponding to the object), viz., the Absolute. The bifurcation of self and object is not a work of the Absolute, however, but of the self through which the Absolute "others" itself. Re-unification must therefore occur in the self, but in virtue of a power in the self which connects it with the Absolute. This power must be simultaneously free and the source of law; and such a power Fichte thought imagination to be. He advances the provocative notion that imagination, in moral action, is "self-developing freedom."[48] Through imagination the "image of God," i.e., the image of the identity of freedom and moral law, is applied to the relation between the self and its objects. In the finite ego, of course, this image is not altogether clear; but through the operation of imagination in moral action, freedom is developing itself toward its ideal, viz., unity with self-legislated moral law. In consequence, moral imagination in man is the single finite reflection of "absolute self-developing freedom."[49] By virtue of that, imagination is the link between the phenomenal and noumenal orders of being, and so is the most divine of powers.[50]

[47] *Ibid.*, p. 129.
[48] Fichte, *Tatsachen des Bewusstseins*, (1813); in *Nachgelassene Werke*, Bd. I, p. 498.
[49] *Ibid.*
[50] Drechsler writes: "For Fichte the riches of spiritual being and the very experienceability of reality are bound up with the imagination. In

(2) Imagination and aesthetic creation. For a second and alternative answer to the question, how the self achieves concrete coincidence with its noumenal ground, it is necessary to return to what was said earlier about unconscious creation of the world. Following Schelling, it was suggested that nature is a dumb, unconscious representation of God or the Absolute: "The objective world is only the primordial, unconscious poetry of Spirit."[51] In so far as imagination works unconsciously, it yields the external world. And in so far as theoretic consciousness encounters the external world, the familiar contrarieties result: necessity (law) and freedom, truth and the good, the real and the ideal. These contrarieties can be overcome only in a concrete representation of that identical source (Absolute Spirit) out of which they arise, viz., in a work of art, which is to say, a conscious act of imagination.[52] In art nature becomes conscious; indeed, it becomes *intelligent*. At this point one can see how radically this view of imagination differs from the "conformation" type. Plotinus said that nature itself cannot be conscious or *intelligent* because it lacks the power of imagination.[53] According to the "conformation" type, nature is *intelligible* precisely because through imagination it can be intellectualized or conformed to the mind. On the present view, imagination represents the Absolute unconsciously as nature; and consciously it represents both the Absolute and nature as art. In a work of art the imagination welds together, with full self-consciousness, the self, nature, and the Absolute. Artistic

---

these respects, imagination discloses its divine character." *Fichtes Lehre vom Bild*, p. 232.

[51] Schelling, *System des transcendentalen Idealismus,* (1800), 3., D.; in *Werke*, Bd. II, p. 349.

[52] Cf. Schelling: "The unity of the ideal and the real is disclosed in the ideal world by means of art. For art in itself is neither a mere acting nor a mere knowing. On the one hand it is an act utterly permeated by knowledge, but on the other it is knowledge that has become act. That is, art is simultaneously act and knowledge." *Philosophie der Kunst,* (1802), I, 14; in *Werke*, Bd. III, pp. 300–401.

[53] *Enneads,* IV, Tract. 4, 13. On the doctrine of imagination, one could say that the major difference between classical idealism and modern idealism is that the former held imagination to be essential to the *intelligibility* of structure, whereas the latter thought it necessary to the *intelligence* or self-consciousness of structure.

363

imagination grasps the infinite in the finite,[54] the identity of truth and beauty,[55] and the unity of freedom and law.[56] Aesthetic imagination of course is not simply an empirical faculty for the combination of images, since it must unite the unconscious and conscious activities of *Geist,* and body forth this unity in a work of art. Schelling, the most ardent champion of this view, goes the full length of identifying artistic imagination with divine revelation itself. He writes:

Through art the divine creation is objectively displayed, for the one rests on the same unification of infinite ideality with reality as that on which the other reposes. The excellent German word *Einbildungskraft* signifies essentially the power of "forming into one"; and that, in fact, is what all creativity consists of. Essential creativity is that power whereby something ideal is at the same time real, whereby soul is also body; it is the power of individuation . . . Through his absolute Identity God is the source of all "forming into one" (*Ineinsbildung*) of the ideal and the real . . . Thus God himself is the immediate cause and ultimate enabler of all art, as he is the source of all beauty.[57]

Unlike the first option above, in which moral action as a human possibility was thought to unite man and God, this view holds that God himself continues his creation through man's artistic imagination; and by that means reunites a bifurcated world.

III. CREATIVITY AND THE NIHILIZING (NEGATIVE) IMAGINATION

Finally, a third view of the creative imagination may be examined very briefly. In many ways, the third view is the second view (just concluded) stood on its head. The two views

[54] Schelling, *Philosophie der Kunst,* III, 70–72; in *Werke, Bd. III,* pp. 500–501.

[55] *Ibid.,* I, 20; in *Werke,* pp. 404–405.

[56] *Ibid.,* I, 19; in *Werke,* p. 404.

[57] *Ibid.,* I, 22-23; in *Werke,* p. 406.

have the same end, the achievement of freedom through imagination. While the second view pursued freedom through ontologically productive imagination, however, the second view holds the goal of freedom to be attainable only through an act of imagination that is ontologically negational. The negative or nihilizing character of imagination may be developed from the thought of Jean-Paul Sartre.

According to Sartre, two types of consciousness should be distinguished. (1) The first is consciousness in general (the *"cogito"* consciousness), which posits the totality of existents; or more accurately, which constitutes the totality of existents in a synthetic "world." (2) Imaginative consciousness, on the other hand, posits the *negation* of existents. That which consciousness in general posits is real, exists, is simply presented to me; it is "given" and so "absurd." What imaginative consciousness posits, as long as it is imagined, is unreal, nonexistent, is in fact *nothingness*. (If I imagine what John is doing in New York, he appears to me as absent. In his *imagined* appearance to me, he is not what he *is*; he is the negation of what he actually is there and of what he would be if he were here.) In imagination "nothing" is given to us; we give it to ourselves, as absent, as nothingness. In short what imagination intends is the *imaginary* (*l'imaginaire*) in something like the popular sense of the word, viz., a nonexistent object, or an object negated.

That is, the imaginative act of consciousness is a negative or nihlizing act; it fends off reality, getting beyond its reach into a realm of freedom.[58] Sartre writes:

To posit an image is to construct an object on the fringe of the whole of reality, which means therefore to hold the real at a distance, to free oneself from it, in a word, to deny it. Or, in other words, to deny that an object belongs to the real is to deny the real

[58] Sartre, *The Psychology of Imagination,* (New York: Philosophical Library, 1948), p. 262. See also *L'Imagination,* (Paris: Presses Universitaires de France, 1950), in which Sartre essays a phenomenological investigation of the nature of imagination. (*L'Imagination* should be distinguished from *L'Imaginaire,* [Paris: Gallimard, 1940]. *The Psychology of Imagination* is an English translation of the latter.)

in positing the object; the two negations are complementary, the former being the condition of the latter. We know, besides, that the totality of the real, so long as it is grasped by consciousness as a synthetic situation for that consciousness, is the world. There is then a two-fold requisite if consciousness is to image: it must be able to posit the world in its synthetic totality, and, it must be able to posit the imagined object as being out of reach of this synthetic totality, that is, posit the world as a nothingness in relation to the image.[59]

The imaginary object will therefore have a two-fold nothingness: nothingness of itself in relation to the world, nothingness of the world in relation to itself; which is to say that it must be constituted on the foundation of the world it denies, yet it truly denies it.[60]

Although "irrational" or "absurd" in its mere givenness, an existent reality tends to "surpass" itself. It carries within itself the possibility of its own negation. This is similar to the Plotinian notion that all finite existents tend to slip into non-being, as it is similar to Hegel's idea of the intrinsic negativity of existents. But it is unlike Hegel's view in that negativity is not *aufgehoben* in being-itself, but rather is objectivized in sheer nothingness or non-being. The actualization of the possibility of negativity in all existents requires the intentionality of imaginative consciousness.

An image is not simply the world-negated; ". . . it is always the world negated from a certain point of view, namely, the one that permits the positing of the absence or the non-existence of the object presented 'as an image.' "[61] This may be taken to mean at least two things. (1) Although man expresses his freedom through imagination, imagination is not absolutely free, or more precisely, absolutely arbitrary. Arbitrarily to imagine a centaur will not of itself cause the appearance of the centaur as an unreal object. "For the centaur to emerge as unreal the world must be grasped as a world-where-the-centaur-is-not, and this can only happen if consciousness is led by different motiva-

[59] Sartre, *The Psychology of Imagination*, p. 266.
[60] *Ibid.*, p. 270.
[61] *Ibid.*, p. 268.

tions to grasp the world as being exactly the sort in which the centaur has no place."[62] Sartre puts the point abstractly by saying that "nothingness can present itself only as an infra-structure of something"[63]; which is to say that imaginative consciousness is tied to the reality that it negates. (2) Imaginative negation is governed not only by the reality negated, but also by *my* consciousness in its freedom: *I* present the unreal object to myself. There is then no general or cosmic or absolute imagination on the present view. While imagination is an intentional structure of consciousness as such, the exercise of imagination, and therefore the content of its own negation, are functions of unique selfhood in its process of defining itself.

From the foregoing it may be concluded that imagination is neither a merely empirical nor yet a superadded power of consciousness; it is the whole of consciousness as it realizes its freedom. The self attains freedom, and so integral authenticity, only as it withdraws from irrationally given existents. By imagination the unreal (the imaginary) is created outside the world by a consciousness which stays in the world. By negating real existents, imagination frees consciousness of absurd restraints which existents exercise upon each other; and in this way "meaning" emerges for the self which would otherwise be enmeshed in an absurd existence.[64]

The self discovers its being-in-freedom only in the non-being of imagination. *Nihilization* of existents through imagination *evokes* the self in its freedom to construct patterns of meaning upon the negated foundations of the world. The authenticity of selfhood is therefore bound up with the *imaginary,* and the concrete forms it assumes. Chief among these is art, for art above all is concerned with the unreal. Of course as a physical object the work of art is "real"; but *qua* work of art it is the

[62] Sartre continues: "Likewise, if my friend Peter is to be given me as absent I must be led to grasp the world as that sort of a whole in which Peter cannot *actually exist and be present to me.* (He can actually be present for others—in Berlin for instance.)" *Ibid.*

[63] *Ibid.*, p. 271.

[64] "The imaginary thus represents at each moment the implicit meaning of the real. The imaginative act itself consists in positing the imaginary for itself, that is, in making that meaning explicit . . ." *Ibid.*, p. 272.

analogate of an image in the artist's consciousness, and so points the beholder into nothingness, where beholder and artist commune as free spirits.[65]

[65] This view is therefore similar to the one above in which the self's destiny was associated with aesthetic creation. But it is altogether unlike the view which connects imagination with moral activity. According to Sartre, imagination is not involved in ethics because the latter has to do with the real.

IV. Pre-Modern Cognates of "Revelation," "Method," and "Theology"

Outline

I. INTRODUCTION

Reflection . . . on a doctrine will be complete only if it succeeds in linking up with the doctrine's history and the extraneous explanations of it, and in putting back the causes and meaning of the doctrine in an existential structure. There is . . . a "genesis of

369

meaning" (*Sinngenesis*), which alone, in the last resort, teaches us what the doctrine "means."[1]

The understanding of revelation as fundament in the preceding chapters (especially Ch. III) was articulated by and large in high abstraction from the history of Christian theology. But it was not *forged* in high abstraction. Indeed the understanding of revelation as fundament and the analysis of the hermeneutical spiral disallow the distinction in principle between systematic and historical theology. The root thesis of this book could be developed in either a systematic-abstract or a systematic-historical frame: could, that is, if either frame were shown to bend into and spiral through the other.

It has not been possible to undertake here a substantive dismantling/recapitulation of the tradition as the means of opening up the problematic or carrying the argument. So large a task would be the work of many volumes. But it is well to recognize that patience with formality may be granny-knotted if the lines of articulation, tracked largely in a systematic-abstract framework, cannot be seen to lead into and out of the material tradition. To trace a few of these lines on a very modest scale is the aim of the remaining pages. Within the space available that aim can be prosecuted only by soundings taken at selected points along the chronological line. We precisely do *not* mean to bemuse ourselves with an historical postlude following on systematic reflexion, but rather to see (again, on a modest scale) from the systematic-historical arc the spiraling genesis of theological meaning. Without *historical* interlacing of regions, theology has neither subject matter nor a place of recommencement in language; without *systematics,* theology has no reflexive way between specific and general reticulations of experience, as it has no way between past and present occasions.

Without some such distinction as that drawn earlier (Ch. III) between revelation as fundament and revelation as category, a very considerable segment of Christian tradition would be simply unintelligible. Revelation as a category has had stellar prominence in theology only since the Enlightenment; perhaps

[1] Merleau-Ponty, *Phenomenology of Perception,* trans. Colin Smith, (London: Routledge & Kegan Paul, 1962), p. xix.

370

one should say, since the dissolution of Protestant Orthodoxy (Protestant Scholasticism). John McIntyre rightly notes that revelation is a category the church got along without for centuries, indeed for the whole pre-modern period.[2] Neither the Christian nor the Hebraic community ever got along, however, without its hermeneutical cognates: without cognate categories through which revelation as fundament came to expression. Just those historical cognates could not be held out of view, without loss of the immanent coign of vantage, even if they were sighted only in an abstract frame, in the start that was made on a formal delineation of revelation as fundament in preceding pages. That delineation should now allow a reading on these cognates at closer range.

To understand why and how the intention of revelation came to expression in various categories in advance of the emergence of the category of revelation itself is to understand at least indirectly the cargo of problems borne by that category as we have inherited it today. Theology is a discipline whose categories cannot be understood without recourse to their genesis and deployment in history. The frontier of a theological category therefore cannot be advanced without mounting simultaneously a substantial rearguard action. Indeed, as Merleau-Ponty says in the passage cited in the beginning as the motto of this section, the participation of genesis is the secret of meaning. If we track revelatory intention to genesis through pre-modern cognates, that is undertaken with a view to understanding how the category of revelation may intersect the genesis of revelatory meaning today.

We wish to see on a limited scale how revelation as fundament came to expression in the pre-modern period through categories other than that of revelation. On an equally limited scale we want to see how pre-modern understandings of *method* and *theology,* in their interaction, served to shape the categories through which revelation as fundament was diversified in categorial expression. The latter desideratum will require amplification when we come to it.

[2] John McIntyre, *The Christian Doctrine of History,* (Grand Rapids: Eerdmans, 1957), pp. 2-4.

371

II. THE PRE-MODERN DEVELOPMENT OF THE PROBLEMATIC IN REVELATION THROUGH CATEGORIES OTHER THAN "REVELATION"

A. Prophetic and Apocalyptic Motifs in the Pre-Christian Hebrew Community: Direct and Indirect Intercourse between God and Man

Martin Kähler, among others, pointed out that the problematic of revelation for Christian theology began in the Bible itself and that its temporal origin antedated the Christian community.[3] This origin, so fateful for subsequent Christian theology, rooted generally in the interplay between prophetic and apocalyptic strands in pre-Christian Jewish piety, and specifically in the transition from oral to written discourse. In all strands God had been understood as opening up intercourse with man, although in different strands by different means. This intercourse was what we should now call revelation. By the prophets God was thought to initiate intercourse with man directly. However much the prophet may have been interpreting some event, sign, or theophany, he was taken to be speaking God's address to man directly. So long as a community of prophets thrived, with its mutually correcting and enhancing power, such a notion of divine-human direct intercourse carried the day. But it was the fortune of Jewish history for prophecy to be silenced, and all that remained was a memory kept vivid in popular lore by oral transmission. We would say that the quality of *immediacy* atrophied with the silencing of prophecy.

As Josephus notes, the silencing of prophetic immediacy was accompanied by the transformation of the prophetic residue into a body of tradition, by the institutionalization of prophetic oracles. In the immediately pre-Christian period it was above all apocalypticism that sought, under the conviction that the old continuous intercourse was finished for the current aeon, to

---

[3] Martin Kähler, "Offenbarung," *Realenzyklopädie für Theologie und Kirche,* 3rd. ed., Vol. XIV, (Leipzig: J. C. Hinrichssche Buchhandlung, 1904), pp. 340–47.

commit the remnants of that intercourse to writing. Therewith the notion if not the fact of scriptural "canon" arose (although to be sure the apocalypticists were not the first to put sacred tradition into writing); and concomitantly that indirect, mediate, and discontinuous quality of divine-human intercourse. One could say that for *immediacy* was substituted *wholeness,* and the problem of the relation between them was bequeathed to all succeeding theological generations. This wholeness was achieved by a vision that bordered on the visionary, anchored to be sure in retrospection but trained as well upon an extrapolated future. In addition to institutionalizing the prophetic oracles which survived in popular memory, apocalypticism attempted, *sub rosa,* to expand the basis for divine-human intercourse by inventing new "prophetic" discourse, which it then attributed to an ancient worthy. Moreover, the basis was eschatologized. There is to be a coming prophet; the prophetic era will return with immediate intercourse finally established by the last prophet. (Here can be seen, concretely within the tradition, the triadic movement of "founding"!) Since apocalypticism drew upon popular lore for the material committed to writing, it carried a surface intelligibility to the common man. But collocated as canon these writings were thought to possess a meaning accessible only to the *cognoscenti,* which further underscored the indirect character of divine-human intercourse and also attached to the notion of canon the requirement of authoritative interpretation.

B. The Mediacy and Immediacy of the Christ-Event: Apostolicity and the Spirit

We cannot easily appreciate the state of shock that apocalypticism and the nascent Christian community must have inflicted upon each other. To be sure, the Christian community (and indeed, Jesus himself) received "the scriptures" as binding without question. But the primitive Christian community emerged, as Kähler says, with the conviction that immediate intercourse with God had been renewed decisively in the event of Jesus Christ; and consequently with the conviction that reflection upon the pre-Jesus past and extrapolations from that past toward the future could not exhaust the meaning of the divine-human intercourse. "Within the community of the risen Christ all are in the most direct communion with God, as were the prophets."[4] The mediated "founded" was put into crisis by the "founding" before the disciples' eyes, a founding which claimed to gather up the past afresh by means of a new future proleptically lived in a single human life. The Word of God was to be heard in the range of full historical temporality.

Two notions, then, were constitutive of the primitive Christian community. First, in one spectrum of events, one lived interlacing of regions (the life and words of Jesus of Nazareth), intercourse between God and man had been decisively and normatively renewed. Second, the force of that renewal was such that, without giving up its historically mediated character, it was held to be continuous and immediate for each and every communicant. But how could the unity of historical mediacy and immediacy be maintained, and above all discoursed upon? How could the fate of the older prophetic tradition be evaded? How could the historical event of renewal continue to function historically? The claim of that event to full triadic temporality was at stake.

For a time, of course, appeals could be made to apostolicity in explanation of continuity; and indeed apostolicity was an accepted test of canonical teaching. But not even apostolicity could account for the immediacy of intercourse between God and man, however much it might shape the direction of such intercourse. In explanation of this immediacy the apostles themselves, notably Paul, made constant reference to "the Spirit." While the account of God's decisive renewal of intercourse with man in Jesus Christ undoubtedly comes to succeeding generations by the route of apostolic witness, something more is required to seal this witness as the believer's own. Nor is it different with the apostle himself: Paul takes the substance of the gospel "not from any man" but from "revelation" (Gal. 1:12). It is clear that, for Paul, revelation cannot be exhausted by what is handed on and around, just as it is clear that

[4] *Ibid.*, p. 341.

374

revelation cannot be exhausted by free-wheeling ecstasy, however much "in the Spirit." While "the Spirit in me prays," care must be taken that "the intellect lay not fallow" (1 Cor. 14:14). The reference could hardly have been lost on his readers when Paul wrote, "The prophet is worth more than the man of ecstatic speech . . ." (1 Cor. 14:5).

C. *Regula Fidei* and *Canon*

In this context the notions of *regula fidei* and canon emerge as exceptionally subtle ones. In a theologically perceptive study of the New Testament canon, Robert W. Funk has drawn together impressive evidence concerning the extreme reluctance in the primitive Christian community to recapitulate earlier apocalyptic and rabbinic practice, viz., to commit the oral tradition to writing.[5] This reluctance was not owing to an Alexandrian sort of mentality, so powerfully represented by the contemporary novelist Lawrence Durrell: truth written is one half lost, and when read the other half goes as well.[6] It was owing rather, in the first instance, to the *eventful* character of revelation, a character that could hardly escape compromise in written form, at least on an ordinary view of written language. In the second instance, it was owing to the kind of future opened up by the decisive renewal of intercourse between God and man in the life and words of Jesus of Nazareth. Funk puts the matter thus:

In refusing to narrow the tradition to a single, internally coherent interpretation, the church perceived that the Christ-event gives rise to innumerable futures just because it is a historical event and has to be appropriated historically. That is to say, the (theological) meaning of the Christ-event is disclosed only in the faith to which it gives rise. Like the Christ-event, faith too is historical. It follows that the Christ-event can be appropriated faithfully only in relation to particular contexts. A single, monolithic tradition would yield

[5] Funk, *Prolegomena to New Testament Theology,* (unpublished manuscript).

[6] Cf. Durrell, *Balthazar,* (New York: E. P. Dutton & Co., 1961), p. 238.

ahistorical faith and an ahistorical Christ. A historical Christ and historical faith necessarily give rise to a multiplicity of traditions and interpretations.[7]

The *regula* in oral transmission, or the canon in written transmission, must accordingly embrace a spectrum of witnesses at once plural and particular.

Yet, particularity attaches not only to appropriation on the part of the faithful but as well and primarily to the Christ-event itself. If that renewal of revelatory intercourse was indeed decisive for the future of humanity, then any such future would perforce be in unity with it, which is just to say that faith would not be faith except in concinnity with its ground. How shall there be proclamation of this new beginning and catechetical instruction concerning it without some account of what it was? This difficulty obviously became acute as the Christ-event receded into the past and as eye-witnesses passed on. There was no choice but to project a written delimitation of traditions out of the materials of the traditions themselves. Funk puts the matter succinctly when he says that the unity of the ground of the traditions (viz., the Christ-event) provided the outside limits for the canon, while the plurality and particularity of appropriation set its inside limits.

While concinnity with the ground of faith is essential to faith itself, not even the canon is able to bear an absolute concinnity of elements within the tradition. The canon, projected out of faith's horizon, was intended as an *invocation* to faith. Repeated efforts to qualify the invocative character of scripture show, however, that the slow establishment of the canon did not settle the question of revelation. This can be seen in two developments that were roughly coextensive with the firming up of the New Testament canon. (1) Distressed by the pluralism of the burgeoning traditions in the wake of the Christ-event, Marcion sought to restrict the future to which that event gave rise by dropping out of the tradition the history that lay behind it (i.e., by eliminating the "founded"). Marcion stands as a much emulated example to those who would purge the tradition

[7] Funk, *op. cit.*

376

of dross in favor of the pure essence, i.e., in favor of an ahistorical concinnity of faith and the ground of faith. (2) Yet another development has had no fewer emulators in Christian history. We have already seen that the Christian community was marked by the renaissance of immediate intercourse with God through "the gifts of the Spirit." The crystallization of tradition in the canon served as a signal to some that their only recourse, in the enjoyment of such direct intercourse, was to "the full dispensation of the Holy Spirit." Thus the firming of the canon was accompanied by Montanism and other ecstatic movements.[8] And indeed every radical emphasis upon *sola scriptura* in Christian history has been followed by libertarian spiritualism. Can we be surprised that even in our own time in the United States, and not alone among the sects, Neo-Reformation theology has been accompanied by a backlash of "speaking in tongues"?

The very concept "canon" achieved strict reference only slowly; and it never reached a point at which it ceased to be a harbor in which to anchor unresolved ambiguities. Not until the fourth century was canon used in clear reference to the New Testament scriptures, even though the church had long since recognized certain writings to be authoritative for Christian life and thought. That canonical scripture did not embrace the full range of revelation, however, is seen in the fact that by the fourth century "canon" was used as well in reference to ecclesiastical dogma, especially in reference to conciliar derees.[9] Here, reflected in the double use of canon, is a manifestation of the polarity in revelation as seized in the early Christian community. The decisively unique renewal of intercourse between God and man in Jesus of Nazareth is testified to by a body of athoritatively circumscribed written materials: scripture. But it is the force of that spectrum of events, when appro-

[8] With Iraeneus we see a theological *riposte* to ecstatic movement, the first attempt to house revelation in an ordered conceptual frame. See the discussion below concerning the emergence of "theology" in Christian usage.

[9] For the history of the use of the term "canon" see *Theologisches Wörterbuch zum Neuen Testament,* ed. Gerhard Kittel, Vol. III, (Stuttgart: Verlag von W. Kohlhammer, 1957), pp. 600–606.

377

priated as the ground of one's faith, that one be placed presently in direct intercourse with God, which intercourse is no less integral to the "content" of revelation. That such "immediate" intercourse should not attain demonically prescriptive force, as in ecstatic Montanism, the Church assembled the Fathers for canonical "interpretation," for the pronouncement of confessional formulae.

D. Confessional Formulae

When the Fathers assembled for confessional pronouncement, the problem of revelation was never out of view; but it was not *revelation* as a theological concept that was front stage and center. For that matter, neither was *scripture*. Arius was unable to gain credibility for his position when, in the famous letter to Alexander in 321, he claimed his faith to be that "of our ancestors" and his God to be "God of the law and the prophets and the New Testament." Nor were the post-Nicene political Arians, the Homoeans (Ursacius, Valens, Germinius, Eudoxius, and Acacius of Antioch), able to make any telling point against the Athanasians by saying they could accept Jesus as "like the Father [*homoios tō patri*] according to the scriptures." No telling point was scored thereby precisely because what was up for debate at Nicea and Chalcedon was the nature of the Christ-event, to which scripture was circulated as testimony. How was God renewing intercourse with man in Jesus of Nazareth "then," and through that "then" renewing intercourse with man "now"? This question could not fail to expose its constitutent elements: How is Jesus related to God, and how is the Spirit (the Comforter of the present) related both to Jesus and to God? As Gerhard Ebeling has put it, the first theological question about revelation can be addressed only through the "*ontological* interpretation of the event of revelation."[10] What revelation really means depends upon what God really is, and what that world really is in which his intention for humanity comes to manifestation. To be sure, the hermeneutical spiral is never escaped:

[10] Ebeling, *Word and Faith,* trans. James W. Leitch, (Philadelphia: Fortress Press, 1963), pp. 30–41.

378

what God and world really are comes by way of revelation. But the "how" of revelation is utterly formal without its "what," and when the church is fighting for its existence, as in this early period, the two cannot be separated. The "gifts of the Spirit" and the written residue of the Christ-event stand in tolerable unity only on the foundation of the activity of the one God, Father, Son, and Holy Spirit: so the Fathers concluded. Their ontological interpretation of the event of revelation took the form of the doctrine of the Trinity.

E. Faith and Reason

That the Nicene and Chalcedonian Fathers relied almost exclusively in their ontological interpretation of the Christ-event upon the Greek metaphysical categories at hand is a fact that has long since passed into the domain of theological and historical commonplaces. The difficulties posed by the use of ahistorical categories in description of a transhistorical God yet active in history have likewise passed into common theological understanding. Less often noticed but perhaps equally fateful is the fact that these metaphysical categories entailed commensurate epistemological categories. The Fathers could not borrow the one without some traffic with the other. Thus an already complex problematic in revelation as fundament, shaped by tension between apocalypticism and the emergent self-understanding of the Christian community, was rendered even more complicated by increasing contact with another (viz., Hellenistic) understanding of revelation. Indeed, this other understanding is not without representation in the New Testament itself, although it came to theological expression in a systematic fashion only after the Fathers. And, again, it came to expression not through the concept of revelation, but through the concepts of "nature and supernature" and "faith and reason."

It belonged to the work of the Middle and the New Academy to sharpen Plato's distinction between the phenomenal and noumenal realms; and to the work of subsequent Neo-Platonists to establish this distinction along religious lines.[11] The sharpen-

[11] This distinction, in relation to the Platonic scale of mental acts,

379

ing of this distinction carried with it, in late Hellenism, a mounting epistemological skepticism.[12] With respect to both the phenomenal and noumenal realms it was held by the Academicians that only the "probable" or "what-is-like-truth" could be attained. Beyond the probable, rational judgment is simply to be suspended. As for the nature of the "probable," it is that which is pragmatically sufficient for action. In Augustine's summary, the Academic skeptic holds to the probable as "that which can induce us to act while we withhold our assent."[13]

Yet late Hellenistic philosophy was marked by a phrenetic passion for "truth" utterly beyond the anxieties and insecurities of Academic interrogation. Here was a *Grundmotif* for many a subsequent theological fugue: cognitive despair is the mother of faith.[14] Correlated with the darkness, tentativity, and mere probability of human judgment is that fulguration of Light which can be neither anticipated nor appropriated in rational terms. This process of fulgurating illumination, called revelation as distinct from knowledge, is in Plotinus and his heirs a process of reversed cosmogony. As the Fall of essentially impartible soul to partitive existence was irrational, so is its return to the impartible One irrational. So occult is this

---

comes under examination obliquely in my article, "The Imagination in Plato," *loc. cit.*

[12] Just this skepticism furnished Augustine his first subject matter for sustained theological reflection after his conversion. At Cassiciacum and in the works written there (*Contra Academicos, De Beata Vita,* and *De Ordine*) he entered upon a lifelong task of saying what revelatory truth could mean in the face of probing doubt, and therefore by implication, how skepticism could serve as a *preparatio evangelium.* For a perceptive study of the encounter and union of Platonist and "prophetic" elements in Augustine's prosecution of this task, see especially Johannes Hessen, *Augustins Metaphysik der Erkenntnis,* (Berlin: Ferd. Dümmlers Verlag), 1931.

[13] *Contra Academicos,* 2, 11, 26.

[14] In modern times one has only to consider what theologians have been able to make of Hume's closing words in *Concerning Natural Religion:* "A person, seasoned with a just sense of the imperfections of natural reason, will fly to revealed truth with the greatest avidity . . . To be a philosophical Sceptic is, in a man of letters, the first and most essential step towards being a sound, believing Christian . . ." Or the even more famous words of Kant (in the Preface to the 2nd ed. of the *Critique of Pure Reason*): "I have destroyed knowledge in order to make room for faith."

revelatory illumination, it cannot be written or spoken; only the initiate will recognize it ("by Light, Light"), and its only celebration is by secret ritual.

In such brief compass one cannot develop, without hopeless superficiality, the "return to the Irrational" as the hallmark of late Hellenism's concern with revelation.[15] We can only observe that its issue, the view of revelation as a kind of truth utterly transcending the canons of mundane cognitivity by courtesy of its mode of communication and source, came to powerful interplay with Christian theology after (and to some extent during) the Age of the Fathers. This view is not found, to be sure, in pristine Hellenistic form, in medieval Christian theology. But that it partially shaped the categories (notably, "nature and supernature" and "faith and reason") through which the problematic in revelation came to expression in the millennium after the Fathers can hardly be doubted. Perhaps this is to be understood best through a more recent parallel: the way in which a modern Age of Reason (the Enlightenment) was succeeded by an ambiguous irrationalism in Kierkegaard, Schopenhauer, Nietzsche, and their theological heirs. No contemporary student can be unmindful of the reconstitution of the problematic in revelation that has occurred in the wake of this tide. *Mutatis mutandis,* the medieval problematic was shaped in relation to the ambiguous mixture of rational and irrational elements in the late Greek-Roman heritage as encountered by theologians over the faltering Roman Empire.

F. Nature and Supernature

It is equally impossible to develop in brief compass the subtle contours of meaning in the categories of nature and supernature as they express the problematic in revelation for such diverse theologians as the Victorine mystics (Hugo and Richard), Bonaventura, Anselm, and Aquinas. Yet all were moved by a passion to delimit a natural and a supernatural intention-

[15] The best work in English known to me, and a valuable introduction to the literature on the subject, is E. R. Dodd, *The Greeks and the Irrational,* (Boston: Beacon Press, 1957).

ality in the created order and to establish for each a proper cognitivity. The notion of two integral orders, each with its proper "knowledge," was fraught with significance far beyond technical theology: for ethics, church life, political organization, and individual piety. (Not even the Reformation, as witnesses the Lutheran doctrine of Two Kingdoms, was able to free itself completely from this form of the problematic.) There is a realm over which reason presides and a realm over which faith presides; and the probabilities bordering on certainty in the one are qualitatively different from the absolute certainties of the other. This view attains modern expression, although through secular alliances quite different from those of medieval theology, in John Locke:

Reason therefore here, as contradistinguished to faith, I take to be the discovery of the certainty or probability of such propositions or truths, which the mind arrives at by deductions made from such ideas which it has got by the use of its natural faculties, viz. by sensation or reflection. Faith, on the other side, is the assent to any proposition, not thus made out of the deductions of reason, but upon the credit of the proposer, as coming from God in some extraordinary way of communication. This way of discovering truths to men we call revelation.[16]

To be sure, this quotation has the disadvantage in this context of perpetuating an egregious historiographical error in much Protestant scholarship, viz., that of interpreting medieval theological categories through their surrogates in Enlightenment Deism. But it shows the "staying power" of that form of the revelation problematic that emerged from the early encounter of theology with late Hellenistic philosophy, i.e., the use of a rationally non-noetic gnosis to explicate the meaning of revelation. And the disadvantage of the Locke reference is offset to some extent by the advantage afforded by the mention of "some extraordinary way of communication" as characterizing revelation. Just this "extraordinary way" characterizes the immediately post-Reformation problematic of revelation.

[16] *An Essay Concerning Human Understanding,* (London: William Tegg & Co., 1849), p. 526 (Book IV, Ch. 18, par. 2.)

We must look now in an even more curtailed fashion to the immediate background out of which the explicit category of revelation arose, the Reformation and Protestant Orthodoxy.

G. Word of God, Sola Scriptura, and Verbum Dei Scriptum

From the presentation thus far it will appear that the Reformers were without precedent in their effort to bring the problematic in revelation to expression exhaustively and without remainder through the notion of *sola scriptura*. Perhaps this statement will be found less contentious if it is qualified to say that the fundamental notion is that of *Word of God* as indissolubly linked with sacred scripture alone. Such a qualification has the merit of rendering post-Reformation polemics more intelligible. At all events, the Reformers declare in principle against a plurality of revelatory modes, and specifically against a duality of testifying scripture and interpreting tradition.

While subsequent Protestant theology has returned again and again to the Reformers' fresh apprehension of revelation as fundament, their transposition of this apprehension into theological key was largely schematic and programmatic. The transposition was marked by a surface although nonetheless serious breach with the scholastic past, while it maintained an unsteady and subsurface continuity with the hermeneutical pluralism of the past.

How to grant that revelation is multi-dimensional (that it involves, *mutatis mutandis,* the sorts of things detailed in Chapter III under "Revelation as Fundament") and yet is one? The Reformers replied by putting scripture to self-interpretation. "Scripture interprets itself": many concerns come into the understanding of revelation, but none requires recourse to a standpoint outside scripture. It was the "extraordinary way of communication," referred to above, that secured to scripture in Protestant Orthodoxy the exclusive rights to revelation. While the original Reformers had drawn an (at least) analytical distinction between the Word of God and scripture, by the end

383

of the sixteenth century the two were largely conflated; *verbum Dei* could only mean *verbum Dei scriptum*. Revelation came to characterize first and foremost the manner of scripture's having come into written form, viz., the verbal inspiration and dictation of scripture. Accordingly Cocceius wrote that the authors of scripture were "assistants and amanuenses, who wrote exactly as they spoke, not by their own will but driven by the Holy Spirit." In what they wrote ". . . it was given them to be faithful . . . whence it follows that they never deviated from the thing to be written by infirmity of memory or of *logismos* nor by lack of skill or care in the use of words. So that every word, as being contained in letters which were sacred as signs, should be accepted and held as the word of the Holy Spirit, useful and most wisely compounded to meet every exigency of edification without the slightest danger."[17]

It was but a short step to bring "doctrine" into the conflation of revelation and scripture. Holy scripture was viewed as the principle of the whole of theology, as the one norm of doctrine and the infallible arbiter of all doctrinal disputes. The vocabulary of scripture, or rigorous inferences from scripture, constitute the substance of dogma. Whatever in dogma cannot be traced directly to scripture is error; and anything else, even if it does not contradict scripture, is indifferent for the soul's salvation.[18] Here no differentiation was allowed in the cognitive scale of revelation; no distinction was permitted

[17] Johannes Cocceius, *Summa Theologiae ex Scriptura repetita,* (Amsterdam, 1665), IV, 39–41; quoted in Heinrich Heppe, *Reformed Dogmatics,* trans. G. T. Thomson, (London: George Allen and Unwin, 1950), pp. 17–18. (Hereafter cited as Heppe.)

[18] Thus the Leiden Synopsis (iii, 18-19): "This Scripture alone is the *principle* from which and the *substance* from which all saving truth is to be deduced, the *canon* and *norm* by which every true and so every false doctrine of things divine must be measured—in a word the *autopistos* and irrefragable *witness* and judge, i.e. its own evidence, by which every controversy raised about divine things should be judged . . . The criterion or norm of judgment is contained in the following axioms; (1) whatever is contained in it or agrees with it either expressly or by valid inference is true dogma; (2) that which disagrees must necessarily be false; (3) while whatever is not contained in it, although it does not directly disagree with it, is not a dogma necessary to salvation." Heppe, p. 21.

between nonreflexive circumspection and doctrinal distance. As in the later idealistic tradition, every scriptural "feeling" was a "nascent idea" to be made explicit and authoritatively binding upon reason.

The Orthodox theologians did not leave the matter there, nor was their identification of revelation, scripture, and dogma as crude as it might appear on first glance. Only one aspect of their ingenuity in explication of *verbum Dei scriptum* can come into the picture here, and that precisely because of the way in which this explication came under attack, and indeed exact contraversion, with the rise of critical historical scholarship. I refer to the much elaborated "attributes of scripture" (*affectiones scripturae*). The number of such attributes was itself a matter of dispute; we shall single out those three (and they are the major ones in all lists) most vulnerable to subsequent critical-historical attack.

Scripture was said to be possessed of (1) *authority*. Calvin had maintained that the authority of scripture "is sealed upon our hearts through the Spirit" and that it rests finally upon the ". . . fact that God in person speaks in it" (*Institutes*, 1, 7, 4). While the authorizing ("sealing") activity of the Holy Spirit was continually emphasized in Orthodoxy, the greater emphasis fell upon the absolute authority of scripture which it possessed in virtue of initial dictation by the Holy Spirit. In the final analysis the authority of scripture was not seen to depend, even *quoad nos,* upon the acknowledgment of the church or even the individual. Yet even this absolutely objective authority admitted an internal distinction that was to prove fateful for the *sola scriptura* principle in nineteenth-century criticism.

Most of the Orthodox dogmaticians, but notably Voetius and Turrettinus, distinguished between the "authenticity of history" (*authentia historiae*) and the "authenticity of norm" (*authentia normalis*) within the authority of scripture. The whole of scripture was held to have the exact authenticity of veridical historical narrative. Not only is the truth of history seized, but truth is as well dispersed throughout the narrative histories of scripture. Yet, this truth is not dispersed in equal degree, so it cannot be said that the whole of scripture possesses

385

the authenticity of norm. While the "words, deeds, and plans" of everyone were reported with strict historical accuracy, there were in the narratives some persons whose words, deeds, and plans are without dogmatic significance, i.e., have not the authenticity of normativity. Thus Turrettinus wrote, "Not everything in scripture has *authentia normae,* as those recorded to have been said by the godless or a devil. Yet everything has *authentia historiae.*"[19] It hardly needs to be pointed out that this last claim fell forever with the rise of critical historical scholarship, and that with this fall the question of the authority of scripture came into a new stage of crisis. And in view of this it is the more ironical that contemporary Biblical scholars are able to say that the authenticity of scripture is the authenticity of *history!* Owing to radically different intentions for the word "history" (we could say, a different hermeneutical use of the word), the identical phrase "authenticity of history" means something for the twentieth-century theologian that contraverts what it meant for the seventeenth-century theologian. Between these uses was interpolated what has to come under notice very shortly, the rise of methodological self-consciousness.

Scripture was said to be possessed of (2) *perfection.* The *perfectio* of scripture was, however, "essential" and not necessarily "integral." Essential perfection pertained to that truth tailored to human need, whereas integral perfection pertained to that plenary preservation whereby no canonical book had been lost and whereby no essential part of such a book had gone astray. The latter perfection can be accounted indifferent if the former is secure; and it is secured precisely by its exact correlation with human need. This can be summarized in the following way. The perfection of scripture is essential, but not absolute, because it is correlated with a need that is essential, but not absolute. It is correlated with a *necessitas ex hypothesi dispositionis.* Were man otherwise disposed than he is, God might well have maintained His truth without the medium of

[19] Franciscus Turrettinus, *Institutio Theologiae elencticae,* Editio nova (Utrecht and Amsterdam, 1701), II, iv, 2; Heppe, pp. 27–28. Cf. also Gisbertus Voetius, *Selectarum Disputationum theologicarum,* Pars. I–V, (Utrecht, 1648–1669), I, pp. 30–31; Heppe, pp. 26–27.

scripture, e.g., in *verbum agraphon*. But given the idolatrous inventiveness of man and church, there can be no perfection attaching to God's Word but that of the *verbum eggraphon*, the written Scripture. Given human disposition, the written Word pertains to the *esse*, not merely the *bene esse*, of the church. So long as this disposition remains fixed there is no need of appeal to an oral tradition or "such mawkishness as the enthusiasts hawk."

We have only to point out the problem of the human "order" that underlies this view of the perfection of scripture. It has belonged to much modern anthropological reflection to call in question the fixity of human disposition, to say nothing of the fixity of language in respect of human being and its dispositions. In the wake of probing the historical character of human dispositions, the old correlation of human need and scriptural perfection has broken down. In question anew is the sort of perfection scripture "essentially" has.

Finally, scripture was said to be possessed of (3) *perspicuity*. This attribute went naturally with the preceding two, but added to them by showing what was meant by the slogan "scripture interprets itself." The essential clarity of scripture is such that, read according to the *regula fidei et caritatis*, it conduces unambiguously to salvation. There are to be sure obscure passages in scripture; but they are illumined by unambiguously perspicuous ones or by the *analogia fidei* based on them. In this context it is clear that the requisite "rule of faith and love" is no extra-scriptural deposit of oral/ecclesiastical tradition, but rather is, minimally, that disposition of spirit whereby man is genuinely desirous of salvation. If that is minimal faith, then *analogia fidei* is mature faith; i.e., is faith dominated by the content of unambiguously clear scripture.

Of course, Orthodox dogmaticians recognized that scripture requires exposition in order that its perspicuity should come into view. Such exposition involves two things, according to Polanus.[20] There must be (1) "an account of the true sense of Scripture" and (2) "it must be made suitable for use (application)." Concerning the former, "all dogmaticians most specifi-

[20] Amandus Polanus, *Syntagma Theologiae Christianae*, (Hanover, 1624), I, p. 45; Heppe, p. 37.

cally declare against a scripture exegesis in principle manifold."[21] The hermeneutical pluralism of previous ages is ostensibly laid aside; specifically, the allegorical, tropological, and anagogical senses are rejected in the determination of the *true* sense of scripture. The only *true* sense is the *literal* sense. Truth is one; and unity can have only a single essential form. This form will be neither single nor perspicuous unless it is literal.

That this single form was exceedingly difficult to hew to is indicated by the fact that Polanus and Turrettinus, among others, distinguished two sorts of "literal sense."[22] There is the *sensus literalis simplex,* in which there is a literal one-to-one correspondence between passage and meaning. There is on the other hand, in connection with obscure passages, a *sensus literalis compositus,* in which the meaning is "figurative," i.e., in which the truth is set forth under a "type." If we add to this distinction the further observation that on (2) above (the exposition of scripture with a view to use or application) Orthodox dogmaticians permitted the use of an allegorical hermeneutic, we see the force of an earlier observation, viz., that the breach with hermeneutical pluralism was more programmatic and schematic than actual.

Perhaps enough has been said to permit us to draw together some threads in support of the claim that it was the encounter of the residue of Orthodoxy's defense of the *sola scriptura* principle with modern critical-historical consciousness that accounts for the emergence of "revelation" as a theological concept in its own right. (A second and equally weighty factor, the rise of methodological self-consciousness, will be taken up shortly.) At most if not all of the decisive points, critical historical scholarship contraverted Orthodoxy's *sola scriptura* principle. The old *literal* sense could only mean: the *historical* sense. And the historical sense could be determined, not by the old *analogia fidei,* but rather only in analogy with what goes on before the researcher's eyes in the present.[23] Thus the

21 *Ibid.*
22 Cf. Turrettinus, *op. cit.,* II, xix, 2; Heppe, p. 38.
23 This note was struck forcefully by the nineteenth-century historian, F. C. Baur. "Where else can he [the historian] obtain the definite con-

machinery for experiencing contemporary reality becomes the analogue from which the sense of any historical analogate is to be determined. This could not fail to call in question the authority, perfection, and perspicuity of scripture as the single framework of revelation.

Another way of stating the point is that "revelation" became a distinct category at the same time that the Bible became a distinct problem in its significance for dogmatics (and, incidentally, it was the latter problem that gave rise to the new discipline, "biblical theology").[24] In the old Orthodox view, the dogmatician put scripture to self-interpretation, a task he could enter upon because of his supreme confidence in scripture's incorrigible *unity*. Under critical-historical hammering the theological unity of the Bible fell apart: decisive differences were found as between the Old and New Testaments. Not only that: the unity of the Old and New Testaments respectively became problematical. Not even overarching doctrines could be called upon to collocate traditions so divergent. This pluralism had the effect of calling in question the meaning of "canon" anew, especially when there was thrown into the bargain the fact that critics found it not only valuable but necessary to call upon extra-canonical ancient literature in order to understand the historical sense of scripture. This had the effect of shaking the normativity of canonical scripture, as it had the result of calling in question the identification of scripture, or valid inferences therefrom, with revealed dogma. In short, it became clear that to settle the sense of scripture by the only means at hand, viz., by critical-historical method, would not be, *eo ipso,* to settle the sense of revelation.

---

ception of the object whose historical movement is the problem with which he ought to concern himself, other than from the consciousness of the present? The historian can move back into the past only from the present." *Vorlesungen über die christliche Dogmengeschichte,* ed. F. F. Baur, Vol. I/1: *Das Dogma der alten Kirche von der apostolischen Zeit bis zur Synode in Nicäa,* (Leipzig, 1865), p. 12. Quoted and discussed by Peter C. Hodgson, *The Formation of Historical Theology: A Study of Ferdinand Christian Baur,* (New York: Harper & Row, 1966), pp. 90ff.

[24] This point is developed obliquely in Ebeling, *Word and Faith,* pp. 79-97.

III. PRE-MODERN COGNATES OF "METHOD" AND "THEOLOGY": MÉTHODOS AND APORÍA IN GREEK AND EARLY CHRISTIAN "THEOLOGY"

In order to understand in depth how "revelation" emerged as a category in its own right in modern theology, i.e., as a category irreducible to one of the categories considered in the preceding section of this chapter, it would be necessary to enter upon three large projects of historical inquiry that are well beyond the purview of the present book. (1) The fundamental task would be an understanding of the preoccupation with *methodology* in modern consciousness, a preoccupation that sprouted in the Renaissance, sprang up adolescently in the Enlightenment, and ripened in the nineteenth and twentieth centuries. (2) A second project would be required to show how modern methodological revolutions have touched those categories which have borne upon the modern category of revelation, such as reason, nature, substance, creativity, history, etc.[25] (3) Finally, it would be crucial to take up the point on which the preceding section of this chapter ended, viz., the critical-historical method, since it has been through *that* method that the modern preoccupation with method as such has intersected the category of revelation most fatefully.

So large and complex a set of tasks must be laid aside, as must also the project of developing the category of revelation in its major ramifications since the dawn of modernity. Returning instead to roughly the same span of history as that covered earlier, we shall look at that pre-modern period with the question of method explicitly in mind. As earlier we saw how the modern category of revelation was pressed through its pre-modern hermeneutical equivalents, so now we may expect to see in selected segments of the same history how pre-modern cognates of "method" and "theology" served to interact in mutual delimitation of the theological task vis-à-vis revelation. This goes to say that, like the modern category of revelation,

---

[25] Such a project is essayed partially and obliquely in Appendices II and III above.

the categories of "method" and "theology" were preceded by categorial cognates; and that the modern categories gather up a host of problems previously pursued under other labels.

To broach the next phase of historical inquiry, it will be useful to comment initially on the tincturing of modern theological consciousness with method; and then to advance some very general remarks about method in modern consciousness.[26]

Had revelation as fundament been able to bring itself forward indefinitely and exhaustively under an earlier categorial equivalent (say, canonical scripture or charismatic Word), theology would never have become tinctured with modern methodological consciousness. (This fact is on display in those retrograde theological movements which—as in Protestant Fundamentalism—pursue "revelation" exclusively under earlier cognates and therefore are entirely unable to make contact with the modern category of revelation as the promontory of methodological self-consciousness in theology.) For method is concerned above all else with access to the subject matter to be thought, with the comport of mind before its properly delineated intention. If the intention of revelation as fundament is already there in appropriate theological mode, i.e., is present for reflection and reflexion, the question of method cannot arise in a grave form; the question of a logical point of departure is already settled in principle. That contemporary theology in the main is unable to coincide exactly with the tradition is evidence of the insertion of the question of method. *Where theology recognizes that it cannot think the same thing the tradition thought without thinking that thing in a different way, the question of method has inserted itself into the heart of the theological enterprise.*

Turning very generally to method in contemporary consciousness, we note a common discrimination: "applied" and "pure" method. Applied method typically refers to scheme, procedure, device, design, plan, technique, formula, rule. Applied method is not a reflexive enterprise, is not to call attention to itself, but rather is to be trained upon and make accessible an object or subject matter. "Scientific method," the technique of

[26] We have already advanced some systematic remarks about method in theology. See above, Chapter VI.

391

clinicians, is the readiest example of this sort of method that has passed into common modern understanding. Its hallmarks are the delimitation of a class of phenomena to be investigated, the formulation of hypotheses bearing upon these phenomena, and the testing of hypotheses by experiment among the phenomena.

"Pure" method is the pursuit of the *how* question in a much broader context of inquiry. Properly speaking a *methodological* pursuit, it seeks the rationale of method itself. The methodological problem in its broadest sense arises whenever the effort is made to discriminate one subject matter from others and whenever, as a part of that, the way to distinctive knowledge of that subject matter is discoursed upon. Needless to say, the history of methodology in this sense has been coextensive with the history of the discrimination and proliferation of subject matter disciplines. One thinks of Descartes' *Discourse on Method,* Bacon's *New Organ of the Sciences,* and Kant's *Critique of Pure Reason;* and one wonders what the organization of human knowledge would look like today without them (and other methodological works of less extensive influence). It is of course no accident that the great methodological treatises have always appeared within the context and at the end of a period of skepticism and broad cultural crisis. The earlier examination of problematic (Ch. II) has shown why this is so. Skepticism is the natural ally of problematic because the latter loosens a subject matter from its hitherto conventional methodological moorings. But genuine problematic embraces as well the nascent terminus of skepticism since, precisely through its novel interrogation of the subject matter, new lines of meaningful inquiry are made determinate.

Before turning to some pre-modern cognates of methodological consciousness, it may prove helpful to specify that consciousness by distinguishing three broadly conceived approaches to methodology in the period that dates from the Renaissance. If labels must be attached, the first can be called "realistic," the second "teleological," and the third either "idealisitc" or "phenomenological" (since the third embraces two distinct subtypes).

(1) For the first view, most similar of all to pre-Renaissance types, whatever shape thought takes will be prescribed by the

392

object of thought and above all by the object's irreducible nature. Methodology is therefore inseparable from metaphysics. The access thought has to an object is governed by its status in being; no "scheme" can circumvent *what* is irrefragably there and *how* it is irrefrangibly there. To be sure, this type of methodological approach has also been inverted in modernity without essential alteration: for a metaphysic of the object has been substituted a metaphysic of the subject, so that access to objects (subject matter) has been thought to be prescribed by the nature of the subject.

(2) A second type of methodology, the "teleological," has concerned itself with the relation between ends and means. Method is an inventive act of mind whereby objects are arranged with a goal in mind, making it possible to discourse upon that goal with substantive reference. An integral discipline, a delimited cognitive endeavor, would be one having a specified or specifiable goal. The discipline as such would not have its "object" in hand but only in potency. Imbued at every point with the attractive force of a final goal, the discipline would order itself by program to the attainment of that end. Method would be the structure of such a program, a program to be conceived by invention, imagination, and abstraction.[27]

(3) In a third type, methodology is devoted to an exact account of the distinguishing marks of integral kinds of thinking. On this view a discipline is discriminated not on the basis of its object or goal but rather because the thinking it embraces is different from that involved in other disciplines. The view assumes that such differentiated thinking is a fact, but from this one is not to conclude that methodology is a sort of commonsense afterthought, a recognition of how thought was executed after the fact. Thus (a) in transcendental idealism, methodology ferrets out the transcendental conditions of legitimate thinking

[27] A classic form of this view of methodology is found in Jeremy Bentham's *Essay on Logic*. "In so far as in any number whatsoever, any objects whatsoever are put together in a particular manner, by design united to a particular end, the operation termed *methodization* or *arrangement* may be considered as performed . . ." See *Works,* ed. John Bowring, Vol. VII, (Edinburgh, 1843), Chs. I, II, VI, IX, and Appendices A and B. Quotation cited and discussed by Justus Buchler, *The Concept of Method,* (New York: Columbia University Press, 1961), p. 9.

393

(in Kant, scientific, moral, and aesthetic thinking; in Cassirer, mythical, religious, and scientific thinking). Or (b) in phenomenology, methodology seeks to "reduce" thinking to that level of what thinking intends, neither the object nor the subject in a realistic sense, but rather the intersection of self and world, whether in bodily perception or conceptual abstraction. In the latter case (b), thinking is described in terms of its intention. Intention in this usage does not mean invented goal but rather that "consciousness of" through which self and world are inserted into each other.[28]

Turning to theology now, we find a question ready and waiting. To anyone who understands a smattering of Greek, does not the very meaning of the word "theology" settle the question of its object, goal, and characteristic thinking? Does not *theología* mean "speech about God," "thought about God in language," perhaps even "God's speech"? Can there be any doubt that the object of theology is God, at the very least that God is the goal of theological *logos?* The answer is: Yes, such matters may be doubted. And that doubt is by no means an exclusively modern phenomenon, as the history of *méthodos* and *theología* amply discloses.

When Plato used the term "theology" he referred to God, the gods, and divine things indiscriminately. That Christians for centuries did not use the term "theology" extensively (and in the beginning scarcely at all) was owing, among other reasons, to the failure of the term to make its substantive reference clear.

Leaving aside the question of objective reference, the term "theology" was applied by the Greeks to two quite different sorts of activity. On the one hand theology was said to describe an essentially mythical-cultic activity; the "theologian" (*theológos*), viz., the poet, cult official, or hymnodist, was an "announcer of the gods" by means of myth and rite. On the other hand theology was said to describe the activity of the philos-

---

[28] A theological equivalent of each of these three views might be stated as follows. (1) Those statements are theological which have God as their object. (2) Those statements are theological which reflect an "ultimate concern." (3b) Those statements are theological which issue from an "existential" (*existentiell*) posture.

opher as he undertook to assess critically the mythical-cultic announcement of the gods.

Not to be forgotten is the fact that Socrates and his hangers-on were charged with impiety, a charge that arose out of the conflict of these two "theological" activities. Greek philosophical theology in the beginning was not so much an attempt to construct a philosophical doctrine of God as it was an effort to abut critical mentality with the independent mythical-cultic (i.e., archetypal) religious tradition in the interest of an ordered state. Plato discussed theology in the context of political education (*Republic,* II, 379a). To the "mythical" and "political" senses of theology, Stoicism added the "physical," according to which the physical world was interpreted as the bearer of the divine. (It fell to Augustine to popularize this three-fold distinction, although he—fatefully—translated "physical theology" as "natural theology" [*De civ. Dei,* VI, 5–10]). The discrimination of the senses of theology arose from the exigencies of statecraft; and when the *polis* as the horizon of Greek thinking receded, in late Hellenism, the discrimination itself became problematical. Whereas in Plato the discrimination had permitted at once the pledging of fealty to the faith of the fathers and the appropriation of that faith to the requirements of an enlightened citizenry, in late Hellenism an *aporía* appeared within the discrimination itself. We shall consider this *aporía* next.

It is worth noting that *aporía* was used as an antonym for *méthodos. Odós* and *poros* were of course common Greek words meaning roughly the same thing in untechnical usage: the way, path, or passage.[29] In philosophical literature the terms took on a metaphorical meaning, as when Parmenides spoke of the

[29] See the perceptive study of Ottfrid Becker, "Das Bild des Weges und verwandte Vorstellungen im frühgriechischen Denken," *Hermes,* Einzelschriften, Heft 4, 1937. While his interest is *aporía* in Plato's dialogues, Becker finds it necessary to examine both *poros* and *odós.* "*Aporia* is founded on the image of the 'way.' Closely related to it is the concept of 'method' (created by Plato) which, mythologically, refers to the way of ascent toward the light from the depths of the cave . . ." (p. 2) Another comprehensive study of the category of *aporía* in Plato will be found in Victor Goldschmidt, *Les dialogues de Platon: Structure et methode dialectique,* (Paris, 1947).

odós which the goddess pointed out to him. (On the contemporary scene a similar metaphorical usage is found in Heidegger who speaks of truth as a "path through the woods" [*Holzweg*], as a "clearing.") *Méthodos,* first used as a technical term by Plato, was a compound of *metà* and *odós* meaning "following after," or less strictly, "getting on down the way."[30] As a technical term *méthodos* for Plato was a *technē* (an art), but an art of a special sort: the art of dialectic.[31] What "gets one on the way" toward the understanding of the nature of something is the artful exercise of *diaíresis* (division, or analysis) and *sunagogē* (collection, or synthesis).[32] Whatever blocks the path or otherwise inhibits getting on down the way is *aporía.* Wherever method fails to open up the way, there *aporía* obtains.

The course of Greek thought, especially in the late Hellenistic age, exposed an *aporía* with respect to theology. Increasingly the *way* between thought of a certain sort (philosophy) and an object of a certain sort (made present by the rites and myths of the cult) was blocked. Philosophical theology depended for the presentation of its object upon a tradition that was independent of philosophy; mythical theology, while responsible for the announcement of its own object, undertook no responsibility for

---

[30] Among modern writers on method, Coleridge relied most heavily on etymology for establishing the proper meaning of the word. ". . . Otherwise than by abuse," he wrote, method cannot "be applied to a mere dead arrangement." For *méthodos* "literally means a way, a path, a transit," it means movement, forging ahead in a single or unified 'way.' Coleridge's views are advanced in *A Preliminary Treatise on Method,* ed. Alice Snyder as *Coleridge's Treatise on Method* (London, 1934), and in *The Friend* (1818), Section 2, Essays IV–XI entitled "Principles of the Science of Method" (Samuel Taylor Coleridge, *The Friend,* ed. Henry Nelson Coleridge, 4th ed., [3 vols.; London: William Pickering, 1850], Vol. III, pp. 103–206.)

Of course *many* modern writers on method have used the metaphor of "way" casually, e.g., Thomas Hobbes, who spoke of method as "the shortest way." (See his *Elements of Philosophy Concerning Body,* Ch. VI.)

[31] See especially *Phaedrus,* 265d–277c.

[32] An extended investigation of *méthodos,* especially in relation to dialectic, will be found in the excellent study by Richard Robinson, *Plato's Earlier Dialectic,* 2nd. ed., (New York: Oxford University Press, 1953), pp. 62–92.

396

developing the cognitivity of its announcement and so could give no account of the connection of its object with other—especially inner-worldly—objects. To philosophical theology fell the heroic task of attempting to break open the cabal of mythical-cultic confessionalism without at the same time robbing that confessionalism of its independence.

But this attempt was beset by the following dilemma. If philosophical theology sticks to its method of critical dialectic, its object becomes less that of mythical theology and more that of its own elaboration; thus the later Plato and Aristotle take steps toward what could later be formulated as philosophical doctrines of God. If on the other hand philosophical theology accommodates itself steadily to the "religious" object and thus to the cultic archetypes, its own critical independence is sacrificed: in late Hellenism philosophical theology is transmuted into mythical theology. In short the dilemma is this, that philosophical theology *either* maintains itself as a critical enterprise but dissolves the object it set out to understand *or* it maintains the object steadily in view but suspends its own critical character.[33] Here *méthodos* fails: the way between religious intentionality and its appropriate "thinking" is blocked (*aporía*).

And here is an early example of a certain parcel of difficulties that beset the effort to construe method as the relation between an object and thought about it ([1] above), especially when the source of the object and the source of critical reflection are in different traditions. The mention of this example, certain difficulties in Greek *theología,* might be thought diversionary: are we not pursuing the question of methodology in *Christian* rather than in *Greek* theology? Indeed. But we have to make our peace with that half-truth so freely bandied about, that while early Christian testimony (*homologia*) managed its own object, it made its ordered way to and from this object by means of Greek dialectical mentality. This half-truth, as briefly spelled out in the preceding section of this chapter, points to one of the most complex periods in the intellectual history of the west. While some types of early Christian thought did accommodate

[33] Cf. Paul Tillich, *Religionsphilosophie*, in *Gesammelte Werke,* Vol. I: *Frühe Hauptwerke,* (Stuttgart: Evangelischer Verlag, 1959), p. 297.

themselves to the Greek pattern of philosophical theology vs. mythical-cultic theology, they did so at the cost of winding up, *mutatis mutandis,* in an equivalent *aporía.* Thus Christian Gnostic thought dissolved the dialectical moment in favor of mythological-cultic theology, whereas the Christian Apologists came close to dissolving the mythological in favor of philosophical theology.[34]

Noticeable here is the fact that we have spoken of Christian "thought" rather than "theology." Notwithstanding our casual references to theology in the New Testament and the Fathers, the term was rarely used to characterize Christian thought before the fourth and fifth centuries, and then only in a highly restricted usage.[35] Theology and its word-group (*theología, theologein, theológos, theologikos*) are altogether lacking in the New Testament and the Apostolic Fathers. Even where one would expect to find the term in abundance, in the Apologists, it is rare (for the reason cited earlier, viz., distrust of the pagan-religious sense of the term). Not until the time of the Alexandrian Christian thinkers did the term emerge in any other than the pagan-religious sense. More striking still is the fact that "theology" was used even less frequently in Latin Christendom; indeed it gained general currency only at the beginning of the high Middle Ages. From all this one may conclude that it is technically incorrect to say that Christian *theology* arose out of the encounter between the early Christian community and pagan philosophy. Indeed, as Gerhard Ebeling has said, the emergence of Christian theology cannot be set down to certain conditions in the history of religions and philosophy. For although all Mediterranean religions of the time encountered Greek philosophy, Christianity alone produced theology.[36]

[34] Actually the second-century Christian Apologists approximated the Greek pattern much less closely than did the Christian Gnostics. That is, the Apologists (notably Justin Martyr) did not restrict the manifestation of the object of Christian reflection (viz., the Logos) to an independent religious-mythological tradition.

[35] See Ebeling, "Theologie: Begriffgeschichtlich," *Die Religion in Geschichte und Gegenwart,* 3rd. ed., Vol. VI, (Tübingen: J. C. B. Mohr [Paul Siebeck], 1962), pp. 754–770.

[36] *Ibid.,* pp. 759–761.

Of course, there was a phenomenon in the early Church, whether or not "theology" can be applied to it without anachronism, which we have called simply "Christian thought." To approach this phenomenon with methodological questions uppermost in mind is an exceptionally frustrating experience. For modern methodological consciousness, directed by one of the free forms mentioned above or by some other, already assumes that the phenomenon is an ordered whole; or at the very least that, if it is not an ordered whole, there is a methodological reason for that (à la Kierkegaard). Yet these assumptions run aground on many of the manifestations of the phenomenon before it took on the label of "theology."

Here only one example must suffice. Can anything comparable to one of the three types of method, described above, be found at work in the Christian thought of the Nicene era? Certainly not (1) as such, for disagreement about the *object* of Christian thought (i.e., whether a generated or an ungenerated Logos) brought the controversy on. Possibly (2), if carefully hedged, and if applied more to the aftermath of the Nicene formula than to the formulation itself. Thus the thought of Athanasius, in defense of the formula, seems ruled by one overriding goal or intention: to understand the reality of salvation. With this goal no "object" is immediately at hand. Yet as means are applied in the execution of this goal, the object heaves more visibly into view. What is meant by "means" here? One thing it seems not to mean is the importation of a neutral Greek philosophical method applicable to any intention whatsoever. The *logical* intent here must be achieved in a way that is in harmony with the way in which the reality of salvation itself is achieved; the logic of faith must be harmonious with the ground of faith; that which is sought (i.e., *qua* object) must guide the means of seeking. Thus Athanasius says that if we are to understand the reality of salvation we must understand that this salvation is owing to nothing other than God. What of the decisive profferment of salvation in and through Jesus, the Logos in flesh? He must be internally continuous with God himself. How is this to be understood? By turning it into the horizon of understanding, which was not the *method* of Greek philosophy so much as it was the metaphysical residue of that method, viz., the categories of *phusis* and *ousia*.

Here then is really a compound of something like (1) and (2) which cannot be divided. Christian thought for Athanasius is governed by a logical intention which in turn is dominated by a real object whose reality must be exegeted in the execution of the logical intention. Surely impressive is the fact that fourth-century Christian thought saw the emergence for the first time, as a unit of itself, of *theology*. This "theology" had a strict and restricted reference: it pertained only to the doctrine of God, and indeed functioned as a technical term for that doctrine. But Christian thought included much beside the doctrine of God; and the unity of the surplus, if there at all, can hardly be set down to anything that satiates modern methodological appetite.

The span of time from theology as exclusively doctrine of God to theology as the science of the whole of Christian thought is a long one indeed, covering possibly eight centuries or so. The methodological turns in the transition from the one kind of theology to the other are as complex, understandably, as is the interweaving of intellectual, political, and cultural forces in this long period in the history of the west. Two facets of the transition attract brief notice.

The first is the compounded subtlety of the relation between Christian thought, only slowly getting itself in hand as a cognitive enterprise, and philosophy, only with great difficulty maintaining itself as an independent party to the relation. Greek philosophy survived the collapse of classical culture, as Ulysses escaped the Cyclops, by clinging to the bellies of (theological) sheep. Onc need only look to Augustine, Dionysius the Areopagite, and Boethius to see how the theological patronage lavished upon philosophy involved its accommodation to ends other than those strictly its own. This very domestication of philosophy served to diminish the methodological question as the modern theologian is forced to ask it (i.e., out of the context of strictly discriminated disciplines). Yet one need not come all the way to modernity; for surely one of the factors bearing upon the emergence of the new sense of theology in the thirteenth-century was the state of problematic into which the Christian domestication of Greek philosophy came in the ninth through the twelfth. Here was a foretaste of what was to occur with even greater force in the Renaissance. Against the parochial Christian sustenance of Neo-Platonism is set now the independent preservation of Aristotle in the Islamic tradition. The renaissance of Islam and its own renaissance of Greek philosophy brought about, through the fortuities of political contact, a profound and fateful alteration in the meaning of Christian "theology." (And it is worth noting that it was in this context that Jewish thought, under the influence of Arabic Kalām, used "theology" as a technical term for the first time. With Saadya Gaon in the tenth century, the first Jewish "theology" [as a scientific, systematic statement of belief] emerged, and that with the Islamic renaissance of Greek studies directly in view.[37])

The second facet of the transition is evident in the changing relation between the unity and the manifoldness of theology's subject matter or material object. This problem was touched in the treatment of the canon earlier in this section; it has been present in every stage of the development of Christian thought. Although the term "theology" arose in Christendom with God as its single material referent, the unity and manifoldness of this object as expressed in the Trinitarian formula were of such an extraordinary sort that no ordinary discipline could embrace them. The strains are especially visible in Chalcedonian christological reflection. Is this Chalcedonian thought "theological"? Is not its material object *God* the Son? An unqualified *yes* to these questions, by the canons of Nicene "theology," would make Chalcedonian and subsequent christological thought unintelligible. Involved in that thought was an expansion of the unity and the manifoldness of theology's material object (intentionality). For christological thought turns theology toward the horizon of humanity—something to be sure already present in nub in the Nicene formula, but hardly worked out as the subject matter of "theology." Bound up with this expansion of the *manifoldness* of theology's object, and thus the complication of the *unity* of its object, was the need to find the form of

[37] See Saadya Gaon, *Book of Doctrines and Beliefs,* ed. Alexander Altmann, in *Three Jewish Philosophers,* (New York: Meridian Books, 1960). I am indebted to my colleague Professor Lou Silberman for introducing me to this important work.

401

speech (redundantly, the logical *logos*) suitable to just such an object. The controversy over universals in the Middle Ages has its theological intelligibility in the light of just such a quest.

*   *   *

To participate the spiraling action of tradition is to extend one's past by proxy; it is so to distend the past as to disclose novel but determinate potentialities within its own interstices. Theology that means to live in the fullness of time will exercise that proxy by conducting an unremitting "search for the neglected factors in our inherited analyses" (John Herman Randall). One such neglected factor, worried in the arguments at Nicea, Chalcedon, and in the thirteenth-century confrontation of theology with Aristotelianism (to recall but three decisive junctures along the chronological line), has been the subject of hermeneutical retrieve throughout this book: the problem of an ontology of revelation and its appropriate rhetoric.

Index of Names

Adams, James Luther, 310 *n*. 52
Albertus Magnus, 207 *n*. 51
Allemann, Beda, 239 *n*. 90
Althaus, Paul, 30 *n*. 13
Anderson, Bernhard W., 285 *n*. 16
Aquinas, St. Thomas, 89, 111 *n*. 2, 121 *n*. 14, 129 *n*. 35, 166, 166 *n*. 89, 171 *n*. 100, 172 *n*. 102, 311, 319–334 *passim*
Aristotle, 125, 162 *n*. 77, 163, 166, 193–194, 233, 251 *n*. 114, 319–334 *passim*
Athanasius, 400
Auden, W. H., 142 *n*. 56, 188 *n*. 12
Auerbach, Erich, 284
Augustine, St., 52, 100, 104 *n*. 34, 130, 139 *n*. 52, 174, 174 *n*. 105, 205ff., 249, 293, 322 *n*. 7, 329 *n*. 21, 332 *n*. 33, 380 *n*. 12, 395, 400
Avicenna, 201 *n*. 35

Bacon, Roger, 322 *n*. 4, 392
Barfield, Owen, 95 *n*. 21, 142 *n*. 56, 213 *n*. 58, 243
Barth, Karl, 30 *n*. 13, 74 *n*. 5, 82 *n*. 11
Basch, Victor, 316 *n*. 3
Baur, F. C., 388 *n*. 23
Becker, Ottfrid, 395 *n*. 29
Bentham, Jeremy, 307, 393 *n*. 27
Berdyaev, Nicholas, 243 *n*. 98
Berenson, Bernard, 244
Bergson, Henri, 73, 124 *n*. 21, 138, 158 *n*. 73, 175, 208
Bochenski, I. M., 147 *n*. 63
Boehme, Jacob, 133 *n*. 44, 353 *nn*. 24 and 25, 354–355
Boethius, 400
Bonaventura, St., 90

Boney, William Jerry, 171 *n*. 100
Bonhoeffer, Dietrich, 39 *n*. 20, 118 *n*. 13
Bosanquet, Bernard, 315 *n*. 1
Bréhier, Emile, 316 *n*. 4
Brentana, Franz, 146
Brown, Norman O., 299 *n*. 39
Buber, Martin, 177
Buchler, Justus, 306, 308
Bultmann, Rudolf, 33 *n*. 17, 77, 78 *n*. 10, 122 *n*. 18, 189 *n*. 13, 294, 310 *n*. 53
Bundy, Murray Wright, 201 *n*. 35, 206 *n*. 51, 316 *n*. 3
Buri, Fritz, 92 *n*. 19
Bushnell, Horace, 303 *n*. 43

Calvin, John, 169 *n*. 96
Campbell, Joseph, 270ff.
Caponigri, A. Robert, 266 *n*. 134
Cassirer, Ernst, 394
Clarke, O. Fielding, 31 *n*. 14
Cobb, John B., Jr., 103 *n*. 32
Cocceius, Johannes, 384 *n*. 17
Coleridge, Samuel Taylor, 196 *n*. 29, 198, 200–204, 227 *n*. 75, 240, 245 *n*. 106, 300, 305, 335–344 *passim*, 396 *n*. 30
Collingwood, R. G., 164 *n*. 83, 215
Corot, Jean Baptiste, 258
Croce, Benedetto, 315 *n*. 1, 352 *n*. 21
Cudworth, Ralph, 161 *n*. 76, 208
Cushman, Robert E., 292 *n*. 30

Davies, Samuel, 22 *n*. 3
Descartes, René, 126–127, 131–132, 138, 146, 319 *n*. 1, 335 *n*. 1, 392
Dewey, John, 131 *n*. 39, 335 *n*. 1

403

404

405

Tillich, Paul, 145, 216, 261, 307, 310 *n.* 54, 397 *n.* 33
Tindal, W. Y., 243 *n.* 100
Troeltsch, Ernst, 283 *n.* 13
Turrettinus, Franciscus, 385–386

Unger, Erich, 201 *n.* 36
Urban, Wilbur Marshall, 167
Vahanian, Gabriel, 176 *n.* 109
Vaihinger, Hans, 347 *n.* 4, 350 *n.* 14
Van Peursen, C. A., 61
Vico, Gianbattista, 194 *n.* 23, 261, 266 *n.* 134
da Vinci, Leonardo, 252
Voetius, Gisbertus, 385

de Waelhens, Alphonse, 140 *n.* 53
Warren, Robert Penn, 248
Waugh, Evelyn, 164 *n.* 84
Weiss, Paul, 63, 65

Welch, Livingston, 315 *n.* 2
Whalley, George, 204 *n.* 43, 225 *n.* 75, 233 *n.* 84, 237 *n.* 87, 240 *n.* 93, 338 *n.* 4
Wheelwright, Philip, 147 *n.* 64, 203, 233, 234, 253 *n.* 116, 261
Whitehead, A. N., 116 *n.* 8, 129 *n.* 37, 131 *n.* 39, 158 *n.* 73, 160, 192, 201 *n.* 36, 222, 272 *n.* 4
Wilde, Oscar, 244
Wilder, Amos, 297 *n.* 37
Wimsatt, W. K., Jr., 263 *n.* 132
Wittgenstein, Ludwig, 112 *n.* 3, 243 *n.* 101
Wolff, Edgar H., 316 *n.* 4
Wordsworth, William, 203, 227 *n.* 75, 240, 246

Yeats, W. B., 290, 299

Zaner, Richard M., 140 *n.* 53

406

Index of Subjects

Constitution (*cont.*)
 in language, 87
 self-conscious unity with, 93–94
 triadic character of, in revelation, 85–88
 with regard to *reference,* 91
Content, of revelation, 75–83 *passim*
Contingency,
 and method, 306ff.
 of revelation, 79–82, 100–101
Continuity,
 of events, 161
 in German idealism and naïve realism, 137 *n.* 50
 and memory, 195ff.
 Merleau-Ponty on, 86 *n.* 15
 personal, and death, 145
 and potency, 152
 pour soi and *pour autrui,* 156
 of revelation, 77–83, 100–101, 296ff.
 the self and "continuous ingredience," 138–155 *passim,* 197ff.
 and theological occasionalism, 79
"Continuous ingredience," 138–155 *passim*
Creation,
 doctrine of, 87, 118, 169–170, 175, 308–309, 326 *n.* 11, 351ff.
 simultaneity of creation and knowledge, 351ff.
Creativity, 307
 and imagination, in modern philosophy, Appendix III, *passim*
 and nature, 345–346
 and nihilizing or negative imagination, in Sartre, 364–368
Custom, and imagination, in Hume, 350–351

Death, 145
"Death of God" theology, 102–103
Demythologization, 13, 122 *n.* 18, 294f.

Dialectic, 138, 169, 271
Distance, (see symbolic extrication)
 and abstraction, 154, 282ff.
 and event, 228
 and feeling, 237
 and historical potency, 217ff.
 and knowledge, 231–232
 and language, 27–28, 241
 and translation, 33 *n.* 17
Dogma, and imagination, 24
Dogmatics, 120, 122 *n.* 19

Ecstasy, and imagination, in St. Thomas, 332ff.
Embodiment, 128, 140 *n.* 53, 288 *n.* 20
 bodily bias of the will, 140ff.
 limit of body upon intention, 148
Entertainment, (see background, foreground, potency)
Epistemology, 182ff., (see knowledge, method, *méthodos,* event, hermeneutical spiral, noesis)
Epoché, 146, 235, (see reduction)
Eschatology, doctrine of, 87
Essence, 166–170
Essential form, 167–169
Eucharist, 241, 253
Event,
 and the circuit of cognition, 47f., 214ff.
 and concentration, 153–155
 and continuity of revelation, 78, 278ff.
 from and *toward,* 283ff.
 and images, 49, 281–285
 and imagination, 228–254
 and "interlacing of regions," 90–93, 159f.
 and language, 43–44, 48–49, 98, 104, 282ff.
 and ontologically antecedent concentrations, 160f.
 paradigmatic, 105, 192, 241, 273, 279, 285–290
 pre-schematical noesis and schematization of, 94
 and truth, 43–44
Evidence, and the will, 116

Existence, and modification of the will, 131–132
Existential, the imaginative, (see imaginative existential)
Extension, (see intension)
  and archetypes, 298f.
  inverse relation to intension, 63–65
  and the self, 113

Faith, 47, 255, 272 n. 4, 309
  and church, 79–80
  cognitive character of, 93ff.
  content of, 78
  and event, 183, 289ff., 301
  fundament of, 83
  and language, 311
  logical unity of, 289ff.
  and the modes of time, 96–97
  and reason, in early Christian community, 379–381
  relation to theology, 94, 102–103
Fall, doctrine of, 118, 175, 178
Fancy, 201f.
Fate, and imagination, 213ff.
Feeling,
  cognitivity of, 237ff.
  generic, 234–235, 292
  and immediate experience, 228f.
  and reproductive imagination, 232–237
  spontaneous, 235
Finitude, scale of, 165
Foreground, of selfhood, 143–153
Form,
  and archetype, 292f.
  expansion of, 167
  fixity of, 232
  what is finished in man, 162–166
Freedom, historical, 165–167
Fundament, (see constitution, constitutive process)
  Husserl's *Fundierung*, 84–85
  temporal-historical character of, 95–96
  triadic character of *founding*, 85–89
Fundamental theology, 72–75
  contrasted with dogmatic theology, 120–121

noemata of, summary, 92–93
  and ontological fundamentals, 119–125

Given, the, in theology, 37–46 *passim*
  and analytic, 200ff.
  and the content of revelation, 76–83 *passim*
  datum, dandum, dator noemata, 87–88
  definition of, 40 n. 44
  as focal actuality, 157, 242–249
  imagination and the modalities of, 242–254
  increase of phenomenological range of, 248ff.
  its immediacy, 42–45
  its mediation, 40–42
  the mnemonic, 210ff.
  modalities of, 183
  not necessarily to be equated with God, 37–39
  not restricted to "the already founded," 87
  and "particular interlacing of regions," 90–93
  as penumbral actuality, 158–161
  relation of, to "subject" and "object," 40f., 78f., 85ff.
  relation to the *withheld*, 62–65, 230
  in revelation, some summary propositions, 278–281
  and the scale of mental acts, 249–254
  schematization, schematism of, 93–96, 102–103
  sundering or dissolution of, 199ff., 245–248, 301
  transition from one mode to another, 250ff.
  and triadic constitutive process, 85–88
God, 255, 265, 272, 284, 289, 299
  in classical metaphysics, 90–91, 168–169
  existence of, 132
  faithfulness of, 306f.
  in Greek philosophical theology, 394ff.
  immediate intercourse with, 183

409

God (*cont.*)

intention of, for personal being, 178 *n.* 113

not one entitative foundation among others, 89

not necessarily *the* given for theology, 37–39, 400–401

potentiality in the divine being, and imagination, 327 *n.* 12

relation to Being, Being-Itself, 120, 122

Grace, 47–49, 78, 177f.

and "deiformed" imagination, in St. Thomas, 328ff.

and the theological given, 296

Hearing, 26

Heresy, 102–103

Hermeneutic, (see hermeneutical circle, spiral)

and memory, 210

relation to epistemology and ontology, 63–65

Hermeneutical circle,

in Bultmann, 34 *n.* 17

in Dilthey, 60–61

rejected in favor of hermeneutical spiral, 60–61

Hermeneutical spiral, 60–68 *passim*, 230ff., 241

from circumspection to schematization, 93–95

and "imaginative shock," 216ff.

and method, 305–309

and reflexive thinking, 111–119 *passim*

revelation in, 99, 218

and systematic symbolics, 298ff.

and translation, 277

Historicism, 41

Historio-personal existential, 178–179, 254–256, 278, 297, 300 (see *potentia obedientalis*)

History, (see being, man, time)

actual historical present, 211f.

distinction between historical being and historical knowledge, 191ff.

and form, 165f.

historical future, 223ff.

historical past, 223f.

historical temporality and imagination, 189–254 *passim*

and modification, 178

universal, 212

Holy Spirit, identical with "deiformed" imagination, as subjective principle of revelation, in St. Thomas, 330

Horizon, (see world)

as function of the polarity of question and answer, and of problematic, 54–60 *passim*

horizon-fusion, 58–60

reconfiguration of, 54–56

Idealism, classical and modern, doctrine of imagination in, 363 *n.* 53

Illumination,

doctrine of, 90

in St. Thomas, 328ff.

Imagery, religious, and American "manifest destiny," 22–25

Images,

archetypal, 209, 235, 290–300, (see archetypes)

as cognitive form of revelation, 279ff., (see imagination)

"crisis" of, 199

and event, 281–285, (see event)

firmament of, 211f., (see world)

"master," 199, 209, 279, 300–305, (see master images)

Imagination,

active, 90, 116, 198ff., 209f., 216

and activity of mind, in perennial realism, 322–334

and aesthetic creation, in Schelling, 363–364

"answering," 259ff., 278, 280–281, 296, 308

and apprehension, in Kant, 339–340

and being, 184ff.

and cognitivity, 224

and concept or category, in Kant, 341–342

creativity and nihilizing or negative imagination, in Sartre, 364–368

creativity and the ontologically

410

Intension (*cont.*)
and the self, 113
Intention, 132
distinguished from *intentionality*, 147
of dominant direction, 149–150, 214ff.
and *foreground*, 143ff.
form of, 208ff., 220–223
and imposition of pattern, 148
modern history of the term, 146
of the specific project, 150–151
Intentionality,
distinguished from *intention*, 147
in the phenomenological tradition, 146ff.
Interpretation, 281, (see hermeneutic, hermeneutical spiral)
and memory, 210ff., (see memory)
and scripture, 285, (see scripture)
and world, 224ff., (see world)

Knowledge, (see epistemology, hermeneutic, hermeneutical spiral, imagination, revelation, theology, will, world)
and imagination, 224, 238ff.
and intensive and extensive "presence," 252, (see presence)
inverse relation between extension and intension, 63–65
relation between being and knowing, 61–62
some general propositions about, 231–232
and theological method, 307ff., (see method, *méthodos*)

Language,
and apprehension, 27–28, (see apprehension)
atrophy and renewal of, 71–72, 87, 99
and background, 142
and being, 41, (see being)
as deposit of reproduction, 243ff.
and event, 282ff., (see event)

event-inverbalizing, 104, (see event)
first- and second-order, 28, 42 *n.* 21, 45, 94, 217ff., 296, 310
and "imaginative shock," 216ff.
and intention, 71ff.
and meaning, 100, (see meaning)
and metaphysics, 111, (see metaphysics)
and perception, 70, (see perception)
and personal history, 71
and plurality of cognitive modes, 98
and reality, 87, (see being, reality)
sedimentation, ossification of, 99–100, (see sedimentation)
and systematic symbolics, 309f.
and thinking, 112ff., (see thinking)
and tradition, 275ff., (see tradition)
and triadic constitutive process, 87
and translation, 32–34, 99, 276ff., (see translation)
Leiden Synopsis, 384 *n.* 18
Limit,
and form, 162ff.
as function of background, 139–143
historical limit, 164–166
natural limit, 165
and the past, 189ff.
and potency, 152
and *situation*, 156ff.
Linguistics, structural, 282, 299
Liturgy, 92 *n.* 19

Man, (see being, history, language, nature)
finished being of, 167–170
human being and imagination, 225, (see imagination)
non-coincidence with himself, 176ff.
ontological instability of, 122–123, 167–170, 174ff.
unfinished being of, 167ff.

412

"Manifest destiny," American, and transmutation of religious imagery, 22–25
Marxism, 176
Master images, 279, 300–305, (see images, imagination)
cognitivity of, 304
and historical causality, 303
relational character of, 302
simultaneously intensional and extensional, 301ff.
Meaning,
and communication, 302
genesis of, 121, 278, 283
increment of, in theology, 34 *n*. 17, 87
as intentionality of consciousness, in Husserl, 146f.
and language, 87, 100
not merely *there*, 61, 85
and perception, 86
and presentiment of being, 247
and significance, 262, 289ff.
and time, 97
Mediacy, mediation,
of the Christ-event in the primitive Christian community, 373–375
and contingency of revelation, 80ff.
of the given in theology, 40–42
Memory,
and background, 143
and events, 43
and imagination, 189–219 *passim*
and intention, 149
passivity of, in classical realism, 193–195
and perception, 196ff.
and personal being, 191ff.
relation to mediacy and immediacy, 43
status of intentional pattern in, 206f.
Metaphor, 237–242, 248f., (see images, imagination, symbol)
Metaphysics, 90–91, 111, 117, 120–121, 130, 168–169, 173, 187, 269, 293–294, (see being, history, God, man, nature, ontology, time)

Method, in theology, (see *méthodos*, hermeneutical spiral, theology, systematic symbolics)
pre-modern cognates of, 390–402
Méthodos, in Greek and early Christian theology, 390–401
Mind, 90, 92
Modification, (see will)
and conviction of *existence*, 132
mark of revelatory relation, 121–122
Montanism, 43
Moral action, (see parable)
and imagination, in Fichte, 361–362
and imagination, in Sartre, 364–368

Natural theology, 168–169, (see metaphysics, ontology)
Nature,
and the bodily bias of the self, 140ff., 148
in classical realism, 162f., 318, 334 *passim*
and creativity, 345–346
imagination in the knowledge of, in St. Thomas, 321–325
and ossified imagination, 244ff.
and potency, 172–175
and supernature, in medieval theology, 381–383
Neighbor, 123, 179
Neo-orthodox theology, 310
"New quest of the historical Jesus," 215
Noema,
definition, 85 *n*. 14
multi-dimensional *noemata*, 88–93
Noesis, 93–96

Obedience, 171ff., (see *potentia obedientialis*)
Object, 157ff., (see hermeneutical spiral)
Occasionalism, 79
Ontic, (see ontology)
the ontically given thing, 62
logic of the movement from, to

413

Ontic (*cont.*)
the ontological, and vice versa, 34 *n.* 17
Ontologism, 89–90, 110
Ontology, (see being, history, metaphysics, nature, self)
discussed generally, 110–119
the "ontological difference," 110–111, 113f.
ontological thinking, 111–119, 156f., (see thinking)
regional, 92
of revelation,
problem of, 100–101
defined, 101, 171 *n.* 100
root of ontological reflection, 65
Otherness, 127f., 156–161
characteristics of the "other," 160

Pantheism, 38
Parable, 225, 304
Paradigmatic event, 192, 241, 273, 279, 285–290, (see event)
Passivity,
of imagination, in memory, 193–198
of prophetic imagination, in St. Thomas, 329ff.
Past, the, 189ff., (see history, time)
modalities of, 213ff.
the ontic past, 190ff., 283
the ontological past, 191ff.
the recollected, 190
and tradition, 283, (see tradition)
transition from one modality to another, 210ff.
Perception, 86, 114, 141f., 184 *n.* 3
and immediacy, 210ff.
and memory, 196ff.
Philosophical theology, classical, 90–91, 390–401
Political intercourse, as enacted parable, 311
possibility, (see potency)
and essence, 166f.
funded in the past, 220
ontologically novel, 167
and projection, 226

potency, 137, 171ff., (see potency)
historical communication of, 173
modalities of, 214ff.
in and *of* nature, 172–175
and the past, 190ff.
and tradition, 283
Potentia obedientalis, 170–179 *passim*
in classical Thomism, 172–173
phenomenological account of, 173ff.
Preaching, proclamation, 264, 291, 309–311
Presence, 265–266, (see being and appearance)
and experience, 161–162
historical and archetypal, 300
of man's ownmost historio-personal existential, 255ff.
and perception, 141–142
Presuppositions,
defined, 57–58
and the formation of horizons, 57–60, (see world)
Problematic, the hermeneutical significance of the *problem* or *question*, 53–60 *passim*, 297
Process, of revelation, 75–83 *passim*
Prophetic or "deiformed" imagination, in St. Thomas, 329ff.
Prophetic motifs in the pre-Christian Hebrew community, 372–373
Proposition,
existential intelligibility of, 132
and the form of intention, 220f.
as *form* of revelation, 77, 80–81
Psychoanalysis, and the archetypal tradition, 298ff.
Psychologism, 147

Question, the, (see hermeneutical spiral, problematic)
hermeneutical/cognitive significance of, 53–60 *passim*
and lines of reference, 55–56, (see reference)

414

Schematism (*cont.*)
historicity of, 245
relation to imagination, 184
of revelation as fundament, 93–
96, 102–105
in "synthetic imagination," in
Kant, 335–344 *passim*
Scripture, 252, 281ff., 300, 309,
(see tradition)
and interpretation, 285, (see
hermeneutical spiral)
as mediate and immediate presentiment of theology's given,
43–44
relation to revelation, 103–105,
296
and tradition, problematic of,
in relation to revelation, 103–
105
what scripture makes accessible,
48–49
Sedimentation, 212 *n*. 57, 216
Self, (see being, hermeneutical
spiral, history, man, revelation)
background and foreground of,
138ff.
and Being, 113ff.
bodily bias of, 140ff.
and "continuous ingredience,"
138–155 *passim*
and "discontinuous ingression,"
156–162 *passim*
embodiment of, 128f.
existentialistic interpretation of,
insufficient ground for theology, 299ff.
imagination, the ultimate status
of the self, and the Absolute,
in Fichte and Schelling, 359–
364
situating and situated, 156–161
"starting point" for a formal
grasp of revelation, 125ff.
terminality and relationality of,
134–135, 302
unity of, 128f., 153–155
Self-image, 149
Sexuality, 166 *n*. 88
Shock, (see ecstasy, rapture)
imaginative, 216ff.

in work of art, 235
and world, 225
Sin, original, 38
Situation, situating and being situated, 156–161 *passim,* 170–
179 *passim,* (see history, self,
will)
developed in relation to classical
ontological categories, 162–
170
initial and terminal, 286ff.
relation to essential form, 167–
170
Spiritomonism, 79
Stoics, 208 *n*. 54
Substance, 335ff.
Symbol, 120, 122, 201, 241, (see
imagination, reference, symbolic tradition, systematic
symbolics)
cognitivity of, 237ff.
contexts for the interpretation
of, 280–281
imagination and symbolic reference, 158, 193, 246ff.
and intentionality, 147–148
and the modalities of time, 225
ontological presuppositions of
symbolic imagination, 248f.
and ossified imagination, 243ff.
symbolic extrication, 237–242
the task of a phenomenology of
the symbolic tradition, 274–
305 *passim*
Symbolic tradition, (see symbol,
systematic symbolics)
a phenomenology of, 274–305
passim
justification of and program
for, 275–280
problem areas in, 378–281
Synthesis,
and imagination, in Kant and
Coleridge, 335–344 *passim*
and "substance," in modern
philosophy, 335–339
Systematic symbolics, 280, 281 *n*.
11, 289, 298ff., 305–311
and the hermeneutical spiral,
298ff.
and language, 309f.

416

417